The Identity of Christianity

The Identity of Christianity

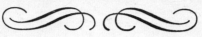

Theologians and the Essence of Christianity
from Schleiermacher to Barth

STEPHEN SYKES

Van Mildert Professor, University of Durham

First published 1984
SPCK
Holy Trinity Church
Marylebone Road
London NW1 4DU

British Library Cataloguing in Publication Data

Sykes, S. W.
    The identity of Christianity.
    1. Christianity
    I. Title
    200   BR121.2

ISBN 0–281–04088–5
ISBN 0–281–04112–1 Pbk

Filmset in Monophoto Sabon by
Northumberland Press Ltd, Gateshead
Printed in Great Britain by Richard Clay
(The Chaucer Press Ltd), Bungay, Suffolk

To Joy

γυνὴ ἀνδρεία στέφανος τῷ ἀνδρὶ αὐτῆς

Contents

Acknowledgements ix

Abbreviations xi

Introduction 1

PART ONE

1 Identity and Conflict in Christianity 11

2 The Tradition of Inwardness 35

3 Power in the Church 51

PART TWO

4 Schleiermacher on the Essence of Christianity 81

5 Newman on the Idea of Christianity 102

6 Harnack and Loisy 123

7 Troeltsch and the Relevance of Epistemology 148

8 Barth and the Power of the Word 174

PART THREE

9 Analysis of the Essence Discussion 211

10 The Unity of Christianity 239

11 Worship, Commitment and Identity 262

Notes 287

Bibliography 327

Index 339

vii

Acknowledgements

I gladly acknowledge the assistance of the very large number of persons who at different stages during the development of this project have given generously of their support. In particular I should mention in the first place the Trustees of the Cadbury Foundation, who did me the honour of electing me to the Cadbury Lectureship in Birmingham in 1977–8, and the members of the Department of Theology who provided me with such a warm welcome, especially Professor and Mrs Gordon Davies.

The Edward Cadbury Lectureship was established in 1941 by Edward Cadbury Esquire, LL.D. for the furtherance of the study of Theology in the University of Birmingham. According to the Regulations there shall be an annual course of Lectures, usually eight in number, to be delivered in either the Autumn or Spring Term. The theme of the Lectures shall be concerned with some aspect of the Christian faith, the original intention of the Founder being that it should be concerned with the relations past, present and future, of Christianity to civilization and culture.

A number of people have discussed the subject with me, or read parts of the typescript and made very helpful comments, including Professor Rolf Schäfer of Tübingen, Professor Nicholas Lash of Cambridge, Professor George Stroup of Yale, and Dr Derek Holmes of Durham. The final draft was given close and careful scrutiny by Mr Ed Kale of Durham, from whose scrupulous criticisms I have greatly profited.

Many people had a hand in the typing of the script, but the burden of dealing not merely with the handwriting but also with the foibles of its perpetrator unquestionably fell upon Mrs Sheila Robson and her team of assistants in the Department of Theology in Durham. No one could wish for a more skilful or cheerful secretarial support-group.

Acknowledgements

Cambridge University Press have kindly permitted me to reproduce (with a few corrections and additions) a substantial part of my chapter on Troeltsch on the essence of Christianity in J. P. Clayton, ed., *Ernst Troeltsch and the Future of Theology* (1976).

Publisher's Acknowledgements

Unless otherwise stated, biblical quotations are from the Revised Standard Version of the Bible, copyright 1946, 1952, © 1957, 1971, 1973 by the Division of Christian Education of the National Council of the Churches of Christ in the USA, and are used by permission.

Extracts from *Church Dogmatics* by Karl Barth (1936–74) are reprinted by permission of T. & T. Clark Ltd.

Extracts from *Brief Outline on the Study of Theology* by Friedrich Schleiermacher, translated by Terrence N. Tice, are reprinted by permission of John Knox Press, Atlanta, USA. Copyright M. E. Bratcher 1966.

Extracts from *The Word of God and the Word of Man* by Karl Barth (1957) are reprinted by permission of Harper & Row.

Abbreviations

Publishing details are given in the Bibliography.

AC   E. Troeltsch *The Absoluteness of Christianity and the History of Religions*

B-H   H. M. Rumscheidt *Revelation and Theology*

BO   F. D. E. Schleiermacher *Brief Outline on the Study of Theology*

BOA   *Birmingham Oratory Archives*

CD   K. Barth *Church Dogmatics*

CF   F. D. E. Schleiermacher *The Christian Faith*

CM   J. B. Lightfoot *The Christian Ministry*

Dev¹   J. H. Newman *An Essay on the Development of Christian Doctrine*

EASP   H. von Campenhausen *Ecclesiastical Authority and Spiritual Power in the Church of the First Three Centuries*

ECH 1   J. H. Newman *Essays Critical and Historical* 1

ER   K. Barth *The Epistle to the Romans*

GC   A. Loisy *The Gospel and the Church*

GS   E. Troeltsch *Gesammelte Schriften II*

Jager   L. Allen ed. *John Henry Newman and the Abbé Jager*

KB   E. Busch *Karl Barth*

MP   R. C. Moberly *Ministerial Priesthood*

NEB   New English Bible

NZSTh   *Neue Zeitschrift für systematische Theologie*

ODCC   *Oxford Dictionary of the Christian Church*

OHD   A. von Harnack *Outlines of the History of Dogma*

OR	F. D. E. Schleiermacher *On Religion, Speeches to its Cultured Despisers*
PRE	*Realencyklopädie für protestantische Theologie und Kirche*
RGG	*Religion in Geschichte und Gegenwart*
RSV	Revised Standard Version
Signif.	R. Morgan and M. Pye *Ernst Troeltsch, Writings on Theology and Religion*
STCC	E. Troeltsch *The Social Teaching of the Christian Churches*
US	J. H. Newman *Newman's University Sermons*
VM 1	J. H. Newman *The Via Media of the Anglican Church, Vol. 1*
WC	A. von Harnack *What is Christianity?*
WW	K. Barth *The Word of God and the Word of Man*
ZKG	*Zeitschrift für Kirchengeschichte*
ZThK	*Zeitschrift für Theologie und Kirche*

Introduction

The distinguished Swedish theologian, Gustav Wingren, once observed that 'the special task which confronts systematic theology both in its historical and strictly systematic functions is to answer the question: What is the essence of Christianity?'[1] This remark would be readily verified if one were to examine the sort of introductions to Christian theology still being reprinted in the 1930s, for example the immensely influential *Einführung in das theologische Studium* of the Swiss reformed theologian, Paul Wernle, first published in 1908, or the posthumously published work of the Chicago philosopher of religion, George Burman Foster, *Christianity in its Modern Expression* (1921). But one might well be less confident about the situation today.

Without doubt we would have to admit, in the first place, that the question of the essence of Christianity has a very old-fashioned ring about it. In 1957, indeed, Professor Carl Heinz Ratschow, the author of the article on the essence of Christianity in the foremost German dictionary of theology, *Die Religion in Geschichte und Gegenwart*, discussed the suggestion that the essence of Christianity had disappeared as a central problem for Christian theology, being superseded by that of the existential decision of the Christian. But the opinion stated in conclusion, namely that, despite its apparent dissolution, the problem is still with us in that of the continuity of Christian existence, seems (at least in the light of the present study) to be fully justified. The essence of Christianity is a matter which has a habit of constantly making its reappearance, irrespective of fashions, though occasionally in slightly different guises. It would be a satisfactory outcome of the labours which lie behind this book if it were recognized that answering the question, What is the essence of Christianity?, continues to be an extremely important task for any systematic theologian to undertake, and for aspiring systematicians to ponder.

The specific purpose, then, of this immodestly entitled book is to learn what there is to learn from the long discussion of 'the essence of Christianity' which took place in the nineteenth century. Why, then, is the title of the book not *The Essence of Christianity*? The simplest way of explaining the significance of the transition from 'Essence' to 'Identity' is to prove a brief account of the stages of my involvement with this problem.

The work had its origin in my long-standing interest in Friedrich Schleiermacher, where the essence of Christianity occupies an obviously central place in his interpretation and transmission of the Christian tradition. The conventional wisdom about the use of this phrase by Schleiermacher, as by Harnack and Troeltsch at the end of the nineteenth century, seemed to be that this was a typically reductionist gambit of liberal protestantism, the whittling away of the rich and complex substance of Christianity into a thin formula specially designed for acceptability in the modern world. But it had already become clear to me that there was rather more to the question than that; accordingly I published two rather general studies of the topic,[2] followed by a close examination of Troeltsch's highly significant contribution to the discussion.[3] In the meantime it had become apparent that considerably greater interest was being shown in the topic by contemporary theologians, and that the question was, from the standpoint of theological method, far from dead.

Nonetheless the term 'essence' continued to elicit antipathy. Some of this was based on sheer misunderstanding, for example, that essence definition is inherently reductive in character. But other more thoughtful and better informed reactions left me with the conviction that the same topic could be treated under a less misleading heading. A consideration which inclined me strongly in this direction was the (in fact, erroneous) belief, enunciated by Ernst Troeltsch and held by very many, both Protestant and Roman Catholic, that the concept of the essence of an historical phenomenon was the creation of the German idealist tradition, and that its application to Christianity was possible only for Protestants.[4] Troeltsch had pointed for evidence to a large number of contemporary works bearing the titles, 'The Spirit of ...' or 'The Essence of ...'. These depended, he asserted, upon a particular attitude towards history which enabled suitably qualified scholars to essay the art of historical abstraction on the basis of vast masses of methodically studied materials. Now it was abundantly clear to me that this kind of writing had gone out of fashion, and that historical scholars eschewed the massive generalizations which the idealists regarded as the pinnacle of historical scholarship – a pinnacle, it should be said, that Troeltsch did not hesitate to scale at the relatively tender age of thirty-eight.

But my objection rested not merely on a question of fashion in historiography. Solid philosophical opposition had been taken to what was termed 'the essentialist fallacy'. Of certain nineteenth-century idealistic theories of aesthetics W. B. Gallie wrote:

> I believe that they are vitiated through and through by the 'essentialist fallacy': they presuppose, that is, that whenever we are in a position to define a substance or an activity we must know its essence or ultimate nature – and know this by methods that are entirely different from those used in the experimental and mathematical sciences or in our common-sense judgements about minds and material things.[5]

The fallacious element in the stance of the essentialist was the claim made or implied for the mode of cognition; and this, as we shall see, is where Troeltsch himself is at his weakest. It is when the 'essence of Christianity' is made the result of ultimately mysterious techniques of intellectual discovery that the enterprise falls into philosophical disrepute.

Accordingly when invited to deliver the Cadbury Lectures at Birmingham University in 1977–8, I chose as my title, not the 'Essence of Christianity', but the 'Identity of Christianity'. By this I meant, in all innocence, the enquiry into what makes Christianity Christianity. In particular I wished to avoid any assumption that I was interested only in Protestant (or at least in non-Roman Catholic) answers to the question, since I had in the meantime discovered how very important the work of John Henry Newman was in the elucidation of what was at stake.

Nonetheless I was under no illusion that by changing the title of my enquiry I had in any way simplified my task. On the contrary, precisely because I had become convinced both of the complexity and the unavoidability even of the 'essence quest', I realized that with a still more comprehensive-sounding, and scarcely less ambiguous heading I had committed myself to an apparently impossible labour. The process of carefully delimiting what I was about became still more urgent.

It was plain that in no sense could this be a survey of Christian history,[6] or a comprehensive review of the multidimensional phenomenon of Christianity.[7] It was to be a theological work arising from a particular modern uncertainty, expressed in the question, What *is* Christianity? That is to say, it presupposes that there are problems arising out of the distinction between form and content in the Christian tradition,[8] or from the post-enlightenment phenomenon of historical enquiry and moral criticism of Christianity,[9] that 'historical-mindedness' and the multiple phenomena designated by the term 'relativism' present peculiar and new challenges to theories of development,[10] let alone of continuity in the Christian tradition, and that the contemporary acquaintance with the sheer diversity of forms of Christianity disturbs the bland parochialism of familiar assumptions. All these give particular urgency to the question, What, then, *is* Christianity? Another way of putting the same question would be to ask directly, Do the differences between Christians matter?

The problem, then, is diversity in Christianity, both historical and contemporary, and the controversy which attends diversity. It is not a problem of antiquarian interest, however, since it is asked with an eye to the present and future. Nor is it merely a problem for church hierarchies which make decisions about the future shape of their Christian churches; it is one which faces every active member of a local church called on to participate or not to participate in a new experiment, a moral or political campaign or an ecumenical endeavour in the name of what Christianity actually stands for.

It is for this reason, if for no other, that I would be glad to have been able to have claimed to have 'solved' the problem. One of the themes of the book concerns the responsibility of the Christian theologian in his exercise of power in the Church, a power which resides in his or her articulacy, or power to communicate. I hold that a theologian must communicate to other than fellow theologians, and that clarification of meaning is one of the few justifications for occupying valuable time and money in the production and reading of works of scholarship. Despite this the claims which I feel able to make for the book are modest indeed, as compared with the apparent presumption of the title. In essence, then, I have tried to carry out two tasks; in the first place, to analyse and exhibit the kind of question which the enquiry into the identity of Christianity is, and, secondly, to propose some modest minimum conditions under which the identity of Christianity may be preserved.

The core of the book, Part Two, remains the nineteenth-century discussion of the essence of Christianity. Foundational are the contrasting, but remarkably similar, approaches of Schleiermacher and Newman to, respectively, the 'essence' and the 'idea' of Christianity. Compared with these Harnack's celebrated public lectures (translated into English as *What is Christianity?*) are methodologically naive, for all the urgency of a new attempt at the problem. Troeltsch and Barth both specifically dissent from Harnack, and reformulate the problem at a new level, Barth in particular attempting to abandon the terms in which the problem has been earlier discussed in the Protestant tradition.

In a sense, then, the essence of Christianity discussion is an episode in the history of Christian theology. Moreover as an episode, it is in truth primarily a Protestant discussion, with Roman Catholic contributions of an apparently disdainful kind. The distance, however, is in my opinion more apparent than real; and the argument of this book is that this nineteenth-century episode is highly instructive for the problem of modern Christianity, in as much as it confronts not merely the problem of Christian identity, but at the same time, the painful role which the theologian appears to play in conflicts about that identity in any of the Christian churches.

The nineteenth-century discussion itself has a context, however, not merely in the immediately preceding centuries, but in certain apparently inescapable constituents of Christian exist ence. Accordingly the central section of this book is preceded by the three chapters of Part One in which these constituent elements are explored. They are, respectively, the fact of controversy about Christianity, the importance of inward dispositions to Christian discipleship, and the power-claim implied in the Church's existence. I do not claim to have any general theory up my sleeve to explain why these features of Christian profession, abundantly evident from the New Testament, should prove to be of such importance. From the sociological point of view they have, no doubt, to do with the phenomena of religious change, of religious commitment, and of the nature of the sacred.[11] But it seems probable that there are other aspects of Christianity which, under different conditions, would also prove to be remarkably significant. Other writers either have attempted, or will attempt, a more comprehensive presentation of the relevant factors.[12] What seems to me certain, however, is that without an understanding of these three factors we remain at a wholly superficial level in our appreciation of the nineteenth-century attempt to formulate the essence of Christianity. Such, then, is the prelude.

The postlude (Part Three) to the central section also consists of three chapters. Their function is to return to the starting point of this investigation and to ask the question whether there is a theory of Christianity which provides us with an adequate containment of the controversy characteristic of Christianity from the start. This is not the same question as that which enquires after the essence of Christianity. Nor is the answer any kind of 'solution' of the identity crisis (if crisis there be) of contemporary Christianity. It is nonetheless a proposal regarding the minimum conditions under which Christian identity may be optimally preserved, offered on both of two assumptions, that there will never be complete theological accord between Christians, and that at the same time church leaders have a responsibility to provide the best conditions for the handing on of the Christian faith to the next generation.

I have already mentioned the fact that my enquiries have forced me to become sensitive to the role of the theologian in Christianity. In effect this question has become a sub-plot in the wider discussion of the maintenance of Christian identity. The matter can be put as follows. I wish to challenge the bland assumption that the theologian's job is to specialize in purely intellectual problems, apart from careful consideration of the setting of the theological disciplines in the wider context of Christianity's identity as a religion. In my opinion the forms of specialism strongly promoted by the compartmentalization of western intellectual life have led theologians into an uncritical adoption of the role of vanguard to the Christian community.

6

This self-portrayal implies, of course, that it is the intellectual realm which leads the way; the bias of the image is inherently towards discovery and intellectual novelty.

My challenge to this assumption is mounted on two major fronts. In the first place, I wish to locate the role of theology in the task of the preservation of Christian identity. The problem of continuity in the Christian tradition is not something which has to be tackled *after* the 'progressive' theologian has led the rest of the Christian community to a brand new redoubt. All too often this is how the matter is presented, leaving the impression that the new defensive position has to be connected with the tradition by some brilliant *tour de force*. To question the assumptions on which such a self portrayal of the role and responsibilities of the theologian is based does not imply a merely static conception of the discipline of theology. That the preservation of Christian identity in changing cultural contexts requires exceptionally serious intellectual work and entails novelty, is not open to serious question. But it is the reality of Christianity as a whole, not just its intellectual content, which is implicated in the problem of continuity.

Secondly, my argument will in due course turn to the difficult matter of the grounds of religious knowledge, that is to the question of epistemology. This, of course, is where the theologian is on home territory. Occasionally, indeed, you will catch an exasperated theologian *prescribing* what can and cannot be known religiously, sometimes to the astonishment and dismay of those who believe they know otherwise. We have to take seriously, it seems to me, the possibility of a tyrannous use of intellectual power; and there has to be somewhere in the remarkable system of checks and balances in the living religious tradition where theology is simply not in charge. In the end I shall argue that the Christian community at worship is such a place, and that here there are grounds for religious knowledge which limit the control which the theologian is tempted to exercise by means of his or her superior articulacy.

All this, as I say, is a sub-plot to the central theme of the book which concerns the reasons why dispute about the identity of Christianity arise. The major part of Christian history has assumed that the community of true believers will actually be of one heart and mind. Discord, on this account, is a phenomenon of the margins. I propose a wholly different picture, to the effect not merely that it is inconceivable that Christians could agree with each other, but also that it is actually undesirable that they should do so – with the proviso that they should share enough in common to be capable of worshipping together. The purpose, therefore, of the sub-plot is to place the discipline of theology and the expertise of the theologian in an explicitly new relation to the total phenomenon of Christian identity, conceived as a body with unavoidable and restless internal conflicts.

I wish to comment on one final question. An Anglican Canon Professor may be assumed to be a Christian, and I would not hesitate to describe this as a work of Christian theology. But could anyone not sharing the Christian faith be expected to accompany the author on this particular journey? Are not certain assumptions constantly being made about the truth or value of the Christian tradition, which detract from the scholarly status of the work? There is no doubt that authors are rarely sensitive enough to the range and depth of their unquestioned presuppositions. But I see no reason why the theological analysis of a phase of a religious tradition from a standpoint within that tradition should not be generally intelligible and illuminating. I would be the first to agree that other methods could be used, and would also be illuminating. I doubt whether a complete perspective on any portion of intellectual history exists, any more than a definitive biography of an individual.

What can, however, be sensibly claimed for this study, is that it is a contribution to understanding the complex dilemma of Christian identity in the modern world. If it enables the general reader to gain an insight into the curious tenacity with which Christians insist on proclaiming their gospel and at the same time quarrelling with each other, it will have fulfilled at least part of its aim. If it enables Christians to conduct their inevitable quarrels to the better accomplishment of their task of proclaiming the gospel, it will not have been written wholly in vain.

Part One

I

Identity and Conflict in Christianity

I

In the present chapter, I propose to tackle two interrelated questions, first, the problem of controversy in early Christianity, and secondly, the fact that Christianity exists in a number of different aspects or dimensions. Both of these themes tend strongly to emphasize pluralism in the Christian movement, and the reason for highlighting pluralism should be obvious enough: if there were no plurality, there would be no problem of Christian identity. But the argument of the chapter will reveal, I trust, considerably more than the scarcely controversial fact that there has been, and still is, a diversity of forms of Christianity. I shall argue that any realistic account of the Christian phenomenon strongly suggests the inconceivability of there ever being complete agreement about the identity of Christianity. That is not to say that Christians may not be able to contain disagreement within reasonable boundaries. But contained diversity is, in fact, what unity amounts to.

Two prefatory remarks must be made, first about my use of the term 'Christianity', and secondly about my use of the New Testament. On 'Christianity' it has been argued by a modern writer that the term is of recent coinage, and that it abstracts and 'reifies' a much less precise phenomenon.[1] That argument will have to be examined in due course. But here it would be as well to indicate that I am fully aware of the danger lurking in the mere use of the collective term. By 'Christianity' I mean, at this stage, only 'the Christian movement', and the less well defined, the better. The fact that the title 'Christian' was itself given to the new movement, apparently by pagans, and adopted only by Christians in the second century, tends to confirm somewhat the comparative informality of the movement's early self-consciousness.[2] The justification for a separate term ultimately lies in the actual outcome of the process of differentiation from the movement's Jewish matrix. At this stage it is relevant to indicate that precisely what is involved in this process is part of the argument of this chapter. Thus, again, it is proper to insist on a provisional lack of precision in the term. 'Christianity', as we shall use it in this chapter, refers to the complex circumstances in which the first and second centuries of our era saw the birth of the 'new' Christian movement.

To speak about these circumstances at all inevitably involves one in the use of the New Testament documents, and with the dawning of this realization systematic theologians have grown accustomed to the need for a ritual rending of their garments. If by systematic theology one understands the attempt to unify the Christian tradition and contemporary thought, then practitioners of this discipline are likely to find themselves in trouble on the highways and byways of modern New Testament criticism. The awkward truth seems to be, however, that New Testament scholarship is an aspect of contemporary thought which belongs to the very definition of systematics. Systematic theologians are obliged to come to some understanding of the history of primitive Christianity. That is to say, they have to exercise some kind of intellectual judgement about the differing theories which are presented by the experts in New Testament history. In this their responsibilities are, at least, not less than those of *any* informed person who desires to take a serious interest in the documentation of the early Christian movement. The excuse of belonging to a separate specialism does not apply.

Why should this be so? Why should the systematician be forced to deal, secondhand, with the debates and conclusions of another discipline? The answer, unfortunately for the systematician, is that the price of abstracting systematics from the New Testament period is abstraction from the teaching and history of Jesus and his impact on his first disciples and their converts. Despite the fact that there have been theologians willing to dispense with the uncertainties of historical scholarship, the costs in a loss of realism are unacceptable.[3] It may be necessary to come to terms with the fact that there are limits to our capacity to be confident about historical judgements, but the mere use of the New Testament forces on the reader an imaginative reconstruction of the early communities' faith. The only practical choice is whether or not that reconstruction is, or is not, an informed one.

Use of the New Testament in systematics entails the use of New Testament scholarship. In this sense systematic theology is a form of professional generalizing, a kind of 'general practice' theology; unless systematicians know a certain amount not merely about the New Testament, but about every relevant theological discipline they will be unable to do their job properly. They will certainly not be adequate to function as specialists in all relevant fields, and will probably be weaker in some fields than in others, but they cannot opt out of a field like New Testament studies and hope to remain in systematics. Accordingly what is offered here by way of reference to the relevant parts of the New Testament is, I trust, recognizable as an adequate form of generalizing.

Another word may be added, *sotto voce*, on the possible value of systematicians asking questions about the state of modern New Testament studies. Systematic theology is obliged to take into account a number of other disciplines also, for example philosophical hermeneutics and the sociology of religion. Sometimes it appears that New Testament specialists are less alert than they should be to the questions raised by the interpretation or the social setting of a religious tradition. Amateur generalizer though the systematic theologian may be in detailed matters of New Testament scholarship, he or she may claim a certain minor role in the formulation of relevant questions for clarification.

II

We consider, first, the problem of controversy, and do not have to look far before encountering a serious instance within a young Christian community. Writing a bare twenty years after the crucifixion Paul shows that he has the severest difficulties with his church at Corinth:

> I appeal to you, brethren, by the name of our Lord Jesus Christ, that all of you agree and that there are no dissensions (*schismata*) among you, but that you be united in the same mind and the same judgement. For it has been reported to me by Chloe's people that there

is quarrelling among you, my brethren. What I mean is that each one of you says, 'I belong to Paul', or 'I belong to Apollos', or 'I belong to Cephas', or 'I belong to Christ' (1 Cor 1.10–12).

The precise nature of these dissensions has been a matter of continuous debate in modern times.[4] F. C. Baur argued that the factions reduced themselves to two, Paul and Apollos versus Peter (and Christ), the latter representing a Judaizing tendency. Reitzenstein, in his celebrated treatment of the hellenistic mystery religions, regarded the principal 'Christ party' as an early species of Gnosticism. Johannes Munck, on the other hand, startled the scholarly world with his denial that there were, in Corinth, parties or factions at all; according to him, the *schismata*, or bickerings as he called them, were entirely the product of internal misunderstandings of the status of Christian leaders as teachers of wisdom.[5]

Whatever their origin and nature, the dissensions concerned Paul's own status very closely, and provoked from him a momentous reflection on the authority of his message and ministry. To this reflection we shall have reason to return more than once.[6] But for an illustration of the kind of difficulty which Paul may have been facing we may turn to a suggestion made by Professor C. K. Barrett. Barrett proposes that, in the account of his activity as a church planter which Paul gives in 1 Corinthians 3, we should see an oblique reference to Peter.[7] The assertion that 'no other foundation can any one lay than that which is laid, which is Jesus Christ' (1 Cor. 3.11) may contain an echo of, or even a reply to 'the tradition (Matt. 16.18) that Jesus had re-named Simon as Peter (*Kepha*, the rock), and given the promise that he would build his church on this rock'. Whether Peter himself approved of the idea or not, this saying might have been taken to imply that Peter himself represented the true foundation of the Church, and would thus constitute the source of authority, not Paul. To this Paul replies that Christ alone, and his message, is the foundation of the Church.

In view of the fact that we know that Paul and Peter had indeed been in sharp disagreement (Gal. 2.11ff), and in view of the exceptionally difficult problem posed by the Judaizers in the early communities, it is by no means improbable that Peter had been used as a focus of anti-Pauline propaganda. The peculiarly poignant character of Barrett's suggestion, however, lies in the fact that the 'Petrine' opposition was able to employ a saying attributed to Jesus in support of their case. In other words, we are already, in the first decades after Jesus' life and death, embroiled in the problems of conflicting interpretations of his teaching. Paul himself is already a commentator lodged in the history of tradition. There is no primitive period of immediate and unambiguous clarity.

But the longing for unity is exceedingly powerful. Indeed Paul again supplies us with evidence for the kind of total conviction and commitment which he thought ought to characterize the reception of the gospel. Writing to his Galatian congregation he exclaims:

> I am astonished that you are so quickly deserting him who called you in the grace of Christ and turning to a different gospel – not that there is another gospel, but there are some who trouble you and want to pervert the gospel of Christ. But even if we, or an angel from heaven, should preach to you a gospel contrary to that which we preached to you, let him be accursed (Gal. 1.6–8).

But ought Paul to have been so astonished? Did he really expect a complete and trouble-free allegiance to the gospel? Had he no realization of the inherent ambiguities in what he was attempting to communicate? He certainly believed that the gospel he preached was no human invention (Gal. 1.11), and that its authority lay in its having been received through a revelation of Jesus Christ (Gal. 1.12). He was convinced that once that gospel had been accepted, and once believers had received the Spirit, a turning towards the spiritual slavery of the Mosaic law was, or should be, impossible. Paul's agony at the discovery that the impossible was indeed possible is what gives the whole of his letter its passionate character.

At the same time the total context in which Paul was writing is much more ambiguous than he can possibly admit. The hints which he drops, however, are eloquent enough. What lies, for example, behind his account of his relations with the Christian community in Jerusalem (1.18–20)? Who precisely are the false brethren who want to maintain circumcision (2.4)? Who are the men of high reputation whose acknowledgement of himself he refers to with a marked lack of enthusiasm (2.6)? Why were there grounds for a dispute with Peter (2.11–14)? Although this evidence manifestly demonstrates a deeply embedded lack of homogeneity within the Christian movement in its first twenty years, Paul himself obstinately clings to the notion of one gospel. As we shall see, this firmness is of considerable significance.

For the moment, however, it is sufficient to note that one can distinguish between two sorts of controversy in the Galatian church; that, on the one hand, which affects the very core of the gospel, involving a ruinous return to slavery of 'beings that by nature are no gods' (4.8), and a relatively minor problem, on the other hand, which entails the misinterpretation of the doctrine of freedom (5.13). Some commentators, indeed, have argued that Paul is battling on a double front, against Judaizers on the one hand, and libertines on the other. But this is not a necessary conclusion; rather, the position which Paul takes against the Judaizers whose distortion of the gospel he treats with such seriousness has to be defended against the misunderstanding that 'liberty' means 'licence'. This misunderstanding may or may not have actually led to misbehaviour by Paul's own supporters. At all events it is reasonably easy, so Paul believes, to establish a rule of thumb for the interpretation of 'freedom', namely the love and service of the neighbour (Gal. 5.13–14).

However, this sharp line of distinction between a major and a minor issue is very far from providing us with an escape from the difficulties with which Paul had to deal. So-called minor matters have a way of becoming the focus of major disagreements, in Paul's day no less than our own. An example of this is to be found in the letter to the Romans. Although for the most part it is less loaded with allusions to specific controversies than other letters, two chapters (14 and 15) are devoted to a tension between those who are 'strong' and those who are 'weak' in faith, basically the Gentile and Jewish Christians respectively. This is not unrelated to an issue also treated in his correspondence with the Corinthians (1 Cor. 8–10), namely that of regulations concerning food and drink, and the observance of periods of abstinence. Paul's attitude here, summed up in the words, 'Whether you eat or drink, or whatever you do, do all to the glory of God' (1 Cor. 10.31), while designed to relativize the status of traditional Jewish regulations, evidently resulted in increasing the gulf between himself and the hard-pressed Christian community in Jerusalem. For this reason, as he makes clear at the end of Romans, he is determined to visit the 'saints' in Jerusalem, ostensibly to bring them a gift of financial support, in reality to strengthen the fragile bond between the fast-growing Gentile mission and the Jerusalem church.[8]

Nothing less than Paul's sense of God's plan of salvation for Israel is at stake. He sees himself in the priestly service of the gospel labouring so that the Gentile world may be presented as an acceptable offering (*prosphora*), consecrated by the Holy Spirit (Rom. 15.16). In the event, the hoped-for 'return' of Israel to the Christ did not transpire, and the Gentile Christians overwhelmed the remnants of a more conservative order. But the problem of the interpretation of Judaism, treated with such profundity in Romans 9–11, did not evaporate, in part because Paul himself may not have been entirely fair in his presentation of his opponents' case.[9] Paul's stance as, simultaneously, a Jew and not a Jew, under the law and free of the law, becoming 'all things to all men, that I might by all means save some' (1 Cor. 10.22), entailed formidable ambiguities which he did not resolve. The alleged clarity and certainty of the principle of accommodation which he adopted by no means disposed of the difficulties of interpretation in particulars.

What these examples show is the reality of conflict in the Pauline church. This conflict concerned not merely moral questions, which invariably entail ambiguities of intention, circumstance and consequence. Rather we find controversies about Paul's authority, based, he believed, on a misunderstanding of the gospel, controversies about the continued applicability of the legal traditions of Judaism, and controversies about his own attempt to mediate between the Jewish and Gentile elements in the Christian movement. The point to be made clear is that these are not in every case external trials brought about by some implacably or demonically hostile agency. They constitute rather a continuous spectrum of difficulty apparently inherent in the complexity of what was being attempted. The Christian movement was the cause of its own dissensions.

But what *was* being attempted? So far we have dealt only with the evidence from Paul – the earliest documentary evidence and, for all the uncertainties of precise interpretation, the easiest to construe. Greater difficulties are encountered the moment we press our enquiry back into the earliest traditions about Jesus, and to Jesus' own intentions. What was Jesus trying to do? Before attempting to answer this question it is as well to offer a philosophical observation about the logical impossibility of total novelty. The hyperbole at the heart of Christian discipleship occasionally commits itself to an unguarded affirmation of the absolute incommensurability of Jesus' teaching with any previous example of religious teaching. But irrespective of what may be stated about Jesus' own person, in respect of what he taught we are dealing with the relative novelties of a process of religious change. Under no other circumstances could what he said have been intelligible to his contemporaries. Those who have new things to communicate do so by means of modifications of previously held beliefs. The modifications may be slight, or they may be far-reaching; but they can never be total.

It follows from this that there can be no answer to the question, What was Jesus attempting to do?, which extracts an account of his teaching from its precise context in Palestinian Judaism. Recent studies have greatly sharpened our focus on the social, cultural and political pressures upon Judaism from the time of Alexander the Great.[10] The religious situation into which Jesus was born can be understood only as the consequence of a series of encounters between Judaism and the dominating cultural force of Hellenism. The problem for the Judaism of Jesus' day was to find a *modus vivendi* of some kind, and the movements of Pharisaism, Zelotism, the Qumran community, and Sadduceeism, like the Jesus movement may be regarded as attempts to modify the Jewish tradition to one degree or another in order to meet the new situation.

The Jesus movement itself may, according to Professor Martin Hengel, have taken two forms from the start; one, an Aramaic-speaking congregation based on Jerusalem, and the second, a Greek-speaking group which dispersed northwards towards Syria.[11] Both groups, it is argued, derive from Jesus, the second emphasizing the more radical elements in his teaching, moving rapidly in the light of them towards engagement in the mission to the Gentiles. The significance of this proposal for our discussion is considerable, since it suggests that from the start there was a diversity of interpretations of Jesus' teaching. But even if the hypothesis is rejected, we have still to account for the fact that, within twenty years of his death, markedly different versions of Jesus' message were current. How was this possible?

An adequate answer to this question can scarcely be given without a more detailed examination of the traditions of the synoptic Gospels than can be attempted here. All I can hope to do is to indicate the kind of reply which is in principle plausible.[12] On the face of it, the heart of Jesus' teaching concerned the Kingdom of God, an expression used with a variety of connotations by different groups in the first century. What Jesus distinctively meant by his use of the expression entailed a reworking of its conventional associations, deleting its nuances of military domination and relating it to notions of forgiveness and joy, and above all by placing the teaching in the context of his own actions of healing and fellowship meals with the poor and outcast. The implications of this message and these actions for the traditional law of purity were entirely radical and in effect constituted a new picture of the quality and implications of God's care for the world and for humankind.

The view of Jesus' intentions which emerges from such an outline is one which emphasizes the possibility for the transformation of a religious tradition by a simultaneous retention of the core-meaning of a familiar term combined with novel treatment of its conventional associations, supported by particularly significant actions.[13] What is given, in other words, are the necessary elements for a new response to the pressing needs of Judaism in first-century Palestine, containing the potential for the transformation of other traditions in other contexts – in short, a universalizable and transforming vision of the nature and acts of God.

If this account is tenable in its major features, then it becomes possible to explain not merely why Paul's gospel was subject to such a measure of controversy, but also why any realization of the transformative potential of the teaching of Jesus is inherently disputable. Given in and with the traditions concerning Jesus is the dialectic between his teaching and a local religious situation. Jesus, we may say on the evidence, attended to particulars. But outside the context of, for example, the Zealot view of the Kingdom or the Qumranic view of purity, the implication of his teaching *required* development. And development necessarily entailed ambiguity. Jesus, we can conclude, transformed

Judaism, but strictly speaking did not found Christianity. Rather, Christianity was founded by Jesus' earliest followers on the foundation of his transformation of Judaism.

Moreover when, after their experiences of Jesus' resurrection, the disciples and their converts increasingly treated Jesus as the focus of the identity of the new movement, a further cause for internal variety was thereby incorporated. The reason for this lies in the immediacy of the relationship said to exist between the believer and Christ, an immediacy which then prompts comparisons or matchings between circumstances of Jesus' life and circumstances in the believer's own life. We may again take our examples of this immediacy from Paul. One of Paul's most vivid images to express the quality of Christian discipleship is that the Christian is like a soldier girt with armour, and that the armour is Jesus Christ himself (Rom. 13.14). Another is an analogy with the growth of a child in the womb; 'I am again in travail until Christ be formed in you' (or 'until you take the shape of Christ', Gal. 4.19). Or again, there is the closest identification made between the suffering of Christ and those of the Christian in the references to 'suffering with Christ' (2 Cor. 1.5; Phil. 3.10).

However, concealed behind the very intimacy of these images is a difficulty, which shows acutely in Paul's defence of his authority in 2 Corinthians. What parts of Christ's example are relevant at what times? 'I, Paul, appeal to you by the meekness and gentleness of Christ' (2 Cor. 10.1) is only part of the appeal. It matters not at all that the appeal to meekness is, in all probability, to the acceptance by the divine Christ of the life on earth, as in the celebrated hymn of Philippians 2, rather than to the early example of Jesus. Christ is, in either case, treated as the ideal focus of identification.[14] The important thing for us to note is that the story of the Christ contains diverse episodes, so that Paul is later able to invoke a very different set of characteristics. Basing himself again on the story of Christ he is ready to tell the Corinthians:

> You will have the proof you seek of the Christ who speaks through me, the Christ who, far from being weak with you, makes his power felt among you. True, he died on the cross in weakness, but he lives by the power of God; and we who share his weakness shall by the power of God live with him in your service (2 Cor. 13.3–4 NEB).

Here there is explicit recognition of two facets to the story, with an appeal being made to the power of Christ rather than to the no less characteristic weakness. The point is that because the acts of Jesus or the episodes in the story of Christ are diverse, on some occasions being acts of gentleness, or the patient suffering of injuries, on other occasions being acts of triumphant power, appeal could be made to one or other as occasion necessitated.

Paul is, indeed, confronted in Corinth with an insoluble dilemma, namely the existence of those who claimed equal right to be regarded as a follower of Christ. 'If anyone is confident that he is Christ's, let him remind himself that as he is Christ's, so are we' (2 Cor. 10.7). This makes clear another ground for the inevitability of conflict, namely that the appeal to the intrinsic authority of a life of close discipleship of Christ can never be final, since, again, what has to be appealed to are diverse acts done in different circumstances. In the following of Christ one can only act *like* Christ, and close though the relation to Christ may be said to be, it is a relation and never an identity. Furthermore, there is no question of perfection here and now (Phil. 3.12–16), and to that extent there is always the possibility of mistake and error, even though Paul himself is confident enough to speak of his own example as a model for others (Phil. 3.17).

I have pressed the arguments for the inevitability of conflict in Christianity from the evidence of the New Testament itself because of the powerful influence of what has been correctly identified as the myth of Christian beginnings.[15] It is important to appreciate that what I am attempting to show is not merely the familiar thesis that the New Testament provides evidence of internal diversity.[16] That diversity may, or may not be as extensive as is sometimes urged. The problem of the unity of the New Testament may or may not be as difficult to resolve as is argued. The point I am seeking to make is that the disagreements which the writers of the New Testament had to encounter are not accidental. Even if all these disagreements were resolved by identical solutions (which, in the light of the data seems implausible), it would still be the case that it was the very nature of Christian profession itself which provoked those disagreements. Internal conflict inheres in the Christian tradition, even in its earliest forms.

It is not, therefore, in the least surprising that conflict and debate should continue to characterize the Christian movement as it expanded into other cultures. Certain problems had to be solved for which there was no precise blueprint or precedent.

Two familiar examples, one ancient and one modern, make this abundantly plain. The simplest way of appreciating the first is to compare a passage on any page of Aristotle's *Metaphysics* Zeta with a passage on any page of the New Testament. It very quickly dawned upon Christians living in the context of later hellenistic culture that some account was necessary of the relationship between God's redemptive act in history on the one hand and philosophical argument on the other. In the writings of Justin Martyr, Clement of Alexandria and Origen various solutions were adumbrated.[17] Also given an airing was the plausible view that philosophical enquiry was actually inimical to the discovery of the truth in Christ.[18] What is certain is that the claims of philosophy, of art, and of science could not be ignored. For not only do they have their proper autonomy and method as disciplines, but the Christian understanding of the world as God's creation means that discoveries and achievements in these areas are matters of theological interest. Needless to say the variety of Christian responses to culture has given rise to conflict;[19] no less conflicting and diverse are the Christian accounts of human rationality, for which the very lack of overt epistemological theory in the Scriptures gives direct occasion.

The second further reason for controversy in Christian theology is the result of the modern critical study of the Bible. Precisely because the records of the life of Jesus and the history of the very earliest Christian communities are relatively uncorroborated, the process of historical reconstruction from the sources provides opportunity for a wide spectrum of views. There is very little testimony which is unchallengeable, in view of the known partisanship of most of the early writers. There is, moreover, almost nothing to break the circularity of the procedure whereby a general view of the material is based on a particular evaluation of one part of it. The resulting controversy between scholars of unquestionable learning has a number of consequences which are very well known; but the chief result of relevance here is the doubt which is sown in the mind that appeal to details in the teaching of Jesus himself can be made in systematic theology with complete confidence. The discussion of differing scholarly views exemplifies precisely what I mean by the necessity of controversy. It is simply not possible, in Christian theology, to circumvent the problems which arise from different views of Jesus, and the relationship of his life, death and resurrection to the preaching of the primitive communities. Much of what I have said above about Jesus or Paul is open to rational doubt, and the moment the given interpretation is challenged in the interests of any alternative explanation, the substantive argument of the chapter is merely further confirmed. Controversy is simply unavoidable.

What is it that I have shown? I have shown that a faith which is spread by appeal to the teaching and example of Jesus has certain inherent ambiguities which will give rise to different interpretations. I have also shown that the way in which the faith claims the allegiance of human beings, heart, mind and soul, creates an inescapable problem for the terms on which intellectual and cultural discoveries and achievements are accommodated to discipleship; of this problem the relation with philosophy provides the most acute example. This is by no means a modern phenomenon. But at the Enlightenment two further features emerge to exacerbate the situation. New political conditions enable the controversy implicit in the very profession of Christian discipleship to be conducted more openly; and critical historical enquiry finally destroys the always unrealistic hope that appeal to the Scriptures would end controversy. The truth, rather, was and has always been that the Christian faith is unprotected from the eruption of disputes both about its content and about the practice of Christian discipleship. The only question was to what extent did these disputes matter, and if they mattered how were they to be contained?

The second stage of this argument is to show not only that controversy is a problem, but that disputes about the Christian faith can raise issues which are of far-reaching importance. The point is put with great force by Friedrich Schleiermacher in his speeches *On Religion*.[20] Christianity, he says, is polemical through and through. Its only chance of making clear what its own innermost nature is is by unmasking every false morality, or corrupt thinking, or impoverished religion. Its very first work was to destroy the expectations of the pious of Jesus' day, and then it went on to challenge the gulf which pagan religion had established between the gods and humankind. But more than that, Christianity is as sharply polemical within its own borders, lest some corruption should be able to take root. Jesus said that he had come not to bring peace but a sword, and by that he meant that the religion he founded would be essentially characterized by an unrelenting struggle for purity of intention. Much as Augustine before him, Schleiermacher interprets true religion as unsatisfied longing for union with the divine.

In asserting that the reason for controversy is concern for the purity of Christian faith, Schleiermacher is only reflecting the anxiety evident in the New Testament itself about the possibility of being misled by false guides. In dealing with that divided Christian community at Corinth Paul goes so far as to suggest that 'there must be factions (haireseis) among you in order that those who are genuine among you may be recognized' (1 Cor. 11.19). Similarly fateful are the words about the false teachers described as agents of Satan, masquerading as agents of good (2 Cor. 11.13–15). The teaching of the Gospels likewise makes clear the reality and danger of false prophets and false messiahs, capable of producing 'signs and wonders to lead astray, if possible, the elect' (Mark 13.22; Matt. 24.24; cf. Mark 13.6; Matt. 24.5,11). Matthew's Sermon on the Mount contains a warning against false prophets 'who come to you in sheep's clothing but inwardly are ravenous wolves' (Matt. 7.15).

The later strands of the New Testament and the literature of the early apostolic age give evidence of apprehension in the face of what Luke, in the farewell speech attributed to Paul at Miletus, also vividly describes as 'fierce wolves'.[21] Their activities will be such that 'from among your own selves will arise men speaking perverse things, to draw away the disciples after them' (Acts 20.29–30). The troubles seem to originate in a counter-attack from the side of Judaism on the Christian claim to be the authentic Israel; but one notes that its results include internal schism. Under no circumstances could such conflict be regarded with equanimity as an acceptable form of religious pluralism.

The danger of being misled is taken with great seriousness for two reasons, the fact that it is by no means easy to perceive the right way and the fact that God is judge of those who apostatize. The various warnings reflect differing situations and different times. But from whatever source the sayings originate, they have profound consequences for subsequent Christian attitudes. The disciple will always be faced with difficulties:

> Enter by the narrow gate; for the gate is wide and the way is easy, that leads to destruction, and those who enter by it are many. For the gate is narrow and the way is hard, that leads to life, and those who find it are few (Matt. 7.13–14).

The vividness of the imagery is the source of the impressively disciplined and alert view of discipleship implied. Similarly with the persons who built houses on rock and on sand, in the verses which follow, a view is powerfully expressed on the future destruction of those who do not act upon the message of Jesus. Both Gospels and Epistles take a serious view of those who begin on the way of obedience, but who do not persist.

It would, on the basis of this evidence, be extremely difficult to think that easy toleration of diversity of opinion came naturally to a mind formed in any way upon the teaching of the New Testament. If controversy is inevitable it is also serious. There are choices to be made about what to believe, to say and to do, and these choices matter, because it is possible to go seriously wrong. For this reason there is a substantial quantity of teaching which relates to the obedience of the believer, both in Paul, who speaks of the pattern of obedience as arising directly out of life in Christ (Phil. 2.6–13; 2 Cor. 10.5; Rom. 6.15–19), and in John, who develops a notion of the believer's dependence on Christ, as an abiding or dwelling in him.

Moreover, apart from this direct teaching relating to the very basis of Christian discipleship, there is some instruction concerning the need for discernment in particular matters. Thus the Thessalonians are advised to bring all prophetic utterances to the test (1 Thess. 5.21), or the Corinthian congregation are assured that a person gifted with the Spirit can judge the worth of everything, 'but is himself to be judged by no one' (1 Cor. 2.15). Similarly in the letter to the Hebrews, the grown persons to whom the writer wants to address his higher thoughts are said to have 'their faculties trained by practice to distinguish good from evil' (Heb. 5.14). In short, authentic Christian discipleship, which is achieved out of the midst of ambiguity and with necessarily attendant controversy, thrusts believers into a position of difficulty and danger where there is need both of guidance and of a power of discrimination.

Given these two factors, the inevitability of controversy, and the seriousness with which the possibility of deviation must be taken, the third stage of the argument follows with a certain historical inevitability. It becomes necessary, in other words, to provide guidance in cases of dispute. I do not propose to do more at this stage than adduce one illustration of this need, in view of the fact that I shall be taking up the question of power and authority in the third chapter. The illustration returns, appropriately enough, to Paul's farewell speech to the elders of the church at Ephesus composed by Luke presumably after Paul's death:

> Take heed to yourselves and to all the flock, in which the Holy Spirit has made you guardians (*episkopoi*), to feed the church of the Lord which he obtained with his own blood (Acts 20.28).

After the death of the first generation of apostles, the danger of being misled is such as to require the exercise of an alert guardianship by those described as elders (*presbuteroi*). The reality and responsibility of leadership is thus clearly envisaged, and with it, as we shall see, a necessary exercise of power.[22]

The three stages of the argument are herewith completed, and yield the following conclusion: the history of the earliest stages of the Christian movement demonstrates that conflicts about the identity of Christianity are not incidental or peripheral, but that they are inseparable from the actual form and content of that movement's origins. It is now necessary to consider the full range of topics over which conflicts are bound to occur, and the implication, for such conflicts, of the fact that Christianity has a diversity of aspects.

III

Christianity is a religion whose identity is perceptible in different aspects or dimensions; it is multifaceted. A simple way of appreciating this important fact is to recall the threefold medieval confession of sin in 'thought, word and deed'. Thinking, speaking and doing are, so to speak, theatres of the Christian warfare in which personal defeat may be suffered. They reflect, it may be, the demand for purity expressed in Psalm 15 as a condition for dwelling on God's holy hill:

> He who walks blamelessly, and does what is right,
>   and speaks truth from (or, in) his heart;
> Who does not slander with his tongue ... (Ps. 15.2–3).

The true living of the Christian faith entails, accordingly, true thought, true speech and true action.

The threefold nature of Christianity, roughly corresponding to the threefold theatre expounded above, but more particularly to the threefold office of Christ as prophet, priest and king, is a thought upon which John Henry Newman briefly touches. 'Christianity is dogmatical, devotional, practical all at once';[23] or, more fully:

> Christianity, then, is at once a philosophy, a political power and a religious rite: as a religion it is holy; as a philosophy, it is Apostolic; as a political power, it is imperial, that is, One and Catholic. As a religion, its special seat is pastor and flock; as a philosophy, the Schools; as a rule, the Papacy and its Curia.[24]

We shall return to this important passage in our subsequent discussion of Newman. For the moment it is sufficient to recognize the three areas of activity to which Newman points, the devotional or religious, the dogmatic or philosophical, and the practical or political. For Christianity to be Christianity, he is saying, it must be simultaneously extended in each of the three areas in an internally coherent manner.

The scheme so established is, however, capable of further analysis. For example, the practical or political sphere is composed at once of teaching about practice, and actual institutional embodiment. Teaching about practice can be broken down further into doctrines about humanity, doctrines about the Church, and Christian ethics. Similarly the devotional aspect can be subdivided into religious rituals, the life of prayer itself, and the theology of worship. Such analyses speedily reveal not merely the interconnectedness of the 'aspects', but the metaphorical status of the language of 'aspect'. In examining Christianity we are not looking at a three-dimensional figure from a variety of perspectives. We are attempting rather to do justice to a complex of elements by the artificial process of separating out now one and now another feature for inspection; the reason for doing so is in fact to prevent ourselves from oversimplifying our mental picture or image of what the religion actually is.

The same remarks apply to the now well-known 'dimension' analysis of religion provided by Professor Ninian Smart:

> Religion is a six-dimensional organism, typically containing doctrines, myths, ethical teachings, rituals, and social institutions, and animated by religious experiences of various kinds. To understand the key ideas of religion, such as God and nirvana, one has to understand the pattern of religious life directed towards those goals.[25]

These six dimensions are, in effect, expansions of Newman's three aspects. Newman's devotional aspect is made up of Smart's dimensions of rituals and religious experiences; the doctrinal is rendered as doctrines and myths; the practical is subdivided into ethical teachings and social institutions. But here again the divisions are artificial, and it is solely for the avoidance of oversimplifications that they are to be invoked.

The reason for going to some trouble to insist on the multi-faceted character of Christianity can be simply explained. The treatment of the identity of Christianity to be offered in this book is confined almost entirely to questions of theological method. Yet Christianity is a religion, not a philosophical system, and one does not participate in Christianity by discussing its methodological problems. The point of acknowledging the many-sided character of Christianity at this stage is twofold. On the one hand, I wish to offer an explicit justification for concentrating on the doctrinal question of method, and on the other hand I propose to return at the end of the book to another dimension of Christianity, and to do so without appearing to alter the character of the discussion. In any case what must be regarded as certain is that a consideration of the identity of Christianity which failed to refer to anything other than its doctrinal content would be a gross distortion of the way it actually appears in history.

However, it has to be admitted that most of what will concern us in this book will be Christianity seen in its doctrinal, specifically methodological, aspect. Is there any good reason for this fact? One might argue, for example, that Christianity of all religions places the greatest emphasis on the 'word', on that which is verbally articulable. 'Faith', says Paul, 'comes from what is heard, and what is heard comes by the preaching of Christ' (Rom. 10.17). On this view that which does not 'preach Christ' (Luther) does not properly belong to Christianity, and the only way to discover whether any non-verbal dimension of Christianity, such as a ritual or an institution, is authentically Christian, is to submit it to rigorous theological analysis and criticism. The objection to this view, which we can without hesitation describe as characteristically Protestant, might well be that it takes sides too readily and too quickly. Indeed it would appear to be typically Protestant to treat Christianity as though Christian iconography or liturgical ritual was of no, or only of minor, significance; and I would want to insist that at this stage of the discussion such an assumption would prejudice the whole enquiry.

It is not, however, for that reason that I shall be concerned principally with Christian doctrine. My reason is, rather, that because, as I have shown above, Christian discipleship necessarily throws the disciple into internal controversies, he or she is forced to employ doctrinal discussion as a means of clarifying and ultimately making the decisions which conflict imposes. There is no dimension of Christianity which is not controversial. For example, rituals differ; some rituals are held to be appropriate and others are not; as ritual develops certain possibilities are adopted, and others are set aside. When one asks how this discrimination is made, the answer is bound to involve doctrine. As an illustration of this fact one might offer the following reasoning:

1   The eucharistic elements are, or are not, in themselves, transformed into the Body and Blood of Christ.

2   Kneeling expresses an attitude of humility and adoration.

3   Therefore one should, or should not, receive the eucharistic elements kneeling.

Although the logic of an argument in ritual is certainly more sophisticated and indirect than this implies, this illustrates the fact that there exists a felt coherence between doctrine and ritual, which makes doctrinal differences of great weight when discriminating between various ritual practices. Indeed, as Smart has himself put it, 'the meaning of ritual cannot be understood without reference to the environment of belief in which it is performed';[26] and as far as the Christian tradition is concerned, one of the major ways in which 'environments of belief' have differed from each other is in respect of their doctrines.

The reason, therefore, for focusing attention on the doctrines of Christianity is that it is in relation to the doctrinal tradition that internal conflict becomes most explicit and manageable. One can observe that Christianity has a ritual dimension; one can point out that different Christian churches have different rituals; but one can only resolve conflicting claims for different rituals in conjunction with an articulation of their coherence with doctrines. This way of viewing the significance of doctrinal discussion does not entail a radical reduction of the significance of ritual, as though ritual was justified, if at all, only as a rather ambiguous (and hence dangerous) substitute for discursive communication and argument. No more does the literary critical analysis of a poem reduce the poem to the philosophical, political or aesthetic views of its author or milieu. Rituals, like poems, can speak directly to people, without analytic interpretation. But because conflict between ritual practices in Christian history has arisen in conjunction with doctrinal divergences, doctrinal discussion is at least of assistance (and I do not put it higher than that) in the resolution of conflict.

In Smart's exposition of the dimensions of Christianity there were six elements. In justifying concentration on the doctrines of Christianity, I have referred only to the relation of doctrine and ritual; but, in principle, the same considerations can be applied both to the myths and to the institutional embodiment, or social reality of the Christian religion. Of these also it may be said that conflict (about which myths to believe and how, or about which forms of institution to adopt) requires doctrinal discussion. We are left with two remaining dimensions, ethics and experiences. Concerning the former it is at least possible to argue for the integration of the doctrinal and ethical aspects of Christianity.[27] Chapter 3, dealing with the problems of power and Christianity, will provide us with an impressive example of this. The tradition which speaks of the power of God holds that that power is an expression of his goodness and love; it is, in other words, power exercised in accordance with moral and person-forming goals. Doctrine and ethics are aspects of a single religious intention.

What then, finally, of the dimension of experience? How is experience, as a dimension of Christianity, to be understood in relation to doctrine? As Smart describes it, religious experiences 'animate' the entire organism of a religion. Experience is, therefore, importantly different from the other five dimensions, in particular in two ways. In the first place, unlike rituals, myths, doctrines, ethical teachings and social institutions, religious experiences cannot be directly inspected. Of the other five dimensions, there is a public act, story, proposition or constitution in which that aspect of the Christian religion comes to expression. Of religious experiences, however, we have no public data, other than reports of internal happenings or sensations. Secondly, religious experiences are themselves an essential aspect of each of the other dimensions. This is particularly clear in the case of rituals, which can be fully interpreted only when the personal state of the participant is taken into account. There is, in other words, both an external and an internal aspect of a ritual, the inner aspect being the accompanying intentions and sentiments giving the ritual its meaning. Similarly, it could be argued, that in the case of myth, doctrine, ethical teaching and social institutions, the external, or public aspect constantly needs to be explicated in connection with the internal, or experiential aspect, with which it is directly related.

If this view commands agreement, then it is plain that a doctrinal discussion of the identity of Christianity has to bear in mind three elements: (a) the public doctrinal inheritance of the Christian tradition, that is, the doctrinal dimension, *per se*; (b) the connection that exists between the doctrinal dimension and the inner experiences of the believer, between, that is, the outside and the inside of the doctrinal dimension; and (c) the fact that, because of the existence of controversy about every other dimension of Christianity, it is necessary that the doctrinal, that is the verbal and intellectual tradition, play a leading part in elucidating the nature of the conflict, and hence that there should be a specific relationship between the verbal and the non-verbal dimensions of Christianity, and their experiential roots.

This last point, of course, adds greatly to the complexity of the picture which I am trying to paint of how the nature and identity of Christianity can be elucidated in a doctrinal discussion. Put at its simplest, what I am saying is that, in addition to the doctrinal tradition *per se*, and to the Christian experiences related to that doctrine, there must be developed an articulate theological interpretation of Christian ritual, of Christian myth, and of Christian institutions. Moreover, I am saying that these theologies must be properly sensitive to the fact that all the dimensions of a religion arise in intimate connection with religious experience. The experiential aspect of a myth, for example, may be (on certain psychological theories) buried deep in the collective unconscious, or contained in the power of stories to provide a context or horizon for human lives. Similarly, because we are social beings, the institutional embodiment and posture of the Church has a profound impact upon our consciousness.

Accordingly, in the concentration upon doctrine which will be evident in what follows, there is no commitment to the view that doctrine and ethics are the most fundamental reality of Christianity. At a time of religious controversy or change, this, certainly, is how they appear, because the conceptual apparatus of a doctrinal and ethical tradition furnish the sharpest tools known to us for making distinctive meaning as unambiguous as possible. But it must never be forgotten that part of Jesus' teaching was parabolic, and that part of the distinctiveness of the community of his disciples was their observance of a common meal. We shall have every reason to mark the imperialistic instincts of the intellectual tradition in the course of this book. For the moment we note both the sufficient reason for handling the topic Christianity by means of its doctrinal tradition, and also the dangers implicit in doing so.

A final qualification must be added about the extraordinarily elusive concept of religious experience. We speak of *religious* experience in order, presumably, to distinguish such experience from other experience. But do experiences fall into distinct categories? Are there particular forms of perception corresponding to different forms of experience? Consider the following account from Smart:

> A religious experience involves some kind of 'perception' of the *invisible* world, or involves a perception that some visible person or thing is a manifestation of the invisible world.[28]

But on such a description the concept of experience is being used to include vastly differing kinds of perception; moreover, some analogy is being drawn between a visible and an invisible world.

The complexity of this relation is well beyond the bounds of the treatment which we can give the matter here. But it would be extraordinarily foolish not to advert to one important factor, namely the historical character of all such experience. Religious experience is also qualified by time and place; that is, it is the experience of persons historically conditioned. The experience of the invisible world is of a world already structured by an historically received religious tradition, at a particular stage of its development. It follows from this that other aspects of historical conditioning are also reflected in religious experience. That is to say, there is a necessary reflection of a particular stage of psycho-social development in the historicity attaching to religious experience. This is important if we are to avoid the temptation of treating religious experience as a source of 'unpolluted' or unambiguous information. On the contrary, the historical character of religious experience is a further reason for conflict. As the early Christian communities discovered, 'prophetic inspiration' was by no means self-authenticating. It, too, had to be tested by discriminating judgement (1 Thess. 5.21). Moreover, culturally transmitted ways of seeing things embedded in the processes of socialization tend to shape the way in which claims are made about religious experience. Not merely does religious experience provide no escape from ambiguity into a kind of direct perception of the eternal world, it may actually create further problems for doctrinal or ethical solution. Once again the subject matter of Chapter 3 provides us with an example; here we have a case where already existing patterns of authority inform the sociological requirements for a growing church, and pose the doctrinal and ethical problems of 'institutionalization'. Changing experience of authority provides the modern Church with problems to which it has all too inadequately responded hitherto.

At the opening of this chapter I stated that it is inconceivable that there should ever be complete agreement about the identity of Christianity. Why should this be so? The argument of this chapter has provided three reasons. In the first place, the controversies or dissensions which occurred in the early Christian communities were caused by certain ambiguities inherent in the gospel as taught by Paul, and in the very nature of what had to be carried out in taking Jesus' teaching and work into new contexts. Secondly, the multifaceted character of Christianity ensures a series of problems in the internal relationship of its various aspects or dimensions. Thirdly, as we have just argued, religious experience, because it is always historically conditioned, guarantees the constant presentation of new problems for solution, which derive from the different personal and social experiences of Christian individuals. So much at least can be argued in principle. But of this third question there is much more to be said. We turn, therefore, to a closer examination of the Judaeo-Christian tradition of 'inwardness'.

2

The Tradition of Inwardness

It is undeniable, from even a cursory knowledge of the Christian tradition, that 'inwardness' has played an important role in the development of Christian identity. But what role precisely? Obviously it is beyond the scope of a single chapter even to survey the evidence as a whole. Accordingly, a different method has been adopted, more strictly relevant to the limited aims of this enquiry. As the previous chapter has indicated, conflict inheres in Christianity; but at the same time Christians find it impossible to regard that fact with equanimity. Decisions have to be made about what to believe and what to do, and these decisions matter. It is from this particular standpoint that the question about inwardness must be raised, namely, What is the relevance for decision-making of the fact that there is an internal dimension to Christianity?

Pursuit of this enquiry leads us to the following: in the first place, we must clarify what this inwardness tradition amounts to, in particular in the teaching about the heart in the Old and New Testaments. For references to the heart occur in a whole series of biblical passages which subsequent Christian writers have cited, when carrying forward into their own times an understanding of the internal dimension of Christianity. Secondly, it will be necessary to illustrate the impact of that dimension on two other dimensions of Christianity, namely upon ritual and ethical teachings. Finally, and very briefly, an argument will be developed about the element of ambiguity which is necessarily introduced by the tradition of inwardness into the decision-making of the Christian Church when dealing with matters of conflict. In this way I hope to prepare the ground for a discussion of the theme of power in the Church, in the following chapter.

I

> But lo, thou requirest truth in the inward parts: and shalt make me
> to understand wisdom secretly ... Make me a clean heart, O God:
> and renew a right spirit within me (Ps. 51.6 and 10).

Coverdale's translation of Psalm 51 has unquestionably had a
special impact upon the modern English spiritual tradition. It
suggests that God requires of each person a kind of ultimate
inner integrity, a correspondence of his will for the individual
and that individual's personal intentions; it further teaches that
it is only by a re-creative act of God himself that the person is
able to attain to such an inner state. For the heart to be clean of
this kind of corruption which afflicts it, it must be renewed by
God.

It is, therefore, with a certain dismay that one encounters in
the New English Bible translation a completely altered sense,
which connects verse 6 with the previous verse:

> In iniquity I was brought to birth and my mother conceived me in
> sin; yet, though thou hast hidden the truth in darkness, through this
> mystery thou dost teach me wisdom (Ps. 51.5–6).

The more conservative translators of the Church of England's
admirable Liturgical Psalter have restored, indeed enriched, the
Coverdale tradition, with:

> You that desire truth in the inward parts: O teach me wisdom in the
> secret places of the heart (Ps. 51.6).

But in fact the phrase 'truth in the inward parts' is a departure
from the Septuagint, the Vulgate and Luther's Bible, and justified
only by one interpretation of an uncertain text.[1]

Happily for the purpose of this chapter, the argument about
inwardness which is to be mounted here does not depend on, or
even begin with, this verse, for all its attractions. The reason for
attending to this particular feature of the tradition has already
been touched on, but can be somewhat more fully explained. The
desire for clarification which the inescapable conflicts in Christianity stimulate, advances the discipline of theology to a position
of importance. The reason for this is that words are the most
precise tools to hand in the pursuit and promotion of an agreed
common meaning. Theology thus becomes the means whereby

a discriminatory perception, a judgement between true and false alternatives, becomes possible. By virtue of the tools employed, and for the purpose of communication the judgement is necessarily given in verbal form (or deeds explained and justified by words). But at once the question arises, Are words adequate? In particular, are they an adequate vehicle for the truth required of the heart? It is for this particular reason that the question of inwardness needs to be investigated at this present stage.

It should also be noted, parenthetically, that the observation and analysis of the Judaeo-Christian tradition substantially expands and undergirds the discussion of the experiential dimension of Christianity in the previous chapter. There we noted that every publicly observable or external dimension of the religious tradition (whether myth, doctrine, ethics, ritual or social embodiment, to employ Smart's categories) needs to be explicated in connection with the internal or experiential aspect by which it is animated. This programmatic statement obviously requires careful assessment in the light of the history of the Christian Church, and it is this requirement also which forces us to consider, in the first place, the Old Testament understanding of the heart in relation to the demand of God.

But first I propose to offer a brief comment on the function of commitment. In a recent general theory of the sociology of religion, commitment is identified as one of the major elements in the sacralizing process.[2] Defined as 'focused emotion or emotional attachment to a specific focus of identity', commitment is said to anchor in the emotions that system of meaning common to a whole society or a group, or even embraced by a single individual.[3] A system of meaning entails a hierarchy of priorities which guide the individual's choices. One of the most important forms of religious commitment is the ritual offering of sacrifice, for it is sacrifice which reinforces whatever is at the apex of the system.[4] An advantage of this understanding of sacrifice is that it creates an intelligible link between material offerings and self-sacrifice. The function of a material offering is to establish a means of communication with the sacred, and by the same action the values for which the sacred stands are affirmed and reinforced. Similarly in relation to self-sacrifice, the values for which the self is consecrated or offered to the divine are those which are ultimate in a particular system of priorities.

The importance of commitment is also highlighted by observation of the negative significance of hypocrisy, in which 'commitment to the actual system of meaning is kept hidden behind an ostensible, usually more acceptable one'.[5]

This understanding of commitment places a strong emphasis on interior intentions. While it is incorrect to say that intentions can never be known to anyone other than the individual intender, there may be occasions when nothing certain can be said about a person's intentions by any other party. Moreover individuals, on looking back at actions they have performed, may not be entirely clear what their intentions actually were. Under these circumstances, it is intelligible why a capacity to inspect and judge intentions with unerring accuracy should be attributed to God.

A further aspect of the importance of commitment arises at this point. Consistency of intention is of great social importance.[6] The benevolence of a ruler who possesses great or even unlimited power is a source of stability in a given society, because subjects can rely upon his or her commitment to a system of priorities in the daily administration of affairs. The stability of the family similarly depends heavily upon consistency in the parents. If religion at least in part consists in the objectification of a system of values, then a substantial part of its function will be to reinforce by teaching, by myth, by ritual and by any other external means the commitment of its adherents to that system of priorities. It will, in short, be concerned with the interiorization of a consistent intention, and upon its success in so doing its stability will largely depend.

These remarks are made of religions in general. The extent to which and manner in which any given religion emphasizes the importance of interior commitment no doubt varies with particular traditions. We are concerned here with the Judaeo-Christian tradition, to whose teaching about the heart we now turn.[7]

The Old Testament narratives show a plain enough recognition of the universal phenomenon of human deceit, that is of the concealment of the intention by misleading external acts or speech.[8] By contrast, the view is repeatedly expressed that a right relationship with God entails recognition of the impossibility of deceiving him, and the catastrophic consequences of trying to do so. In a series of passages from the psalms attention is drawn to the necessity of self-examination, in which reference is made to the heart.[9] In these passages the term 'heart' stands, in the first place, for the focal point of a whole range of psychical activity, especially at the emotional level. But it is also, and more prominently, used to refer to the seat or instrument of human intellectual and volitional activity. The dual usage is surely significant in its recognition of the emotional or affective element in all intention. The 'heart's desire' (Ps. 20.4) is precisely that towards which one's resolve or purpose is ultimately bent.[10] Significant too, is the mysteriousness and inaccessibility of this interior seat.[11]

The self-examination, therefore, which is enjoined on the worshipper amounts to a seeing of the heart as God himself sees it.[12] This has especially to be true of the believer's worship.[13] For a true sacrifice to be offered the heart must be broken of its proclivity towards disobedience.[14] What is required is so exacting and so total that it can be spoken of as possible only if given by God.[15]

The purpose of referring to this aspect of a long and complex history of worship and reflection is to illustrate what amounts to a fundamental assumption of the literature which was the matrix of the early Christian communities. For them too discrepancy between religious actions and the disposition of the heart is scandalous, and God is spoken of as the tester of human hearts.[16] The heart, moreover, is one of Paul's most characteristic terms usually understood as the centre and source of human willing, thinking, emotion and affections.[17] It is the heart which is the dwelling place of God's Holy Spirit, given by God himself.[18] In three passages, two of them indubitably Paul's own writing, the phrase 'the inmost self' (*ho eso anthropos*) is used in contexts suggesting an analogy between the ultimately mysterious depth of human personhood, and the inwardness of the mind or *nous*.[19] Elsewhere the phrase 'the hidden person of the heart' suggests the interior source of the virtue of obedience.[20]

We may say that, for the Judaeo-Christian tradition as a whole, the heart stands for the locus of human commitment, and that at that 'centre' human intentions are open only to God. If a person is to be attentive to God, it is in the heart that the necessary transformation of attitude will occur. Moreover, so radical is the required surgery, it is God alone who can successfully carry it out.

The unity of this testimony is impressive. It is by no means invariably the case that a consistent tradition is maintained over a long span of time, while other elements of the tradition are subject to substantial reinterpretation and modification. None the less it would be misleading to speak of 'biblical anthropology', as though there is a consistent terminology or set of concepts. What we have, rather, is the affirmation that the depths of human psychology are mysterious, combined with the conviction that, however mysterious they may be to us, they lie open to God. How this tradition has contributed to the problem with which we are dealing must now be further explored.

II

The teaching concerning the heart which we have expounded above has had a profound impact upon the formation of the identity of Christianity. In particular it was bound to be the case that a religion with so strong an emphasis on the internal response to God would also show evidence of interaction between that response and the visible or external phenomena in which it is embodied. The variable nature of that interaction I propose to examine in the next section. Here I want to give some illustrations from two of Smart's external dimensions, namely those of ritual and ethical teaching, in order to demonstrate the direct impact which emphasis on the theme of the heart has had.

As we have already seen, strands of Old Testament tradition are conscious of the complex relation between external rituals and the inner dimension of the heart. The remarkable phrases concerning the 'foreskin of the heart' (Jer. 4.4 and Deut. 10.16) or 'an uncircumcised heart' (Lev. 26.41) demonstrate sensitivity towards the problem of bringing about an undeviating allegiance to the covenant. For Paul, too, circumcision of the heart requires an act, not of an agent in a ritual, but of God himself.[21]

How, then, do matters stand with water baptism? This, too, is an external rite, and it is appropriate to ask whether there is a similar tension to be observed. Examination of the evidence suggests that this is so, and that the external ritual of water-baptism stands in an unclarified relationship to the reality of salvation,[22] or to the gift of the Holy Spirit.[23] However, the rite has a highly dramatic content in the transference of the Christian from an old to a new life, and no New Testament writer has any interest in minimizing its significance. Thus though Paul shows quite unequivocally the vanity of thinking that baptism constitutes a kind of guarantee against falling into damnation,[24] he has every reason to associate the ritual of baptism as closely as possible with the participatory reality of being 'one in Christ'. The 'interest' of the writer is also crucial to the interpretation of a passage from the letter to the Colossians:

> In him [i.e. Christ] also you were circumcised with a circumcision made without hands, by putting off the body of flesh in the circumcision of Christ; and you were buried with him in baptism, in which [or, in whom] you were also raised with him through faith in the working of God, who raised him from the dead (Col. 2.11–12).

The passage occurs in the context of warning to Christians not to become embroiled in human traditions, philosophized forms of Jewish legalism. The convert is being recalled to the spiritual significance of an actual event in his or her life, namely his or her baptism in water. The appeal to an impressive physical occurrence which can stick in the memory has even more power in it than the appeal to 'circumcise the heart', which, by definition, is not externally perceptible. It may well be that the reference to the old rite of circumcision prompted in the writer's mind the thought of the new rite of baptism. But we may surely say that it is typical of the New Testament as a whole that in this passage too the relation between internal and external is open to more than one interpretation.

Precisely the same ambiguity can be observed in relation to the Eucharist. As in the case of circumcision the Old Testament itself sponsors what has, somewhat ambiguously, been termed a 'spiritualization' of the external rite of sacrifice.[25] The early Christian movement concurred with an established section of contemporary Judaism for which true religion did not depend on the sacrificial system.[26] Once the death of Christ was itself interpreted as covenant sacrifice, the superfluity of the sacrificial rituals was further emphasized.[27] But it remains an open question in modern interpretation whether or not the new ritual of the eucharistic meal has residual sacrificial connotations. Indeed, here again Paul (who is virtually our only witness in the matter) has no conceivable interest in distinguishing with precision between the ritual actions and the inner participation in Christ.

In this matter, by far the most important New Testament text is Paul's allusion to the meaning of participation in sacrifice: 'Consider the practice of Israel: are not those who eat the sacrifices partners in the altar?' (1 Cor. 10.18). The context of the reference is the discussion of the Gentile practice of sacrifice to idols which Paul regards as nullifying the force of participation in Christ. Baptism in Christ is no more a protection from destruction than eating miraculous manna was to the Israelites in the desert. For one who participates in Christ by the bread and the cup, participation in pagan sacrifice is similarly ruinous; it is a participatory union excluding one from union with Christ. It is at this point that Paul introduces his allusion to Israel's sacrifices. He is not arguing for a theology of participation; that is his assumption. But how does the analogy work? Does it assume the reality of Israel's sacrificial ritual, and apply that reality to the new (sacrificial?) ritual of the Christian? Or does it rather extract the principle of sharing in the benefits of worship (in this allusion, Israel's worship), without affirming or denying the sacrificial character of the Christian Eucharist? Needless to say, the commentators differ.[28]

Thus although the rituals of baptism and Eucharist occupy an important place in the life of the new Christian movement, they inherit some of the ambiguity attaching to the rituals of the old covenant. More precisely, the Christian movement strongly developed the theme of the change of heart which had figured in the Old Testament, but in so doing it necessarily left ambiguous the precise status of its new rituals. Accordingly, subsequent Christian reflection shows a characteristic oscillation between emphasis on inward transformation, and an emphasis on the importance of the cult, with a large number of possible ways of conceiving the relationship between the two.

This last statement concerning subsequent Christianity requires some substantiation, and in general the history of realist and symbolist interpretations of the Eucharist provides persuasive illustrations.[29] But the most remarkable contribution and one which stands at the fountain-head of the whole Western tradition, both Catholic and Protestant, is the thought of Augustine. Central to a description of the character of the Christian life, as Augustine conceives it, is the longing characteristic of the lover. Commenting on the text, 'No man cometh unto me except the Father draw him,' he writes:

> Give me a lover, he will feel that of which I speak: give me one who longs, who hungers, who is a thirsty pilgrim in this wilderness, sighing for the springs of his eternal homeland: give me such a man, he will know what I mean.[30]

'Longing' he says, 'is the heart's treasury', and he proceeds to enumerate all the external forms of the Christian life (Scripture, congregational worship, sacraments, and preaching) as directed towards the growth of a capacity to long for God. The frustration of longing in this life is the impetus for devotion; 'you have made us for yourself, and our heart is restless until it rests in you'.[31] This longing for God is, indeed, what Augustine means by prayer. Both prayer and praise can be offered perpetually, that is literally without ceasing, because they proceed from the inward 'voice of the heart', and are thus not restricted to the external utterance of words.[32]

That the true worship of God is a matter of the heart, is the presupposition of the well-known discussion of sacrifice in *The City of God*. Having defined true religion as the love of God and the love of neighbour as oneself, Augustine shows that the intention of Jewish sacrifices, as of our sacrifices, was 'to cleave to God and seek the good of our neighbour for the same end'.[33] The visible sacrifice is the sacrament or sacred sign of the invisible sacrifice, the broken heart (referring to Psalm 51.18). The true sacrifice is characterized by its end or intention, expressed in the words of Psalm 73, 'As for me my true good is to cling to God' (v. 28). Augustine continues:

> This being so, it immediately follows that the whole redeemed community, that is to say, the congregation and fellowship of the saints, is offered to God as a universal sacrifice, through the great Priest who offered himself in his suffering for us.[34]

This living sacrifice of the Christian community unified into one body *is*, for Augustine, the sacrifice celebrated in the eucharistic sacrament. The Eucharist contains visible sacrifices, but it does so as symbols of the invisible sacrifices of the heart.

In offering our sacrifices we shall be aware that visible sacrifice must be offered only to him, to whom we ourselves ought to be an invisible sacrifice in our hearts.[35]

The thought expressed here by Augustine is certainly a development beyond the ideas of Paul, rather than a mere reproduction of them. But I do not think it can be said that the method is other than Paul's method. For, like Paul, Augustine has everything to gain and little or nothing to lose by reminding Christians of the extraordinary internal reality which the external rite represents. As Burnaby puts it, 'the Eucharist is there to keep the Church in mind of her sacrificial character'.[36] Therefore Augustine will speak of the Eucharist as a sacrifice, and assert that at the sacrifice what is offered is the Body of Christ (in its twofold sense).[37] But he will also say that in the eucharistic oblations the Church celebrates the mystic symbol (*mysterium*) of the sacrifice of ourselves.[38] The language is at once whole-heartedly realist, and yet at the same time non-literal. Both inwardness and exteriority are fully affirmed, qualifying each other without a clear synthetic statement, and bequeathing to subsequent thinkers a series of problems in the theory of sacramental symbolism which can hardly be said to have been solved.[39]

The third illustration to be offered of how inwardness qualifies the external dimensions of Christianity is in the area of ethical teaching. It needs only to be briefly characterized. According to the synoptic gospel tradition Jesus identified the heart as the source of human defilement (Mark 7.21–3). There is a prior adultery in the heart which is forbidden no less than the act of adultery (Matt. 5.28). Accordingly the ethical teaching of the early Church is marked by a recurrent tendency to lay emphasis not merely on the outward acts of good and evil, but on the intention of the heart. If the human good is defined as cleaving to God, so human evil is 'the will's aversion from the changeless good, and its conversion to the goods that are changing'.[40] Augustine correctly interprets the Psalms as teaching a secret impulse of the heart known only to God. This may be, as we have seen, a continuous stream of interior praise; or it may be the intention to commit a crime. In either case the cry of the heart (*clamor cordis*) is already known to God, and subject to judgement.[41]

The emphasis Augustine placed on the will as the principle by which actions are guided became part of the accepted teaching of medieval theologians. But among them the one to emphasize the significance of intention most strongly was Peter Abelard. For him 'works ... are all indifferent in themselves and should be called good or bad only on account of the intention of the agent'.[42] The formulation of this thesis is carried out with reference to those passages from Old and New Testaments relating to God's observation of the human heart. The inwardness tradition ensures what has been termed 'the interiorization of morality'.[43] Morality cannot become, in the Christian tradition, the due performance of right deeds.

Particularly striking also, in the lively ethical treatise in which this intentionism is propounded, is the moral criticism of the way in which certain of the Church's rituals had developed. Thus fear as a motive for penitence, priestly cupidity in the sale of masses, unskilled and imperceptive confessors, and the arrogation to the entire episcopate of the power to remit or retain sins are strongly attacked.[44] In each of these cases the emphasis which Abelard has placed on intention has given him a standpoint from which to open up the external rituals of the Church to critical examination. Not that Abelard believes the rituals or ordinances to be wrong in themselves, or that there are no objective criteria of right and wrong; though he went further in his emphasis on intention than most medieval thinkers, he held back from drawing such conclusions. Rather it is always the case for him, as for the tradition as a whole, that the moral act is inseparable from the internal movement of the heart toward God. This is the 'truth in the inward parts', that interior and ultimately secret conformity of human willing to the divine will.

III

What we have so far examined has consisted of examples of how the performance of and justification for external rites are related to the truth of interiority. It has been strongly suggested that the biblical documents which themselves exhibit this relationship offer a less than precise resolution of the difficulties to which it gives rise. It is certainly a fact that modern New Testament writers dealing with, for example, baptism and Eucharist are by no means agreed on how the texts are to be interpreted.

What is to be concluded from this fact? There seem to be three possibilities. In the first place, it might be the case that we must in this matter simply follow the different arguments which purport to state what Paul or any other of the New Testament writers actually thought, and then make up our minds which of them was right; for example, that Paul did, or did not ascribe a particular efficacy to baptism in water, or that he did, or did not, believe that the Eucharist was a new cult to be performed by a Christian priesthood.

Another possibility, secondly, is to conclude that while a certain ambiguity attends the discussion of these questions in the New Testament, the Christian Church in due course and at greater leisure was able to supply the missing precision; and that it did so in a manner which is at least adequately comformable to the less precise traditions of the Old and New Testaments. This proposal, of course, presupposes that it is possible to identify which of the numerous subsequent attempts at clarification genuinely and authoritatively achieves this result.

A third possibility also presents itself. This is, to suggest that the conflict between differing interpretations is not resolvable because the words in which the element of inwardness is expressed are intrinsically inadequate to the task of conveying the necessary meanings. A verbal resolution of the tension between external rite and internal intention, so the argument would go, necessarily belongs to one of the external dimensions of Christianity; it is theology. No matter how precise theological formulations may strive to be, or indeed actually are, they are never immune from the charge that they have failed to capture the ultimately mysterious meaning and truth of the heart. On this account of the matter Christians had better reconcile themselves to the perpetuation of internal conflict; indeed they would do well to go beyond mere resignation, and seek the positive advantages to be gained from such disputes.

The existence of those three possibilities will have to be borne in mind when we examine the nineteenth- and early twentieth-century debates about the essence of Christianity. But there exists one quite limited example of the difficulty of conceiving the relationship of outer and inner which is instructive for our purposes here. It concerns two leading Anglican theologians of the second half of the nineteenth century, and a disagreement about the theology of the Christian ministry.

The title, 'The relation between inward and outward', was given by Professor R. C. Moberly to the second chapter of his book, *Ministerial Priesthood*.[45] The work was written as a theological introduction to the Anglican ordinal and necessarily in the light of the encyclical of Leo XIII, *Apostolicae Curae* (1896), which had condemned Anglican orders as invalid through defect of both form and intention. But as a whole the book was written as a reply to, or corrective of, an essay on the Christian ministry written by the Cambridge theologian and later Bishop of Durham, J. B. Lightfoot, some twenty years earlier and published as his commentary on Philippians.[46] This particularly influential treatment of the early development of the ministry Moberly regarded as 'upon the whole very misleading'.[47] In particular he believed that it was based on a presupposition, never examined, about the relation between inward and outward, a relation which supposes that

> the outward represents the inward, and the inward which is represented is far higher than the outward which represents it; therefore while the inward is essentially necessary for the reality of the outward, the outward is only conventionally necessary for the reality of the inward.[48]

It is this representation of the relation between outward and inward which Moberly desires to criticize and replace.

Lightfoot had indeed written a Janus-like treatise. Though wrongly celebrated by certain Presbyterians as abandoning the Anglican claim that episcopacy derives from the apostles, and as justifying their own presbyterial order, the conclusions of the essay were somewhat sober and historical. According to Lightfoot, the episcopate had developed out of the presbytery and only gradually acquired its powers, especially in the second and third centuries; nonetheless he believed that the institution of the episcopate 'cannot without violence to historical testimony, be dissevered from the name of St John'.[49] Lightfoot was sufficiently perturbed by the subsequent misunderstandings of his essay to issue in 1888 a collection of extracts from his works, including the essay on the ministry. These illustrated his belief that Anglicans had inherited the threefold ministry 'from apostolic times',[50] and were published in the twelfth and subsequent editions of his commentary.

Moberly is, however, less concerned with the historical question than the theological, or indeed the philosophical one. The relation between external form and internal reality is conceived by Lightfoot, he believes, in such a way as to downgrade the external as something accidental or 'only conventionally necessary'. The passages he cites from Lightfoot certainly tend to give this impression. For all that Lightfoot is essentially a historian and exegete, the opening paragraphs of his essay on the ministry express a fully theological statement of 'the ideal of the Christian Church'.[51] In this ideal there is, according to Lightfoot, no sacerdotal system mediating between the believer and the divine realm, since each member has immediate and personal contact with God. However, 'no society of man could hold together without officers, without rules, without institutions of any kind':[52] submission to natural (sociological) law is the condition of realizing the ideal in history. As an example of the nature of this realization Lightfoot adduces the relation between law and gospel. In this analogy 'the ideal conception and the actual realization are incommensurate and in a manner contradictory',[53] but nonetheless practically necessary. As the Christian movement grew in size and distribution, the ideal had to be supported by rules, by officers, and by special observances. But these were all aids and expediences, and 'no part of the *essence* of God's message to man in the Gospel'.[54]

In his reply Moberly seizes on the contrast alleged between ideal and actual, and the accidental character of the external aids. Though there may indeed be a contrast between the ideal and the less-than-ideal performance of the Church, nonetheless there is a real identity between the Church as it should be, and the Church as it is. This identity he illustrates in two ways, by reference to the continuous personality of an individual saint, and to the spirit-body unity of the human organism. The latter appeal is particularly important to Moberly who constantly deals with the Church in the language of body and spirit. What, he asks, is the individual person? Not, he argues, a mere representation of the spiritual life. Bodily life '*is* spiritual life, expanding, controlling, developing under bodily conditions'.[55] The bodily and the spiritual are mutually related truths relating to the one personhood.

This, says Moberly, is how the relation between the outward and the inward in the Church must be conceived. The Church's real meaning is the spiritual meaning, but there is no working of the spirit which is not through the body. The body is not a regrettable necessity; one cannot imagine an ideal church which had abandoned special seasons, places, ordinances, ministers and sacraments.

> On the contrary, being, as they would by hypothesis be, the perfectly undimmed and faultless expression of the higher spiritual possibilities, they would be – not merged, but accentuated, not obscured but illuminated; they would be more conspicuous, more dominant, more profound and august in their reality than they are in any form of the Church that now is.[56]

Moberly, accordingly, protests against Lightfoot's statement that externals are no part of the essence of the gospel. He observes that while he would be ready to agree that the life of the Church is the life of the Spirit of the incarnate Christ, he would want to insist that the bodily methods for maintaining that life, if included in the divine plan of revelation, must themselves be part of the essence of the gospel.[57] Methods or means are not necessarily 'mere' methods or means. Furthermore Moberly draws attention to a distinction between the noun 'essence' and the adjective 'essential'. Ordinances and externals may be essential to the Church's life, without being the essence of the Church's life. As essentials, moreover, they could in a certain sense be regarded as indispensable to the essence.[58] In any case indispensability could only be predicated in respect of those features of the Church which were divinely ordained, and in so far as they were divinely ordained. They would, in this case, be 'essentially necessary', that is, they would constitute those methods by which God has revealed that he is at work.

I have outlined the substance of Moberly's objection to Lightfoot in order to illustrate one point. Even among those who are fully aware of the inwardness tradition, the problem of relating outside and inside offers a variety of possibilities. Moberly's remarks about the ambiguity of Lightfoot's use of the term 'essence' are fully justified. But it is less clear that the analogy of spirit and body which Moberly deploys to illustrate the relation of outside and inside in the Church is as persuasive as he imagines. For the boundaries of the Church are not like the boundaries of a human being; they are not even as definite as the boundaries of the covenant with Israel, which the rite of circumcision was interpreted as denoting (Gen. 17.11). The inwardness tradition is, potentially, much more disruptive of unambiguous identification of the 'body' of the Church than the uncritical use of that metaphor allows. Certainly Moberly is far too incautious at this point.

Lightfoot, on the other hand, is, for a notably cautious historian, remarkably confident in his assertions about the true relation of actual and ideal as contrasted with each other. Why is Lightfoot so negative, or at least grudging, in his acknowledgement of the necessities of everyday existence? He does not tell us. But the answer has doubtless to do with the critical stance he adopts towards the 'sacerdotalism' in which the concept of the Christian ministry was, he believes, later engulfed. Here again we see the critical potential, which we observed in the case of Abelard, in a certain sort of emphasis on the inwardness tradition. It appears that the more conscious one is of the inward response, the more likely one is to adopt a critical distance from the external forms of the institution. Moberly is by no means uncritical of failure in the Church. But it is impossible not to detect in his work a certain optimistic, evolutionary tone in his description of the Church's forward progress, which so grows 'as to realize actually and perfectly the whole ideal character of the Kingdom of God'. Moberly represents, we may say, the progressive-utopian potential in the inward-outward relation, whilst Lightfoot stands for its critical-disruptive potential. But can we say that either one or the other is the only valid stance on the basis of the evidence? It appears not to be the evidence itself, but the tools with which the evidence is evaluated which determines the issue.

3

Power in the Church

The enquiries undertaken in the previous chapter have, I believe,
established two extremely important results, whose impact is felt
acutely in the nineteenth-century discussions of the essence of
Christianity. In the first place, the Christian movement was
shown to contain inherent ambiguities whose resolution was
bound to cause conflict. Moreover, the ambiguities might relate
to matters of very great importance, on which it was possible
for Christians to go seriously astray. Then, secondly, it was
demonstrated that, because Christianity lays strong emphasis
upon the hidden intention of the believer, no theological decision
about the external aspects of Christianity could be immune from
the challenge that it fails to do justice to the real substance of
the faith.

But is conflict really inevitable throughout Christian history?
After all, it might not unreasonably be said that if there were
ambiguities in the very early days, further reflection might well
be expected to clear them up. In one of Newman's later letters
there is an ingenious depiction of the problem-solving character
of the later Church:

> The Church is, so to call it, a standing Apostolic committee – to
> answer questions which the Apostles are not here to answer concern-
> ing what they received and preached.[1]

It is entirely typical of Newman to have added a caveat which
would not have commended itself to every member of that
standing committee, before or even contemporary with him.

> As the Church does not know more than the Apostles knew, there
> are many questions which the Church cannot answer.

To answer questions, and even to admit ignorance, may well be
one of the normal functions of the Church's leadership. But the
conclusions of the two previous chapters when taken together
point to a more disturbing possibility. Not merely is conflict
inherent in the early days of the Christian movement, it is

inherent in the very existence of the Christian Church at every stage of its life. Moreover, in the case of the early Christian movement we argued that the ambiguities giving rise to many of the conflicts were not the result of deliberate misunderstanding or malice, but were the indirect consequence of carrying out Jesus' intentions in new contexts. Similarly, in the later history of the Church, it may not be sheer bad faith, pride, or wilful disobedience which gives rise to disputes. Conflict arises because there is real difficulty in determining the proper relationship between the internal dimension of Christian commitment, and decisions or teaching about its diverse external dimensions. Emphasis on this inherent difficulty by no means entails accepting the insolubility of all controversies, nor validating all dissent. It is possible to make mistakes about Christian doctrine or ritual; it is also conceivable that arrogant self-assertiveness may be the root cause of certain controversies. But the argument of the second chapter pointed to two conclusions which I would regard as well grounded; first, that the internal dimension is of great importance to Christian identity, and secondly, that in some arguments about Christianity uncertainty about the relation between internal and external dimensions may play an important role.

On the basis of these considerations it would not be unreasonable to suppose that conflict in Christianity is not accidental or occasional, but intrinsic and chronic.[2] Whether or not this is tolerable for a religion which sets such public store by peace and reconciliation is a matter to which we shall attend in Chapter 10. For the moment, this supposition has the merit of at least bringing out into the open the unexceptional character of Christian divisions. Western Christians are, it seems to me, in some danger of so interpreting their own rhetoric about unity as to conceal from themselves some fundamental reasons for their actual diversity. Diversity, I would argue, is the norm for Christianity, though not necessarily that form of diversity consisting in separated churches with independent and self-perpetuating traditions. If the sociology of theological disagreement were to be taken more seriously, however, the churches might be in a better position to find their way out of the institutionalized divisions in which they now languish.

Conflict, of course, may have damaging consequences, and it

is obvious enough from the letters of Paul that he takes many of the disputes in which he is involved with very great seriousness. But the important point about his involvement is not merely that the outcome of the conflict is regarded by him as a matter of extreme gravity; rather it is the implication for himself of the very fact that he is in conflict. In a word, he is drawn into a power-struggle. Conflict entails the use of power, and power is the theme of this present chapter.

This important and difficult subject requires a much more comprehensive treatment than can be given here, and the course we shall pursue is dictated by the necessarily limited purposes of the present argument. First, we shall examine how Paul's authority, and the problem of authority after his death, has been interpreted. Secondly, an account will be given of one example from Troeltsch of a sociologically informed theory of how the centre of power developed by stages in the Christian community. Then, thirdly, I shall attempt a general presentation of the theme of power in the New Testament. And in a final section we shall consider the challenge to modern theology, or, more specifically, to modern theologians to deal adequately with the issues raised by conflict and the use of power in the Christian Church.

I

It is convenient to start with Paul, not least because the question of his own authority is one of the issues in his letters to the Galatian and to the Corinthian congregations. Challenges to a person's authority are not, however, always made directly; there can be an indirect challenge implied in a struggle about a quite different matter. On that understanding, any of Paul's numerous difficulties has the potential for focusing the question of his own status. What is certainly true is that, in his conduct of controversy, his language, his arguments and his appeals are intended by him to effect something. They are elements in a clash of intentions and purposes into which he is drawn by the mere existence of important disagreements.

But is the exercise of authority the same thing as an exercise of power? It is part of the modern theological reluctance to have anything to do with power that the unavoidable questions concerning power have been discussed under the religiously more acceptable term authority. It is widely held, indeed, that there is a crisis of authority.[3] But is that the same thing as a power crisis? How are the terms power and authority related to each other?

For the sake of clarity, a decision has to be taken about the range of meaning of the term power. With a recent sociologist, I shall define power as 'the capacity of some persons to produce intended and foreseen effects on others'.[4] This is a very broad and general definition, and establishes a continuous spectrum of power-terms and power-relations from forceful coercion or manipulation at one extreme to the give-and-take of mutual influence at the other. One may identify four major types of power as force, manipulation, persuasion and authority.[5] Authority itself has many forms, but it is distinguished from persuasion by its command–obedience connotation.[6] The one who obeys usually recognizes grounds for the obedience, but these grounds are other than persuasion by argument.[7] Authority may be coercive, induced, legitimate, competent or personal. In religion the authority of clergy is quite frequently legitimate, that is, it is based on the mutual acknowledgement of the divine source of authority, and thus of the right to command and obligation to obey. It may also be personal, indeed charismatic in the precise sense; quite often personal and other forms of authority are combined in a single instance.

Accordingly, so far as the use of terms in this chapter is concerned, Paul's authority is an exercise of power. His is conscious of being in no way inferior to those whom he ironically calls 'superlative apostles' (2 Cor. 11.5; 12.11); he is himself an apostle, albeit most unworthy because of his past history, and entirely subject to the grace of God (1 Cor. 15.8–11). That indeed is the hall-mark of Paul's claim to authority, that it does not reside in himself, but in his endowment.

> For what we preach is not ourselves, but Jesus Christ as Lord, with ourselves as your servants for Jesus' sake. For it is the God who said 'Let light shine out of darkness,' who has shone in our hearts to give the light of the knowledge of the glory of God in the face of Christ (2 Cor. 4.5–6).

However, the way the claim is phrased does not make him a less powerful person. It is a common misunderstanding that in order to be powerful one has to be self-assertive. On the contrary, great power can be exercised by those who locate the origin of their authority outside themselves, in God. However self-effacing Paul may (or may not) be, however humbly he may refer to himself as an earthenware pot (2 Cor. 4.7), there is contemporary revelation in Paul's apostolic testimony to the knowledge of God.[8] Thus the authority is exercised by Paul, though it does not originate in him. 'There is no question of our being qualified in ourselves: we cannot claim anything as our own. Such qualifications as we have come from God' (2 Cor. 3.5 NEB). Indeed, a few verses earlier Paul has suggested that his qualifications are based in the blessing God has bestowed on his ministry. He has no need of letters of commendation from others: the Spirit of God has supplied his own letter of commendation on his own, and on their hearts (2 Cor. 3.1–3).

It is not to be wondered at that some found Paul's statements less than persuasive. Neither the claim to divine commissioning nor success in planting churches are by themselves adequate criteria for authority. Many could assert spiritual gifts of various kinds, and success in evangelism is notoriously various. Paul adds to these the appeal to himself as founder, and therefore, father of the community (1 Cor. 3.10 and 4.15). The former would be of considerable weight in the Graeco-Roman world, which attributed great *auctoritas* to the *auctor* or founder of a new city or colony. But, of course, the same concept produces acute difficulty in the relations between different founders of neighbouring communities, and Corinth was certainly large enough to have different groups tracing their origins to different founders.

It is perhaps this situation which is reflected in the carefully subordinate role which Paul assigns to Apollos. Though neither he nor Apollos are more than servants doing the work of their Master, yet he, Paul, 'planted' the church, whilst Apollos watered the plants (1 Cor. 3.5–6); and if anyone else contributes to church-growth it must be on the same basis, and in accordance with the same gospel (vv. 12–16). The letters to the Corinthians convey a strong sense of Paul's possessiveness about his 'dear children' (1 Cor. 4.14), whom, of course, he cannot treat literally as children, even though they are 'babes in Christ' (1 Cor. 3.1). But precisely because he has a special relationship with them as their founder, the Corinthian letters cannot provide us with a general theory of the authority of a church leader. Another basis than Paul's had to be developed.[9] The only question was, how many of the diverse elements in Paul's claim to divinely legitimated authority would be transferred to the later period once Paul himself had died.

Various alternative solutions to the question of church organization are already in evidence in the later documents of the New Testament and the early so-called apostolic period. The Pastoral Epistles, the Gospel of Matthew, and the Johannine writings are evidence for the fluidity, but at the same time increasingly definite outline, of church office. There are numerous studies of this confused and variously interpretable situation.[10] Here it is necessary merely to observe that a need was felt, at least in some quarters, for a certain precision in the location of authority. 1 Clement and the epistles of Ignatius are instructive in this respect. Clement, for example, using an analogy from the subordination of military officers and ranks to the king and governors, that is, an explicitly hierarchical structure, urges the mutual interdependence of the levels of the ecclesiastical hierarchy for the explicit purpose of the salvation of the whole. There is a divinely given order, and those who follow the institutions of the Master cannot go wrong. As Christ and his apostles 'came of the will of God in the appointed order', so the apostles themselves appointed bishops and deacons, and provided for continuance.[11]

In Ignatius' case, likewise, the main concern is the unity of the Church, and for this unity the only appropriate analogy (in Ignatius the analogy is elevated into a piece of typology) is not the law or the army, but the unity and singularity of the Godhead.[12] In like manner let all men respect the deacons as Jesus Christ, even as they should respect the bishop as being a type of the Father and the presbyters as the council of God and as the college of the Apostles'.[13] However it is also clear that it is not the mere existence of one bishop and a group of presbyters which is the sufficient condition of Christian unity. Holding to the bishop is but one of a number of different appeals, expressed, for example, in the following way: 'Do nothing without the bishop; keep your flesh as a temple of God; cherish union; shun divisions; be imitators of Jesus Christ, as he himself also was of his Father.'[14] Needless to say these attitudinal and moral commitments are present also in Paul. Moreover we find Ignatius, like Paul, claiming in the same passage to speak with divine authority on the prompting of the Holy Spirit. The point to observe is the connection both writers see between the preaching of the gospel and the unity of the congregation. The gospel does not cease to be the 'power of God for salvation' (Rom. 1.16) merely because it is not Paul, but another, who preaches it. Those who preach the gospel after Paul are empowered, just as Paul was empowered; and disunity is just as serious a threat to the preaching of the gospel after Paul's time, as it is in Paul's time.

Yet it is precisely at this point that one of our authorities, Hans von Campenhausen, in his most influential work, *Ecclesiastical Authority and Spiritual Power*, instructs us to observe a sharp distinction between Paul's approach to, and understanding of, his authority, and Clement's. In Paul there is a unique combination of unequivocal assertion of his authority as an apostle, and a direct refusal to allow this authority to be set up 'in a sacral relationship of spiritual control and subordination'.[15] The Pauline congregation, which lives entirely by the Spirit, is not given any basis for any fixed forms of 'office', and Paul teaches no kind of obedience towards those in authority, such as is demanded towards Christ, and himself, as Christ's apostle.[16] Clement's letter to the Corinthian church, however, contains none of this dialectic. Although Clement draws repeatedly on 1 Corinthians, order for him has become an abstract and autonomous principle of an abstract kind. Von Campenhausen leaves no doubt of his disapproval of this letter; it shows 'an impoverishment of spiritual content'; it revives a notion of cultic officialdom and a sacral system which Paul had pronounced dead and obsolete; it represents a victory of church officialdom over the 'slackening energies of Christian proclamation'; it strengthens the trend towards an 'unbalanced ascendency of office', which continued unchecked in the second century – itself an age of spiritual decline.[17]

Now it is a feature of von Campenhausen's work that he is determined to overcome some of the earlier confessionally-dictated antagonisms in the presentation and discussion of the origins of the early Christian ministry.[18] Nonetheless the source of the criterion for these sharp judgements is familiar. Even granted the fact that 1 Clement is, compared with Paul's major letters, of lower intellectual stature, the movement towards a closer definition of authority of church leadership can only be said to be 'unbalanced' if we accept von Campenhausen's presuppositions about what is 'balanced'. Moreover his evaluation of the situation in the Pauline congregation turns on the assertion that 'Paul is the true founder and discoverer of the Christian concept of authority'.[19] Once he has explained that this authority consists in the apostolate, and that the apostolate can neither be continued nor renewed, but only safeguarded or handed on in an apostolic tradition, then it simply follows that any theory, such as Clement's, which involves justifying order by placing it under the protection of an apostolic injunction can only be a departure from the proper understanding of 'evangelical authority'.[20]

Two major criticisms must be passed of this position. The first is that Paul's theological position has apparently been abstracted from its social setting.[21] Paul's letters to Corinth are reactions to a specific (and very unsatisfactory) situation, not a blueprint for a church order. The theology of charisma, of the bestowal of gifts for specific functions in the body, is a theological interpretation of, not a normative basis for, a structure of interactions in a Christian community. Von Campenhausen has in effect confused two different senses of the term 'the Pauline church'. In one sense it refers to churches which Paul actually founded, but whose structures have developed on lines governed as much by social needs and particular circumstances as his own teaching; in another sense 'the church' is a theological construct, which Paul does not see as a sociological phenomenon or human entity at all.[22] This latter church certainly does not have a 'church order' – or if it did, it has never existed in any actual church of Paul's. It is no coincidence that von Campenhausen's single (foot-noted) reference to Max Weber dismisses his categories as 'developed in too schematic a manner to be useful as they stand for throwing light on early Christian situations'.[23]

In the second place the work as a whole demonstrates an underestimation of the chronic power vacuum left by the departure of the so-called 'apostles'. It is true that Paul says nothing about the provision of any formal structure for his churches; but once Paul himself had died, the churches he founded could not possibly continue on the pattern illustrated from his letters. No doubt the story of Paul's assembly of, and address to the Ephesian elders, to which we have already referred, reflects Luke's, rather than Paul's, conception of the necessities of a congregation bereft of the principal representative of its source of authority.[24] But the demonstration of the need for leadership in the face of 'savage wolves' and false brethren is wholly realistic. What separates Clement from Luke, or indeed from Paul, is not that 'the abstract concept of order has become completely detached from any specifically Christian meaning – that is to say, one connected with Christ and the Gospel',[25] but that what would in any case be necessary in a congregation committed to Christian mission, to Christian worship and to Christian discipleship, namely a measure of communal discipline, is said to have been created on the instruction of the apostles themselves.

There is, as one would expect, not merely an historical, but a conceptual or theological issue involved. Certainly there is a change of emphasis between Paul and Clement. But the change is not a great one. The concept of a revealed religion which is communicated by means of human beings entails some kind of personalization of religious authority. 'To believe that there has been a divine revelation, but that there is no means of establishing its content, no means of resolving disputes about its content, or its meaning would invite the question what point could there be in such a revelation'.[26] Nor is it possible for there to be a merely written authority; there must be a speaking, interpretative authority. What Clement in fact is claiming is that there is a speaking authority to be heard, both in Rome and in Corinth. The fact that the authority is claimed to be divinely legitimated is merely a continuation of Paul's precedent. It does not, in fact, differ from the device of pseudonymously writing a letter 'from Paul', whose intention was to continue on Paul's apostolic foundation.[27] The difficulty of the claim is rather that *all* external norms, including authoritative persons, have to exercise their discrimination on matters concerning the inwardness of the Christian life. This was no less a difficulty for Paul than it was for Clement. Paul was no less challengeable than Clement; despite Clement's theory of authority, he was no more invulnerable than Paul.

The need for increased precision in the location and criterion of orthodoxy is amply demonstrated by the encounter with

Gnosticism in the second century. Here we may properly speak of a crisis of identity because what was determined in the course of the controversy was not merely important matters of the content of the faith, but ways of solving disputes. As we know, the chief result of these conflicts was the development of the appeal to apostolicity; the exhibition of the list of bishops going back to apostolic times and the manifest agreement of the present preaching of the orthodox with the apostles, were the supports for the assertion that the orthodox were heirs to the apostles and had entered into their estate.

The dangers in this position are obvious. The internal diversity of the Scriptures was suppressed in the interests of the argument that the apostles were all in agreement. It was never clearly explained how some aspects of the faith emerged for special emphasis, while others remained, so to speak, instinctive in liturgical and pastoral tradition. In practice the degree of the knowledge and insight of the apostles was exaggerated in order to claim their backing for subsequent theological clarification. It became fatally easy to overlook the possibility that bishops, and even large parts of the Church as a whole, might go astray. A large, and even unspecified, measure of power was handed over to certain office-bearers, which might in due course wholly lose touch with the very teaching which the theory was designed to safeguard. Nonetheless it seems reasonable to say, with S. L. Greenslade, that 'in practice the early Church could probably not have preserved its identity and saved itself from dissolution through syncretism without such confidence in apostolicity.'[28]

All this history is very well known, and extensively commented on. A judicious historian will take the view, in all probability, that what is spoken of in the language of historical development involves a complex mixture of gain and loss – gain, in that on no other conceivable conditions could the Church so effectively have maintained the degree of unity it did; loss, in that the very same procedures were justified by less than valid arguments and led, on occasion, to injustice.

But what, precisely, is crucial in evaluating this development? My contention is that the situation is unintelligible apart from the question of the distribution and exercise of power. Only if the reality of the power situation is taken with full seriousness will a fully persuasive picture emerge of the implications for the

Church of its numerical growth and geographical expansion. The odd thing is, however, that we are very far from having such a picture. As I have already shown, it is only comparatively recently that New Testament scholars have taken closer interest in the sociology of power, with reference to the obvious conflicts in which Paul was embroiled. The lack of such an interest among historians of the early Church is, if anything, more marked. And yet it is, or should be obvious, that with the growth in size of the Church, there must be a growth in complexity in the distribution of power. The comparatively informal remarks of J. B. Lightfoot about the necessary conformity of the Church to human laws governing organizations positively invite further precision.[29] But hitherto the field is comparatively bare.

II

One exception to the general dearth of scholars with a qualified interest in the sociology of power in the early Church is Ernst Troeltsch, and he is an exception for a very good reason.[30] Troeltsch's major attempt to depict the history of Christianity was published in 1911, after Harnack's massive efforts at synthesis, the *Lehrbuch der Dogmengeschichte* (1886–9) and *Die Mission und Ausbreitung des Christentums in den ersten drei Jahrhunderten* (1902).[31] Moreover, Troeltsch presented his work openly as an addition to, or corrective of, Harnack, precisely because he believed the necessary sociological dimension was missing. Part of his qualification for providing the alternative lay in his appreciation of the sociological theories of Max Weber, whose personal friendship he enjoyed, though he claimed independence of specific borrowings.[32] The significance of Troeltsch's contribution to the discussion of the essence of Christianity will be presented more fully in Chapter 7. Here, however, he must be introduced as an example of a thinker who both understands the importance of power in religion and who has an explicit theory about the transformation of the power situation in early Christianity. Despite the fact that, as I shall hope to show, Troeltsch's solution has considerable theological difficulties, nonetheless he is one of the few writers to make the sociological dimension in the development of early Christianity unambiguously plain.

Troeltsch holds a three-stage view of the development of the gospel ethic to the form it assumed in early Catholicism. In the first stage, constituted by the teaching of Jesus, the gospel ethic is centred upon the idea of God.[33] The ethical demand is that the individual surrenders his or her will to God, and the satisfaction is that the individual is united with the will and with the being of God. This wholly inward occurrence is the meaning of the Kingdom of God, 'that state of life in which God will have supreme control'.[34] The power of this ethic is its capacity to elicit absolute single-mindedness and purity of intention. It is severe, but not, strictly speaking, a form of asceticism. From the sociological point of view it is utterly individualistic, and at the same time absolutely universalistic. It implies no severence from national religion; Jesus organized no church.

By the times of Paul a considerable change has overtaken this ethic, under the impact of the mystical faith in the exalted and risen Lord. Here Troeltsch indicates his agreement with Deissmann, that 'the central happening in Primitive Christianity was the rise of a Christ-cult out of faith in Christ, and that only then there arose a new religious community because there was already a new cult'.[35] Sociologically speaking this amounts to a great transformation, the fundamental feature of which is the growth of an independent religious community possessing the essential ideas of the gospel and equipped with its own powers.[36] In this community the gospel ethic acquires a new shade of meaning. Purity of heart becomes sanctification; love of the neighbour becomes brotherly love; and the universalism of Christ's preaching becomes the missionary effort to draw the whole world, which is lost without Christ, into redeeming participation in the death and resurrection of the Pneuma-Christ (as he terms the new 'focal point'). Individualism remains, but is narrowed into the transformation achieved by baptism and participation in the Lord's Supper.[37]

The transition to the third stage, which is termed 'early catholicism', is already implicit in the position accorded to the Pneuma-Christ in Paul's teaching.[38] Both the individualism and the universalism of the gospel ethic required an independent centre of organization, which would give it anchorage in the growing complications of its relations with the contemporary world. Belief in the living presence of the Pneuma-Christ gave it that foundation. 'This conviction was the driving force and organizing power of the new community; it created its only new article of faith, faith in the Christ who is identical with the Spirit of God.'[39] It created, furthermore, the new cult, the worship of God in Christ, and the new ethic, the dying with, and rising again in Christ to newness of life.

The presence of Pneuma-Christ was the 'sociological point of reference';[40] and for this reason the first fundamental dogma of the faith became that of the Father and the Logos, in due course expanding into the doctrine of the Trinity. This doctrine was not able of itself to constitute a secure enough contemporary foundation. Hence the need for a new point of reference, which was satisfied in the episcopate and the development of an organized sacramental system. Troeltsch's view of episcopacy was as follows:

> The episcopate meant that the endowment with the Spirit was clearly defined within fixed limits; it formed the channel through which the miraculous powers, the authority, and the power of celebrating the Sacrament, could be conveyed to the official ministry which had been called forth by the needs of the organization; such an emphasis in fact was suggested by the actual authority of the Christian tradition and of its close relation with the original founders of the new religion. In a concrete way the episcopate was substituted for the earlier faith in the Exalted Christ and the Spirit; it is the successor of Christ and of the Apostles, the Bearer of the Spirit, the extension or externalizing of the Incarnation, a visible and tangible proof of the Divine Truth and Power, the concrete presence of the sociological point of reference.[41]

These three stages represent a massive reorganization and transmutation of the phenomenon of power in the Christian community. From a state where power resides solely and simply in the claim of God upon the individual to live a life of purity and humble submission to the divine will, by the second century we are confronted with a community highly conscious of its own status as the channel for the miraculous powers by which alone humanity can be redeemed. Particularly noteworthy is Troeltsch's claim that in early Catholicism the episcopate replaces the earlier faith in the Pneuma-Christ. The bishop is the 'concrete sociological point of reference', and, as such, is the natural focus of power.

It is worth noting that this historical analysis of the early centuries and Troeltsch's own personal view of the situation of the modern Church are complementary. Although he is engaged on what he claims to be value-free research in this particular work, he made his own interpretation of the matter unambiguously plain in a lecture, published in the same year (1911), entitled, 'The Significance of the Historical Existence of Jesus for Faith'.[42] Here he simply states that the question of the significance of historical research into the life and teaching of Jesus arises only if one entirely rules out the claim of Catholic Christianity. The historical question is quite simply the 'death-certificate' of that kind of belief.

> This question makes sense only if one presupposition is granted. It would be pointless if one assumed the Christianity of the early church with its dogma of the God-man, its church and sacraments established by Christ and the redeeming effects of his saving work of reconciling God.[43]

This essay, as we shall see in Chapter 7, contains Troeltsch's most revealing constructive statement about the phenomenon of power in the contemporary Church. There can be no doubt that he held the view that the second great development of the Christian ethic after its transformation by Paul had to be radically undone in any conceivable post-Enlightenment form of the Church. Once again historical writing on early Christianity and theological restatement proceed hand in hand.

This remarkable reconstruction of the stages of development in early Christianity is of such interest that I am bound somewhat to anticipate my commentary on Troeltsch's contribution to our discussion, which will be examined in Chapter 7. That there is a process of development involving a serious question of power in the Church, its distribution and exercise is not, I think, open to doubt. That the bishop becomes, in a certain sense, a mouthpiece for divine authority, a manifestation of the contemporary presence of Christ, is likewise a plain fact of church history. What is disputable in Troeltsch's thesis is the transition he depicts from a teaching or doctrine to an office. Is it true that the episcopate *replaces* faith in the exalted Christ? Does not Paul himself qualify, for example in the Corinthian congregation, for the title 'sociological point of reference'? And are we to deny that the later Church also believed in a presence of the exalted Christ, distinct from that of the bishop? Troeltsch's schematization admirably suits the polemical point he is making against 'early catholicism', but it is inadequate to the complexity of the question of power in the primitive Church. To this we must now turn.

III

Having discovered that an appreciation of the power situation in early Christianity is integral to an understanding of its development, it is necessary now to step back a stage to ask a more general question. Given that any religious movement is bound to distribute power in one way or another once it grows in size and complexity, what sense of its own power does the Christian movement have? How powerful does it see itself to be? This is a quite separate question from the political question, how powerful was the Christian movement? In the early decades we are dealing with an obscure sect of minute proportions; but, as is obvious enough from the New Testament, Christians entertained remarkable convictions about the importance of what they were undertaking.

How, then is the issue of power handled in the New Testament? The brief answer to this is that the New Testament writers show themselves to be members of what one might call highly power-conscious communities. I propose now to illustrate this statement in three ways:

(a) By the power implications of the kingdom, or kingly-rule of God, which is so central a part of Jesus' own ministry.

(b) By the power believed to have been conferred on Jesus' followers.

(c) By the teaching on power in Pauline and deutero-Pauline writings.

In synthesing this material I am again conscious not merely of entering the field of New Testament studies as a systematician, but of doing so on a topic where the guidance of the experts is more than a little uncertain.⁴⁴ However, it is essential that the full significance of the question of power for the early Christian movement be grasped, and to do this there is no alternative but to seek an understanding of the New Testament material.⁴⁵

The background to the teaching of Jesus on the Kingdom lies, it is usual to argue, with the coming together in the traditions of Israel of a version or versions of the ancient Near Eastern creation myth with a summary of God's saving acts in history.⁴⁶ A psalm, such as Psalm 136, shows the fusion of the two, with part of its verses (4–9) celebrating his creative activity, and part (10–22) his deliverance of Israel, the whole being in praise of 'the God of gods' and 'the Lord of lords'. The language of the kingdom is, in fact, inseparable from the concept of power, because both creation and the deeds of God are conceived as triumph over opposition, in the case of creation over the forces of chaos (Ps. 89.10–11), in the case of history over Pharaoh and other famous kings (Ps. 136.15–22). The praise of God is, accordingly, praise of his power.

> All thy works shall give thanks to thee, O Lord,
> And all thy saints shall bless thee!
> They shall speak of the glory of thy kingdom,
> And tell of thy power   (Ps. 145.10–11).

What carries the symbol of God's kingship into the times of Jesus is its place in Jewish myth and piety. In the light of the importance of the association of the kingship and the power of God in future Christian worship it is relevant to cite the terms of an address of praise to God from 3 Maccabees, a book variously dated between 100 BC and 70 AD, and probably written in Greek: 'Lord, Lord, king of the heavens and ruler of all creation, holy among the holy, monarch, all-powerful ruler (*pantokrator*).' The evident point of so emphasizing the kingly power of God is its association with confident hope in future triumph over adversity. The God who was believed in was a God of undeviating goodness, whose 'steadfast love endures for ever' (Ps. 136. *passim*). Thus in the Psalms of Solomon (commonly dated in the years 70 BC–40 BC) an ingloriously defeated invader is depicted as having forgotten that he stood under the infinitely greater judgement and power of God.⁴⁷ In Rabbinic literature, likewise, the kingship of God is associated with the assurance of the covenantal relationship. When a person accepts the Kingdom of heaven, what is entailed is not subordination to despotism, but agreement to obey the commandments.[48]

But hope in God's future kingly rule lends itself also to a specifically political interpretation, particularly attractive to a subjugated people. Thus in the so-called war scroll of the Dead Sea Scrolls there is an incitement to believe that God will intervene with power in a military confrontation with his enemies.[49] Merely to use the term 'Kingdom of God' in the context of first-century Palestine is evidently to invoke a whole range of connotations, unless these are specifically deleted or denied. This is where the analysis of Jesus' teaching which distinguishes between core meaning and conventional associations seems to be particularly helpful.[50] Plainly if Jesus is to use the term Kingdom at all, the core meaning of an act of God consistent with God's creative and saving purpose for humanity must be conveyed. Nationalistic, militaristic or ritualistic connotations may, however, be deleted, if the kingdom language is associated with types of activity carried out by Jesus which are compassionate and forgiving rather than destructive or burdening.

But on such an analysis how would the power connotation stand? Would the symbol of the Kingdom carry with it the connotation of power? Here a critical analysis of the texts of the synoptic Gospels containing or implying the concept of power becomes unavoidable; and fortunately the task has been carried out by Barrett.[51] Jesus both performed miracles (*dunameis*, though Luke does not use this term) and has miraculous power (*dunamis*, understood virtually as a physically communicable substance Mark 5.30). Luke, in particular, sees Jesus as being endowed with the power or energy of the Spirit (Luke 4.14), which in the book of Acts he connects with the eschatological prophecy of Joel (Acts 2.16–21, cf. Joel 2.28–32). Similarly eschatological is the Marcan saying, 'Truly, I say to you, there are some standing here who will not taste death before they see the kingdom of God come with power' (Mark 9.1; cf. Mark 13.26). Quite apart from the controversy which has raged over the translation of the perfect participle 'come', it is clear that Mark intends to associate 'power' with the 'glory of the Father' in the previous verse. The pouring out of God's power at the end of time when the will of God for humanity is completed is a frequent theme of both Jewish and Christian eschatology. For Jesus it appears to have been associated in particular with the resurrection of the dead, in which he specifically believed (Mark 12.24, where the resurrection is said to be the manifestation of God's power).

The Gospels attribute to Jesus not merely power (*dunamis*), but also authority (*exousia*), sometimes without discernible difference of meaning. Nonetheless, as Barrett observes, *exousia* tends to refer to potential energy or divine resource, where *dunamis* is more often actual force in operation.[52] In Mark, Jesus is represented as teaching and healing with authority, meaning either without proper or official authorization, or with higher and divine inspiration and approval. The latter sense agrees closely with the story of his absolution of the paralytic (Mark 2.10); the authority to forgive is God's alone.

In summary, the picture given by the synoptic Gospels of the power of Jesus can be seen to be double-sided. On the one hand Jesus both has authority, and is powerful; on the other, despite the miracles, there is no unambiguous exercise of power, such as is reserved for the last day. There are many puzzles about the authenticity of the sayings, and historicity of the particular descriptions of Jesus' miracles. Moreover the status of the language concerning the Kingdom, whether it is myth, symbol, image, or concept, is far from certain. Nonetheless the survey has at least established the crucial point for our purpose, namely that the power connotation of kingdom language is part of its core meaning. However Jesus spoke precisely of the presence or futurity of the Kingdom, his own activity was intimately connected with its realization; and both speech and action concur in the view that in this matter, the kingly rule of God entails the triumph of God's enduring goodness.

In view of this conclusion, Paul is hardly innovating when, in exasperation with his Corinthian congregation, he reminds them that 'the kingdom of God does not consist in talk, but in power' (1 Cor. 4.20). The power here is, indeed, his own divinely–given authority – here we see the interrelation of divine and human power – in the light of which he will obliterate (if need be) the influence of certain self–important, but ultimately powerless persons (1 Cor. 4.19). The Kingdom of God is, as we have seen, an eschatological concept, more frequently employed in the synoptic Gospels than in Paul. But where Paul uses it, it has formidable power connotations. In Paul's apocalyptic thought there seems (the exegesis is disputed) to be a period before the coming of Christ, when Christ disposes the evil powers who have come to dominate the world. The coming of Christ then brings in the end of all things, when Christ hands over the Kingdom to God the Father, 'after destroying every rule (*arche*) and every authority (*exousia*) and power (*dunamis*)' (1 Cor. 15.24). There is, in other words, literally a power-struggle in progress at the moment, in which the last enemy to be defeated is death.

The New Testament document giving the most vivid, not to say bizarre, picture of the struggle is, naturally, the Revelation of John. In the course of the revelations the seer is shown how various agencies have been given various degrees of authority for limited periods of time. The issue, however, is never in doubt. Not merely is God, the sovereign Lord, worshipped as one worthy to receive glory, honour and power (Rev. 4.11; and similarly the Lamb, Rev. 5.12; and cf. 7.12 and 19.1), but also the other powers are clearly stated to be ephemeral.

And I heard a loud voice in heaven, saying, 'Now the salvation and the power and the kingdom of our God and the authority of his Christ have come, for the accuser of our brethren has been thrown down, who accuses them day and night before our God' (Rev. 12.10).

This, of course, is high cosmic drama, composed at a considerable remove from the preaching of Jesus. Nonetheless the apocalyptic teaching contained in Mark 13 shows the readiness of the early Church to see in Jesus' proclamation of the Kingdom a specific prediction of the coming of the Son of Man in the clouds 'with great power and glory' (Mark 13.26; cf. 14.62). This may be a development of Jesus' teaching, and an alteration in its form; but the framework remains the mythology of God's kingly rule, and the power connotation is preserved.

But does not this power reside in Jesus alone? On what grounds is the historical claim made that Jesus himself bestowed power on his followers, or on a group of them? This question, it must be admitted, is exceptionally complex. The stories of the mission charges to the apostles (Mark 3.15; 6.7–13) include on both occasions the power to cast out unclean spirits. In the Lucan doublet of this story, the seventy-two who are sent out return jubilant, and are told of Jesus' vision of the fall of Satan (Luke 10.17–20). Barrett, Jeremias and Kümmel see no good grounds for supposing that these stories are creations of the resurrection community.[53] Others, for example Conzelmann, clearly think that the identification of the twelve (who figure in 1 Cor. 15.5) and Jesus' apostles (Mark 3.14) is a later idea.[54] But the precise historical question turns not so much on whether or not Jesus himself chose, commissioned and empowered particular persons, as on the convictions of the post-resurrection Church. Luke's understanding of the situation is that, just as the power, or Spirit of God had moved in the womb of the Virgin (Luke 1.35), just as Jesus himself had set out 'armed with the power of the Spirit', (Luke 4.14), so the disciples had received power from above (Luke 24.45, cf. Acts 1.8), at Pentecost (Acts 2). It may be that the narrative of Acts 2 has been strongly shaped by Old Testament motifs; yet, at the same time, what distinguishes the disciples from Jesus' own companions during his life-time is the conviction that the Church itself had been given, in the gift of the Holy Spirit, a unique and special endowment of divine power.

The most obvious power saying from the standpoint of the future of the Christian Church is the unique Matthean saying:

> I tell you, you are Peter, and on this rock (*petra*) I will build my church, and the powers of death (Gk. gates of Hades) shall not prevail against it. I will give you the keys of the kingdom of heaven, and whatever you bind on earth shall be bound in heaven (Matt. 16.18–19).

Some commentators accept this as a saying of Jesus, others deny it. But at the least it expresses the self-understanding of the Matthean community, and in view of its language and structure goes back quite probably to a primitive Aramaic-speaking community, who saw themselves, under Peter's administration, as the eschatological community of salvation. As such the community participates proleptically in the power to judge, which is one element of God's kingly rule. Jeremias connects the magnitude of the authority so claimed with that asserted in the words, 'He who receives you receives me, and he who receives me receives him who sent me' (Matt. 10.40; cf. Luke 10.16).[55]

Luke's formulation of the power of the apostles is consistent with his presentation of the power of Christ. Thus they perform powerful healings whilst invoking the name of Christ (Acts 4.7–10), but the power of God is also associated specifically with their preaching of the resurrection (Acts 4.33). Stephen, like Peter and John, is a person 'full of grace and power' (Acts 6.8), both working miracles and speaking with the aid of the Spirit.

Seen, therefore, from the standpoint of the power involved, we may hold that Paul's aggressive understanding of the authority lying behind his preaching of the gospel involves no radical transformation. He is dependent on Jesus' own insight into the nature of the power conflict into which all are born when he affirms, to his Thessalonian congregation, that 'our gospel came to you not only in word, but also in power and in the Holy Spirit and with full conviction' (1 Thess. 1.5). His gospel was a matter of spiritual power, and faith is built not on sophistry but on the power of God (1 Cor. 2.5). The gospel is 'the power of God for salvation to everyone who has faith' (Rom. 1.16).

Crucial for Paul is, of course, the resurrection. 'God raised the Lord and will also raise us up by his power' (1 Cor. 6.14; cf. 2 Cor. 13.3–4). All he cares for is to know Christ and 'the power of his resurrection', which will involve, before the resurrection, a sharing in Christ's sufferings and death (Phil. 3.10–11). Perhaps with sharper insight into the essentially veiled nature of Jesus' own exercise of power, Paul perceives that the crucifixion itself, and the weakness of Christ, is a message of great power (1 Cor. 1.18 and 24). This indeed was a lesson he himself had learnt by experience; 'My grace is sufficient for you, for my power is made perfect in weakness' (2 Cor. 12.9).

Here one must note particularly the dialectic between weakness and power in Paul. It is not that human weakness is identical with divine power; rather that human weakness constitutes a vacuum which the power of God can fill.[56] This is why Paul claims to be able to do everything 'in him who strengthens me' (Phil. 4.13). He sees the whole of his activity as an apostle as the work of Christ in him 'by word and deed, by the power of signs and wonders, by the power of the Holy Spirit' (Rom. 15.18–19).

So, though the letters are doubtfully Pauline, the cosmic drama disclosed in Colossians and Ephesians is, theologically speaking, a consistent expression of the fundamental situation.

The dominion of darkness (Col. 1.13), a phrase found also in the Gospel of Luke (22.52), has been overcome. The principalities and powers have been mastered on the cross (Col. 2.15), and the Christian is bound to acknowledge Christ as the head of all power and authority (Col. 2.10). However, Christians still find themselves engaged in a serious conflict against cosmic powers, in which the power of the Lord is to provide them with their decisive resources (Col. 1.11; Eph. 6.10–18), of which unceasing prayer in the spirit is among the most potent. The profound prayer of the author for his readers is 'that according to the riches of his glory he may grant you to be strengthened with might (*dunamis*) through his Spirit in the inner man, that Christ may dwell in your hearts through faith' (Eph. 3.16).

From this survey of the way in which the theme of power is handled in the New Testament we may conclude without any reservation that the early Christian communities were highly power-conscious bodies. More specifically they interpreted their own significance in terms of an overarching mythology of the kingly power of God. This Kingdom is conceived as the ultimately victorious outcome of a massive power struggle into the midst of which the disciple is cast.[57] From the teaching of Jesus to the testimony of some of the later parts of the New Testament there is a basic consistency of conviction: to be a Christian is to be equipped with power – real power, as distinct from the outward form of piety (2 Tim. 3.5). This power is the divine power, the power of the Spirit. It dwells in the gospel, and is evident at the points where it overcomes challenge, opposition and conflict. It is the power to convince, to bring about new life, to create loving harmony in the community, to withstand persecution, and to triumph over death; it is powerful, in other words, over indifference and rejection, over law, over internal dissent, over external oppression, and over the last enemy itself. The Psalms, which continue to be used in the worship of the new communities, have now a new range of associations, not least the Psalms interpretative of the passion, Psalms 22 and 69, and of the resurrection and ascension, Psalms 110 and 114. The sense of dependence upon the power of God is thus not merely a matter of myth and of doctrine for the primitive Church, it is embedded in the liturgy; it becomes not merely an integral part of the proclamation and a presupposition of its catechesis, it also lodges itself in one other of the dimensions of the new movement, that is, in its ritual.

The evidence also permits us to conclude that as soon as the new communities expanded to a size which required a measure of formality in structure and discipline, the deployment of considerable power would characterize its understanding of its arrangements. Those who preached the gospel of the power of God were themselves seen as powerful people—similarly, those who baptized or who led the worship, whoever they may have been. The argument here, it should be noted, is neutral as regards the establishment of any particular order; rather we may conclude that whatever order came into being would serve as a focus for identifying the presence of the power of God. Even if the prophets, the preachers, or the leaders rightly claimed that the power originated not in themselves, but in God, they were undeniably and perceptibly co-operators. For the power to function it required localization in authorized persons, rites and places. Totally diffused power is indistinguishable from no power at all.

IV

The original reason for setting out on this discussion of power lay in its relation to conflict. If, as we have shown, conflict is endemic in Christianity, then there will be power struggles within the Christian Church. This led us to a discussion of Paul's understanding of his authority as an apostle, and from this we moved to what I called the power vacuum after Paul's death and the death of the other original church founders. This in turn brought us to consider power as a theme of the New Testament.

But it has not been made clear what the connection is between the Church's consciousness of itself as a powerful body, and the question of internal conflict. Even if the Christian sees himself or herself as engaged in a cosmic fight against 'the principalities, the powers and the world rulers of this present darkness' (Eph. 6.12), what has this to do with internal dispute about the true identity of the faith? A second question arises from the very manner in which the first is phrased. How is the mythological language of cosmic struggle to be interpreted? Once we perceive the myth as myth, then it becomes relevant to enquire about the function of the symbolic language out of which it is constructed.

The answer to the first question about the relation between the external and the internal struggles of the Church is on the following lines. A Church which perceives itself to be involved in an ultimately serious struggle against evil, is a Church which is capable of evoking the full commitment of its membership. Commitment, as we have seen, is a standard feature of religion and self-sacrifice is its hall-mark. Every individual person committed to the system of values constituting a religion is capable, with the support of his or her group, of resisting and rejecting contrary values in other groups of society as a whole. The mere fact that early Christian churches were politically and socially insignificant in the Graeco-Roman world by no means inhibited them from utter dedication to their vision of reality. That vision of reality cast them in roles of the highest significance as bearers of the power of the Lord of hosts.

The same commitment, of course, is responsible for the resolute defence of their own value system from compromising incursions. Since the group values so highly its own task, it will be insistent on high standards of identification, and the norms of behaviour will be sharp and enforced. The development of rules of behaviour in the Christian community, by no means impossible even in its earliest days, is not necessarily a sign of degeneracy.[58] On the contrary, regulations are an inevitable consequence of growth in size, and an indication of seriousness of intent. The sharp definition of boundaries and the enforcement of discipline within the community are developments wholly to be expected in the light of Jesus' preaching of the Kingdom, and of Paul's understanding of the gospel. Both, as we have seen, are understood as exercises of divine power, and this power is available to the entire Christian community which is gathered to fulfil the divine intention for the whole of humanity.

But what, secondly, is the real significance of this talk of kingly power? Here we raise a serious question in modern theology to which it is possible to give no more than an outline answer. It is undeniable that power is avoided as a topic in modern Christian theology;[59] the word authority is likewise held to be in crisis. Why should this be? First, it is patent that the rapid growth of secondary education in the western world has brought to the attention of very large numbers of young people the appalling abuses of political power for which the established churches of the Christian world are responsible. In democratic cultures which have become acutely suspicious of arbitrary force, and in which capital punishment is rejected as barbaric, the execution, let alone the slow burning to death, of even one heretic is an inexplicable crime, and the power to commit it utterly unacceptable.

Then, again, the undeniable fact is that modern western cultures have developed a huge range of activities, which make numerous demands on the individual's time and skill, and inevitably disperse his or her capacity for single-minded commitment. 'Lack of commitment, lack of identity, meaninglessness, anomie, and alienation are all very much related symptoms of societies in which definitions of reality are no longer taken for granted because competition has relativized them all.'[60] Under such pressure, Christian theology has a natural tendency to justify a less intense form of faith. The result is tacit abandonment of the power claim.

A third reason for avoiding the themes of power and authority lies in the diminished political influence exercised by the Church in western societies. The theological celebration of powerlessness, based on what appears to be a misunderstanding of Paul's theology of the cross, has an altogether too suspicious air of *post factum* justification for loss of political influence.[61] Correlations of this kind are notoriously difficult to verify, and I refer to this possibility for no other reason than to arouse suspicion. But when confronted by the evidence of early Christian communities, without political influence of any kind, rejoicing that God has given them knowledge of 'the immeasurable greatness of his power in us who believe' (Eph. 1.19), one is inclined to ask whether there are social reasons why modern theologians fail to make any such claim. Alternatively, if it is said that the early Church was, in such exaggerated language, over-compensating for its social and political impotence, may not the modern Church be suspected of a similarly relativistic adjustment to the history of its somewhat more complex social situation?

For whatever reason it may be so, it is a plain fact that in modern theology the mythological character of the language of God's kingly rule is open to a variety of interpretations. One example will have to stand for many. At the end of his impressively fair and sophisticated review of modern New Testament scholarship on this topic, Norman Perrin refers to his own personal response to the language of the Kingdom. He sees it as a challenge to explore 'the manifold ways in which the experience of God can become an existential reality to man' and to understand the Kingdom as something 'which every man experiences in his own time.[62] He added that he regarded all talk of God as acting, and persons as experiencing the event of the Kingdom as mythological language 'to be taken seriously but not necessarily literally'.

A full discussion of the status of language of divine intention and divine action would take us far beyond our brief at the moment. What I wish to draw attention to is the contrast between the hesitancy implied in the words 'take seriously but not necessarily literally' and the confidence of, for example, the passage quoted from Ephesians above. This is a perfectly relevant consideration. If one of the functions of the mythological language of God's kingly rule is the mobilization of the person to total commitment and to a sense of confident participation in an ultimate victory of the divine intention over contrary forces, then any response to that language which fails to elicit a corresponding confidence may be justly regarded as inadequate. Hermeneutics must under no circumstances become a sophisticated way of clinging to the evacuated shell of a once living religion.

The problematic element in the situation I would identify as the discipline of theology itself. In a situation of internal conflict about the identity of Christianity, as I have already argued, the necessary decisions are taken in the light of the clarification of the issues provided by theologians. Theologians are active across the entire range of dimensions of Christianity, from doctrines and ethics to ritual and social embodiment, because in each case a theological, or interpretative discipline has grown up in order to make meanings as precise as possible. Theologians are, therefore, necessarily involved in the internal power struggles which conflicts provoke.

It is, nonetheless, very rare to discover a theologian who has taken full stock of the power which he or she exercises. Theological responsibility is commonly defined solely in terms of obedience to the truth. In this case, of course, the epistemological questions raised by theology become determinative of the theologian's attitude, and I shall hope to show in a subsequent chapter why epistemology and the issue of the power of the theologian are inseparable. But even if it be true that obedience to the truth is one of the aspects of the theologian's responsibility, it is demonstrable that other aspects entail the formidable use of power in the modern Church. How else are we to interpret the activities of presiding over, or addressing large congresses of experts, of writing large works which figure on theological reading lists, of compiling reading lists, of framing syllabuses, of recommending students for appointments, including and especially appointments at theological seminaries, and of participating (or not participating) in church commissions? All these activities, especially those connected with the theological education of the ministry of the Church, embody interventions both in the Church's distribution of power and in the Church's participation in the external power conflicts.

But theologians seem remarkably reluctant to expose their own activities to this disturbing analysis. They are happier, for obvious reasons, to write large and impressive works exploring the reasons why the traditional authorities are supposed to have collapsed, than to ask questions about the power which such books tacitly deliver to the theologian in the new situation. It is perhaps fortunate that modern churches have devised ways, sometimes rather crude ways, of diminishing the impact of theology within its own structures. But it is my argument that the quality of theological judgement would be improved if theologians understood the significance of power in the Church, and the role of theological judgement in the elucidation of the complex issues concerning Christian identity with which theologians inevitably deal. For theology or doctrine is but one of the dimensions by which the identity of Christianity is conveyed over time. To make a theological judgement about myth is by no means necessarily to appreciate the role which myths perform, especially when associated with the other dimensions of Christianity, for example ritual. To be a theologian means to be conscious of the diversity of Christianity's dimensions, and to be a responsible theologian means to be conscious of the power that intervention in conflicts entails.

Part Two

4

Schleiermacher on the Essence of Christianity

The purpose of introducing at this point certain *historical* examples of 'early modern' theologians writing on the identity of Christianity is to show something of the complexity of issues involved. I have decided to deal with Schleiermacher, Newman, Harnack and Loisy, Troeltsch and Barth. That is a substantial enough selection, but it could manifestly have been still broader. Why, for example, is there nothing on Hegel or Feuerbach or Ritschl? And why, in the twentieth century, have Tillich and Rahner been omitted? To these questions, if what was being attempted was a thorough modern history of the question, there would be no answer. My present justification is nonetheless simple enough. The theologians chosen for analysis are important in their own right, and adequately demonstrate what enquiry into the identity of Christianity involves; further examples would not add to the analysis which it is possible to offer.

What precisely then are the concerns of this section of the book? First, I desire to show what two *modern* theologians of unquestionable stature, 'fathers' of, respectively, modern Protestant and modern Roman Catholic theology, are driven to do once they abandon certain naive traditions for solving the problem of continuity and identity in Christianity—hence the chapters on Schleiermacher and on Newman. Secondly, I wish to show how two modern historians of similar stature fare when they try to write on this same question—hence the discussion of Harnack and Loisy. And thirdly, I wish to demonstrate the acute problem which two mutually exclusive patterns of epistemological argument have bequeathed to the contemporary theologian—hence the treatment of Troeltsch and Barth. It is at the last stage that I become most aware of the apparent arbitrariness of my choice of examples. Why, for instance, is there no extended discussion of that well–cultivated tradition of contemporary theology which sees the identity of Christianity as realized in *praxis*, rather than in *theoria*? An answer to this question is most certainly implicit in the last three chapters, but I must simply plead guilty to the charge of manipulating my examples to suit the total thesis for which this book is arguing. To tackle Troeltsch, as an acute philosophical commentator on the problems into which Harnack and Loisy tumble, then to tackle Barth, as the theological antithesis to Troeltsch, leaves my enquiry at the precise point at which I want to pursue it further. The nature of what follows is, therefore, not to be construed as a comprehensive survey of one aspect of the modern history of ideas, but as the deployment of certain useful examples for illustrating the nature of a peculiarly teasing problem.

I

The importance of Schleiermacher for the consideration of our topic can be briefly stated. Though not by any means the first theologian to use 'the essence of Christianity' (*Wesen des Christentums*) as a prominent element in his thought, he is the first systematic theologian to show unequivocally how the concept functions in his system. Thus although Wagenhammer is correct in his contention that already by the end of the eighteenth century the methodological problem of essence definition had been appreciated by such thinkers as Semler, Steinbart and Lessing,[1] nonetheless the originality of Schleiermacher lies in his actual demonstration of how a systematic theology looks when based on a thorough mastery of the issues at stake.

The work of Schleiermacher which most obviously gives us an insight into how he deploys his concept of the essence of Christianity is *The Brief Outline on the Study of Theology*, produced first in 1811 in connection with his appointment to the new University of Berlin, which opened in 1810. Schleiermacher had already lectured on the topic of a general outline, or *Enzyklopädie*, in Halle in the winter semester of 1804–5 and did so again in Berlin in 1810–11.[2] The resultant publication, which Schleiermacher revised in 1830, provides us with his most comprehensive presentation of the structure of the theological disciplines in relation to the essence of Christianity, and is also a useful bridge between the earlier works, such as the speeches *On Religion*, and the later works, such as the *Christian Faith*. A view of the various editions of his three major productions illustrates the point.

On Religion	Brief Outline	Christian Faith
[1]1799		
[2]1806		
	[1]1811	
[3]1821		[1]1821–2
[4]1831	[2]1830	[2]1830–1

What I propose to do here is to present and discuss certain of Schleiermacher's major contributions to the discussion of the essence of Christianity on the basis of the final editions of his major works, especially the *Brief Outline*. It will emerge that five points are of importance; first, the implications of the concept of a 'mode of faith' (or *Glaubensweise*), which lead directly to the problem of the relation of philosophy and theology; secondly, Schleiermacher's description of theology as a 'positive science' and the practical character of the task of maintaining Christianity's identity; thirdly, the technique of defining Christianity's essence; fourthly, the place accorded to the 'original form' of Christianity in Schleiermacher's essentially Protestant conception of the essence; and fifthly, the tasks to which essence definition are put in the structure of Schleiermacher's mature theology. These five points encompass the whole of Schleiermacher's highly sophisticated use of the concept, and constitute, in effect, a fascinating way of appreciating his theological achievement as a whole.

The opening proposition of the *Brief Outline* reads as follows:

> Theology is a positive science whose parts join into a cohesive whole only through their common relation to a particular mode of faith (*Glaubensweise*), i.e. a particular way of being conscious of God. Thus, the various parts of Christian theology belong together only by virtue of their relation to 'Christianity'.[3]

Schleiermacher is concerned with the cohesiveness of the theological disciplines. What is it that makes theological study more than an arbitrary assemblage of disparate enquiries? The answer is a 'common relation to a particular mode of faith (*Glaubens-weise*)'. By this Schleiermacher means that orientation of the human heart which pervades Christianity in all its aspects. For an explanation of the thought we have to turn to the fifth of Schleiermacher's speeches *On Religion*, where he outlines an extremely important and influential theory about the principle of individuality in a religion. Religion (in the sense of conscious-ness of God) is always, according to him, 'positive', that is, organized according to a particular determining content. To the question whether religion is a system or not, Schleiermacher had already returned the reply that it is a system in the sense that each particular manifestation of it, from the great historical religions down to the religious consciousness of a single individual, is 'formed according to an inward and necessary connection'.[4] Christianity is, indeed, 'a whole in itself' (*in sich ein Ganzes*),[5] in words exactly echoing the terms of the *Brief Outline*. With every other religion, Christianity sustains its identity by means of an inner principle of adhesion (*Anziehungsprinzip*), which one learns not by examining and detailing its external features, but a general view taken from its centre (*von innen heraus*).[6]

Naturally enough this method of interpreting a religion as an internally coherent whole excludes the traditional method of construing it as a particular quantum of religious matter (*ein bestimmtes Quantum religiösen Stoffs*).[7] Schleiermacher's argument against this is twofold; first, were there no inner principle of coherence it would be unintelligible why religions have persisted side by side for so long without becoming slowly assimilated to each other, and secondly, the growth of indi-viduals in a religious tradition would amount simply to a matter of the truths at which they consciously arrive, an implausible explanation of the actual phenomenon of common patterns of development. Moreover, he adds, it is characteristic of the false, quantitative approach to a religion that quarrels should con-stantly break out among adherents of that view about essentials and inessentials.

They do not know what is to be laid down as characteristic and necessary, and what to separate as free and accidental; they do not find the point from which the whole can be surveyed; they do not understand the religion in which they live and for which they presume to fight, and they contribute to its degeneration, for, while they are influenced by the whole, they consciously grasp only the details. Fortunately the instinct they do not understand guides them better than their understanding, and nature sustains what their false reflections and the doing and striving that flows from them would destroy.[8]

As we shall see, the theme of acquiring the correct point from which the whole can be surveyed re-occurs in precisely the same words in the work of Karl Barth.[9] Schleiermacher's concern is to escape from the toils of the externality tradition; and the method of escape involves the attempt to determine the essence of Christianity by means of a grasp of Christianity's inner structural coherence, that is, its particular mode of faith (*Glaubensweise*).

This latter expression was introduced by Schleiermacher into the second edition of his *Brief Outline*, and is more characteristic of the later period of his theology, especially of his *Christian Faith*. Earlier he tended to use the phrase 'a particular intuition of the Universe' (*Anschauung des Universums*),[10] which cohered with the terminology of his philosophical and theological psychology. For an 'intuition of the universe' to constitute the central factor in a particular religion implies a whole way of interpreting religion as a human phenomenon. 'I would show you', said Schleiermacher at the very outset of his speeches *On Religion*, 'from what human tendency (*Anlagen der Menschheit*) religion proceeds'[11] – and doing so involved him in the outline of a psychology of religious knowledge, a theory of the nature of religious language, and a rudimentary sociology of religion. The first of these is to be found in his interpretation of 'feeling', especially in the first edition of the speeches; later to be replaced by the brief discussion of 'absolute dependence' and 'religious self-consciousness' in the early chapters of *The Christian Faith*. The second is evident in his suggestive comments in the speeches *On Religion* on the communicability of the Christian faith, and is elaborated in the most important essays on hermeneutics, on which he lectured on a number of occasions.[12] The third, Schleiermacher's sociology of religion, is implicit in his repeated attempts to understand the phenomenon of 'church', or assembly of religious believers, in relation to fundamental traits of human beings.[13]

The sophistication of Schleiermacher's approach to this topic now begins to become clear. For him, the identity of Christianity does not consist in a specifiable quantum of propositions handed down invariably in a particular community from generation to generation; nor can it simply be constructed out of a reading of certain infallible texts. It consists, rather, in the perception and maintenance of a particular mode of faith (*Glaubensweise*) which permeates the whole, and causes the whole to cohere as a whole; and in order to understand both *that* this is the case and *how* it is the case, you need to become aware both of what it means to believe, and how believing relates to all other human activities.

The direct implication of Schleiermacher's argument is that there can be no adequately reflected and thought-through grasp of Christianity's identity which is not grounded in a set of preparatory considerations dealing with the human person as a religious being. This is the reason for the more than a hundred pages of introduction on the definition and method of dogmatics which open *The Christian Faith*. This, moreover, validates the explanation which he gives there of the significance of the speeches *On Religion*, Schleiermacher's first attempt to portray the human person as an essentially religious being. This, too, explains his confidence that 'it must be possible to show that the existence of such associations (i.e. religious communities) is a necessary element for the development of the human spirit'.[14] Only when you have attained some systematic clarity about the nature and function of religious belief in human beings can you state with any precision what a 'mode of belief' or *Glaubensweise* might be.

It was, therefore, an entirely natural thing for Schleiermacher to say that the preliminary philosophical investigations take their stance 'above' Christianity.[15] A percipient, and otherwise not unfriendly reviewer expressed his shock at the expression,[16] and it is fair to say that in doing so he placed his finger on a recurring doubt, which Schleiermacher's revision of the phrase does not wholly remove. For him to explain that a preliminary investigation into the 'general concept of a religious community or fellowship of faith (*Glaubensgemeinschaft*)' is 'over' Christianity only in a 'formal' sense disposes merely of the crude objection that Christianity is being *evaluated* in the light of some prior notions about religion.[17] The doubt remains, however, when one asks whether or not it is possible to pursue a purely 'logical' enquiry into the nature of persons as religious beings and not to employ some far-reaching philosophical doctrines about human nature which *must* have consequences for the form of any subsequently articulated Christian doctrine of humanity. At the start of his preliminary investigations in *The Christian Faith* Schleiermacher asserted that, since the process of the definition of a science was not part of the science itself, none of the introductory propositions belonged to dogmatics. In the strict sense that is correct. But it would not be correct to say that Schleiermacher the theologian saw humanity differently from Schleiermacher the philosopher; and there is manifestly a process of mutual interaction of extraordinary complexity in the formulation of the strictly philosophical material in order to match the needs of the theological standpoint.

II

The precise nature of the relationship of theology and philosophy is, however, for Schleiermacher decisively qualified by the peculiar character of theology as a 'positive science'. In the words of the opening definition of the *Brief Outline* quoted above, 'theology is a positive science'. The meaning of this expression deserves to be explored, and to this we now turn.

To say that theology is a positive science, he explains, is to draw attention to the practical tasks for which the parts or elements of Christian faith are assembled as a whole. Theological activity came into prominence in Christianity precisely because leading a Church which rapidly grew into so many cultural and linguistic areas posed acute theoretical and practical problems.[18] To lead the Church one must be theologically educated (Schleiermacher was, after all, lecturing to theological students). There must be a 'vital interchange' between theologian and minister, which can come about only if both have a working knowledge of each other's spheres of operation.[19]

Therefore, if one is to deal with any one of the theological disciplines in a truly theological sense and spirit, he must master the basic features of them all.[20]

This is Schleiermacher's plea for an educated church leadership; this, he believes, is the only hope for the preservation of Christianity from the invasion of 'diseased deviations'.[21]

The practical character of Schleiermacher's organization of the theological disciplines under the concept of the peculiar essence of Christianity is of the utmost importance, and yet has been rarely acknowledged. The reason for this failure is that it has not been appreciated that controversy about the identity of Christianity has important implications for the deployment of power within the Christian community. In the *Brief Outline* Schleiermacher is remarkable for perceiving that the cultivation of an intellectual tradition in Christianity is a direct consequence of the problems and controversies caused by its expansion; he is also particularly acute in his observation that 'the contrast between leaders and ordinary members and the rise to prominence of theology mutually condition each other'.[22] In other words, theological education is an integral element in acquiring access to the power structures of the Church. The importance such a view naturally bestows on the theological professor scarcely needs pointing out. It is as if he has the implicit danger of such an importance exactly in mind when Schleiermacher portrays the balance of a true 'prince of the Church', in whom a religious concern and a scholarly spirit are finely conjoined for the purposes of theoretical and practical activity alike.[23] This is a theme to which we shall have cause constantly to return. Although it is not further developed by Schleiermacher at this point, it is a mark of the quality of his insight into the issue of Christianity's essence and into the root of the intellectual (*wissenschaftlich*) task of defining it, that he should see the sheerly practical reference of the process of definition.

III

This brings us, thirdly, to the point of asking how precisely Schleiermacher conceived the movement from awareness of the issues involved to making the definition explicit. Schleiermacher, for all his methodological sophistication, is plainly not a methodologist pure and simple. He actually defines the essence of Christianity and uses the definition in his system. The question is, How does he arrive at his definition?

We answer this question best by returning to the progress of the propositions in the *Brief Outline*, which is arranged according to numbered paragraphs. The first twenty paragraphs of the *Brief Outline* deal with the preliminary explanations justifying the writing of an outline and explain its fundamental purpose; paragraphs 21 to 31 outline the reasons for the following divisions and subdivisions of theology, in which Schleiermacher expounds his threefold division of philosophical, historical and practical theology. Here again the definition of the essence of Christianity is presented as absolutely foundational. Schleiermacher opens his discussion with the following statement:

> Insofar as one tries to make do with a merely empirical method of interpreting Christianity, he cannot achieve genuine knowledge of it. One's task is rather to endeavour to understand the essence (*das Wesen*) of Christianity in contradistinction to other churches and other kinds of faith (*Glaubensweisen*), and to understand the nature of piety and of religious communities in relation to all other activities of the human spirit.[24]

The denial of an adequate grasp of Christianity from an 'empirical' standpoint is made elsewhere in Schleiermacher's works. The complaint against 'empiricism' is that it has no standard or formula for distinguishing the essential and permanent from the changeable and contingent.[25] By contrast, as we have already seen, the task of the preparatory disciplines is to make clear what concept of church (*Glaubensgemeinschaft*) is entailed in the peculiar mode of faith (*Glaubensweise*) characteristic of Christianity. Here three preparatory disciplines are involved.[26] First, the understanding of the essence of Christianity in contrast with other faiths; secondly, the understanding of the nature of piety in contrast with other human activities; and thirdly, the perception of the authentically Christian in the historical development of the Christian community. To take the second of these disciplines first, Schleiermacher speaks of this as 'ethics'. Thus we note that the first of the 'propositions borrowed from ethics' to be found in *The Christian Faith* runs:

> The piety which forms the basis of all ecclesiastical communions is,

89

considered purely in itself, neither a Knowing nor a Doing, but a modification of Feeling, or of immediate self-consciousness.[27]

The discipline of 'ethics' is of extraordinary importance for Schleiermacher, and it makes a further appearance in the third of the preparatory disciplines.

The second discipline (the first detailed above) is the philosophy of religion. It is concerned with the manner and degree of the differences between different 'societies of faith' (*Glaubensgenossenschaften*).[28] It yields a taxonomy, or classification of religions according to type, and creates certain terms (such as monotheism, polytheism, pantheism and so forth), by means of which the characteristic type of a particular religion can be determined.[29] In Schleiermacher's discussion Christianity emerges as a monotheistic faith of the teleological type of religion with its outward unity constituted by a reference to an original relation. It is not now necessary to discuss the meaning of the term teleological, nor its differentiation from so-called aesthetic religion.[30] The importance of the philosophy of religion is, rather, that the proper cultivation of it creates a link of great importance with the third preparatory discipline, namely philosophical theology (or, in *The Christian Faith*, apologetics). 'Philosophical theology utilizes the framework developed in philosophy of religion', as Schleiermacher puts it.[31] Whereas philosophy of religion arrives at an understanding of the essence of Christianity by considering its relations with other religions (and hence studying its *differentia*), philosophical theology studies Christianity from the standpoint of its own internal history of development (and hence of its *characteristica*). In *The Christian Faith* Schleiermacher explicitly acknowledges that the 'philosophy of religion', as he has depicted it, is an intellectual discipline in its infancy. Recent 'philosophies of religion' (he is thinking of Schelling, or conceivably of Hegel, the outline and main drift of whose lectures on the subject Schleiermacher would most certainly have known) 'do not sufficiently maintain the balance between the historical and the speculative for us to be able to appeal to them in our theological studies as admittedly satisfactory'.[32] Hence greater importance attaches to the third discipline, philosophical theology, on which most of the burden of defining the 'essence of Christianity' falls.

For all the preliminary and rather sketchy quality of this

material we should be willing to acknowledge that Schleiermacher has articulated a principle of great importance, namely that the study of Christianity should not be isolated from the wider study of religion. He decisively points Christian theologians away from a cultural parochialism which is still embedded in its system of theological education, and is undergirded by a misleading sense of western economic superiority. It is true that Schleiermacher's own attempt at the 'philosophy of religion' has, as its outcome, the depiction of the superiority of the Christian religion. But it is also the case that he is totally innocent of any attempt at proving the superiority of Christianity; his method is quite consistent with the development of less value-laden tools of analysis of the phenomena of religions, and in this respect he deserves recognition as the founder of the study of religions as carried out within the context of western cultures.

The third, and most important, of the preparatory disciplines is 'philosophical theology'. Its task is to define and depict the distinctive nature (*das eigentümliche Wesen*) of Christianity, or its idea (*Idee*). Since Christianity is now divided into a plurality of communities there is both a general and a special philosophical theology, the latter (in Schleiermacher's case) being Protestant philosophical theology. Its task is to survey the history of Christianity and elucidate it *critically*.

> The distinctive nature of Christianity ... admits only of being defined critically by comparing what is historically given in Christianity with those contrasts by virtue of which various kinds of religious communities can be different from one another.[33]

The 'critical' method (distinguished by Schleiermacher from 'scientific' or speculative, and from empirical methods) rests, as the latter part of the sentence makes clear, on the foregoing disciplines of ethics and philosophy of religion. The method involves a *comparison* of the actual history of Christianity with certain abiding elements in man's religious history. Although Schleiermacher goes into no further detail, it seems that he believes that as a result of bringing the two areas of study to bear on each other a conclusion may be reached about Christianity's true identity.

How this works in practice is illustrated in *The Christian Faith*. Here he writes:

The only way of discovering the peculiar essence of any particular faith and reducing it as far as possible to a formula is by showing the element which remains constant throughout the most diverse religious affections within this same communion, while it is absent from analogous affections within other communions.[34]

Schleiermacher quite explicitly recognizes the difficulty of this in view of the great variety of forms of Christianity, and the disputes among Christians about the boundaries of Christianity. He quite deliberately, therefore, chooses a broad and inclusive definition, which specifies the focus as 'the redemption accomplished by Jesus of Nazareth'. Two inter-connected points are involved; that all religious emotions in Christianity are given their particular 'tone' and 'colour' (the words are Schleiermacher's)[35] by the sense of redemption from captivity which all Christians share, and that the accomplishment of this redemption universally and completely is attributed to Jesus and to no other.

To elaborate these points would be to launch into dogmatics itself, but the definition, once launched, as it were, experimentally,[36] can be tested against Christian history. One observes, for example, that exaltation of the founder of Christianity and a sense of redemption rise and fall together; as do the opposite tendencies, to depreciate the distinctiveness of Christianity and to regard Jesus as a teacher of moral truths.[37] Or again one observes that what have been traditionally regarded as heresies relate precisely to redemption and Jesus, either presenting humanity in such a way as to make redemption impossible (so Manichaeism and Pelagianism) or presenting Jesus in such a way that he cannot accomplish redemption (so Docetism and Ebionism).[38] Thus 'the more it turns out that what is thus set up problematically as heretical is also actually given in history, the more ground have we to regard the formula upon which the contruction is based as a correct expression of the essence of Christianity'.[39] The inquiry into the heretical serves to supplement the inquiry into the essence of Christianity.[40]

This experimental inquiry constitutes that same process of comparison, of which Schleiermacher has already spoken as the critical handling of essence–definition. Defining the essence of Christianity does not rest on a crude 'deduction' of dogmatic conclusions from history; nor does it presuppose the prior acceptance of some externally constituted authority, such as a council or a document. But whilst there is no proof to be had from any simple set of norms, nonetheless there is the possibility of advancing arguments in favour of the position taken. Each theologian has the responsibility of working through the process to his own conclusion.

> Everyone's philosophical theology essentially includes within it the principles of his whole theological way of thinking. Thus, every theologian should produce the entirety of this part of his theology for himself.[41]

IV

Schleiermacher has already admitted that there will be both general and special tasks of essence definition. There is, in other words, an appropriate way of defining the essence of Christianity in general *and* an appropriate way of defining Protestant Christianity, Catholic Christianity and so forth (Eastern Orthodoxy is treated as moribund, and Anglicanism would not at this time have been regarded as distinctive enough to be separately considered).[42] The two tasks are to be done in the same kind of way, that is, 'critically', not 'empirically'.[43] In taking the Protestant stance Schleiermacher is conscious that he is laying particular emphasis upon Christ. His formulation of the 'antithesis' between Protestantism and Catholicism is, indeed, that

> the former makes the individual's relation to the Church dependent on his relation to Christ, while the latter contrariwise makes the individual's relation to Christ dependent on his relation to the Church.[44]

This antithesis amounts, he claims, to a modification of the essence of Christianity, not a subversion of it in its entirety; and, moreover, it is 'destined some day and somehow to disappear'.[45]

It would be strange indeed if the imprint of Schleiermacher's own Protestant convictions were not apparent in his definition of the essence, not merely of Protestantism, but also of Christianity in general. We find this feature, as one would expect, in the emphasis which he lays upon the original form of Christianity.[46] This forms a special section of the major subdivision of the study of theology, entitled historical theology. The importance of the earliest expression of Christianity lies in the fact that here the distinctive nature (*das eigentümliche Wesen*) of Christianity emerges in its clearest and purest form. 'Exegetical theology' is, accordingly, devoted to elucidating 'the original, and therefore for all times normative, representation of Christianity'.[47]

Two careful qualifications are, however, added to this wholly predictable and Protestant thesis. The first is a careful statement about the uncertainty of the temporal boundary or canonical documents of primitive Christianity. The concept of normative value can be ascribed to Christ alone, and not to documents which themselves may contain actual deficiencies and inadequacies. The second qualification is that the Protestant Church, in the development of 'higher criticism' is continually occupied in the process of determining the canon; no decision of the Church can possibly be held to have closed the question.[48] Nor can this task ever be said to have been achieved definitively. Two criteria are used in canon criticism whose concurrence Schleiermacher holds to be especially powerful: first, whether external signs indicate a derivation of the text in question from circles remote from 'the centre of the Church' (*der Mittelpunkt der Kirche*) and, secondly, whether internal signs indicate that the matter is dealt with in a manner not in agreement 'with what is essential in the canonical representation' (*mit dem Wesentlichen der kanonischen Darstelling*). Both of these criteria are themselves dependent on the theologian's judgement about the essence of Christianity. On the 'centre of the Church' Schleiermacher adds the typical comment:

> That by 'the centre of the Church' neither any given realm nor any official post is to be understood here, but only the fullness of Christian sensitivity and insight (*die Vollkommenheit der Gesinnung und Einsicht*), doubtless needs no further explanation.[49]

His view, then, of 'original Christianity' amounts to this: there is a primitive period, containing the original impetus of Jesus himself and the first apostolic establishment of the Christian Church, of which the Christian theologian must become a student. The documentary evidence must be studied with the maximum care, in the light of an already formed set of convictions about the essence of Christianity (itself based on the study of the history of Christianity), so as to enable one to make ever more careful judgements about what is to be held to be authentic in Christian faith. The circularity, or repetitiveness, of the procedures is obvious; and the continuous correction of insights in the light of new data is precisely that *critical* process which Schleiermacher was determined to commend.

V

Finally, it remains to refer to the tasks to which the definition of the essence of Christianity may be put. The most obvious of these are in relation to the two sub-divisions of philosophical theology, named by Schleiermacher, apologetics and polemics.[50] Both of these arise out of the particular and practical concerns of church leadership, apologetics being the laying of foundations for the task of communicating the lively faith of the community, polemics being the activity of criticizing distortions within the community. Both entirely depend on 'an authentic representation of the essence of Christianity' (and also, for the Protestant Church, of the essence of Protestantism).[51]

The discipline of apologetics works, according to Schleiermacher, in the following manner. Having set out a formula for the essence of Christianity and having critically tested it in the manner already described, the theologian must seek to validate the claim of the community to be a 'distinct historical existence' (rather than, let us say, a derivative movement within a larger complex). This involves the development and use of such concepts as revelation, miracle and inspiration which express the novelty and divine origin of the new Christian movement.[52] Similarly the continuity of the new movement with earlier forms of religious community in Judaism and paganism is expressed in the use of concepts such as prophecy and type or pattern.[53] Next, the unity of the essence of Christianity in the midst of its historical changes in the course of time requires the concepts of canon and sacrament.[54] Finally the historical existence of the Christian community in the midst of common life demands the analysis of the concepts of hierarchy and church authority.[55]

All these concepts constitute, in effect, the development of a kind of fundamental theology, whose task is to secure the basic terms in which the Christian community explains its distinctiveness. However, the breadth of scope which they represent is accompanied, in Schleiermacher's exposition, by a certain lack of clarity in the way in which the concepts operate. Moreover, when we examine *The Christian Faith*, we find that these concepts (revelation, miracle, inspiration and so forth) do not recur in the precise way in which they are presented in the *Brief Outline*; it is evident that the over-formal schema of the *Brief Outline* gave him severe problems. But the task achieved by essence–definition is clear enough in broad outline. On the basis of this definition it becomes evident that there is need of conceptual clarification. A new religious community, for example, must clarify both its novelty and its continuity with the past; if it persists through time it must explain how it does so; if it exists with other human organizations it must make clear on what terms. All these are acute *practical* needs. If people are to have a clear idea of what Christianity is, these questions must be answered. And the answering of them, so Schleiermacher says, is based in the study of apologetics which takes its start from the fundamental proposition about the essence of Christianity, as formulated by each theologian. Moreover, the very process of meeting the questions which arise in a satisfactory way constitutes the best test of the original formula.[56]

If, then, apologetics is a discipline designed to meet external needs, polemics, on the other hand, is an internal discipline, practised within the Christian Church in order to keep it in a healthy state. Schleiermacher had cherished this idea from the very first. Integral to his earliest conception of the nature of Christianity is its vigorously self-critical character, relentlessly unmasking 'every false morality, every bad religion, every unhappy union of both for mutual covering of nakedness'.[57] Now, in the *Brief Outline* he establishes polemics as a task of philosophical theology, charged with the detection and exposure of 'diseased deviations' caused either by the recession of vitality or by the incorporation of extraneous matter.[58] Just as the distinctive nature (*das eigentümliche Wesen*) of Christianity can express itself in doctrine and in polity (*Verfassung*) so a diseased condition can arise in either area, by indifferentism or heresy in doctrine, or by separatism or schism in polity.[59] What is meant by these conditions must be analysed in the light of the formulation of the essence of Christianity. The critical method also operates in this area, and yields, by a process of checking the hypothetical formulation against the phenomena of church history, an increasingly reliable conclusion.[60]

Apologetics and polemics are, however, not the only areas where the essence of Christianity is put to work. Schleiermacher makes it clear that the whole interpretation of the history of Christian theology rests on the same formulation.

> The order in which the various points of doctrine arise and in which the main constellations of didactic language are formulated must be capable of being directly conceived, on the large scale at least, from the distinctive nature (*das eigentümliche Wesen*) of Christianity.[61]

By this Schleiermacher means that the earliest controversies in Christian theology ought to reflect most accurately the crucial points in the understanding of Christianity, if, that is, the essence has been correctly conceived. From this proposal the whole structuring of historical theology may be ordered as a discipline, showing how, why and when particular sorts of terminology ('didactic language') were developed for particular purposes.

When we come, however, to the proper subject matter of dogmatic theology, the concept of the essence of Christianity totally disappears from the scene. Contrary to what one might expect, the content of dogmatics is not said, in the *Brief Outline*, to consist in the elaboration and explanation of all that is implicit in the formulated essence. Why should this be so? Part of the answer is certainly that Schleiermacher saw no need to re-emphasize what he had already made quite clear, namely that the principles of the whole theological way of thinking had been formed by the theologian in his development of a philosophical theology (see above p. 91). But it is also true that in dogmatics Schleiermacher saw not the exposition of the timelessly true essence of Christianity, as critically constructed by the individual theologian; rather all dogmatics arose out of the state of a given church at a given time.[62] The analysis of the situation for any given dogmatics is thus of great importance. The 'principle of the present period' (*das Prinzip der laufenden Periode*) must be ascertained on the basis of a carefully constructed periodization of historical theology. This periodization has itself, of course, been developed in close connection with the definition of the essence, so that the doctrinal tasks of the present can be more clearly ascertained. Moreover the whole hermeneutics of the period of the primitive Church, yielding the sense or instinct for a view of authentic Christianity, is brought to bear in assisting the presentation of a dogmatics adequate to the present and true to Christian identity. But Schleiermacher had learnt a decisive lesson from Semler. A pure expression of Christianity simply does not exist and never has existed. No claim, therefore, can be made for any dogmatic theology, that it is the straightforward articulation of all that is implied in the proper definition of Christianity's essence.[63]

Nonetheless the influence of all that has gone into the understanding of the essence of Christianity is fundamental. The whole structure of *The Christian Faith*, Schleiermacher's dogmatics, bears numerous signs of this influence. Two examples makes this sufficiently clear: the implications drawn from the study of the human person as a religious being account for the use of the concept of religious consciousness in the threefold framework of the body of the work, and the fact that redemption is focused upon Christ accounts for the pivotal position of the doctrine of Christ's person and work. Both of these utterly fundamental and structural considerations are a direct consequence of the particular way in which essence–definition has been undertaken. The conclusion we may reach is that the method of writing a Christian dogmatics is, for Schleiermacher, determined by the decisions and judgements made in the definition of Christianity's essence.

VI

One of the problems in the study of Schleiermacher is the achievement of what one might call an adequate middle distance perspective. At close quarters he presents an exceptionally dense and demanding text, over which at every other sentence the modern interpreter has to wrestle for a sympathetic understanding of the allusions of the argument. In the generalized histories of thought, on the other hand, he is plausibly rendered as a typical Romantic, or a post-Kantian theologian of religious experience, or an anthropocentric subjectivist. What is his significance, however, in the kind of outline which we are here attempting to present of a decisive change in the theological handling of this central question of Christianity's identity?

In part the answer has already been given by recent theological research. It has been shown that what I have termed the inwardness tradition was already long established in Christianity, especially in Protestantism, where it had been deployed to meet the onslaught of rationalism. Schleiermacher's central convictions that Christianity must always be engaged in a process of re-evaluation, and that no external form can ever represent Christianity in pristine purity, are already familiar to the student of Luther and Semler. That there is an epistemological price to be paid for this doctrine he learnt above all from Kant. For obvious reasons Schleiermacher's teachers were, for the most part (apart, that is, from Plato himself) German Protestant theologians, and if we analyse the separate elements of his rich and mature synthetic achievement we find without difficulty remoter or closer precursors in most of its individual features; though, as we shall see in Newman's case, the influences at work are not restricted to their impact on Protestantism.

The 'middle distance' answer to our question, however, seems not to lie in these areas. Rather, I would argue that, more or less by accident, Schleiermacher stumbles on a theological tool, namely that of the critical definition of the essence of Christianity, which meets the future exigencies of the impact of the biblical–critical movement on doctrinal theology. Not merely does he make essence definition central to his theology, as I have shown above; he specifies the processes involved in this definition in a highly sophisticated and nuanced way. To name but two lastingly important features of this process, he seeks to establish a permanent relationship with the non-theological disciplines, and he expects the theologian's definition to be subject to a process of continuous checking against the whole history of Christianity, as presented by contemporary historical research. In both of these respects Schleiermacher makes a *methodological* contribution to theology which, I would argue, is of lasting significance, and to which I shall return in Chapter 10.

This method meets in a remarkable way the demand for a

thoroughgoing internally applied criticism of theology, which neither on the one hand imports alien criteria in order to judge the rationality of theology according to some supposedly universal standard, nor on the other hand merely presupposes the immunity of its revealed foundations.[64] Schleiermacher's openness to criticism reaches back to the very notion of faith itself and to its communal expression in a Church. He may be right or he may be wrong in his particular definition of either or both, but he is at least exposing both concepts to critical scrutiny with the aid of tools from psychology and sociology. In his day, psychology meant philosophical psychology and sociology a rudimentary study of society which he termed 'ethics'. In our day, a critical theologian working on Schleiermacher's principles would prepare a dogmatics by submitting the concepts 'faith' and 'church' to an analysis which had first been disciplined by a Freudian and a Marxist critique.

That such an analysis would be forced in the end to make its own perhaps somewhat eclectic psychological and sociological appraisal of religion seems most probable, rather as Schleiermacher himself found that he needed his own, home-made 'philosophy of religion'. Theologians perforce have nowadays to operate at what Rahner called, somewhat grandly, 'the first-level of reflection', which I take to be an intellectually responsible kind of generalization.[65] Again their generalizations may be right, or they may be wrong, but they are doing something which theologians ought to do if their discipline is supposed to be in open and critical dialogue with the culture of which it is part.

The same appreciation of Schleiermacher's merit rids us of two superstitions about definers of the essence of Christianity. The first of these is that essence–definition is necessarily reductive in character. One could not credibly suggest, on a close examination of Schleiermacher's procedures for the delineation and use of the concept, that he had in mind the abandonment of whole areas of Christian existence. Nor will the second dogma stand, that essence–definers employ historical research as a substitute for the appeal to authority.[66] We shall in due course see the extent to which such a charge can properly be made against Harnack, but against Schleiermacher it will not run. Indeed it is a remarkable fact that none of the disciplines preparatory to the task of Schleiermacher's dogmatics is in any simple sense history, and it is by these disciplines co-operatively that the essence of Christianity is determined, and then checked against history.

A serious doubt remains, however, in the mind of any critical student, even after due acknowledgement of Schleiermacher's theological insight. This doubt concerns the absolutely crucial presupposition of the unitary character of Christianity (*in sich ein Ganzes*). I do not at this point wish to anticipate a fuller discussion of what may be implied in this ambiguous expression. But at the very least we must note Newman's severe reservations about the instinct towards systematization which he believed was characteristic of Protestantism, and Troeltsch's acute analysis of the internal tensions within Christianity which keep it in a state of perpetual oscillation. Schleiermacher was an unrepentant systematician.[67] He did not imagine, as we have seen, that definitive systematics could ever be written, but it was, nonetheless, the duty of at least some theologians to conceive of Christianity as a whole. His entire conception of the study of theology, in which he was so remarkable an innovator, was systematic to the core.

But what, precisely, did that entail? Is the cost, as Barth was to argue, an inevitable pull into subjectivism and anthropo-centricity? Or is the loss otherwise specifiable, as a certain lack of realism, of attention to the particular and the unassimilable, in the very observation of what it is to be Christian in the midst of the dense and intractable stuff of human living? These are, in my view, the major doubts about Schleiermacher's inheritance, with which a modern critic must wrestle. They are, moreover, the very questions which concerned Newman as he attempted to relate his own sense of the divinely given wholeness of Christianity to his aversion to what he believed to be arbitary human systematization.

5

Newman on the Idea of Christianity

It would be manifestly unfair to John Henry Newman's handling of our theme if we were to approach his work in the same way as we approached Schleiermacher's. We are precluded from this course of action by the fact that Newman did not formally give the question of Christianity's essence the careful methodological consideration which we have seen in Schleiermacher. Newman's references to the theme are, for the most part, occasional and passing. Nothing of great moment appears to turn on how he treats the question, and it is not in the least difficult to show his uncertainty and even inconsistency on the subject.

To score cheap points in this way would be an absurd misuse of Newman's fertile and exceptionally suggestive contribution to our discussion. The argument here will be, by contrast, that the very importance of what he has to tell us lies in his sensitivity to the different traditions of thought and the different considerations which he allows to tell at different places. It is, therefore, of the very essence of our approach to Newman that we should give full weight to the often extremely personal qualifications of received opinion, expressed sometimes in quite tentative fashion, which characterize his writing on the subject. We will look in vain for a systematician, but it is pure gain for the argument of this book that Newman was constitutionally incapable of reflecting any tradition of discourse without at the same time transforming it.

When Newman left Anglicanism to become a Roman Catholic, part of the process of reflection which led to the change concerned his dissatisfaction with the Anglican tradition of 'fundamental articles'. He had been forced to give careful thought to this tradition in the course of his rather confusing exchange with the Abbé Jean-Nicholas Jager, a French Roman

Catholic who later became Professor of Ecclesiastical History in the Faculty of Theology in the University of Paris.[1] The controversy occupied Newman for a substantial part of the latter part of 1834, and the formulation of his view over against Jager constituted the nucleus of his work in a course of sermons given in 1836 which were subsequently published as *Lectures on the Prophetical Office of the Church*.[2] From here it is a bare six years to the sermon on developments in religious doctrine (preached on the Feast of the Purification, 1843) and eight years to the events of 1845, the writing of *An Essay on the Development of Christian Doctrine*,[3] and Newman's reception into the Roman Catholic Church. Although for our purposes it is the period of transition which is chiefly of interest, inasmuch as it contains Newman's attempt to elucidate the problem of continuity and change in Christianity, evidence both from the previous decade and the subsequent years also has its importance. Especially, on the one hand, the University Sermons,[4] and, on the other, Newman's Preface of 1877 to the third edition of the *Via Media*[5] and his substantial rewriting in 1878 of the *Essay*[6] provide us with some vital insights into both the seed and the fruit of the period of transition.

The structure of this discussion falls into three parts. In the first we shall review, in Newman's Anglican period, the terms in which he rejected the systematization of the gospel under a 'leading idea' and his modification of the Anglican 'fundamental articles' apologetic. In the second section we shall treat the terms in which Newman sought to explain the preservation of Christianity's identity, as a whole, even in the midst of change. Finally, the question will be pursued, in what respects Schleiermacher and Newman can be intelligibly compared in their understandings of, respectively, the 'essence' and the 'essential idea' of Christianity. As a whole the chapter will demonstrate that, contrary to expectations, the similarities are considerable and significant.

I

Newman's first major attempt to handle the question of the 'leading idea' of Christianity occurs in connection with a strong criticism of two Protestant theologians of the early nineteenth century, Thomas Erskine of Linlathen and an American, Jacob Abbott.[7] Both are unsurprisingly accused of the 'introduction of rationalistic principles into revealed religion' in a tract written in 1835 for the *Tracts for the Times*;[8] the same essay contains an appendix dated February 2, 1836, sharply critical of Schleiermacher's work on the doctrine of the Trinity, the only explicit reference to Schleiermacher in Newman's works.[9] Erskine and Abbott are accused by Newman of having ignored the fact that the Christian revelation is a mystery, 'a doctrine *lying hid* in language, to be received in that language from the first by every mind ... of depth unfathomable, and illimitable in its extent.[10] Religious truth is, therefore, neither light nor darkness, but both together, that is, both illuminating and perplexing.

> Revelation, in this way of considering it, is not a revealed *system*, but consists in a number of detached and incomplete truths belonging to a vast system unrevealed, of doctrines and injunctions mysteriously connected together; that is, connected by unknown media, and bearing upon unknown portions of the system.[11]

Newman details the chief of these 'detached and incomplete truths'. They are: the Trinity, the Incarnation, the Atonement, the Church, the Sacraments, Regeneration, Faith and Works – 'each stands in a certain degree isolated from the rest, unsystematic, connected with the rest by unknown intermediate truths, and bearing upon subjects unknown'.[12]

The contrast between this view and 'the popular theology of the day' is, he holds, extreme. This latter takes the atonement, especially in its experiential aspect, as 'the chief doctrine of the gospel', to which 'as if to the point of sight in a picture' the parts of the 'Gospel system' are directed.[13] The result is the production of 'an intelligible human system',[14] of which humanity is itself the centre.[15] Newman, we may remark, has correctly observed the inherent tendency to anthropocentrism of all theologies which exalt the atonement over the incarnation.

Turning particularly to Thomas Erskine, Newman directs his criticism specifically at the notion of a leading idea of Christianity. He will grant that God's revelation of himself operating on the moral characters of persons is an element of Scripture, but not that it is 'the chief and sovereign principle of it'.[16] Again, against Erskine's view that the doctrine of the atonement is the 'corner-stone of Christianity ... to which *all the other doctrines of Revelation are subservient*',[17] he urges that the prominence of a doctrine does not entail its pre-eminence or paramount character.

It is important to advert to Newman's own standpoint in relation to this criticism. First, he is convinced, with Bishop Butler, that 'Christianity is a scheme quite beyond our comprehension'.[18] But Newman also fears that systematization of the kind proposed by Erskine and Abbott leads to a distortion of the language and ordinances of the Christian religion, as they were given. Constantly he uses the doctrine of the Trinity as his example, and it is no accident that this heads the list of chief doctrines. He fears that the subordination of the essential to the economic Trinity is but the first stage of the road to the abandonment of Trinitarian theology altogether. The objection to a system is thus not to any kind of system whatsoever, but rather to that urge to systematization which springs from the desire to make Christian doctrine immediately intelligible. Some elements of a scheme or system are evidently revealed (Newman refers to the death and resurrection of Christ and the sending of the Spirit as being revealed portions of a system);[19] others, again, are equally evidently unsystematizable, such as the doctrine of the Trinity ('a mere juxtaposition of separate truths, which to our minds involves inconsistency, when viewed together').[20] A door, one might say, is left slightly ajar for the further development of the idea of system, inherent indeed in revelation, but in part at least mysterious ('a vast system unrevealed', see above). Finally one must note Newman's readiness to speak of revelation as consisting in 'facts'.

That essay was written in 1835; in the previous year Newman had become involved in the discussion of the idea of 'fundamental articles' with the Abbé Jager. As background to his side of the argument Newman had had to give a close reading to certain Anglican apologists, such as Laud, Stillingfleet, Hall and Jewel, who had treated the same question at some length in earlier controversies with Roman Catholics. The importance of this study, we should note particularly, is that it brought Newman actively to consider a particular tradition of interpretation of the identity and continuity of Christianity stemming from the Reformation, about which a word of explanation must be added. According to this tradition the Christian Church is characterized by the invariable profession of certain 'fundamental articles', distinguished from variable elements, otherwise known as non-fundamentals, which should never be absolutized. The importance for Anglican apologetic of this distinction between fundamentals and non-fundamentals is well-known. As evidence it is usual to point to Hooker's references to the subject in Book III of the *Laws of Ecclesiastical Polity* (1594) ('The visible Church of Jesus Christ is therefore one, in outward profession of these things, which supernaturally appertain to the very essence of Christianity, and are necessarily required in every particular Christian man'),[21] it is less frequently noted than it should be, however, that the whole principle of the Henrician reformation rested on Melanchthon's doctrine of *adiaphora,* or things indifferent, in implicit distinction from things necessary to salvation.[22] Adopted originally to justify the abandonment of Roman supremacy, the doctrine was extended to cover all the non-scriptural elements of Roman practice (such as clerical celibacy), which might quite properly be varied from place to place and time to time. Far from promoting toleration, on the other hand, the same distinction could be used to bolster authoritarianism. Thus things indifferent might also be properly insisted upon by lawfully constituted church authority, if they tended to good human order.

Thus the doctrine of 'fundamentals' came to be a vital and highly flexible plank of Anglican apologetic against Roman Catholic additions, Presbyterian rigidity, and Independent wilfulness, as opportunity demanded. However, by observing the actual history of the use of the distinction we note one important element of it, namely, the variability of its content. What Henry VIII himself regarded as belonging to the necessary doctrines and practices was different from what Cranmer eventually so regarded. Who, then, was to decide what was necessary, and what merely accessory?

To invest their answer to this question with the required measure of authority, the Anglican apologists laid particular stress on the early Church. Thus Hooker himself in the same passage in Book III referred explicitly to the 'few articles of Christian belief' as summarized by Tertullian and Irenaeus, the so-called *regula fidei*, or rule of faith;[23] to these he adds merely the (two) sacraments of the Church of Christ. The point of this appeal to the early Church was primarily polemical. The intention was to convict Rome of *adding* to the faith by demonstrating that she was guilty of innovation (one of the patristic marks of heresy). But the *basis* of the appeal to the early Church was the production of evidence that for many centuries the Church had retained the faith taught in holy Scripture. Hence (as Article V of the 42 Articles of 1553 puts it):

> Holy Scripture containeth all things necessary to salvation: so that whatsoever is neither read therein, nor may be proved thereby, although it be some time received of the faithful as godly, and profitable for an order and comeliness: yet no man ought to be constrained to believe it as an article of faith or repute it requisite to the necessity of salvation.[24]

It is this position which Newman is at pains to defend and interpret in his controversy with Jager: 'The main principle', he writes, 'which we of the Anglican Church maintain is this: that Scripture is the ultimate basis of proof, the place of final appeal, in respect of all fundamental doctrines.'[25] By 'fundamental doctrine' Newman explicitly notes that he means 'such doctrines as are necessary for Church Communion';[26] he is referring in fact to 'the articles of the Creed'. Furthermore, in his second letter in explanation of this position, he is prepared to reduce the foundational doctrine of the Church to its simplest expression in the Petrine confession, 'Thou art the Christ, the Son of the Living God'.[27] This, he suggests, is the source and root from which the articles of the Apostles' and Nicene Creeds have developed. The proof that these, and these alone, are fundamental is historical; and like Hooker, Newman at once quotes Irenaeus and Tertullian.[28] 'To be simple and precise in fundamentals', he adds, following Locke, 'is a socially charitable arrangement, so that all classes might profess the same faith in the same terms, the totality be easily memorable, and minds be saved from perplexity'.[29]

It is at this point that Newman adds a characteristic qualification to the received view. This qualification, which is of major importance both for construing his own theological position and also for understanding his movement out of the Anglican church, consists in a particular view of the language of revelation. As we have already seen, revelation for Newman is a mystery, 'a doctrine *lying hid* in language'. Thus although the creed in which the fundaments of Christianity are expressed consists in few, simple and precise words, nonetheless its meaning is 'incomprehensible in its depth and indefinite in its extent'.[30] No candidate for baptism can know, at the time when he is repeating its words and binding himself to it, precisely whither he will be carried by its implications. Moreover it is a property of faith to 'wish to conceive rightly of sacred doctrine, so far as it can be conceived at all, and to look towards the Church for guidance how to conceive it'.[31]

It is precisely at this point that Jager inserted his knife. What sort of a church is it, he asked, to which people look for guidance, and which for the sake of wise and simple alike claims to give certain guidance on matters said to be fundamental, but which can actually err on the prior question of what is fundamental?[32] To cope with this difficulty, Newman at first tentatively in a letter to Froude, and then more confidently in the *Prophetical Office*, sought to bring out his distinction between what he calls the Episcopal and the Prophetic traditions. The first is precise and official, resting on the apostles themselves; the second is less precise, interpretative and supplementary to scriptural or fundamental doctrine.[33]

When, in the *Prophetical Office*, Newman came to give an account of the difference and relationship between the two traditions so conceived, he had to admit that no precise distinction could be drawn between the two. After all, there was nothing in the creeds about original sin, or justification by faith, or election, or the sacraments. It could not, therefore, be said that the prophetical tradition was coterminous with the 'non-fundamentals', sure though he was that the episcopal tradition contained the fundamentals. Newman's description of the prophetical tradition represents, accordingly, a characteristically independent adaptation of the usual Anglican apologetic, in part forced on him by valid objections from his Roman Catholic interlocutors, but also corresponding to his long-held sacramental view of language. He writes as follows:

Let this maxim be laid down concerning all that the Catholic Church holds, to the full extent of her Prophetical Tradition, viz. that her members must either believe or silently acquiesce in the whole of it. Though the meaning of the Creed be extended ever so far, it cannot go beyond our duty of obedience, if not of active faith; and if the line between the Creed and the general doctrine of the Church cannot be drawn, neither can it be drawn between the lively apprehension and the submission of her members in respect to both the one and the other. Whether it be apprehension or submission, it is faith in one or other shape, nor in fact can individuals themselves ever distinguish what they spiritually perceive from what they merely accept upon authority.[34]

We may remark that although at this stage Newman still believes that he can show that Rome has added to the essentials of the gospel, it is manifest that he has provided himself with the basis of the idea of an infallible *developing* authority. Only the existence of such an element in the day-to-day life of the Church could correspond to that 'duty of obedience' laid on Christian believers when faced with an, in principle, illimitable divine mystery.

II

What, however, is the appropriate response to the mystery of revelation? As Newman faced the implications of this question with greater precision and determination, he found himself compelled to undertake a more far-reaching reappraisal of the Anglican apologetic, even than that contained in his own modified form. In his 1843 sermon on 'The Theory of Developments in Religious Doctrine' he creates a link between the response of the faithful individual to the divine mystery, and that of the Church. Mary, who is 'our pattern of faith', ponders upon divine truth, uses it, develops it, reasons upon it. Similarly the Church in the course of centuries has investigated the doctrines of faith and reared 'a large fabric of divinity ... irregular in its structure, and diverse in its style ... nay, anomalous in its details'.[35] This is, surely, a reference to and description of the prophetical tradition; and although it is Newman's intention to deal in the Sermon primarily with the Trinity and incarnation (that is, with the 'high doctrines' which have to do with the 'objects of Faith'), nonetheless the 'theory of development' outlined is applicable to 'doctrinal developments in general'.[36] Thus all Catholic doctrines, whether to do with the Trinity and incarnation, which Newman considers to belong to a special category, or to do with original sin, sin after baptism, penance, the Eucharist or justification – all these are equally doctrines developed as a result of reflection and investigation, based upon revelation and according to fixed and fundamental laws of human nature.[37] Newman explicitly excludes from consideration the question of who might be 'the legitimate framer and judge of these dogmatic inferences'.[38] But of the fact that the tendency of his thought now urgently requires an act of identification there can be no doubt.

The Sermon on 'The Theory of Developments' is, on any view of it, a document of extraordinary importance. Not merely does it illustrate the transition in Newman from the tradition of Anglican apologetic to a position in which he can envisage the validity of that view of Christianity which Roman Catholicism embodies; it also advertises in a fascinating way the extraordinary fertility and originality of Newman's whole approach to Christian doctrine. Certain ways of speaking of doctrine are tentatively reintroduced. Thus, whereas 'system' has previously been a negative term, implying undue rationalism, especially in Protestantism (though also in Romanism),[39] it is now offered as a criticism of heresy, that it 'tends to no system'.[40] The body of Catholic theology is, indeed, referred to explicitly as 'the dogmatic system'.[41] Consistent with this evidence of increased respect for order, is the depiction of the battle for an orthodox expression of a dogma as the achievement of balance and harmony 'till the whole truth "self-balanced on its centre hung", part answering to part, one, absolute, integral, indissoluble, while the world lasts!'.[42]

The unitary character of this conception of Christian doctrine is based, for Newman, on the nature of revelation itself. Although in one passage he speaks in the plural of 'certain supernatural facts and actions, beings and principles'[43] as constituting the content of revelation, the more characteristic way of speaking is in the singular:

As God is one, so the impression which He gives us of Himself is one; it is not a thing of parts; it is not a system; nor is it any thing

imperfect, and needing a counterpart. It is the vision of an object ...
This being the case, all our attempts to delineate our impression of
Him go to bring out one idea, not two or three or four; not a
philosophy, but an individual idea in its separate aspects ...

Creeds and dogmas live in the one idea which they are designed to
express, and which alone is substantive; and are necessary only
because the human mind cannot reflect upon that idea, except
piecemeal, cannot use it in its oneness and entireness, nor without
resolving it into a series of aspects and relations.[44]

It would be a mistake to imply that this unitary concept is a new
feature in Newman's thought; he had, after all, referred to
'Revealed Religion' as 'one comprehensive moral fact' as early
as 1831.[45] But its presence in the context of an argument about
the necessity of developments in religious doctrines provides the
element of organic integrity if development is not to incur the
risk of radical mutation. If there develops something as diverse
and irregular as the prophetic tradition, then the argument which
secures its internal homogeneity is one which establishes, or
seeks to establish, the singularity and unity of its original *and
continuing* inspiration. Ultimately, as Newman has argued, this
is nothing less than the divine Unity itself. Nothing is more
bluntly indicative of Newman's thought-process in this matter
than the following:

Surely, if Almighty God is ever one and the same, and is revealed to
us as one and the same, the true inward impression of Him, made
on the recipient of the revelation, must be one and the same; and,
since human nature proceeds upon fixed laws, the statement of that
impression must be one and the same, so that we may as well say
that there are two Gods as two Creeds.[46]

Although this astonishing series of false premises and non-logical
conclusions by no means does justice to the sophistication with
which Newman can develop his argument, the direction and
tendency of the argument is clear. The language of Christian
doctrine stands in relation to the divine reality as type to arche-
type.[47] If God is one, so ultimately must be our conception of the
truth concerning him, inadequate though our realization of that
truth may be.

On one further feature of 'The Sermon on Developments' must remark be made. Newman speaks of his way of treating Christian doctrine as 'an inward view of these doctrines, distinct from the dogmatic language used to express them'.[48] What does he mean by 'inward' in this context? The answer is inevitably multi-layered. In the first place it clearly refers to the intimacy of the kind of knowledge referred to in the New Testament as the knowledge of Christ Jesus, especially as an 'indwelling' in the believer.[49] Secondly, Newman desires to draw attention to the priority and interiority of the 'sacred impression' over all external and demonstrating reason. When enlightened by the regulating principle which that impression supplies, the believing mind is, as it were, inhabited.[50] Finally, and most fundamentally, Newman appeals to common human psychological states, such as the existence of unperceived impressions and unconscious ideas, as evidence for 'the reality and permanence of inward knowledge'. Although Newman's application of this last argument is in its context to the history of the Church (just as humans have to make explicit what they implicitly know, so also does the Church), the conceptual apparatus constitutes a much more generally significant position vis-à-vis the nature of Christian doctrine. It proposes, in Newman's own words, 'the inward idea of divine truth', which we have seen to be the Judaeo-Christian tradition of referring truth to the ultimately mysterious depths of the human heart.

We come now to consider the evidence provided by the two main versions of Newman's *Essay on the Development of Christian Doctrine*, of 1845 and 1878 respectively. The first of these reproduces views which he has already expressed at one time or another in the previous decade. The problem of the *Essay* is to offer an hypothesis to account for the apparent variation and growth in Christian doctrine and worship. The procedure is 'to consult history for the true idea of Christianity',[51] armed with the prior assumption that 'the external continuity of name, profession and communion is a *prima facie* argument for a real continuity of doctrine'.[52] The *Essay* opens with a disquisition on the Process of Development in Ideas, and an explicit alliance of the 'idea of Christianity' with that category of complex and living ideas whose capacity for sustaining a persistent identity after prolonged and variegated inspection constitute a claim to be considered 'the representative of an objective truth'.[53]

En passant, though consistently with earlier writings, New-man dismisses the (Protestant) attempt to ascertain the 'leading idea' of Christianity:

> a remarkable essay as directed towards a divine religion, when, even in the existence of the works of man, the task is beyond us. Thus, the one idea of the Gospel has been decided by some to be the restoration of our fallen race, by others philanthropy, by others the spirituality of true religious service, by others the salvation of the elect, by others the union of the soul with God. All these representa-tions are truths, as being aspects of Christianity, but none of them is the whole truth. For Christianity has many aspects: it has its imaginative side, its philosophical, its ethical, its political; it is solemn, and it is cheerful; it is indulgent, and it is strict; it is light, and it is dark; it is love, and it is fear.[54]

This passage, of course, closely recalls the terms of Newman's argument against Erskine in Tract 76 of 1835. The same opposition is expressed to the apparent arbitrariness of the Protestant 'reduction' of Christianity to one of its aspects. How-ever the difference between the writing of 1835 and that of 1845 is that in the meantime Newman had learnt a greater respect for the implicit order and system bestowed on Christianity by the unitary character of its original inspiration.

Accordingly, when he comes to deal with the question of distinguishing between developments and corruptions, he enunciates the rule that

> that development ... is to be considered a corruption which *obscures or prejudices its essential idea*, or which *disturbs the laws of development* which constitute its organization, or which *reverses its course of development*.[55]

The presence in the same work of this passage affirming the existence of an 'essential idea', and that (quoted above) denying the existence of a 'leading idea', is perfectly intelligible in the light of Newman's intellectual pilgrimage. As far as he was concerned the 'essential idea' of Christianity was not an arbitrarily chosen 'leading idea' from a collection of possible candidates. It was, rather, that 'one view of the Mystery', 'the Catholic idea', 'that one impression concerning Almighty God', which *he* had given to be the ruling principle of our minds.[56] The application of the test of 'preservation of [essential] idea' is, Newman readily admits, by no means easy in particular cases. Bearing in mind the unsystematic character of the biblical documents and 'the all but silence of contemporary history' (that is, presumably, the failure of the contemporary world to bear unequivocal testimony to the singularity of the true form of Christianity), it is all too easy to lapse into 'those eclectic and arbitrary decisions' censured earlier.[57] As evidence of such arbitrariness Newman quotes a particularly stunning example from the autobiography of an Oxford contemporary, Blanco White.

The point evidently lies not so much in the allegedly reductive character of attempts to determine the 'leading idea' of Christianity, as in their arbitrariness.[58] A 'leading idea', after all, cannot logically be the sole idea; and although Newman slides from the term 'leading idea' to 'one idea' and 'whole truth' in a way which certainly misrepresents his opponents, it is the sheer arbitrary confidence of their diverse pronouncements which manifestly offends him. Nonetheless the position which he now occupies requires a principle of continuity and internal order; continuity, so as to preserve an original idea of type, and order, so as to correspond to the singularity and unity of the Godhead. He needs, in short, an 'essential idea'; but how is it to be conceived, and, particularly, how is it to be protected from the charge of being *arbitrarily* conceived?

In the third edition of 1878 Newman strives to make his meaning clearer. Lash is undoubtedly correct in his contention that there is no reversal of judgement in the 1878 acknowledgement of the convenience of positing a 'central idea' in Christianity; nor is this to be seen merely as a practical concession on Newman's part, since it but makes explicit the perspective from which in fact he had viewed the mystery of revelation for a considerable number of years.[59] The passage quoted above (p. 113) is now rewritten to allow the harmlessness of using one idea as a means of organizing the totality of Christian truth, a concession to his Protestant discussion partners which is no more than just. He adds:

In this sense I should myself call the Incarnation the central aspect of Christianity, out of which the three main aspects of its teaching take their rise, the sacramental, the hierarchical, and the ascetic. But one aspect of Revelation must not be allowed to exclude or to obscure another; and Christianity is dogmatical, devotional, practical all at once.[60]

The 'I should myself' with which this passage begins shows clearly enough the recognition of the personal, though not for that reason *arbitrary*, nature of the proposal. Both of the other 1878 passages in which the incarnation is thus spoken of as the 'central truth' or 'the central doctrine' likewise emphasize that what is in view is 'convenience of arrangements'.[61] Newman evidently does not wish to seem to be claiming too much for his proposal. However, the *use* to which he puts his proposal is more eloquent of its importance. Thus in a passage which summarizes the kinds of development to which Christianity has been subject, Newman makes clear that from the doctrine of the incarnation has sprung the political development of the episcopate, the logical development of the doctrine of Mary, the Mother of God (*Theotokos*), the historical development of the determination of the date of Christmas, the moral or ethical development of eucharistic worship, and the metaphysical development of the ideas of the Athanasian Creed.[62] These are used as illustrations of kinds of development; but the centrality of at least some of them to Newman's conception of Christianity is hardly accidental.

Further confirmation of this fact is to be found in the passage in which Newman proposes to expound the 'principles' on which the continuity of Christianity reposes. These nine principles (of the many which might be enumerated) are all drawn out from the incarnation, when regarded as the 'central truth' of the gospel; it is their source.[63] The natural question to ask is, of course, if he had, 'for convenience of arrangement', taken another doctrine, would he have been able to draw out those same principles? The answer is instructive. Although the first three principles are of an entirely general nature, numbers four to nine are quite explicitly related to the incarnation. Further, although not all of them could be drawn out from the incarnation alone, it is not difficult to think of a substitute for the incarnation (let us say, the preaching of the Kingdom) from which it would be impossible to infer some of the last six principles which Newman enunciates. Either, then, the decision to take the incarnation as central is crucially important, or the 'principles of continuity' are so indeterminate and potentially variable as to be useless for Newman's purpose.

So clearly, however, does the doctrine of the incarnation stand at the centre of the whole of Newman's thought, that we are bound to ask the question why he hesitated to announce the fact openly and with confidence. One answer seems to be given in a draft for the 1878 edition where, qualifying the idea of 'convenience of arrangement', he added: 'Not as presuming to master and analyse what comes to us from the infinite heavens above'.[64] Newman was determined never to lose sight of both poles of the patristic, especially the Greek, view of theology, that it was at once based on something divinely revealed and yet, at the same time, constituted a mystery. The confident tone of the theological rationalist revolted him, at one stage scarcely less in its Roman Catholic than in its Protestant form. A proper hesitancy in this area corresponded to the characteristically negative formulation of the argument concerning development (that here is the form of Christianity *least unlike* its original type, rather than its perfect reduplication).

A second answer, however, to the question about Newman's hesitation suggests itself. Above all he was impressed by the complexity of the nature of a developmental process. In a passage of consummate prose Newman depicts the struggle of a new idea fully to exhibit its capabilities. How and where it must expand and exert its influences is never fully clear, certainly not at its earliest stages. There is, then, a necessarily provisional quality about each attempt to depict the 'essential idea' of which any particular point in time is an incomplete realization. He is sufficiently satisfied that the incarnation provides a clue of genuine insight into this process; but further than that he is unwilling to go.

It is in the last of the documents which we are to consider that Newman writes with the utmost clarity on his conception of Christianity. The Preface to the third edition of *Lectures on the Prophetical Office of the Church*, now retitled, *The Via Media of the Anglican Church*, was written in 1877. It contains both a statement of how it comes about that Christianity has the form that it has, and a recognition of the inevitable existence of inconsistencies and apparent anomalies. There is, in other words, both order and disorder.

The order stems from the representative character of the Church, the bequest of Christ himself. As Christ was at once prophet, priest and king, so the Church 'after His pattern, and in human measure' has a threefold office, of teaching, of ministry and of rule. He writes in words we have already had cause to cite:

> Christianity, then is at once a philosophy, a political power, and a religious rite: as a religion it is holy; as a philosophy, it is Apostolic; as a political power, it is imperial, that is, One and Catholic. As a religion, its special seat is pastor and flock; as a philosophy, the Schools; as a rule, the Papacy and its Curia.[65]

The sheer fact of its multi-faceted character accounts for the complexity of the actual administration of the Church. Each of the three offices has both to further its own aims and to attend to the claims of the others. Hence the inevitability of internal conflict; hence also, so Newman urges, the wise foresight of the promise of infallibility in the Church's formal teaching, and protection from serious error in worship and political action.

The finely nuanced further discussion of the relation of these three offices need concern us only in one further particular, namely Newman's recognition of the position which must be accorded to theology. Complaint against 'Popery' for political malpractice leads Newman to affirm the primacy of the theological.

> I say, then, Theology is the fundamental and regulating principle of the whole Church system. It is commensurate with Revelation, and Revelation is the initial and essential idea of Christianity. It is the subject-matter, the formal cause, the expression of the Prophetical Office, and, as being such, has created both the Regal Office and the Sacerdotal, and it has in a certain sense a power of jurisdiction over those offices, as being its own creations.[66]

This is not to say that theology is self-sufficient or autonomous. But to ascribe to it a position as the 'regulating principle' on the grounds of its being 'commensurate with Revelation', is to raise the theologian to a position of considerable importance, over against (if need be) the proclivity of the human mind towards power (in the regal office), and self-indulgence (in the priestly). The theologian, therefore, has a duty to articulate not merely the doctrinal dimension or aspect of Christian, but also to explore the doctrinal dimension or aspect undergirding the political and the devotional dimensions or aspects of Christianity; that is, its rites and usages.[67]

This argument is the same as that deployed in the 1878 edition of the *Essay*, where, as we have already seen, the incarnation is said to be that from which the three main aspects of Christianity take their rise (see above p. 115). Nor is there any disagreement in speaking of 'revelation' as the 'initial and essential idea of Christianity'; because, as has been noted, the unity and singularity of revelation is rooted in his self-revelation. The one mystery of Christ is the standpoint from which the whole circle of Christian truth may be viewed in its essential interconnectedness.

III

Finally, we must enquire into the extent to which Schleiermacher's and Newman's respective contributions to our topic can be intelligibly compared. A thorough treatment of Schleiermacher and Newman is, indeed, long overdue; and the delay is doubtless the result of the markedly parochial character of our national and denominational divisions. What follows here can be only a partial and preliminary sketch.

An initial question of general importance is the 'platonism' with which both Schleiermacher and Newman are frequently credited. The fact that Schleiermacher translated Plato's dialogues, and that Newman studied the works of the 'Christian Platonists of Alexandria', is sufficient reason for taking the question seriously; though it is hardly surprising that, when studied in detail, the extent and manner in which they received and appropriated philosophical doctrines deriving from Plato himself turns out to be both complex and obscure. The attaching of the generalizing labels of intellectual history to men of the calibre of Newman and Schleiermacher scarcely advances any deeper appreciation of their thought. In all the diversity of interpretation, however – Newman's epistemology is roundly declared to be Aristotelian, it must be noted[68] – there is something close to scholarly agreement that, as theologians, both Schleiermacher and Newman owed a profound debt to a long-standing tradition of Christian Platonism.[69] The close relationship between Newman's thought and Coleridge's, Pusey's evident regard for Schleiermacher, Newman's background in English Evangelicalism, and the unanimity of both Schleiermacher and Newman in opposition to rationalism, together with their copious use of the term 'mystical', establish at least a presumption in the mind that we are dealing with thinkers who received help and stimulus from a similar source.

Lest, however, one be thought to exaggerate this similarity, it must at once be said that the standpoint from which they viewed the problems of theology were markedly separate. Schleiermacher, in particular, seems only remotely to have encountered the Roman Catholicism of his day, largely through the conversion of his close friend Friedrich Schlegel in 1808. Newman, for his part, despite having been an Anglican and once having had Evangelical leanings, swiftly became resolutely anti-Protestant. 'Romanism', he said, 'has the principle of true Catholicism perverted; popular Protestantism is wanting in the principle'.[70] Moreover, both Schleiermacher and Newman are thoroughgoing apologists for their respective positions, concerned with the different controversial questions of their own immediate circles. Both were fervent patriots; neither had the remotest desire to understand the immediate national situation of the other. Finally, insofar as Newman had any information about Schleiermacher whatsoever (second-hand through Pusey, and at first hand in the translation of Schleiermacher's long article on patristic trinitarianism), he was firmly of the opinion that here was a man guilty of promoting 'a serious doctrinal error . . . being the result of an attempt of the intellect to delineate, philosophise and justify that religion (so called) of the heart and feelings.'[71]

Nor is this all that must be said on the negative side. Precisely as a result of the restricted range of their sympathies, it is manifest that they both failed adequately to consider the force of certain kinds of objections to their views, and of the intrinsic limitations of the arguments in which they felt unduly secure. In Newman's case this is true of his response to the impact of biblical, especially historical criticism; Schleiermacher's weakness, for all the unusually irenic quality of his reaction to Roman

Catholicism, lies in the ambiguity with which he treated the reality of the Church. It is in relation to the Church, indeed, that their divergence is most obvious and fundamental. Where Newman from a very early date holds the existence of a visible body, united in a determinate polity, to be the necessary outcome of the revelation of God in Christ, Schleiermacher only by slow and painful steps released himself from a deeply-felt antipathy to the visible Church as he knew it. Though convinced that religion was, in its essence, a social matter, Schleiermacher was at heart a republican and congregationalist; hierarchical notions were totally inappropriate to his understanding of church order. Friedrich Schlegel, in a letter of 1817 (that is, when already a Roman Catholic) would have correctly identified Schleiermacher's view in referring to the Anglican tradition of episcopal church order as that 'terrible Anglican ecclesiastical despotism'.[72]

What, however, can be said on the positive side, especially with respect to our topic, is neither inconsiderable, nor marginal to their activity as theologians. In the first place neither Schleiermacher nor Newman adopt the position which sees the continuity and identity of Christianity as guaranteed by the possession of certain externals. Schleiermacher in particular, as befits a Protestant who had learnt much from Semler, does not believe that Christianity comes to definitive expression in any of its outward manifestations. Newman, though educated in one of the most static versions of guaranteed external continuity, that of the Anglican fundamental articles apologetic, first of all decisively qualifies that tradition and then remarkably imports his own qualification of it into another static theory of continuity, that of late eighteenth-century Roman Catholic scholasticism. Although they clearly differ on the authority of creeds and dogmas, they are united in being primarily concerned to draw attention to the inward reality of Christian believing. Commentators are no doubt right in drawing attention to the Evangelicalism of Newman's grasp of the indwelling presence of Christ in the believer;[73] but the language of indwelling is developed considerably further, as we have seen, to the point of what has been rightly called a sacramental theory of language. The whole attempt to speak of the divine mystery of revelation is conditioned by the fact that, in Newman's understanding of faith, the heart may have certain knowledge of what it can only inadequately express.

Moreover the whole of Christian believing is characterized by the unique individuality and unity of that to which Christian doctrine is trying to do justice. For Newman the 'idea' of Christianity is a unity; this opinion, as Lash pertinently observes, is at one and the same time an historical, descriptive claim, a heuristic recommendation, and a complex prescriptive argument.[74] Precisely the same words could be used to describe Schleiermacher's attempt to identify the unitary *Glaubensweise* or form of faith, characteristic of Christianity. Here too there is a descriptive element, an attempt to provide an experimental criterion for the interpretation of Christian history, and a basis for the constructive discipline of Christian theology.

If we take two aspects of the use to which both Schleiermacher and Newman put their respective concepts of 'essence' and 'idea', further similarities emerge. As we saw, in Schleiermacher's case the identification of the 'essence of Christianity' was advanced hypothetically, for testing against the actual history of Christianity. There is no trace here of that arbitrary dogmatism which Newman found so offensive. Moreover the gap separating Newman's proposal of the incarnation, and Schleiermacher's apparently Protestant preference for redemption, is narrowed somewhat when we read a note scribbled in the margin of Newman's 1845 edition of the *Essay*: 'Surely the leading idea of the Gospel is the Redemption "Xt crucified". There are other ideas subordinated to this – e.g. "Call no man yr. master."'[75] Neither proposal is reductive in character; both carry the widest range of implications.

The second aspect of the use of these proposals is their critical function. As we noted in Schleiermacher's case, the purpose of an accurate identification of the 'essence of Christianity' was to facilitate criticism of 'diseased deviations'. If, in Newman, the scope of the possibility of deviation is greatly diminished, it is by no means eliminated; and it becomes the function of theology, by virtue of faith's correspondence to its divinely given ground, to purify the political and devotional excesses to which the spread and development of religion naturally give rise. In both their schemes of thought, the theologian occupies a position of prominence and great responsibility. It is quite intelligible why, in a later clash between ecclesiastical authority and the authority of the scholar, Newman was appealed to as having articulated that view of Christianity which made the scholar's contribution so important. Newman's work is not a sufficient condition for the activities and views of the Abbé Loisy, but it cannot seriously be doubted that he is a necessary condition. Newman's sophisticated view of the plurality of aspects of Christianity and the complexity of their interrelationship, together with his argument about the primacy of theology, would give sufficient support and encouragement to a man like Loisy to bring forward his convictions about the next necessary stages of Christianity's development – irrespective of the (anachronistic) consideration of whether Newman could ever have entertained such convictions himself.

What I desire to demonstrate by this comparison between Schleiermacher and Newman is that, important and far-reaching though the differences between them are, their views on the identity of Christianity show a fundamental similarity of pattern. This pattern is comprised by four features; the explicit abandonment of the externality tradition, the necessity of a preliminary, but constructive proposal for construing Christianity as a whole, the importance of the inward dimension of Christian allegiance and its relation to theological epistemology, and the power conflicts which reflection about the identity of Christianity necessarily precipitate. Each of these is in evidence in both Schleiermacher and Newman, even if in characteristically different form and despite their obviously different conceptions of the problem-complex with which they are dealing. If one were baldly to conclude that, with respect to construing the identity of Christianity, both the main branches of Western theology are in the same boat, that would be to generalize beyond the evidence. What can be said with confidence is that it is a superstition to suppose that reflection on the 'essence of Christianity' is solely a Protestant preoccupation. Furthermore our examination of both of these two thinkers strongly confirms the view that their weighty contribution to the discussion needs to be carefully pondered by the modern theology of either tradition.

6

Harnack and Loisy

I

Harnack's book on the essence of Christianity (English title, *What is Christianity?*)[1] is the one work on our theme which is widely and popularly known. Indeed it is precisely because the phrase 'essence of Christianity' is so closely associated with Harnack, and thus with Liberal Protestantism, that there is something of a problem in suggesting that the question is of continuing importance. It is, therefore, a little paradoxical to have to admit that for our purposes Harnack's work is not of first rank significance. What, however, is both important and instructive is the controversy to which the episode gave rise, and in particular the remarkably important responses which followed it.

In what follows I have decided to present an analysis of the dispute between Harnack and the French Roman Catholic biblical scholar, the Abbé Loisy, and in the following chapter the major treatment of the methodology of the dispute provided by Ernst Troeltsch. The chapter on Troeltsch is concerned with more than Troeltsch's response to Harnack's *Das Wesen des Christentums*, and it will become plain that Troeltsch's lifelong interest in the problem of Christianity's identity fully justifies separate and extended treatment. But what is the justification for reviewing, yet again, the disagreement between Harnack and Loisy?

The answer to this question can be put with a certain simplicity. In essence both Harnack and Loisy were historians of Christian origins. The nineteenth century had witnessed a tremendous growth of basic historical research into the life and times of Jesus and the early Church, yielding a variety of possible reconstructions of the received narrative. These reconstructions were plainly in competition with the received tradition, some more sharply than others. The uncomfortable question could not be evaded as to their authority, and the authority of their proponents. The point about both Harnack and Loisy was that they *were* authorities in their own fields, by no means unchallenged, but certainly scholars of considerable stature as historians.[2] Their deliverances on the question of Christian origins, therefore, could not fail to be of remarkable public significance in any informed attempt to understand the relationship between original Christianity and the modern Church. This would be the case despite the fact that they could not be said to be anything more than amateurs in the matters already canvassed with such sophistication by Schleiermacher and Newman.

Our interest in Harnack and Loisy may be said, therefore, to be based on their significance as historians, or rather, as historians with Christian instincts and convictions. For it is precisely the relationship between their work as historians, and the constraints which this work imposed upon their faith, which made the episode so fascinating to their contemporaries, and still compels our attention. In two respects the clash of these Christian historians continues themes we have already noted in Schleiermacher and Newman. In the first place, we have discovered the status of the study of Christian origins to be controversial. Is 'original Christianity' normative for the modern Church or not? And if so, in what sense or respect? Then, secondly, particular stress has been laid on the theme of power in the Christian community, its source and distribution, especially with reference to the power of the theologian. Both of these two themes play an important role in the controversy between Harnack and Loisy, and are subsequently picked up with very great perception by Troeltsch.

One further reason, however, can be given for including the dispute in our treatment of the theme. The secondary literature on Harnack, and especially on Loisy has grown rapidly in the last twenty years.[3] But despite the fact that we now possess a remarkable quantity of documents interpreting the context and motives of the separate protagonists, there is more than a certain tendency for the literary treatment to fall into denominational and national camps, French Roman Catholics concerning themselves hardly at all with Harnack, and German Protestants (and, most recently, Roman Catholics) virtually ignoring Loisy. Quite apart from a natural tendency to handle Harnack and Loisy according to the still lively demands of denominational allegiance, there still exists an almost wilful blindness to take care over the precise delineation of their respective views, and to the precise extent to which they actually answered the questions they themselves posed.[4] In what follows, therefore, I shall attempt such an analysis, prefaced by a necessary comment on the method which (so it seems to me) is appropriate to use in elucidating their differences.

One important acknowledgement must be made in relation to the Roman Catholic context of the views of Loisy. For obvious and understandable reasons it was Protestants who were angry with Harnack, and Roman Catholics with Loisy. In general, Protestants and Roman Catholics contented themselves with the customary dismissals in their references to each other. The Roman Catholic discussion of Loisy became known as 'the modernist crisis', and brought to a head a fierce debate about tradition, authority and the limits to the concept of development, which has returned with renewed life in modern times.[5] So many studies now exist of modernism, and so extensive are the requirements of an adequate account of Loisy's challenge to contemporary Roman Catholicism, that in this place we must rest content with allowing Harnack to set the agenda for the debate. This restriction is in part justifiable inasmuch as Harnack made little attempt, apart from a review of Loisy's book, to respond to Loisy's counter-theses.[6] What follows, therefore, is a study of the provocation given by Harnack to the debate, and the extent to which Loisy's reply actually constituted an answer to Harnack's questions, neither of which themes have been adequately treated hitherto.

II

But first a word must be said about how controversies of this kind ought to be elucidated. Controversies in theology are rarely simple matters to interpret; and the more acute they are, the more grounds we have for presupposing that they operate on a number of different levels. Consider, for example, Arius versus Athanasius. Even if we agree that the subject matter of the controversy is the nature of the divine Sonship, we can identify different levels at which the controversy is conducted. It is a controversy about exegesis; it is a controversy about the nature and role of tradition, that is, of the *ekklesiastikos skopos* to which Athanasius appealed; it is also a dispute, left over from Origen and chronic in all subsequent Christian theology, about the role of philosophical argument; and who will deny that, on a philosophical level, there are acute and separable problems of metaphysics and epistemology which play a virtually unacknowledged role? We have restricted this list to the consideration of what emerges from the texts of Athanasius and Arius (such as they are). If we put these texts in their proper historical context and consider the social and political circumstances in which not merely the main protagonists, but also their precursors and disciples, did battle, the agenda grows still further.

Faced with this complexity, modern interpreters are forced to a measure of selectivity. A decision has to be taken, if the issue is going to be clarified, about which of the numerous levels of the controversy lies closest to the heart of the matter. Frequently, for example, it is said (with Harnack) that whereas Arianism lays the stress on cosmological and rational considerations, Athanasius is more concerned with redemption.[7] Such a view is, of course, an interpretation. Its intention is threefold. First, it summarizes a large mass of material in a brief and easily memorable form. Secondly, it creates a hierarchy of levels within the available texts, establishing the point at which certain considerations lie in relation to the heart of the matter. And, thirdly, it conveniently generalizes the conflict in such a way that similar problems can be picked out in other circumstances.

In themselves these observations amount to no more than a few elementary steps in the direction of a proper discussion of hermeneutics, but they are perhaps sufficient to alert us to the theoretical issue which underlies the interpretation of the controversy we are to discuss. First of all, it is axiomatic to my argument that the Harnack–Loisy controversy is conducted at a number of different levels, not all of which were immediately apparent even to the protagonists. Secondly, the way in which this controversy is interpreted reveals, as one would expect, an acute selectivity about what is said to be the central issue at stake. My argument here will be that one common interpretation is hopelessly superficial; further, that an improved view of it leads us to postulate a hierarchy of levels on which the controversy is conducted, according to which somewhat different things lie at the heart, or at the circumference, of the matter. And thirdly, I would be the first to admit that I am not offering a 'true historical interpretation' of the controversy, whatever that may be. When one consults the exhaustive, biographical studies of what both Harnack and Loisy *intended* at the time of writing, one speedily discovers their radically different personal agenda in the writing of, respectively, *Das Wesen* and *L'Evangile et l'Eglise*. Interesting though this conclusion is as a contribution to understanding the controversy, it does not in my view constitute the whole of the story, nor would it constitute the historical truth of the episode. My understanding of historiography is that history can be written in a variety of mutually illuminating ways. What follows is a theological perspective on their disagreement, informed by the preliminary studies we have undertaken.

III

On the face of it the controversy between Harnack and Loisy presents itself for interpretation on the following lines: here, on the one side, is Harnack, the great German liberal Protestant, the disciple of Albrecht Ritschl, the leading figure, if not the pope, of the Protestant professorial curia, handing down to the masses the final verdict about the future of Christianity, after its examination by scores of scientific historians working impartially on its history and literature. Here, on the other side, is Loisy, the great French Roman Catholic modernist, student of Newman, disciple of Louis Duchesne, penning a controversial writing of subtlety and refinement whose attempt 'tactfully to instruct the Catholic clergy about the real situation of the problem of Christian origins'[8] brings down upon his head the whole might of papal condemnation. To treat Harnack and Loisy as 'representative figures' of certain 'movements' in the history of late nineteenth and early twentieth-century thought, has obvious pedagogical attractions. The typically academic qualifications applied to this thesis, which raise doubts about whether either were as 'representative' as supposed, or whether these movements were as homogeneous as is sometimes depicted, are hardly more than would be expected of an academic. Harnack turns out, on close inspection, not to be in any simple sense a disciple of Ritschl;[9] Loisy's work can scarcely be regarded as 'the classical exposition of Catholic Modernism' which Tyrrell saw in it, once that so-called movement has been shown never to have attained a sufficient degree of unity or coherence.[10]

Reputations, however, have an insidious way of surviving the pedant's qualifications and footnotes. It is unquestionably true that Harnack has, not least in England, a poor reputation. This seems to have a number of grounds. Liberal Protestants as a whole share in the general scorn and disfavour heaped upon their English counterparts, the modern churchmen.[11] In the difficult years preceding and following the First World War, there were a number of modern churchmen who were at some pains to distance themselves from their German colleagues.[12] Harnack's works themselves, especially those translated into English, have been in the course of time superseded, and the *History of Dogma* in particular has acquired the worst of all possible reputations, that of an overschematized and, at the same time, over-long text book. Finally, and more pertinently to our topic, there has crept into the standard works a particularly impoverished interpretation of Harnack's lectures on the essence of Christianity. One may cite the most recent edition of the *Oxford Dictionary of the Church*:

> In the winter of 1899–1900 he delivered a celebrated course of lectures stressing the moral side of Christianity, esp. the claims of human brotherhood, to the exclusion of all that was doctrinal.[13]

If Harnack languishes in undoubted disrepute, one may surmise that this fact has something to do with his prolonged occupation of the very pinnacle of esteem in pre-World War Wilhelmian Germany. Loisy, by contrast, possesses the hero's advantage in modern eyes of having endured papal reproof and finally excommunication for his doctrinal errors without officially recanting. Moreover he had, since the early twentieth century, a number of able English defenders, both Roman Catholic and Anglican. His reply to Harnack, also, has the enviable reputation of being totally devastating;[14] and in any case, Loisy's intellectual courage is not to be doubted, as manifest in his determination in no way to avoid the problem of the recalcitrant eschatological beliefs of Jesus and the early Church.

In this respect, at least, he allied himself with a school of New Testament interpretation which subsequently grew in importance, a fact which, as we shall see, has much to do with the way the controversy has been interpreted.

There are two major points on which it is necessary to take issue with the received view. In the first place, it is necessary to emphasize the extent to which Harnack and Loisy shared, not merely respect for historical scholarship, but actually a view of the relationship between religion and theology which subordinated the latter to the former. Loisy's programme 'to renew theology from top to bottom, to substitute the religious for the dogmatic spirit, to seek the soul of theological truth and leave reason free under the control of conscience' has a closer similarity to Harnack's endeavours than he could allow himself to recognize.[15]

However, the challenge which I particularly wish to mount to the received or standard view of the controversy, concerns what is said to lie at its heart. It is often asserted that the issue is between a reductionist with a static view of the invariable, predominantly ethico-religious content of Christianity, and a developmentalist with a dynamic or organic view of the historical process. Harnack, it is said, reduces Christianity to a fixed essence or kernel, and the point about a kernel is that it comprises an entity of an exactly quantifiable kind lying inside a husk which can be discarded. Loisy, on the other hand, replies to Harnack that in the living organism of the Church, kernel and husk are not so clearly separable that you can have one without the other. The conclusion of this view of the controversy is implied in the analysis, namely that Loisy is greatly to be preferred, because he is both a better historian, in not falling into the temptation of manipulating the past in the supposed interests of the present, and a better theologian, because an organic theory is always preferable to a static one.[16]

The problem with this view of the controversy is that it can only be made credible by a falsification of what Harnack actually says. The falsification itself springs in part from regarding Loisy's presentation of Harnack's position as accurate; but it also springs from an over-simple perspective on the nature of the questions which Harnack and Loisy were respectively attempting to answer. Greater clarity in this area will help us to see the considerable extent to which Harnack and Loisy were in agreement, as an acute English observer of both sides of the controversy, Alfred Fawkes, had already observed in 1904.[17]

To what precise question, then, is Harnack addressing himself in his lectures on the essence of Christianity? Harnack came to deliver his lectures on *The Essence of Christianity* as a well-established theologian, bruised by conflict first with his own, conservatively-minded father, and secondly, on a number of occasions, with conservative church authorities.[18] It is right and proper to regard the lectures as a personal confession of faith, but not to separate them from the rest of Harnack's intellectual endeavour. Accordingly, the background to the answer lies, as one would expect, in the massive labour of intellectual history in which he sought to separate Christian gospel from ecclesiastical dogma, the *Lehrbuch der Dogmengeschichte*. Harnack summarized his own view of the matter in 1889 in the following way:

> Religion is a practical affair with mankind, since it has to do with our highest happiness and with those *faculties* which pertain to a holy life. But in every religion these faculties are closely connected with some definite *faith* or with some definite *cult*, which are referred back to Divine *Revelation*. Christianity is that religion in which the impulse and power to a blessed and holy life are bound up with faith in God as the Father of Jesus Christ. So far as this God is believed to be the omnipotent Lord of heaven and earth, the Christian religion includes a particular *knowledge* of God, of the world and of the purposes of created things; so far, however, as this religion teaches that God can be truly known only in Jesus Christ, it is inseparable from historical knowledge.[19]

Christianity thus entails knowledge both of God and the world, and also of Christ. In its natural inclination to formulate such knowledge into articles of belief it is forced into relationship with the worlds of both science and of history. Since knowledge in these spheres is fluctuating and variable, and since Christianity desires a permanent statement of its beliefs, an inherently insoluble tension is created at the heart of theology. The rise of dogmatic Christianity is, however, the most thorough-going attempt at a solution of this difficulty, in which faithful acceptance of a system of doctrine is required of every mature member of the Church. This synthesis is, however, exploded by modern historical research. The claim that dogma is simply the exposition of Christian revelation deduced from Scripture is shown not to be tenable. The same research illuminates, more-over, the processes by which theological activity leads towards the formulation of dogma, which in its turn requires the oblitera-tion of the prior history of the theological development. It is the study of the history of dogma, therefore, which helps free Christianity from dogma. At the same time, however, this study

> testifies to the *unity* and continuity of the Christian faith in the progress of its history, in so far as it proves that certain fundamental ideas of the Gospel have never been lost and have defied all attacks.[20]

Conspicuously, therefore, there are two further tasks apart from a writing of the history of dogma itself: one is to establish a valid method for discerning 'the fundamental ideas of the Gospel', and the second is the tracing in broad outline of their handling in the course of history. These, in effect, are the tasks tackled in *Das Wesen des Christentums*. Dogma is a temporary phenomenon characteristic of a past period of the Church's history; the future lies with something different, but something which has been characteristic of the Christian faith in all its periods. The question is, What is it? In his answer Harnack makes certain assumptions which he never questions: First, he asserts that religion is a 'practical affair with mankind'; secondly, that it is something simple, and by being simple essentially profound (over this he was to quarrel bitterly with Barth); and, thirdly, that Christ is the centre of faith, and that if religion and theology is to be freed from dogma, such liberation must come about through a renewed exposure to him. For this last task, of course, the sober and painstaking work of the biblical historian is a precondition. Axiomatic, too, is the assumption that the religious impulse in Christianity always leads to the creation of theology, the articulation of the intel-lectual implications of the faith, and that theology is never at a standstill, because both scientific and historical knowledge constantly advances.

Loisy, likewise, has a particular problem to solve. It was, in words already quoted, 'to substitute the religious for the dogmatic spirit', an early programmatic utterance of 1892. Of *L'Evangile et l'Eglise* he subsequently wrote:

I thought it opportune to sketch a history of Christian development from the Gospel onwards, to show that the essence of the Gospel, in so far as an essence existed, had been truly perpetuated in Catholic Christianity.[21]

En tant qu'essence il y avait. Loisy's scepticism about Harnack's language and method cannot, however, disguise the fact that the aim of his work is to demonstrate the continuous perpetuation of the gospel. In some studies of Newman's *Essay on Development*, published in the *Revue du clergé français* between December 1898 and October 1900, Loisy makes clear his three-stage view of the development towards dogma.[22] First comes the moment of the real, the life of the Church in its entirety; secondly, the theological moment, when intellectual articulation is given to that life; and thirdly, the dogmatic, a stage which is never closed, because dogmas are always in need of restatement, completion and explanation.

How does this view differ from Harnack's? It is manifestly wrong to say that whereas Harnack believes that the intellectual developments of the Church are corruptions of its historic mission, Loisy affirms that the emergence of the Church enables the message to survive. Harnack clearly maintains that the Church in history was necessary. It is true that he believes that the survival of the gospel in the era of dogma entailed a corruption and distortion in its presentation of the faith, which must now be corrected. But this belief he shares with Loisy, who quite as certainly believes that the modern Catholic church embodies a dogmatic corruption which requires correction. The problem for both writers is, manifestly: In accordance with what criteria must these corruptions be criticized?[23] This is the point which we must press in the enquiry which follows. Part of the difficulty between Harnack and Loisy is, I shall argue, that whereas Harnack's assertion of criteria is relatively unambiguous (though more subtle than generally recognized) Loisy's response is acutely vague and rhetorical. Comparatively invulnerable unclarity is often at an advantage over vulnerable clarity in theological questions. But whether Loisy's stance incorporates, nonetheless, important advantages can only be elucidated if we take the trouble to be entirely fair to the detail of Harnack's proposed solution.

IV

The first substantial question to be examined is, What, according to the two writers, *is* the identity of Christianity? In Harnack's case this question is best answered, not from the pages of *Das Wesen*, but from the two paragraph summary of 'The Gospel of Jesus Christ according to His Own Testimony' in the *Outlines of the History of Dogma*. There are, according to Harnack, three major themes: namely, the Kingdom and the secure citizenship of the same bestowed on all who give themselves to God; the law of whole-hearted love to God and one's neighbour, exemplifying a better justice for mankind corresponding to God's perfection; and the necessity of a change of heart, guaranteeing the forgiveness of sins.[24]

By selective quotation of certain statements, for example that 'the Gospel is the good news of the reign of the Almighty and Holy God, the Father and Judge of the world and of each individual soul',[25] it can be made to seem as though Harnack's summary of the gospel is devoid of relationship to Jesus. However, what Harnack actually says is quite different. He continues:

> In the three-fold form, however, in which the Gospel is set forth, (God's sovereignty, higher justice [law of love] and forgiveness of sin) it is inseparably connected with Jesus Christ. For in the proclamation of the Gospel, Jesus Christ everywhere called men unto himself. In him is the Gospel *word* and *deed*; it is his meat and drink, and, therefore, it is become his personal life, and into *this life* he would draw all men ... This close connection of his *Gospel* with his *person*, Jesus by no means made prominent in *words*, but left his disciples to experience it. He called himself the Son of Man and led them on to the confession that he was their Master and Messiah.[26]

Furthermore in his interpretation of his death as an imperishable service for the forgiveness of sin, he claimed a unique significance for himself as Redeemer and Judge, and then proved his power by awakening in his disciples the conviction that he still lives and is Lord of the dead and the living.

> The religion of the Gospel rests upon this faith in Jesus Christ, i.e. looking upon him, that historical Person, the believer is convinced

that God rules heaven and earth, and that God, the Judge, is also Father and Redeemer.[27]

In *Das Wesen* the presentation of Jesus' own gospel is slightly reorganized. 'The Kingdom of God and its coming' remains the first feature; it, says Harnack, is the comprehensive category with which all else is connected.[28] The second becomes 'God the Father and the infinite value of the human soul'. This has been developed out of a theme in his earlier first feature. The closer attention given to the problem of eschatology in *Das Wesen* evidently led Harnack to separate out the theme of inwardness, the 'inner relation of the soul with God',[29] and to associate with it an important apologetic statement, namely that Christianity is 'religion itself'.[30] The third theme, 'the higher righteousness and the commandment of love', is similarly a potentially all-embracing summary of the gospel.[31] Forgiveness and the change of heart have, as themes, been assimilated into the first of Harnack's *Das Wesen* themes, the Kingdom. Here, if anything, there emerges a greater emphasis on the divine initiative; the Kingdom is supernatural, a purely religious blessing, and the most important thing a person can have. 'It permeates and dominates his whole existence, because sin is forgiven and misery banished.'[32]

The reorganization of aspects of Jesus' teaching is of significance, therefore, only insofar as it enables Harnack to make an apologetic claim about Christianity's relation to other religions. Critics, however, who know all too little of Harnack's other works have been considerably thrown off course by the fact that in *Das Wesen* Harnack entirely separates the christological material, which we have examined in the *Outline of the History of Dogma*, from the summary of Jesus' own teaching. The reason for this is that Harnack wants to discuss in a group six problems arising from the content of Jesus' message, of which the christological problem is the fifth.[33] The first four have to do with the social implications of Jesus' teaching, asceticism, the 'poor', public order, and culture.[34] The fifth, however, resumes the theme which in Harnack's earlier works had never been separate from the outline of Jesus' preaching, namely, 'What position did Jesus himself take up towards the Gospel while he was proclaiming it, and how did he wish himself to be accepted?'[35] A discussion follows of two titles which, Harnack argues, Jesus uses of himself, 'the Son of God' and 'Messiah' (or 'Son of Man').

Does this mean, then, that Jesus himself occupies a position in his own gospel? To this question, Harnack replies, there are two answers, one negative, one positive. The negative answer is that Christology is not a part of Jesus' own message, a view summed up in the subsequently notorious sentence, that '*the gospel, as Jesus proclaimed it, has to do with the Father only and not the Son*' (Harnack's emphasis).[36] The positive answer is that the basic reason for the gospel is the uniquely redemptive act of Christ; 'it is not as a mere factor that he is connected with the Gospel; *he was its personal realisation and its strength, and this he is felt to be still.*'[37] This is merely to state again what Harnack had made clear in his earlier publications. What Harnack wishes to deny is clear enough; 'it is a perverse proceeding to make Christology the fundamental substance of the Gospel'.[38] By Christology here he means a theory about the constitution of Christ's person and what kind of nature he had. These are precisely what Bonhoeffer, a pupil of Harnack, was later to call the 'How' questions, the questions of immanence.[39] The question of transcendence, the 'Who' question (again Bonhoeffer), lies in the mystery of the relationship of Father and Son, on which Harnack so emphatically insists.

The identity of Christianity is to be found, then, in the combination of Jesus' teaching and his person, and the person of Jesus is to be apprehended as an experienced relationship not as another piece of teaching. This identity is to be observed at every stage of the history of Christianity, like a 'red thread in the centre of the web'.[40] Here we come to another factor which has played a large role in the interpretation of Harnack, the metaphors used by him to distinguish the abiding from the merely ephemeral. It is commonly said, as has already been noted, that Harnack likens the contrast between the gospel and the mass of other elements to a kernel and the husk. This metaphor is used throughout *das Wesen*. At its first introduction the problem with it is explicitly noted:

We must not be like the child who wanted to get at the kernel of a bulb, went on picking off the leaves until there was nothing left, and in the end could not help seeing that it was just the leaves that made the bulb (*dass eben die Blätter der Kern selbst waren*).[41]

Nonetheless the metaphor is used repeatedly, and a reader may be forgiven for thinking both that it is the most appropriate image for what Harnack wants to say, and that it entails the essential worthlessness of the husk. Both of these propositions are, however, false. In the first place, Harnack can also be found to use the metaphor of bark and sap, which on closer thought is a more appropriate image for what he wants to say. And, secondly, it can without difficulty be shown that what is spoken of as the husk is not undervalued in Harnack's understanding of that which does not belong to the inner and essential features of the gospel.

To take the second point first, the intention of Harnack is clear from the following passage discussing developments in the Christian religion in the third century.

> This religion had, no doubt, already developed a husk and a covering; to penetrate through to it and grasp the kernel had become more difficult; it had also lost much of its original life. But the gifts and the tasks which the Gospel offered still remained in force, and the fabric which the Church had erected around them also served many a man as the means by which he attained to the thing itself.[42]

To view the husk as a means of attaining the thing itself rather than as an obstruction is at least a step in a positive direction.

Similarly positive are the implications of the metaphor of bark and sap. This comes into play early in the work where Harnack is insisting, vainly so far as some of his critics are concerned, that the examination of the original teaching of Jesus is not sufficient to establish the proper answer to the question, What is the Christian religion? The point about Christianity is its life. Christ and his apostles believed that 'the religion which they were planting would in the ages to come have a greater destiny and a deeper meaning than it possessed at the time of its institution'. Then follows this significant passage:

> Just as we cannot obtain a complete knowledge of a tree without regarding not only its root and its stem but also its bark, its branches, and the way in which it blooms, so we cannot form any right estimate of the Christian religion unless we take our stand upon

a comprehensive induction that shall cover all the facts of its history.[43]

The metaphor of kernel and husk is used, I believe, simply to illustrate the necessity of making a distinction between the types of material which face us when we contemplate the history of Christianity. Christianity itself is not actually like the relatively inert, apparently fully grown object which we perceive on cracking a nut. Christianity is a living thing, planted by Christ, but developing. In the course of its life it creates, of necessity, bark to protect it. But bark is not the life itself; the life is in the sap.

Evidence for this view of the matter is to be found in a passage in which Harnack is evaluating the apostolic belief of an early return of Christ. What constantly happens in religion, says Harnack, is that a fundamental religious experience constantly associates itself with another factor which enhances it.

> What we are thus taught is that the most inward of all possessions, namely, religion, does not struggle up into life free and isolated, but grows, so to speak, clothed in bark and cannot grow without it.[44]

The same view is to be found in the *Mission and Expansion of the Christian Church*, where Harnack is to be found roundly asserting that

> Like every living plant, religion only grows inside a bark. Distilled religion is not religion at all.[45]

On the evidence of Harnack's own statements, therefore, Loisy's charge that he views Christianity 'as a fruit, ripe, or rather overripe, that must be peeled, to reach the incorruptible kernel' is a gross misrepresentation.[46]

If we turn now to Loisy and seek to elucidate his view of the identity of Christianity, we encounter a certain difficulty. His criticisms of what he takes Harnack's position to be are clear enough. Harnack, he maintains, seems to fear that the essence of Christianity will be spoilt if it contains within itself life, movement or development. Further he sees in Harnack one who finds the essence of Christianity in a sentiment, that is, in filial confidence in God, the merciful Father. There are, he states, two objections to this; one, that it is highly unlikely that the apostles and Herr Harnack thought alike even on this subject; and secondly, that sentiment is not independent of thought, and that if ideas change (as they do) then sentiments must change likewise.

Valueless though these views are as representations of Harnack's position, they give a clear indication of the tendency of Loisy's own, otherwise rather cloudy, concept of the identity of Christianity. Against Harnack's allegedly reductive procedure he asks:

> Why not find the essence of Christianity in the fulness and totality of its life, which shows movement and variety just because it is life, but inasmuch as it is life proceeding from an obviously powerful principle, has grown in accordance with a law which affirms at every step the initial force that may be called its physical essence revealed in all its manifestations?[47]

All that is put in the interrogative, but it is so highly developed a question that it doubtless contains the substance of Loisy's positive proposal about the identity of Christianity. Christianity is a totality constantly generating new life according to a principle of lawful growth and reflecting a powerful initial impulse.

The same point, differently expressed, is made in the passage which immediately follows. Referring to the parable of the mustard seed, he depicts early Christianity as the grain, containing *en germe*, implicitly, the tree which we now see.

> Charity was its sap; its life impulse was in the hope of its triumph; its expanding force was in its apostleship, its pledge of success in sacrifice; for its general form this budding religion had its faith in the unity and absolute sovereignty of God, and for its particular and distinctive feature that faith in the divine mission of Jesus, which earned it its name of Christianity. All this was in the little seed, and all this was the real essence of the Christian religion, needing only space to grow to reach its present point, still living after all its growth.[48]

The rhapsodic character of this passage and its plethora of images (sap, life-impulse, expanding force) tend to emphasize the lack of exactitude in Loisy's thought at this point. What he is clearly trying to say, however, is that primitive Christianity is composed of a number of elements, all of which have a part to play in its historical growth. When we examine the elements, charity, hope, the apostolate, sacrifice, sovereignty of God, the divine mission of Jesus, they hardly differ from Harnack's own. Only the apostolate and sacrifice are not clearly dealt with in Harnack's summary of Jesus' teaching, and these are quite clearly brought in later in the sections on the apostolic reception of the teaching and person of Christ.

What is plainly different from Harnack, however, is the attempt to outline a theory of how Christianity as a totality preserves its identity whilst constantly changing.

> The particular and changing forms of this development, in so far as they are changing, do not themselves constitute the essence of Christianity, but they follow one another, as it were, in a framework whose general proportions, though variable, are always balanced; so that if the figure changes, its type never varies, nor the law which governs its evolution. It is the general traits of this figure, the elements of its life and their characteristic properties which constitute the essence of Christianity, and this essence is immutable like the being of a living being which is the same to the extent and in so far as it is living.[49]

The language of preservation of type and of internal balance is clearly borrowed from Newman;[50] and it represents a substantially more sophisticated imagery than Harnack's talk of a red thread. The difficulty with it is that, without any attempt at illustration or exemplification, it remains a pure assertion. It may, indeed, be the case that by the operation of providence in all its changes Christianity has remained the same; this miraculous preservation may be pictured to our minds by the image of a framework or outline which even as it grows or develops retains a similar internal arrangement of elements. But in the absence of any attempt at historical demonstration that this is what has in fact happened, the idea floats in a vacuum. The difference between Harnack and Loisy on this point is once again that whereas Harnack lays himself wide open to criticism by dealing with the history of Christianity in the broadest of strokes, Loisy fails to offer any historical demonstration of his favoured imagery; it is, again, a case of vulnerable clarity and relatively invulnerable unclarity.

Even so, it is possible to point out the basic similarity between

Harnack and Loisy. Both use the imagery of organic growth;[51] both affirm that the origins of Christianity contain its basic impulse; both are prepared to admit that development is not uniform, and can be more or less in accord with basic principle; and both deny that there is any complete or perfect realization of Christianity, not even in its beginning. Yet one can understand the somewhat weary tones in which Harnack reviewed *L'Evangile et l'Eglise* in the *Theologische Literaturzeitung*, agreeing with much of it and failing to recognize his own opinions in the views opposed.[52]

V

The impression I have sought to give of a greater degree of unanimity between Harnack and Loisy on the essence of Christianity is further confirmed by the examination of their handling of the theme of power. Indeed if we ask of them both not merely what is their conception of the essence of the gospel, but what is their view of the power of the gospel, the answer is most enlightening. The problem of power, divine power and human power, and their interrelation in history, is a major theme of late nineteenth-century theology and its importance deserves much more explicit recognition. Once one perceives this, the appropriate terms of the comparative analysis of Harnack's *Das Wesen* and of the positive content of Loisy's *L'Evangile et l'Eglise* become increasingly clear.

For Harnack the power of the gospel has first of all to be utterly separated from all notions of coercive force. His highly critical sections on Roman Catholicism reveal opposition to two forms of power. In the first place he is implacably opposed to any view that 'it is just as essential to this church (i.e. the Roman Church) to exercise governmental power as to proclaim the gospel'.[53] This constitutes, for Harnack, a total perversion of the gospel. Secondly, he regrets that, in its struggle with Gnosticism, the Church was forced 'to put its teaching, its worship and its discipline into fixed forms and ordinances, and to exclude everyone who would not yield them obedience'.[54] *La mediocrité fonde l'autorité*; it is the semi-religious who prefer an ordinance to a gospel.[55]

Let it be noted, in passing, that this does not constitute Sohm's position that the Church and the realm of law are essentially antithetical, an idea against which Harnack had already written.[56] Harnack's view is, rather, that laws tend to become regarded as the substance of religion, which is a false, if natural, view of their importance.

Against these perversions of the understanding of the power of the gospel Harnack sets his own thesis; Christianity contains the power of total inner convinction and transformation. The Kingdom of God, he writes, 'is the rule of the holy God in the hearts of individuals; *it is God himself in his power (Kraft)*'.[57] Thus the Kingdom 'is in its very nature a spiritual force (*Grösse*), a power (*Macht*) which sinks into a man within, and can be understood only from within.'[58] Its power is the power of simplicity speaking to us with such elemental force that it cannot readily be mistaken.[59] It consists of 'eternal life in the midst of time, by the strength (*Kraft*) and under the eyes of God'.[60]

This power expresses itself in personality. Here Harnack harnesses the 'character of Christ' apologetic, common at the end of the nineteenth century. To say that Christ taught with authority means, for Harnack, that the power of his personality stands behind his words. The root of Harnack's understanding of Christ, namely the unique character of his knowledge of God as a Son, is a consciousness of power, a mystery of personality into which 'no research can carry us further'.[61] The secret of the success of the gospel lies in the fact that Jesus addresses the whole of humanity at the depth of its being; a statement from which stems the often-repeated insistence on the timelessly constant nature of man. The 'timeless' quality of the essential elements of the gospel are addressed to the 'timeless' inner constitution of man (Harnack has the grace to place the adjective '*zeitlos*' in inverted commas), and 'since that is so, this Gospel remains in force ... for us too'.[62]

Similar features show themselves in Loisy's handling of this theme. For him, too, political power is not essential to the Church, which has a quite different end in view. 'Seen from within, the ecclesiastical organisation is essentially of a religious order, and has no other reason for its existence than the preservation and propagation of religion in the world.'[63] Catholicism, despite its apparent desire to augment the authority of the Pope, has in reality no other fundamental principle than that of the gospel. Ecclesiastical authority is not in its true nature domineering, but educative. 'In principle, Catholicism aims, as much as Protestantism, at the formation of religious personalities, souls masters of themselves, pure and free consciences.'[64]

Even in the very section where Loisy is at pains specifically to deny Harnack's assertion that the Kingdom is the power of God acting in the heart of the individual, his positive assertion differs little in substance from Harnack's. The Kingdom is faith in God, the love of God and hope in the Kingdom; this, moreover is a purer, deeper and more living way of understanding and realizing God than ways found in the Old Testament. Once one clears away the polemics and ignores the fitful light shed by the exploding exegetical fireworks one perceives that both men had a broadly similar purpose.

VI

The proper question to ask now is how it has come about that so many intelligent people have failed to perceive this 'broadly similar purpose'. Some explanations I have already offered. It is undoubtedly true that one or two careless critics have relied upon Loisy, or even worse upon Tyrrell, for their view of Harnack. Others are quite clearly guilty of selective quotation, demonstrating their failure to read to the end of Harnack's *Das Wesen*, or to relate it to his other works.

Defensiveness about Loisy has also played a major role, especially among Anglicans who have seen in his tortured wrestling with Catholic sacramental practice and acute exegetical problems a mirror of their own pilgrimage in post-*Lux Mundi* liberal Catholicism. For such persons there is an obvious attraction in stressing the gap between Protestant and Catholic, especially if it is the Protestant who can plausibly be accused of modernizing the Scriptures.

Here, of course, we touch upon an interpretative crux of the issue between Harnack and Loisy. There is absolutely no doubt of the propriety and effectiveness of two points which Loisy makes against Harnack. The first is the denial of Harnack's claim to handle Christianity 'purely historically'. It is undeniable that Harnack has a thesis to argue, and it is only with Troeltsch, who on this topic takes Harnack's part, that we find someone successfully unpacking what Harnack means by history. The study of history is not pure antiquarianism; it includes the duty of perceiving the essential and the lasting in the historical phenomena being studied, as Harnack strongly insisted in his introduction to the first edition of *Das Wesen* in 1900, and again in the editions of 1903 and 1925. The historian is, in fact, a judge deciding on the future.[65] Harnack's problem, the relation of the personally appropriated stance of the historian towards the material which is objectively there to be studied, is also Troeltsch's problem. Neither solved it, and Loisy was well within his rights in pointing out the suspicious similarity between Harnack's own convictions as a Protestant and the supposed solution to certain exegetical problems. The very same problem of stance is nicely considered by the Anglican, T. A. Lacey, in his 1904 pamphlet, *Harnack and Loisy*:

> In his conscientious endeavour to abstract everything that savours of the French ecclesiastic, he (Loisy) approximates perhaps rather too closely to the French layman of the pious unlettered sort; even as Harnack by means of a corresponding abstraction arrives at something very like a pietist of Halle. This sets me wondering whether any modern European mind can be trusted to depict these lineaments. One could wish for the work of a Jew, not too modern, not too Western.[66]

Harnack's problem does not lie in the *general* likelihood that an exegete's solutions to certain central questions of belief will betray the signs of his own deepest convictions; that can hardly be otherwise. It is the *particular* demonstration of instances of weak arguments being accorded too much force that is so damaging to Harnack.

Here is the second fact of substance which has played such a large role in the interpretation of this controversy. It cannot seriously be doubted that Harnack's exegesis was at fault in many particulars. Subsequent research has tended to support Loisy's conviction of the radically eschatological frame of reference of both Jesus' and the early disciples' preaching. Inasmuch as Harnack truly bases his view of the inwardness of the appeal of the gospel on the exegesis of Luke 17.20–1, he is, as Loisy maintains, guilty of an infringement of an elementary rule of historical judgement. But at the same time the inwardness tradition does not depend on the exegesis of this one text.

A more far-reaching set of considerations arises when we question whether, in fact, the dispute is really about exegesis? Has not Loisy, the exegete, transferred the argument to his own sphere of competence, where he feels confident that he can master his opponent? Is not for Loisy the major question *la question biblique*, namely, the extent to which an authority which had just pronounced on the Johannine Comma (an interpolation into the Latin text of 1 John 5.7) might be expected to face exegetical reality?[67] The real subject of Harnack's work is not, however, the exegesis of the New Testament. It is here that the language of levels becomes valuable, as a means for separating out the complex way in which a controversy is conducted. The subject in which Harnack was interested was *Das Wesen des Christentums*, by which he understood the source of the persisting identity of Christianity. The assumption of his discussion was that there was a problem about the plurality and variety of the changes which Christianity had undergone in its history, and the difficulty of discernment of its true identity as a practical matter for the leadership of the modern Church. This was how the subject had been discussed by Protestants since Semler and Schleiermacher; modern exegesis simply exacerbated the problem.

Loisy, as Newman before him, realized that there was a problem here which the older-fashioned Roman Catholic apologetic had ignored, but which modern historical study made unavoidable. It was Newman who had given him a more sophisticated understanding of the various 'aspects' of Christianity in all of which, and in the balance and harmony of which, continuity in Christianity is preserved. But for Loisy it seemed as though the refutation of Newman's hypothesis lay all too visibly in the actions and pronouncements of legitimate church authority. Only by changing the present situation could what Newman had urged *become* true. Thus the exegetical argument was integral to what Loisy wanted to achieve. For the Catholic Church actually to be what Loisy said it was, it was necessary for church authorities to recognize the rights of a biblical scholar to use the tools and methods of a trained historian. The verification (or falsification) of Loisy's thesis turned on official reaction to critical scholarship.[68] Arguing exegetically against

Harnack, in other words, was necessary in order to achieve a non-exegetical point. But that non-exegetical point was not simply the establishment of academic freedom; it carried the force of an argument about the changing nature of the Church's contemporary exemplification of the unchanging gospel; hence the separateness and interconnection of the levels of the controversy.

What have we gleaned from the controversy? In answer to this question I turn back to my reference to the question of power in their respective presentations. So important is the issue of power in every strand of the New Testament that anyone who deploys arguments about the identity of Christianity based on a study of Christian origins is bound to come to a view of it. To put it more sharply, in the very act of commenting upon, or attempting to discern the shape of Christianity for the present and the future the theologian deploys his or her own power in one way or another.

We see Harnack doing this in one way, Loisy in another. For Harnack, as a Protestant, power lies in what he speaks of as 'the gospel'. But the 'gospel' has become in the course of history 'dogmatized', its power being thereby diminished by transformation into external forms such as dogmas, rites and institutions girded about by law, and thus incapable of achieving a radical change of heart and mind. He offers, by means of an historical enquiry, to pinpoint its *original force*. That force is first evident in the *impact* made by Jesus on his original followers, by word and deed. In every way it suited Harnack to emphasize Jesus' personality or character. For a post-Kantian era which had given up proving Jesus' divinity by prophecy or miracle, the personality of Christ was still a potent argument, personality being, for a certain type of idealism, the highest category of created reality. In presenting the power of Christianity, therefore, as the agent *par excellence* in the formation or moulding of personality Harnack was performing a double apologetic service. But at the same time, by insisting on the professional obligation of the historian to act as judge deciding on the future, he plainly occupies a position of truly remarkable importance, as our discussion of both Troeltsch and Barth will illustrate.

Harnack did not, however, in any way escape from the dilemma of all who strenuously seek to articulate the inward reality or experience of a transformed personal existence, which, as soon as it is expressed in words, has a strong tendency itself to be interpreted as doctrine. The reality of the communion of the soul with God becomes the doctrine of the affinity of the soul and God. What happens in effect is that the power of the gospel is identified with the continuous reiteration of certain sentences formulated by professional theologians, but supposedly representing fundamental experiences. For all his strenuous efforts to point to the power of Jesus, unfriendly critics have little difficulty in representing the results as 'Harnack's gospel'.

Loisy's solution is less exposed to the same difficulty. I have sufficiently laboured his unclarity; it is time to emphasize the real advantages of his position. His is a multidimensional model of Christianity. It is the ever-changing whole, not a never-changing part, which guarantees its continuous identity. Although for him, too, personality, conscience, the soul are primary categories of interpretation of the human situation, so, too, are community, myth and ritual. His only tasks, it seems, are to combat the well-developed late nineteenth-century distaste for the recent political history of the papacy and to promote the cause of modern biblical scholarship. Newman himself had assigned to the theologians the right to check the religious and political excesses of popular religion. Loisy exercised that power, and was cut down for doing so.

As our review of the dispute between Harnack and Loisy will have made clear, there is nothing in either of these two authors' treatment of the essence of Christianity which matches the sophistication of Schleiermacher or the nuanced discussions in Newman. In most important respects the combatants fail to observe, or else were elusive about, vital questions on which the earlier masters had already written. Nonetheless, it is evident that the agenda for Christian theology had changed with the advent of radical biblical criticism. Both Harnack and Loisy struggle with the question of 'original Christianity' in a way which makes them instructive to ourselves. On the one hand, historical scholarship is an autonomous discipline with its own conventions: on the other, Christian identity is a problem which cannot be loosed from the historical study of Christian origins. These two propositions constitute the new parameters for the distinctively modern treatment of our theme. Considerable freedom, however, still exists even within those constraints; indeed the proposition concerning the conventions of historiography turns out to contain a rather bewildering series of philosophical possibilities, if grasped at full epistemological depth. It was the achievement above all of Ernst Troeltsch to illustrate precisely the relationship between historiography and epistemology, and to make that relationship central to the further theological treatment of the essence of Christianity.

7

Troeltsch and the Relevance of Epistemology

I

Loisy's *L'Evangile et l'Eglise* was only one small fragment of a vast outpouring of comment upon, and abuse or appreciation of, Harnack's lectures. The volumes of the *Theologischer Jahresbericht* from 1901 until 1906 refer to over one hundred and fifty reviews and books from the pens of European and American theologians. Virtually all of this writing is now forgotten, with one exception. That is, Ernst Troeltsch's essay, 'What does "Essence of Christianity" Mean?', first published in instalments in 1903 and reprinted in Volume II of Troeltsch's collected works in 1913.[1]

Troeltsch provides us with the most sophisticated commentary not merely on Harnack, but also on Loisy's reply. Baron von Hügel, a great dispatcher of books to other people, had sent Troeltsch a copy of Loisy's book, and in their correspondence of 10 March 1903, Troeltsch makes clear that he is impressed with the extent of the points of contact between himself and Loisy.[2] In particular he mentions their common interest in ethics, in the standpoint of the history of religions, and in their grasp of Christianity as the summation of the religion of late antiquity, grasped from a new and deeper centre. These similarities are not, he recognizes, restricted to himself and Loisy; he notes that someone had already adverted to the closeness of his basic standpoint to that of Newman. It is important for us not to lose sight of the fact that, despite what we shall observe to be Troeltsch's acute selfconsciousness as a Protestant thinker, there were Roman Catholics who perceived in him a more promising conversation–partner than they had found in Harnack.

Troeltsch's main importance for our discussion of the essence of Christianity lies in his preoccupation with the epistemological problem of modern historiography. If the essence of Christianity was to be approached from the standpoint of history, as Harnack had insisted, then how is the quest for Christianity's essence to be related to the basic philosophical presuppositions of historical knowledge? Are such presuppositions compatible with Christian commitment? Can one work *both* as a historian *and* as a believer? As Van Harvey has observed, 'Troeltsch's problems still haunt us';[3] and this dictum is true not least because of the explicitly epistemological twist which Troeltsch gives to our theme and which it is impossible, subsequently, to ignore. Thus it is in relation to Troeltsch's epistemology that Barth develops his own, allegedly annihilating response. In Troeltsch and Barth we encounter, in other words, rival epistemological strategies, whose implications allow no place to the other's position.

The point can be made more sharply by observing the importance of epistemology for what we have called the inwardness tradition. As we have seen, Harnack was fully persuaded that the truth and the force of Christianity was perceived by the inner eye of faith. 'No one', he had said, 'who possesses a fresh eye for what is alive, and true feeling for what is really great, can fail to see it and distinguish it from its contemporary integument.'[4] Troeltsch was to endeavour a deeper analysis of this 'fresh eye' and 'true feeling', precisely as historian *and* believer. The slight air of pious enthusiasm in Harnack's lectures was to be dispelled by philosophical enquiry into the precise conditions of this perception. This is the epistemological quest on which Troeltsch embarks, and which leads to huge complication in his attempt to understand the method of determining Christianity's essence.

Troeltsch at no stage of his life wrote anything remotely as clear and popular as Harnack's treatise. He was a complexifier, but a complexifier with a conscience. He knew perfectly well that Christianity did not originate as a philosophical movement appealing primarily to the intelligentsia, but as something simple, clear and imaginative, capable of appealing to the unlettered. No matter how Christianity might subsequently develop, to be Christianity it must retain its naivité. What he set out to achieve, therefore, even while he insisted on the impossibility of the naive supernaturalism of the biblical world view, was 'a scientifically informed restoration of the naive outlook now raised to a higher level'.[5] As we shall see, such an achievement eluded him. But, nonetheless, the attempt was valuable in that it raised questions which under no circumstances can a modern treatment of the questions ignore or circumvent. Complex though his thought is, a complexity compounded by the development of certain inherent tensions in his approach to the topic, there is much to be gained from arguing through each stage of his fascinating engagement with our problem.

The material of this chapter will be grouped in three sections. In the first (section II), Troeltsch's attitude towards the question of the essence of Christianity prior to his discussion of Harnack will be briefly examined. In the second major section (section III) the writing on Harnack, in its two forms of 1903 and 1913, will be analysed and discussed. Thirdly (section IV) the significance of the encounter with Max Weber will be evaluated, and his mature position on the 'power of the Gospel' described and discussed. Troeltsch leaves us at the point where it must be realized that only a treatment which reflects seriously on the position occupied by the theologian in the Church can possibly be adequate to the subject; and this, above all else, is where the discussion of Karl Barth must begin.

II

As we have already remarked, Troeltsch's principal contribution to the discussion of the essence of Christianity consisted in an article he published in six instalments in *Die christliche Welt*. But it is far from the case that the essay of 1903 provides us with the first literary evidence of Troeltsch's concern for this topic.[6] There is an early apologetic essay of 1894 which contains numerous references to the 'essence', 'spirit', 'kernel', 'heart' and 'fundamental idea' of Christianity, in contexts which treat the problem of the continuity of the Christian Weltanschauung in the post-Enlightenment world.[7] This context is significant. For Troeltsch was convinced that a radical rupture separated the genuinely modern period of European culture and history from the pre-modern period, and that since what was achieved by the Enlightenment was a total alteration of modern thought in every department, nothing less than a total reconstruction of theology could meet the situation.[8] The 'old supernaturalism' is referred to with a variety of opprobrious designations, such as 'superficial', 'anthropomorphic biblico-ecclesiastical', 'ancient naive biblico-ecclesiastical' and so forth, and those who continue to trade in such coin are contemptuously dismissed.[9]

Such over-emphatic judgements are not simply symptomatic of Troeltsch's youth (he was, it should be remembered, twenty-nine years of age); they also reflect the insecure sense of superiority felt by a whole group of theologians who had taken over the Kantian and Hegelian analysis of the situation of the churches in the modern world. In the vivid phrase, reminiscent of the early correspondence of Hegel and Schelling, Troeltsch compares the disputes of standard learned theology to children's squabbles in a burning house.[10] The theologians simply do not seem to be aware that Kant, Goethe, Hegel, the historical school and scientific theology have laid a completely new foundation.[11] Naturally enough, whose who, like Troeltsch considered themselves alive to the new context of theology, faced the grave question whether an identifiably Christian faith could persist despite the necessary radical changes. It was precisely to meet this situation that Troeltsch, as an apologist for neo-protestantism, availed himself of the already conventional essence of Christianity argument. It is as easy, he maintained, to conceive of 'the spirit of Christianity' apart from its original historical form, as it was to conceive of the spirit of hellenistic culture without the trappings of Greek mythology.[12] The following is typical of his position: 'The salvation of persons, united with the holy and loving will of God in a kingdom of love is the innermost kernel of the gospel. The special nature of Christianity is determined by the formulation of its purpose alone.'[13] In the modern context, however, this fundamental characteristic of Christianity can be presented only with the help of idealism, the intellectual tradition with which Christianity was inextricably fused in its earliest centuries. In achieving this, two difficulties have to be met. In the first place, the new emphasis on development from within (as distinct from supernatural interference from without) tends towards an optimistic moralism, whereas Christianity is basically a religion of redemption. In the second place, a purely immanental notion of development has no room for a final and unsurpassable revelation, which is, Troeltsch asserts, 'of the innermost essence of the Christian principle'.[14] In other words, he recognized as the terms of the problem he had to solve, a particular view of what is integral to Christianity. The obvious question is why he chose to stick at these points. Was it anything other than sheer assertion that distinguished what he strives to preserve as 'fundamental dispositions' from what he is ready to dismiss as mere 'passing form'? These were the issues which Troeltsch was having to face before Harnack's contribution to the debate, but which the remarkable response to Harnack's lectures forced him to take up with greater urgency.

III

Before we consider Troeltsch's article in detail, a word must be said about his understanding of Harnack's theological position. Troeltsch, together with most commentators to the present, interpreted Harnack as a disciple of Albrecht Ritschl, inasmuch as both saw the essence of Christianity to lie in the idea of the Kingdom of God.[15] In this respect Harnack's work is set in contrast to the Hegelian school, which takes the idea of incarnation as central. But the matter is not quite so simple. In the *Absoluteness of Christianity* (1902), Troeltsch used Harnack's *Das Wesen des Christentums* as an example of that type of 'evolutionary apologetic' which ultimately stemmed from Hegel. As evidence he quoted the sentence: 'It is evident, then, that the gospel is not a positive religion like the others, that it has nothing legalistic or particularistic about it, that it is *therefore religion itself*.'[16] The importance to Troeltsch of evolutionary apologetic was considerable, since it represented the attempt to rule out every means of isolating Christianity from the rest of history on the basis of miracle;[17] and that was the presupposition of the *religionsgeschichtliche Schule* of which Troeltsch was a member.[18] Thus, although it is convenient to regard Harnack and Troeltsch as respectively a supporter and an opponent of the Ritschlian theological tradition, the truth is more complex. Although Harnack was less radical theologically than some of the 'Kleine Göttinger Fakultät' including Troeltsch himself, and although Troeltsch made it clear that he regarded his own work on the social context of Christian teaching as an improvement on Harnack's *History of Dogma*, nonetheless their work belonged recognizably in the same problem-complex and shared many presuppositions.

Troeltsch's starting point in his essay, 'Was heisst "Wesen des Christentums"?', is the sheer variety of the standpoints from which Harnack's work has been assessed, attacked and commended. Such variety called, Troeltsch felt, for a methodological investigation into the presuppositions involved in the quest for the essence of Christianity.[19] He observed that the quest in its modern form had arisen together with the labours of modern historiography. German idealists and Romantics had assumed the habit of surveying an historical phenomenon in its totality and of attempting by abstraction to grasp its driving idea (*treibende Idee*). Their use of the expression, essence of Christianity, presupposed the view 'that large coherent complexes of historical events are the development of an idea, a value, or a line of thought (*Gedankenkreis*) or purpose (*Zweckgedanken*), which gradually develops in detail and consequences, which assimilates and subordinates alien materials and which continually struggles against aberrations from its leading purpose and against contradictory principles threatening from without'.[20] This form of abstract thought Troeltsch considered to be quite unavoidable in history, and wholly proper provided it remained in close contact with the study of detail. He pointed to other examples in contemporary historiography where other cultures and religions had been submitted to a similar analysis. Christianity is no different in principle from any of these; the same methods apply to all. He therefore endorsed Harnack's proposal to view Christianity in a purely historical manner, though, as we shall see, this in fact constitutes only the first step of the total task.

For the moment, however, Troeltsch wished to press home the proper significance of accepting the presuppositions of the historiography of German idealism. Consistently with all his previous writing he insisted that this meant the end of the dogma of Christianity's normativeness, accredited and recognizable on the basis of divine authority or miracle. Christianity cannot preserve inviolate its own internal criteria of interpretation. It must now be viewed in its totality, and within the whole of human history (i.e. not as a self-sufficient entity). With a reference, added in 1913, both to Schleiermacher's *Glaubenslehre* and the Hegelian programme of universal history, he emphatically stated his approval of the comparative approach for the determination of essence, and praised Schleiermacher's *Ethics* for its breadth of view over the spiritual life.[21] Although this form of essence–definition is a 'purely historical matter', the formulation of the necessary abstractions is a task beyond what he termed 'inductive–empirical history', and lies at the point of transition to the philosophy of history. The former, of course, uses general terms, but never concerns itself very self-consciously with abstraction. This was Troeltsch's complaint against Harnack, who had not, in his view, sufficiently pondered the difficulties of the transition. It was not enough historically to have analysed the teaching of Jesus, and to have presented it as the simple essence of the total and complex phenomenon of Christianity. Nor, on the other hand, would it do with Loisy, simply to presuppose the view that the Catholic Church superseded the concept of essence; that would be to lapse into the old unhistorical realm of dogma. The only way of avoiding these mistakes was to operate the correct method. One ought to proceed not on the basis of dogma, but 'from history in general, and its methods, to a view of Christianity in its overall extent, and to the question of its validity'.[22]

But even the correct method itself presented new problems. The only easy way of avoiding these was to suppose that a single force of some kind underlay the basic idea, and expressed itself in history as a single law of development (*Entwickelungsgesetz*). This was the solution offered by the Hegelian school, and might be seen especially in Baur and his pupils.[23] The trouble with this theory of a single law is that it explains too much. All the forms of Christianity would have to be shown to be teleologically necessary; and that, declared Troeltsch, would be impossible for a Protestant, who considers Catholicism to be 'a deviation from the essence of Christianity'.[24]

At this point the differences between the two editions of the text become important. In the original edition of 1903 Troeltsch, after offering his objection that the theory of a single law of development was biased in favour of Catholicism,[25] immediately drew from the opposition between Catholicism and Protestantism the conclusion that the history of Christianity contains absolute opposites.[26] This, he admitted, was a Protestant judgement (a sentence omitted in the later edition), but at the same time a result of purely historical consideration. The idea of essence in any case only existed as a construct of the historian. In the later edition, he evidently felt obliged to admit at once that in offering his objection as a Protestant he had departed from 'purely historical thinking';[27] and subsequently he added that the justification of his objection was a matter of 'our own conception and interpretation of Christianity'.[28] The difference is significant. In the original edition he seemed content to be understood to be saying that the Protestant and the purely historical, or impartial, view of Christianity simply coincide. It was a view which, as we shall see, Troeltsch did not really abandon. But it seems that in his later edition he proposed to be more circumspect, and, so to speak, to set his 'Protestant' objection within brackets by raising the (wholly theoretical) possibility that even Protestantism itself might be viewed as 'a falling away or peripheral variety of the essence'.[29] The conclusion of the argument is thus made much more general in the later edition. The oppositions apparent in church history (he has now reinforced the original argument by reference to the history of heresy and sectarianism) presuppose the necessity of criticism from a particular standpoint; but that statement is at the same time a historical judgement. 'It cannot be otherwise even for the most impartial approach, if one considers it possible to achieve a concept of the essence at all.'[30] The qualification in the conditional clause is vital. Troeltsch was now arguing that, if one wants to do essence reconstruction at all, one is bound to accept the fact that the concept will be formed by the judgement of the historian. Thus the 'impartiality' claimed for the judgement cannot literally mean non-partisanship; it must refer, rather, to the conscientiousness of the historian in the handling of material from his or her own particular standpoint. The difficulty in which he has landed is seen repeatedly throughout the essay.

Troeltsch, however, was thoroughly aware of the point, and gave it at once an airing. If essence definition was at the same time criticism, what provided the criterion? To this his immediate answer was: 'It is a criticism of historical formations in terms of the ideal which lies within their main driving force.'[31] Here he was referring to Heinrich Rickert's programme of the elucidation of 'immanent values', a theory whose importance for his essay he acknowledged in a subsequently added footnote.[32] The critical character of essence definition is still part of the historical task, even if the transition to philosophy of history has taken place. Its criteria are, therefore, supposed to be objective; and this is why Troeltsch, though manifestly now on difficult ground, defended the impartiality of the critical viewpoint he felt compelled to adopt.

> When partisan spirit and personal wishes are left in the background, and if one simply gives oneself over to the impression made by the material and attempts to distinguish the specific within the whole, and to judge the distortion and the accidental additions in terms of the whole, then such a problem is soluble, at least to the extent that unprejudiced persons ready to learn may be brought to a sympathetic understanding or at least inducted into the main direction of the conception and evaluation of the essence.[33]

The objectivity of the solution thus depended on its being tackled by people with the necessary intellectual, moral and spiritual gifts; it was a matter both of historical competence and ethical insight.[34]

Troeltsch was thirty-eight years old when he wrote this essay, and we look in vain for any self-effacing disclaimers about his own competence to fulfil the task. Not even when banning 'the amateurs, the doctrinaire, the fanatics, the narrow-minded, subordinates and specialists' from the work does he hint at the enormity of the claim he is making on his own and his like-minded contemporaries' behalf. It is clear, too, from other work he was doing at the time, especially his long discussion of Rickert in his essay, 'Modern Philosophy of History' (1904), that this new theory was intended to replace the old theological dogma that norms had been given by 'an isolated divine revelation'.[35] But he was clearly torn about the extent to which personal factors influence the historian's judgement. The method for defining the essence of Christianity with the aid of immanent criticism could in principle be used on every other historical phenomenon; but there existed the truth that 'history is ceaselessly striving to realise values which have an objective, inner necessity', and this was no ethically indifferent standpoint. Ultimately, Troeltsch's view was circular, as he frankly recognized.[36] But he defended its circularity on the grounds that it necessarily arose out of the structure of our consciousness. The values which we detect by impartial enquiry into history, we order according to a criterion personally convincing to ourselves which spontaneously arises in the course of a comparative estimate. This criterion emerges in the active correlation of a historical heritage and the living present.[37] Troeltsch's own deployment of the criterion led him to the view (which he did not attempt to alter in his later edition) that the critical definition of the essence was in fact only possible in Protestantism, 'which is based precisely upon the principle that personal insight into what is essential in Christianity is able to evaluate selectively the mass of actual historical manifestations'.[38]

As hitherto described, Troeltsch's method for defining the essence of Christianity, which has striking points of resemblance to Schleiermacher's, is as much art as science, and depends heavily on such qualities as sympathy, maturity of judgement and insight. Troeltsch recognized, however, that the peculiar problem of Christianity lay in the importance for its whole development of its origins in the person of Jesus. Not just artificial dogmatism, but the historically developed tradition of Christian teaching as a whole, recognized in Jesus the founder of the religion in an exceptionally strong sense. Troeltsch preferred the term, 'classical time', to designate the importance of the New Testament period for subsequent developments, and within this classical time further pinpointed the historically reconstructed preaching and personality of Jesus as the 'finally decisive point'.[39] Here it is again instructive to observe the development of Troeltsch's thought from the writing of the original article to the edition published in the collected works, as mirrored in the changes to the text. They begin at once in the answer to the question, at what point is the pre-eminently important revelation of the essence to be found. 'To begin with', affirmed the Troeltsch of the first edition, 'the answer is very simple'; by the second edition it only 'seems' simple. Accordingly, the difficulties which Troeltsch proposed to introduce in the second edition are of a more radical kind. In the first edition Troeltsch touched on the following three complications: first that there can be no artificial isolation of the canon; secondly that within the New Testament it is the words and personality of Jesus, as elucidated by the historian, that are pre-eminently important; and thirdly that these are only mediated to us by the faith of the community, influenced (and rightly so) especially by

Paul to emphasize the spirit of Christ, always active in its midst. From this last the conclusion is drawn that the essence of Christianity is not exhausted by an examination of the teaching of Jesus.

Retaining all that, Troeltsch by 1912 wanted to complicate and radicalize the problem considerably. Much earlier in the discussion he signalled the fact that Jesus' preaching of the Kingdom was not for him the essence of Christianity; also the novelty of the influence of Paul on early Christianity was greatly emphasized, and his Christocentrism was bluntly stated to be a 'new picture of Christ'. Whereas earlier Troeltsch had himself affirmed that the spirit and meaning of Jesus' preaching was contained in Paul, he now presented this position as an argument likely to be brought forward, but one with which he did not fully agree. Paul cannot be understood as preaching, like the Fourth Evangelist, a spiritual Christ, leading the Church into all truth. 'Paul's preaching has a quite different relationship to the present and to the possession of salvation'; it contains 'a substantively new religious element of the highest significance'.[40] Thus Christianity contains from the start different basic trends; it has 'two distinct accents, if not indeed two altogether distinct elements'.[41] This conclusion is used to justify the introduction of a stronger reference to 'the truths of Platonism and Stoicism', without which Christianity is actually said to be culturally inconceivable,[42] or even, in the case of Platonism, untenable scientifically and as a philosophy of religion.[43] Where the first edition spoke of the essence being a complex entity containing in itself an oscillation between several basic ideas, the second edition radicalized the statement by asserting that it 'must go so far as to bear opposites and tensions within itself'.[44]

Even without the addition of this new perspective, the problem of recognizing the essence had become, at Troeltsch's hand, incredibly complex – too complex for any single Hegelian 'law of development'. Nonetheless Troeltsch persisted in maintaining that the careful historian may acquire a sense (*Gefühl*) for what is Christian.

> Our sense for this is corrected by history and yet at the same time our sense for it plays a leading part in our grouping of the historical facts. According to our own inward reflection on the Christian idea and according to the conscientiousness of our grasp of the historical

material we shall arrive at differing conceptions of the course of development, and from these positions conceive differently the seminal potential of the original form.[45]

To counterbalance the inescapable subjectivity of this position Troeltsch quickly added his usual reservation about the need for 'real historical mastery' in the execution of the task.[46]

Thus the continuum so discerned must be capable of accounting for the tendency of Christianity to reformulate itself ever anew. Especially it must take into account the ambiguity of its attitude towards culture, in which it experiences a fundamental polarity. Troeltsch expressed it thus:

> Christianity is an ethic of redemption whose world-view combines optimism and pessimism, transcendence and immanence, an abrupt polarisation of the world and God and the inward linking of these two, a dualism, in principle, which is transcended (*aufgehoben*) again and again in faith and action. It is purely religious ethic which refers man baldly and onesidedly to the values of the inner life, and yet again it is a humane ethic which forms and transfigures nature, overcoming the struggle with her through love.[47]

The original form of Christianity, however, was a 'onesided and abruptly transcendent ethic'; the immanent ethic was a subsequent development, as Christianity was forced to abandon its belief in an early end to the world order. The significance of the 'classical time' was and still is, however, that through the gospel of redemption characteristic of this time, the Christian would be preserved from total immersion in the world and culture. Troeltsch saw the tension resolved not in a synthetic viewpoint balanced between extremes, but in a temporal process of circular movement between the two poles, in which the preaching of Jesus is the stronger. This, at least, is the message of the first edition. But Troeltsch's radicalization required an emphatic strengthening on the side of the legitimate incorporation into Christianity of genuine novelty. Accordingly he later added two sentences expressing the view that the changes and assimilations which have occurred within the history of Christianity 'themselves belong to the essence, as it has now become and as alone it is capable of carrying a general culture'.[48] The supporting reference is not to Paul, used earlier as the grounds for introducing novelty, but to platonic philosophy, social ethics and art.

Thus the concluding words of the section, which are identical in both editions, are given in the later edition an entirely new meaning. Whereas in the first edition the circular movement occurs between two poles found in Christianity virtually from the start, of which the redemptive pole (emphasized by Jesus and original Christianity) is the stronger, in the later edition the idea is conveyed that Christianity itself is being progressively altered by its encounters with culture, and that its essence for today could not be the same as in earlier centuries. Any contemporary essence of Christianity would therefore be construed out of the interrelationship between a progressively transformed accommodation of original Christianity and general culture on the one hand, and the preaching of Jesus on the other.

Troeltsch does not, however, pursue this thought; indeed it is not entirely clear that he wholly envisaged the extent to which the addition changed the sense of the original discussion. But the radical tenor of the alterations in the section is good evidence for supposing that he was ready to defend the increased possibility it gave for accommodating novelty in the Christian tradition. Indeed his own theological position by 1912 demanded such a defence.[49]

Troeltsch now turned his attention to a theme which had been implicit from the start in his concept of the essence as the 'driving force' in Christianity, namely whether that which had carried forward the historical phenomenon in the past had any power to do so in the future. The plain fact is that a historian would view Christianity very differently according to whether or not he considered it had any future. Thus the attitude adopted to the Christianity of the present would decisively influence one's view of the whole phenomenon.[50]

Troeltsch, in admitting this, sought to mitigate the further impression of subjectivity it imported by insisting that, in this situation, Christianity was in no different case from any other phenomenon, such as classical culture, the Renaissance, Buddhism, Islam and so forth. 'The purpose of history is indeed never simply to reflect a past world in the memory. Quite apart from the fact that this is impossible it would also be empty and superfluous.'[51] Yet not even the most distant past is without an indirect relevance to the present and future. History is never merely antiquarian curiosity.

The purpose of Troeltsch's rather confused introduction was to attempt to show that the historian's personal attitude towards the future validity of Christianity conditioned his or her view of its essence. The carefully defended objective status of the definition was not destroyed, however, because, according to Troeltsch, all historical abstractions (in Troeltsch's sense of historical) contained this evaluative element, and, in any case, the conditioning of the historian is only partial.[52] Nonetheless Troeltsch was emphatic that he was pinpointing one of the conditions of the definition of an essence. 'Almost all essence concepts have the tendency to be transmuted into ideal concepts.'[53] The historian has to attempt to foresee how the basic idea of the essence will unfold in the future.

No exposition of Troeltsch's view at this point can avoid the question whether he now flatly contradicts all that he said above about the impartiality or objectivity of the historian's approach to the material. The issue turns on whether sense can be made of the notion that the historian is only 'partially conditioned' by a positive or negative decision about Christianity. Once he has asserted, however, that 'none of the possible decisions about the problem can be absolutely presuppositionless and impartial',[54] it is my view that his protestations about objectivity become redundant, and his further defence of it mere rationalization. What Troeltsch speaks of in a 1912 addition as 'a thoroughly personal matter conditioned by personal religious feeling (*Empfindung*) and attitude towards the Christian idea'[55] is, in fact, in Lonergan's useful notion, the acquisition of a horizon.[56] Such a perspective of history is all-embracing, and, in this specific sense all-conditioning. The case is *not*, of course, that because of his or her attitude the historian is free, for example, to invent the past. In this sense the actuality or facticity of past events continues to 'condition' one's work; and, indeed, new considerations may in due time bring about a change of horizon. But the sheer impossibility of being neutral in the matter of the decision about Christianity's claims requires the conclusion that what is at stake is our whole way of viewing the world. Troeltsch's personal presupposition that

no physics and no biology, no psychology and no theory of evolution can take from us our belief in the living, creative purpose of God, and that no anti-teleology, no brutality and no fortuitousness of nature, no contradiction between the ideal and the real, can take from us our belief in redemption as the destination of the whole world[57]

is an all-embracing affirmation of faith. The historian who makes such an affirmation already has a view about the past, present and future of Christianity, which his or her work on the historical material will certainly exemplify. For should the historical work turn out otherwise, he would, by strict logic, fall into self-contradiction; and from this position, the only release would be, as Troeltsch himself admitted, the negative decision on Christianity's future.

It is thus noteworthy that Troeltsch's defence of the objectivity of the work became, in the pages which followed, an intra-Christian discussion. Having roundly stated that the combining of objective and subjective considerations is a creative act, which shapes the essence of Christianity afresh, and having spoken of 'an ever-renewed, purely factual and irrational combination of that which is recognized to be necessary and true with historical tradition and experience',[58] he is forced to consider whether he has not now permitted a dangerous subjectivism to creep in. But the objection is tackled only from the standpoint of the needs of the *Christian* community. At this crucial point in the argument, in other words, he is principally contending with those conservative theologians worried about the loss of authority and direction, which Troeltsch's method seems to import into the consideration of the Church's future. Thus his replies do not by any means touch the crucial point, namely the utter gulf he has introduced between the Christian's and non-Christian's conclusions about Christianity's future.

This is not to minimize the importance of Troeltsch's contribution to the discussion. By speaking of the relation of the historian or theologian to Christianity's past as involving his own will, and by emphasizing the creativity of the statements about Christianity's essence, Troeltsch was bringing into the open what was implicit in much of the previous history of essence talk. Essence definition frequently had a reformatory intention, a judgement upon the present by means of a hoped-for future. Harnack made much the same point when he said:

> There is no doubt that, with respect to the past, the historian assumes the royal function of a judge, for in order to decide what of the past shall continue to be of effect and what must be done away with or transformed, the historian must judge like a king. Everything must be designed to furnish a preparation for the future, for only the discipline of learning has the right to exist which lays the foundation for what is to be.[59]

That this was the intention of Harnack's book on the essence of Christianity Troeltsch recognized in a passage inserted in 1912.[60]

Similarly important are the terms of the discussion of the limits to subjectivism. Troeltsch quite rightly says that 'the less effort one spends in self-deceit, trying to find a theoretical escape from subjectivism, the more one's hands are freed to limit it in practice and to render it harmless'.[61] The open acceptance of the possibility of novelty, confidence in scholarly conscientiousness, awareness that the laity are often more flexible than official church circles, and the sense of continuity achieved in 'the abiding relationship to the Christian community'[62] – all these considerations comprise a genuinely important contribution to understanding the theological task implicit in the quest for Christianity's essence.

But they are considerations persuasive only to those already concerned about the integrity of the future of Christianity. At this point in the discussion Troeltsch does not introduce any objection stemming from a historian convinced that Christianity has no future, or discuss the 'objectivity' of the very radically different picture which such a view-point would provide. Nonetheless he does consider the work of Eduard von Hartmann, who had attacked the whole tradition of neo-Protestantism, and Harnack especially, as an abandonment of Christianity, in the interest not of orthodoxy but of a philosophical transmutation of orthodoxy. The discussion of von Hartmann is especially interesting, because here Troeltsch entirely rewrote the meagre paragraph assigned to the question in 1903, expanding it to cover seven pages of his collected works. In the original version Troeltsch contented himself with a brief description of von Hartmann's 'pantheistic' transmutation of the idea of incarnation into the essential unity of divine and human spirit. Von Hartmann, too, clearly saw as the essence of Christianity those features of it which had in his eyes future value. He was accordingly, said Troeltsch, operating the same method. The difference lay both in historical interpretation and in personal conviction. In both respects Troeltsch believed his to be a sounder view, but would not have expected a neutral tribunal to be able to arbitrate between them. There is a reciprocal effect of ideas; 'the historical conception works on the conviction and the conviction on the historical conception.' Hence it is not a matter of proof, but of conscientious historical study and personal religious judgement.[63]

By 1913 Troeltsch was evidently convinced that von Hartmann's thesis needed to be met head-on, if the claims for an objective basis for essence definition were to carry much weight. The blandness of the 1903 article was replaced by a slashing attack on von Hartmann's interpretation of Christianity, said to constitute 'an extremely violent construction which distorts all real history'.[64] In support of this assertion Troeltsch argued that the philosophical interpretation of the incarnation was quite new and alien to the orthodox tradition, that pantheism was ruled out by the essentially Christian doctrine of the living God and that the suffering of the Incarnate had nothing to do with any 'pessimistic' view of a suffering God. The true historical connections of such ideas 'are with Brahmanism and Buddhism, and not with Christianity'.[65]

Historical argument is also adduced to dispense with the objection which von Hartmann raised against the non-Christian, innovatory character of neo-Protestantism. It is said to be certain 'on the grounds of objective history' that what for von Hartmann is mere limitation and husk (namely the personalist doctrine of God and belief in salvation) is actually the essential. Of course, it is true that in neo-Protestantism the old Christology of Protestantism falls away with the advent of a new understanding of the relationship of God and history; similarly a new understanding of culture has emerged to meet present needs. But the genuine link with the actual history of Christianity is perfectly clear.[66]

Now whether Troeltsch had actually contributed more to the argument than increased vigour of assertion may be doubted. His own doubts are possibly evident in the defensiveness of the following paragraphs of the discussion. Here he admitted, yet again, that continuity cannot actually be *proved* in an exact historical sense, but claimed that religious subjectivity can find its inner rapport confirmed by conscientious historical research.[67] He also appealed for confirmation to the future, which he feels will support the basic correctness of the movement of neo-Protestantism, and refute von Hartmann's pessimistic monism. Ultimately, however, the appeal was to the truth; compared with this, the argument about whether what we believe is 'no longer Christianity' or 'still Christianity' is unimportant.[68]

But none of these appeals extracts Troeltsch from his difficulty. They may successfully defend his own construction as a *possible* view of the essence of Christianity, against von Hartmann's charge that it was a fundamentally new religion. But that is to offer an *argumentum ad hominem*. The supposed refutation of von Hartmann is otherwise sheer rhetoric. Von Hartmann was not obliged to prove that his 'development' of Christianity was identical with historical Christianity any more than was Troeltsch, and the appeals to the future and to truth could equally have been made by him. The weakest facet of the whole discussion remains, however, its essentially intra-Christian character. Von Hartmann, because he was operating within the Hegelian notion of development was only apparently a non-Christian opponent. Troeltsch had still to discuss a case where a serious and qualified historian conscientiously studying the history of Christianity had reached the conclusion that its course has run into the sand. Only in the context of such a discussion would the true nature of his assumed 'horizon' have become apparent to him, and his protestations about objectivity seem less like special pleading.

It remains to enquire why the impression conveyed by the essay is so muddled. To make sense of his work on this topic one must suppose, I believe, that while he had proved by his own discussion that the definition of the essence of Christianity necessarily involved the historian's whole approach to history, for various reasons he was unwilling to accept the theological consequences of this view. What could these reasons be? One is certainly obvious, namely that he was rightly convinced that personal conviction was no substitute for expertise. Here however he failed to distinguish between the capacity of the expert historian to point out the mistakes of improper historical reconstructions, that is, the technique of falsification, and the requirements for the task of construction. The objectivity which properly belongs to the former task, he imported into the latter. The verification, however, of a *total* way of viewing history, such as is implied in the Christian's decision to accept a Christian account of this matter, is a vastly more complicated business. Troeltsch attempted to unravel the complications by speaking of an initial *foundation* of objective history, followed by a subsequent personal act. 'The concept of the essence seeks and has, at any rate in the first instance, an objective, historical foundation.'[69] But the metaphor of 'foundations' is notoriously ambiguous in intellectual matters, and the temporal precedence accorded to history is at the very least problematic. Then the problem was further complicated by his talk of the essence 'changing automatically' or 'tending to turn' into an ideal concept.[70] Since Troeltsch was not in the least unaware of the unity of all human thought, and affirmed that any divisions and distinctions he had made were 'admittedly only provisional and hypothetical',[71] one is puzzled to know why he was so intent on making them in the first place.

The reason has evidently to do with his sense of the gains made in the understanding of the past by contemporary historians. These gains Troeltsch attributed to the operation of a method, specifiable under the three headings of probability judgement, analogy and correlation.[72] The method had resulted in objective gains in human knowledge. Moreover, if you admitted its usefulness in even one instance you were obliged to accept the revolution which the whole method implied, and this revolution consisted in that new view of the relationship of God and history, the very hallmark of the modern world, with which it was Christianity's duty to come to terms. Troeltsch was especially scornful of those who tried to mediate between the methods imposed by the modern world, and the old dogmatic supernaturalism. Even the 'evolutionary apologetic', which appeared thoroughly to immerse Christianity in the stream of history, was presented by him as 'the philosophical substitute for the dogmatic supernaturalism of the Church'.[73] Troeltsch believed himself, therefore, to be committed to following the new method wherever it led; to do otherwise would be implicitly to put himself in the position of those theologians he most scorned. Yet, on the other hand, he was convinced that it was necessary to stop short of scepticism. Contemporary critics, both theologians and sceptics, were glad to impale him firmly on the horns of this dilemma. His route of escape they were quick to identify as the covert smuggling in of a religious presupposition, biased towards Christianity for no better than cultural reasons.[74] Indeed, in due course, Troeltsch frankly admitted that no better ground existed for maintaining the truth of Christianity as against that of the 'great world religion' than that it was the religion of western culture;[75] and as for the escape route being a religious presupposition, Troeltsch was fully prepared to acknowledge that the real existence of an absolute value as the *a priori* of all knowledge was 'a belief and to this extent a religious thought'.[76] The question then is whether his analysis of what the membership of 'the modern world' implies simply stopped short at an arbitrarily chosen point – a point which, for example, Bertrand Russell and A. J. P. Taylor would certainly not accept. This point is arbitrary, not in the sense of haphazard, but in respect of its character as a chosen point, beyond which the implications of relativism are termed 'spiritual suicide', and before which the imported belief–presuppositions are termed 'dogmatic supernaturalism'. The intellectual mapwork implied in the emotive labels is correlative to the chosen sticking-point. We can therefore remain wholly unconvinced by the implicit threat that in not accepting Troeltsch's depiction of the modern world we are ruling ourselves out of serious consideration as 'modern' theologians. Von Hügel's gentle, but perceptive observation of Troeltsch's proneness to vehement judgements of an apparently quite subjective kind, was wholly appropriate.[77]

But within the terms laid down by his chosen method Troeltsch had given himself a narrow ridge on which to balance. He must polemicize against dogmatic orthodoxy and maintain the sharpest gulf between it and modernity; yet he must stop short of naturalism, empiricism or scepticism. He must depict the orthodox as hopelessly compromised by their dogmatic commitment; yet he must preserve the right of a Christian to decide for a redemptive view of the world. He must insist on the necessity of a modern Christian belonging to and participating in the aristocracy of scholarship so influential in the German state; yet he must allow for the simplest of naive commitments to a Christian life-style. Throughout the essay we feel the tensions in this proposed course threatening to pull the structure of it apart; and despite the fact that Troeltsch returned to the discussion a number of times, most importantly in the essay of 1913, 'The Dogmatics of the "Religionsgeschichtliche Schule"', the problem of connecting the gains of a genuinely historical treatment of Christianity with the positive task of Christian dogmatics manifestly persists in its old form.

IV

One potential source of liberation from the impasse was to be found in the work of Max Weber, whom Troeltsch personally encountered at this time. We find that in Troeltsch's essay on 'Modern Philosophy of History' (1903),[78] devoted to a discussion of Rickert, an explicit parallel is drawn between the formation of the concept essence of Christianity and Weber's idea of an 'ideal type'. Almost at once, however, Weber developed an important distinction, which he expounded in an essay 'Die "Objektivität" sozialwissenschaftlicher und sozialpolitischer Erkenntnis' (1904). As against Rickert, on whom Troeltsch had largely relied, Weber distinguished between value–related judgements, necessarily made by any historian in his selection of material for study, and value–judgements, made as a response to moral dilemmas. The historian's selectivity is not to be turned into a bridge on which to pass from observation to value–judgement.

Weber's discussion of ideal types and theory construction makes clear that the ideal type is constructed as a logical possibility, whose usefulness turns on its adequacy. It is a heuristic tool designed to help elucidate the actual character of specific events. He will have nothing to do with the notion of the type as a *force* working itself out in history. Thus it is we who create the artificial construct, Christianity, in order to explain to ourselves the 'chaos of infinitely differentiated and highly contradictory complexes of ideas and feelings' which make up, for example, the 'Christianity' of the Middle Ages. The relation of an ideal type to the history of a phenomenon as many-sided as Christianity needs careful specification. Turning specifically to the recent essence of Christianity discussions, Weber observed that essence definition is exceedingly problematic if it is supposed to be taken as the historical portrayal of empirically existing facts. On the other hand it is useful as a conceptual instrument for comparing and measuring reality. There is then to be no confusion between the heuristic and the evaluative use of such a definition; an ideal type has nothing to do with a profession of faith.

> The *elementary duty of scientific self-control* and the only way to avoid serious and foolish blunders requires a sharp, precise distinction between the logically comparative analysis of reality by ideal–*types* in the logical sense and the *value–judgement* of reality *on the basis of ideals*. An 'ideal type' in our sense, to repeat once more, has no connection at all with *value–judgements*, and it has nothing to do with any type of perfection other than a purely *logical* one.[79]

Troeltsch clearly attempted to go a certain way to meet this position, especially in the methodology of the *Social Teachings of the Christian Church*. This is not, of course, a direct study of the essence of Christianity, and the 'ideal types' employed are types observed within the total phenomena of Christianity. But what he had learnt by the study was applicable to his discussion of the essence. For example, at the close of the work he asks himself the question whether anything of lasting significance could be learnt from this study about the future form or content of the Christian social ethos. His reply is characteristic:

> It certainly is in the position of being able to teach us something of this kind. But perceptions of eternal ethical values are not scientific perceptions, and cannot be proved along scientific lines. These perceptions [i.e. the 'permanent ethical values' he is about to expound] have been selected from life in history, which the living conviction and the active will fully apprehend in the certainty that here we perceive absolute Reason in the revelation which is addressed to us and formed in the present connection.[80]

He then offers a list of four social and ethical 'ideas and energies' springing out of the Christian religion. What these are is less important than the fact that he sees them as having been 'selected', despite this selection, however, the 'living conviction and the active will' have provided 'certainty' about their status as revelation. The separation of the tasks of history and evaluation, so strongly insisted on by Weber, is only thinly disguised; but it is achieved at the cost of making the subjective 'certainty' of the perception of 'eternal ethical values' hardly distinguishable from the privileged supernaturalism he so scornfully dismissed.

Similarly in the conclusion to the discussion of the essence of Christianity, which he added as a wholly new section in the collected works, he explicitly recognized that in the present situation it was 'perhaps good to separate more sharply the properly historical and philosophically normative in history'.[81] This, he remarked in a footnote, was his procedure in the *Social Teachings*, which he claimed had 'consciously ... no direct connection to doctrine or ethics and may seem to many to be over-realistic or sceptical'.[82] The normative and systematic task, on the other hand, by which the essence is defined anew with reference to future development, is quite distinct; but the distinction is a gain both for the impartial understanding of history, and for the free creative nature of the act of normative essence–definition.[83]

That should in effect have been the conclusion of the whole essay. Indeed it thoroughly accords with what Troeltsch was to say in his article of 1913, 'The Dogmatics of the "Religionsgeschichtliche Schule"', in which the definition of the essence is presented as a matter of personal intuition, and has nothing to do with a single force working itself out in history.[84] The 'essence of Christianity differs in different epochs; to formulate it means to draw on the historical tradition and to reinterpret and shape it according to the needs of the present.'[85] This conclusion had, indeed, been hinted at already in a 1912 addition to the text.[86] But the more emphatically he affirmed the separation of history and constructive reinterpretation, the weaker became the whole purpose of his argument to associate the prestige of the historical movement with the necessity for *his* reconstruction. Hence the final paragraph of the whole essay tried to re-establish some semblance of unity to the tasks he now had come to feel must be separated.

Just as history and the philosophy of history can only be separated artificially and methodologically, while in reality the first of these always contains an element of the second, while the second can only be built up on the first, so too the historical essence and the essence of faith will have to seek and find each other again and again. The task of theology consists in their unity, whether the two tasks are carefully shared out and solved as far as possible independently, or whether they are brought together again in a great comprehensive account of Christianity which is at once both history and faith.[87]

But behind this sober, even somewhat tame conclusion to Troeltsch's 1913 re-evaluation of the problem of essence definition, lies the daunting recognition of the massive gap he had opened up between modern civilization and the apostolic Church. The separation of historical study and constructive reinterpretation is acutest in relation to Jesus himself. It is in an essay of 1911, 'The Significance of the Historical Existence of Jesus for Faith',[88] that Troeltsch confronts the christological core of his dilemma in terms of the residual power of his new version of Christianity. For Troeltsch had never lost sight of the fact that Christianity would not be Christianity if it were merely a religion for intellectuals. What, then, is the continuing nature of its appeal to ordinary people, once Catholicism has been dismissed as incompatible with historical thought, and the halfway house of moderate Protestantism has been subjected to corrosive criticism?

Troeltsch's answer to this question is cast entirely in terms of a discussion of the power said to inhere in Christianity, and this offers striking confirmation of the analysis offered in previous chapters of this book. Troeltsch believed that there could be no effective form of religion which did not have its roots in cult and community. 'There is no possibility of a sure and powerful redeeming knowledge of God without community and cult';[89] that is not a dogmatic or conceptual judgement, but one based on sound principles of social psychology. Christianity cannot, therefore, cut loose from Christ, its concrete focus or *Mittelpunkt*,[90] without entirely running into the sand.

For social psychological reasons he is indispensable for cult, power, efficacy and expansion, and that should be sufficient to justify and assert the connection ... All hope of a non-cultic, purely personal and individual religion of conviction and knowledge is mere illusion

... Lectures on religious philosophy will never produce or replace a real religion.[91]

Moreover Jesus will not do as a merely mythic focus of the religion. For the Christian believer it is and always will be 'a truly significant fact that a real man thus lived, struggled, believed and conquered, and that from this real life a stream of strength and certainty flows down to him'.[92] Historical critical research inevitably has a part to play.

Is then Troeltsch's position any different from that of the mediating theologians in the tradition of Schleiermacher and Ritschl, of whose half-and-half attitudes to history Troeltsch was so critical? Does he too not need, in the end, a form of doctrinal Christocentrism supported by historical enquiry? Troeltsch believes not. The central position which Christ is to hold in the cult is justified not on the grounds of his unique redemptive significance, that is on christological dogma, but on the grounds of social psychology. Religions need a central symbol, and Christianity may be congratulated that its central symbol is no dogma or moral law but 'a living, many-sided and at the same time elevating and strengthening personality'.[93] This is what fills the Christian idea with living power. The old dogmatic Christocentrism was based on a doctrine of original sin. Without Christ there could be no escape from damnation; therefore Christ was the centre of all.

> Today we understand it all in terms of the inner and necessary arrangement of nature ... With the central place it [sc. the social–psychological law] gives to the personality of Jesus Christianity does not have something special which distinguishes it from all other religions and makes redemption possible here alone. Rather, in this it only fulfils in its own particular way what is a general law of man's spiritual life.[94]

In this picture of terms on which the modern Christian community may preserve Jesus as its central focus there are two respects in which the academic theologian holds a vital position. In the first place, it is he who undertakes historical research into the historical actuality of Jesus' life and teaching. Troeltsch recognizes the impossibility of withdrawing historical facts from 'scientific criticism', and admits and defends that degree and extent of dependence upon scholars and professors.[95]

A second, and more insidious dependency he does not, however, recognize. This dependency arises as a consequence of
justifying the centrality of Jesus for the Christian community not
on a view of who Jesus was, but on a doctrine of what the
Church, or any church, needs as a matter of social–psychological
necessity. The important point to recognize is that the second
opinion (Troeltsch's) is a description ('this is the way churches
behave') not a justification ('this is the way we are justified in
behaving') since social psychology is not a prescriptive science.
How then is Troeltsch to justify the immense devotion of time,
money and energy (not to say love, loyalty and self-discipline)
involved in the whole-hearted membership of the Christian
Church? The answer plainly requires a further development of
theology by which 'the inner and necessary arrangement of
nature' according to which Christians hold Christ as their focus
is itself an element of some larger and more comprehensive
vision of the relation of God and the world. For this task
Troeltsch was himself ready. But it entailed the view that the
divine wisdom had established a world in which persons should
seek and find the truth by means of the religion natural to their
cultures. The cost of justifying doctrinal Christocentrism on
socio-psychological grounds was to make its truth relative to the
cultures in which it had established itself.

Inevitably this massive transformation of the inherited
Christian tradition was attainable only by a theological *tour de
force*. Should the theologian fail to articulate and communicate
the religious appeal of such a vision, multitudes of Christian men
and women would be left with no greater assurance, in their
worship of Christ, than that they were acting on the basis of
some readily intelligible cultural or psychological necessity. This
second dependency on theologians to which he subjected the
Christian community was not realized or admitted by Troeltsch.
Its inescapability was rooted in his basic epistemological
doctrines. It was these which had forced him to reject the whole
dogmatic tradition of the Christian centuries before the Enlightenment. It was on these that the whole of post eighteenth-
century theology had to be reconstructed. Epistemology and the
power and status of the theologian in the Christian Church are
thus seen to be inescapably intertwined, an analysis further
confirmed by the rival epistemology of Karl Barth.

8

Barth and the Power of the Word

The major point which needs to be made in respect of Barth's treatment of our theme is that he makes preaching central to his view of what is involved in the maintenance of the identity of Christianity. On the face of it this is a radical change of gear. Hitherto, it might be said, we have been concerned with the major and fundamental questions of epistemology, of historiography, and of exegesis. Preaching, it might be urged, is a practice consequent upon decisions taken in the fundamental disciplines. One would expect no more illumination from examining Christianity from the standpoint of preaching than one from the practice of hymn-singing. There are good and bad sermons and preachers, as there are good and bad hymns and hymn-writers. But all the crucial criteria for excellence and soundness would seem to be derived from the basic disciplines of theology.

On this point Barth must be allowed to speak for himself, since he was thoroughly aware of the objection. One clarifying explanation needs to be made, however, without delay. By preaching Barth does not mean merely the delivery of a sermon; rather, he intends to signify the totality of the Church's proclamation of the word of God, by which it identifies itself as the Church of Jesus Christ, in speech and act.[1] The identity of Christianity is related to preaching, therefore, by definition. The Christian Church is what it is in its acts of self-identification (i.e. its proclamation, *Verkündigung*). Barth's concern with the human word of preaching (*Predigt*) is not with the art or manner of preaching, but with its substance and criterion. Hence concern with preaching is Barth's mode of proceeding to the central problems of theology.[2]

A certain defence of Barth's procedure may be offered here by reference to the point to which our examination of Ernst Troeltsch has brought us. As we have seen above, a central problem in Troeltsch's treatment of the maintenance of Christian identity is the relation of what the theologian knows about Christian origins and the history of the Church, or about the social psychology of religious groups to the lives of ordinary Christian men and women. Precisely because the theologian understands what makes religions powerful, he or she becomes a powerful person in the Church's life. The question of Christianity's future is the question of how the power of its naively-founded faith in Jesus Christ continues to flow in cult and community. As we shall see, it is this same theme of power in the community which Barth confronts in relation to preaching. Why? The reason is because Barth makes central to his theological endeavour the freedom of God to speak, to be heard, and to be obeyed. In the exposition of the threefold form of the word of God, the Word incarnate, the holy Scripture, and the proclaimed word, Barth returns again and again to the question of freedom and of power. God's freedom is preserved only if human beings do not artificially and arbitrarily restrict his power to act in the present. Accordingly, as we shall see, a vigorous doctrine emerges of the contemporary self-proclamation of the word of God in the work of Christian preaching. The preacher, accordingly, is – or rather, may be, in God's grace – a powerful person; and it is only in view of the preacher's status that the theologian, the preacher's critic, is likewise empowered.

But even so much is to anticipate the exposition of Barth's mature thought on the matter, and to err dangerously on the side of unqualified statements. It is sufficient to have to affirm that there is every reason to discuss Barth's contribution to our theme inasmuch as he treats Troeltsch's unresolved question of the role of the theologian in the Church in a fascinating and original manner.

In the second place, moreover, what we have seen of Troeltsch's treatment of the epistemological dilemma of a theologian concerned for Christianity's essence, arises likewise in Barth. For Barth, as one would expect, it occurs precisely in relation to the preacher's question of what he or she is to say. In other words, the relation of the preacher to his or her subject matter can be theoretically articulated in the form of an epistemological thesis. What knowledge does the preacher have of the word of God? Because of Barth's determination to make possibility dependent upon actuality, God's making of himself known to us in Jesus Christ imposes upon theological reflection God's own conditions of intelligibility. Christology and epistemology are inextricably intertwined; and it is only in this frame of reference that the historical questions which necessarily arise from Christian origins can be tackled.

Thus the third question with which we have been principally concerned is likewise given its answer. The persisting identity of Christianity is given in and with the acknowledgement by the theologian of his or her subject matter, and not in any arbitrary decisions he or she may want to make about how it may be regarded. As we shall see, Barth, like Newman, rejected the essence of Christianity tradition from liberal Protestantism (and before), precisely because of its apparent arbitrariness. He did, however, write about 'the centre of theology', and the relation between convictions about Christianity and convictions about Christian theology will need to be explored. Despite (or is it because of?) his ready concern for the situation of the preacher, he treats previous Protestant writing with originality and insight. This is the case not least in respect of most of the authors with whom we have previously dealt. His lifelong engagement with Schleiermacher was profound and mature. After being a deeply respectful pupil and admirer of Harnack as a student, he came to think that Harnack's view of theology was intolerably old-fashioned and inadequate. And we now discover that Barth's copy of Troeltsch's essay on the essence of Christianity (held in the Karl Barth archive in Basel) is covered in numerous underlinings in his own hand. Only Newman, of our 'early moderns', eluded him, participating in the general absence of English and specifically Anglican theology in his comprehensive theological embrace.[3]

But there is another and deeper reason for applying ourselves carefully to what Barth has to say both about the essence of Christianity and the centre of theology. The essence of Christianity has the reputation for being a gambit in Protestant theology, specifically in liberal Protestantism. It appears to be the device used for saving the continuity of Christianity, when aspects of so-called orthodoxy are subjected to criticism. The notoriously conservative Barth, on this reading of the history of the idea, can be expected to be (and is in fact) hostile to it. But the nature of Barth's opposition is neither predictable nor without ambivalence. What precisely is his account of the role performed by theological criticism in preserving the identity of Christianity in all its aspects? As a Protestant theologian Barth lays great stress upon the importance of 'pure doctrine', that is on an authentic, Christian theology, specifically in relation to the preservation of Christian identity. But there are questions to be put to this tradition in relation to the history which we have attempted to uncover. What, for example, differentiates Barth's rejection of the liberal, critical tradition from Newman's? Do either of these two allow enough validity to particularities in their grasp of a comprehensive scheme (if not a system)? Neither Barth nor Newman spoke willingly of the essence of Christianity. Both, however, responded forcefully to what they believed that concept implied, and embodied a tradition of response which discernibly belongs to the same problem—complex. The discussion of Barth is, I believe, fruitful for our own elucidation of the larger problem of the identity of Christianity, and closes the discussion of particular episodes in modern theology at a helpful point for the final chapters.

The organization of this chapter will be, as before, primarily historical. In the first section, I shall be concerned with the way Barth deals with the position of theologian and preacher in the years 1922–3, and with his engagement with Harnack and Schleiermacher. In the second section we must examine the grounds for the specific refusal of the essence of Christianity apologetic, as set out in the first volumes of the *Church Dogmatics*. Thirdly, Barth's use of the metaphor, the centre of theology, will be examined, with special reference to the epistemology of the *Fides Quaerens Intellectum* of 1931 and to volume IV/1 of the *Church Dogmatics*. And finally, in section IV we must investigate the nature of Barth's explicit treatment of the theme of power.

In English-language theology one cannot presume familiarity with the subtlety of Barth's mature thought. Accordingly I have taken the view, rightly or wrongly, that it is advisable to expound what Barth has to say on those matters with some fulness. Although this necessarily involves the repetition of reasonably well-known tenets, it is the case that this material has not previously been assembled and examined before from this point of view in English. Both indirectly and directly Barth significantly advances the discussion of the identity of Christianity, whilst at the same time helping to terminate the popularity of the term essence of Christianity. Without apology, therefore, one turns to the starting-point for these important developments.

I

The critical situation of the preacher itself became to me the elucidation of the essence [*Wesen*] of all theology. For what else can theology be but the truest possible expression of the quest and questioning on the part of the minister, the description of the dilemma into which a man falls when he ventures upon this task [sc. Christian preaching] and out of which he cannot find his way – a cry for rescue arising from great need and great hope?[4]

In explaining (and apologizing for) the rise of interest in the marginal note which he, Barth, desired to make to contemporary theology – he was speaking in 1922 – Barth unambiguously affirms that it was to the situation of the Christian preacher that he wished to address himself. His *Romans* was, he said, crystallized from 'the familiar situation of the minister on Saturday at his desk and on Sunday in his pulpit'.[5] It is best understood as the answer to the minister's question, 'What is preaching?'[6] Barth denies, indeed, any desire to develop a new theology, a new school or a new system; rather he has the entirely practical aim of a response to 'the need and promise of Christian preaching'.

Behind these statements there lies a personal history of considerable interest. In 1909, in the distinguished periodical, *Zeitschrift für Theologie und Kirche*, the twenty-three year old Barth argued that there was absolutely no reason why the modern theological student, trained in 'religious individualism and historical relativism' should shed his views on taking up pastoral work.[7] Once ordained he gave very great attention to the preparation of sermons, sometimes spending days on a single sermon and finding it necessary to revise them frequently.

'Later', he said, 'I was sorry for everything that my congregation had to put up with.'[8] He was persuaded that to a considerable extent he had failed as a pastor.

Barth's ministry in the agricultural and industrial village of Safenwil began in 1911. By 1912 he was already at odds with the owner of a local works because of an article published in a local socialist paper. He got to know the religious socialist, Hermann Kutter, and began to take a greater interest in eschatology in relation to politics, at the same time learning a more 'revolutionary' or 'discontinuous' use of the term God. 'The little phrase "God is" amounts to a revolution', he said in a sermon at this time.[9]

With the outbreak of the First World War Barth's developing dissatisfaction with his earlier theological masters began to crystallize in a sense for a new beginning with the doctrine of God. In 1916 he delivered a lecture on the righteousness of God, which he subsequently chose as the first essay in a book of essays published in 1924. Declaring himself an atheist in respect of the god of European culture, he demanded that the Christian Church once more recognize the true and living God as God. Such recognition is only the result of a fierce inner personal conflict. The will of God is not a continuation of our own, but its basic recreation.[10]

This new, radical concern with the living God merely exacerbated the problem of preaching. Writing to his brother, Peter Barth, in 1932 he stated: 'From the beginning my question was how to develop my thinking about what I should say as a pastor, starting from the presupposition that God is.'[11] But the radicality of that presupposition only dawned about 1915, when he came to believe that the whole of human independence and self-assurance is made questionable in the light of God's existence. It was against this background that he and his friend Thurneysen began to re-read the Old and New Testaments, and in particular to apply himself to the Epistle to the Romans. The first fruit of this new labour on the Bible is the lecture of 1916 on 'The New World within the Bible'. This 'new world' is, predictably enough, the world of God.[12] But more important than the explicit theme of the lecture is the tone of excitement, as of a barely suppressed volcano, which reverberates throughout. The word 'new' is made to bear the weight of a rediscovery that the

Bible is not concerned with the questions of modern civilization, but with its own theme, God; 'not the doings of man but the doings of God'. Thus 'it is certain that the Bible, if we read it carefully, makes straight for the point where one must decide to accept or to reject the sovereignty of God.'[13] This sovereignty means the power of God to establish a new world, a new redeemed humanity, 'new men, new families, new relationships, new politics'.[14] In short, the answer to the impasse of the preacher, face to face with the moral and political problems of modern Europe, is to affirm the reality and promise of 'the power of God to salvation'.[15]

Thus it is that we come to Barth's commentary on the text from Romans:

> For I am not ashamed of the gospel: for it is the power of God unto salvation to every one that believeth; to the Jew first and also to the Greek (Rom. 1.16).

This, with the verse which follows, is, for Barth the theme of the entire epistle, and Barth's exposition of it lays the basis for what is to follow. Thus the gospel is not to be regarded as a truth among other truths. Anxiety and competition is absurd, since 'by the Gospel the whole concrete world is dissolved and established'.[16] The 'power of God' is the gospel of the resurrection. This constitutes the disclosing and apprehension of his meaning, the means of the unknown God. The power of this God is not, therefore, disclosed in the world of nature or in human souls; it is not the most exalted of observable forces, nor even their fount or sum. It is completely different, the *krisis* of all power, both before and after, beyond and above. The power, therefore, that lies behind Jesus, and his appointment as the Christ, can be apprehended only in the Spirit. This appointment is utterly new, and the decisive turning point in human consideration of God. This is what the whole of the activity of the Christian Church is exclusively concerned with. Indeed, in itself, the community is like the crater formed by the explosion of a shell, a void in which the gospel reveals itself. When it tries to be more than a signpost to the Holy One, the community of Christ degenerates into Christendom, a compromised affair moving with its own momentum, and to that extent devoid of relation to the power of God.[17]

As with the community, so with individual men and women. Whenever they desire to comprehend God for themselves, they terminate in the 'criminal arrogance of religion'.[18] The only alternative is a perception of God which proceeds from God outwards. It is the gospel alone which speaks of God as he is, and which is 'pregnant with our complete conversion', the harbinger of a completely new world.[19] But the world as it is remains in existence, and lies under God's decisive, No! This barrier is, however, also an exit. In the power of God we have a lookout, a door and a hope, received in faith as a contradiction.

> Faith is awe in the presence of the divine incognito; it is the love of God that is aware of the qualitative distinction between God and man and God and the world; it is the affirmation of resurrection as the turning-point of the world; and therefore it is the affirmation of the divine 'No' in Christ, of the shattering halt in the presence of God.[20]

The faith which makes open confession of that contradiction, lives of God. It is this conviction which, in the definition of Johann Albrecht Bengel, constitutes the *centrum Paulinum*.[21]

As the central theme of Romans, the exposition of the radical disjunction between the old and the new worlds naturally returns with great frequency, and we take but one example. In commentary upon Paul's treatment of baptism into the death of Christ (Rom. 6.3–5), Barth states:

> In the resurrection, the full seriousness and energy of the veritable negation, of our being buried, are displayed and ratified. By the creation of the new man, the truth of the redemption which Christ effected is made known (v.10, 11); by our existence in Him our existence in Adam is manifestly dissolved. By this radical conception of death the autonomy of the power of the resurrection is guaranteed as independent of the life which is on this side of the line of death.[22]

The phrase 'the autonomy of the power of the resurrection' neatly encapsulates the point which I have been striving to make. In the context, and against the background of a theological tradition which had exhaustively tried to *relate* the gospel to culture and the human psyche, Barth returns to the biblical images of radical novelty and discontinuity, and deploys them as the grounds for a reassertion of the contemporaneity of divine power.

In Barth's *Romans* there is comparatively little about preaching. But this omission is neither surprising, nor accidental, since the entire work, as all his critics noted, is conceived as proclamation. In the exceptionally combative preface to the second edition of 1921, Barth returned to the theme of his earlier lecture on the new world of the Bible, namely the actual *content* of the biblical documents. Do not the academic theologians realize that their students' future in the Church cannot be dismissed as a matter for 'pastoral theology'?[23] In his own ministry he had discovered, he asserts, the emptiness of the concepts offered in university courses of theology as the substance of Christian hope. The implication of the remark is that a union of 'academic' theology and preaching is the avowed aim and method of the whole commentary. In confirmation of this, two years later in public correspondence with Harnack, Barth was to formulate the thesis that 'the task of theology is at one with the task of preaching'.[24]

All this substantial personal history of debate and reflection (except the last thesis) lies behind the words quoted above at the beginning of this section. They derive from a lecture of 1922, entitled 'The Need and Promise of Christian Preaching', significantly given in response to a request for an introduction to his theology. Barth had, through the publication of the second edition of Romans, and his appointment to a chair in Göttingen, attained a certain theological notoriety. Despite this, it was, he said, the problem of the sermon which still preoccupied him, just as it had provided the original stimulus for the development of a theological viewpoint. The event of Sunday worship creates an air of expectancy – but what precisely is expected? All the elements of the service combine to affirm that God is present, but the question which underlies all, asked or unasked, is, Is it *true* that God is present? People are not to be put off with entertainment or good advice. The symbolic opening of the Bible at Protestant worship indicates the centrality of the word of God, and commits Protestants to an affirmation of the presence of God in the preaching of the word.[25]

Here Barth argues that 'the Reformation wished to see something better substituted for the mass it abolished, and that it expected that the better thing would be – our preaching of the Word'.[26] *Verbum visible*, indeed, the objectively clarified

preaching of the word, is the only sacrament left by the Reformers. By the preaching of the word Barth means specifically,
the word of the cross, God's No of judgement and Yes of grace.
When this is faithfully uttered, the preaching of the word is an
event of momentous significance, the act which in Protestantism
is the crux of the whole service.

> However, as we know, preaching consists of human words. The
> word of God on the lips of a man is an impossibility; it does not
> happen; no one can envisage it or bring it about. The event toward
> which the expectancy of heaven and of earth is directed is none the
> less *God's* act.[27]

Barth exposes the apparently chronic presumption of the
preacher. Only a person who knows that he stands under the
judgement of the cross, and thus knows his unworthiness, may
lay hold of the promise of preaching. Barth emphasizes again
that the route of the Catholic altar sacrament is closed to the
Protestant:

> In this most ingenious symbol of its sovereignty, the church depicts
> its fancied *escape* from judgement, though its escape is actually from
> grace; it is not satisfied with the promise but must possess, enjoy,
> and experience the fulfilment – to *experience* it, as if the way to the
> experience of fulfilment did not lie through the death of all human
> sovereignty, and first of all that of the Church![28]

This flight from judgement, this unwillingness to live in the
shadow of the cross, has also penetrated deeply into modern
Protestantism. What, therefore, is needed is careful thought
about what is being said and done, and Barth sees his own role
as attempting to recollect the meaning of what is said and done
by the churches today. Given such an effort of thought there
would be no reason why agreement might not one day be reached
with Catholic theologians over the altar sacrament. The divine
judgement and justification is the source of the life of the Roman
Church no less than the Protestant, if only Protestants would
realize how much their own churches are in need of a new
reformation, and a new resurrection.[29]

All this is to do no more than confirm a statement of Professor
Torrance that Barth's primary concern from his Safenwil days
onwards 'was the question as to what preaching really is as a task

with its own independent right and action'.[30] The connection between the problem of preaching and theological method is clearly exemplified by Harnack's challenge to Barth in 1923. Harnack had already heard Barth lecture at a student conference in 1920 ('Biblical Questions, Insights and Vistas') and had been profoundly disturbed.[31] When Harnack published his '15 Questions to the despisers of scientific theology', in *Die Christliche Welt*, he sent Barth a postcard explaining that he did *not* have him particularly in mind.[32] His anxiety was, nonetheless, for the future of 'scientific theology', and one of the questions explicitly raised the issue of how there could be a non-fanatical preaching of the gospel which did not in the first place rely upon historical knowledge and critical reflection.[33] The fourteenth question returned to the same theme:

> If the person of Jesus Christ stands at the centre of the gospel, how else can the basis for reliable and communal knowledge of this person be gained but through critical-historical study so that an imagined Christ is not put in place of the real one? What else besides scientific theology is able to undertake this study?[34]

The general question is that of the significance of the modern historical study of Christian origins which principally concerned Harnack in his dispute with Loisy. But the particular problem is the one we have seen in Troeltsch's 1911 essay on 'The Significance of the Historical Existence of Jesus for Faith'. Here Troeltsch had asserted the necessity of the centrality of Jesus for community and cult, and the relevance of historical scholarship for laying bare the fact that what we have to deal with is a real man who lived and died; and it is precisely this which creates a necessary, if relative, dependency upon scholars and professors.

What was to be Barth's answer? Essentially that there is no distinction between the 'objectivity' of the scholar and the 'commitment' of the preacher.

> The task of theology is at one with the task of preaching. It consists in the reception and transmission of the Word of the Christ. [Further] ... the reliability and communality of the knowledge of the person of Jesus Christ as the centre of the *gospel* can be none other than that of the God-awakened *faith*. Critical-historical study signifies the deserved and necessary end of *those* 'foundations' of this

knowledge which are no foundations at all since they have not been laid by God himself.[35]

There is no knowledge of Christ according to the flesh, as recent critical study of the Bible reveals. The more radical the shock modern readers receive from critical study the better; this is the service 'historical knowledge' can render the actual task of theology.[36]

In effect the answer is the playing of an epistemological grand-slam. It is only by faith that the theologian and the preacher have knowledge of Christ. If the conventions of historiography lead us to despair of historical knowledge of Christ, so much the better. Harnack, in his reply, seizes on the epistemological point at once. There is only one kind of knowing, common to humanity from the dawn of human thought. Harnack denies that preaching is in any way relevant. 'The task of theology is at one with the task of science in general.'[37] Specifically with reference to Christ, Harnack protests that Barth has failed to answer his principal question. Is there knowledge of Jesus Christ, the centre of the gospel, which is unrelated to his historical existence? As to radical biblical scholarship disposing of the need to worry about the historical Christ, we have, says Harnack, thereby opened the gate to a theological tyranny which tortures the conscience by its own heuristic knowledge.[38]

This last point is of very great importance. Harnack was persuaded that 'the simple gospel', to the exposition of which he had devoted himself in *Das Wesen*, was comprehensible by all. All that was needed was the clear testimony of the preacher (backed by adequate scholarship); normal human insight would bring a sympathetic person to the point of decision. Barth profoundly disagreed, and in this, it must be said, he had Luther on his side. With Luther he argued that the gospel is by no means simple, and that normal human insight is in contradiction to it. There is, moreover, a profound correlation between Scripture and Spirit which cannot be overlooked.[39] Agreeing quite readily that different techniques are applicable in the pulpit and at the academic rostrum, he held that the theme of both is identical. What is totally ruled out is any 'simple gospel' supposedly extracted from the Scriptures after the basis for the cognition of all revelation, namely the correlation of Scripture and Spirit, has been eliminated. The epistemological point about cognition is crucial. The existence of one called Jesus of Nazareth, discoverable historically, is not the same cognition as faith in the incarnation. Faith, he had learnt from his teacher Wilhelm Herrmann, is not mere credence in historical facts apart from the unprecedented activity of the Holy Spirit.[40]

Harnack's final postcript to the debate is, in effect, an acknowledgement that a distinction ought to be drawn between scientific theologians and those such as Paul and Luther, Barth 'and all those who express their Christianity as prophets or witnesses like preachers'. The scientific theologian does not aim to inspire and edify. For the rest Harnack rejects the attempt to grasp the word of revelation as objective apart from all human speech and understanding; that is, no matter what may be said about the Holy Spirit, it must be said in such a way that *some* human account can be given of the cognitional processes involved. Barth's 'dialectic' in the matter he depicts as 'an invisible ridge between absolute religious scepticism and naive biblicism'.[41]

How are we to evaluate this controversy? It contains, needless to say, a variety of themes, and it is marred on both sides by a wilful refusal to take with maximum seriousness the points made by the opponent. Harnack, in particular, refuses to discuss the question of the Holy Spirit – it is remarkable that the term only occurs incidentally in a quotation from Barth. Barth, on the other hand, consistently refuses to assign to historical scholarship of Christian origins a consistent and intelligible role; his evasions on this issue make a most unpleasing impression. For all this unsatisfactoriness, however, the central point emerging from the debate is clear enough and plainly demanded greater clarification from both parties. That is the relation of divine and human in the human speech of both preacher and theologian. It is for this reason that the issue of preaching is not an irrelevance, but constitutes a most important contribution to the discussion of the identity of Christianity. What needs to be discussed in relation to preaching is whether or not we have to do with the powerful active presence of the word of God *in our own day*. Barth is surely correct to parallel the issue of preaching with the question of the 'miracle' of the eucharistic sacrament.[42] If one is to believe in contemporary miracles at all, the divine presence in the eucharistic elements is plainly a less demanding form of belief. Unlike the proclamation of a human preacher, the elements of bread and wine do not lend themselves to critical or hostile analysis of various kinds. Both the onus and the scandal of preaching is patently greater than that of 'performing' the miracle of transubstantiation.

In future years Barth was entirely to dispense with the somewhat minimizing tone with which he discussed the Eucharist, and to argue for the restoration of a weekly Eucharist, as both Luther and Calvin had urged.[43] But at no stage did preaching cease to be central to his thought, although, as we shall see, in the later volumes of the *Church Dogmatics* the word 'preaching' is allowed to fall into the background, behind the more all-encompassing notion of the whole prophetic task of the Church.[44]

It was in Berlin, whilst an enthusiastic student–admirer of Harnack's, that Barth bought his copy of Schleiermacher's speeches *On Religion*, edited by Rudolf Otto.[45] The process of separation from his earlier theological masters entailed an alienation from Schleiermacher. Antipathy to human religiosity and desire for a satisfactory account of God's sovereignty led Barth, in his speeches and commentary on *Romans*, to warn readers against Schleiermacher. It is, however, interesting to hear that when in the winter of 1923–4 he lectured on Schleiermacher, he interpreted him in the light of his sermons.[46] He was, therefore, in an excellent position to review Emil Brunner's exceptionally hostile Schleiermacher book, *Die Mystik und das Wort* (1924), which he did with a certain reserve, not sharing the terms of Brunner's unqualified rejection. Subsequently, Barth returned frequently to deal with themes from Schleiermacher's writing, often with very considerable insight.

Barth's rejection of Schleiermacher is rooted in a number of considerations, of which two are of prime importance for our purposes. In the first place, he greatly objects to the argument of the introduction to *The Christian Faith*, where Schleiermacher sets out, as an explanation of the method and structure of his book a series of considerations drawn from other disciplines. It is precisely these other disciplines (of ethics, philosophy of religion and philosophical theology) which provide Schleiermacher with the terms of his definition of the essence of

Christianity. Barth directly contradicts Schleiermacher at this point. The prolegomena to dogmatics are, he says, part of dogmatics itself. Schleiermacher, in developing his understanding of piety, of the higher self-consciousness and of the Church as a body devoted to promoting piety, has not developed a neutral conceptuality in terms of which the substance of Christian doctrine can be rendered. Rather he has taken over some earlier heretical doctrinal thinking, traceable, Barth believes, to seventeenth-century English congregationalism.[47]

Secondly, Barth believed that Schleiermacher had been mesmerized by the romantic 'principle of the centre', the realm in which the contradictions and tensions between finite and infinite, or between knowing and acting, are harmonized and brought into unity.[48] According to Barth, Schleiermacher craved a haven of peace and reconciliation in which there would be no ambiguity; he found it in piety, in religious self-consciousness. This higher realm contains within itself a necessary reference to the transcendent. Barth acknowledges that it is Schleiermacher's intention at this point to speak not merely of human faith but of the Holy Spirit. At the end of his life, in a remarkable review of his relationship to Schleiermacher's massive theological achievement, he specifically raised the, for him, unresolved question of the propriety of a Spirit-centred theology on the lines of Schleiermacher.[49]

If Barth's ultimate verdict on Schleiermacher's stance as a whole is ambiguous there is no mistaking the firmness of the objection which he advances to the definition of an essence in Christianity. This, as we have seen, is integral to Schleiermacher's whole treatment of religion, and was the most heatedly discussed topic of the early years of the twentieth century. To Barth's response to the quest for the essence of Christianity we accordingly turn.

II

Barth's dismissal of Protestantism's attempt to speak of, or to define, the essence of Christianity is brief and categorical: 'The Word of God may not be replaced even vicariously by any basic interpretation [he uses the Schleiermacherian word, *Grundanschauung*] of the "essence of Christianity", however pregnant, deep and well-founded.'[50] The sentence makes abundantly clear that the reason for abandoning this form of theological construction lies in the view Barth takes of the word of God, the subject indeed of the whole second introductory volume to the *Church Dogmatics* (1/2). It is the 'freedom of obedience' imposed by that word which makes questionable the entire tradition of systematic theology proceeding from the adoption of a *Grundanschauung*.[51] This is yet another statement of Barth's challenge to Schleiermacher, and all that followed from him.

The question to which Barth is attempting to give an answer in this passage is whether dogmatic method requires a system. No, he replies, because system tends to mean the presupposition of 'a concretely formulated first principle or a whole series of principles', followed by a development consisting of an analysis of it or them.[52] But how can such a procedure allow for obedience to the word of God? At best it can only result in a more or less faithful attempt to derive the principle or principles from the word of God. But the correct question to ask is, according to Barth, By what right is this derivation made?

Barth then produces a whole series of examples from the late nineteenth and early twentieth centuries of different theological 'basic principles'. He implies that their very diversity cancels out their authority, and he adds:

> Is it not almost comical to see how, after many authors had long enough boasted of their christocentric dogmatics, it occurred to someone to present his as theocentric, whereupon someone else preferred to be 'staurocentric', and someone else again 'hamartio-centric'? What next?[53]

This caustic observation of the sheer arbitrariness of the rival theologians scrambling to acquire patent rights over ever new terminology reminds one at once of Newman's criticism of the same (Protestant) phenomenon.[54] As for Newman, so for Barth, the individual theologian is not in a position to survey and control the subject matter of the discipline. That has already been given; it is a *datum*, which for both is constituted, although in somewhat different style, by the prior act of God in Jesus Christ.

> The object, which must dictate dogmatic method, is the Word of God itself. It is not a conception of it. It is not, therefore, a basic

dogma, tenet, principle or definition of the essence of Christianity. It is not any kind of truth that can be controlled.[55]

How then is the word of God the basis, foundation and centre of dogmatics (Barth, as we shall see, is to speak more precisely of the reconciling work of God as the centre), without there being a corresponding central or foundational *conception*? Something of the same problem had already haunted Newman in his attempt to escape from mere arbitrariness. His critics, indeed, were quick to point out the apparent fogginess of his idea of Christianity. Was this 'idea' any less arbitrary than the solutions of those he criticized? Was he simply not profiting from the relative lack of clarity in his own portrayal of the identity of Christianity, whilst operating a reductive procedure on the efforts of others? It is with similar problems in mind that we must press the question on Barth, how the word of God can be central to dogmatics without there being a central *concept* in dogmatics. The answer takes us to some of the most fundamental aspects of Barth's whole theological endeavour.

In the first place, dogmatics has to be governed, according to Barth, by obedience to the word of God. Observation of the human tendency to want to control the content of revelation is absolutely fundamental to Barth's understanding of his own place in the history of theology. At numerous points in the dogmatics he sets his own position, usually, though not invariably, in agreement with Luther or Calvin, especially the latter, over against Roman Catholicism on the one hand (a sacralized version of Christianity) and Liberal Protestantism on the other (a secularized version).[56] Not infrequently also he is able to show that Protestant orthodoxy of the later sixteenth and seventeenth centuries, is also guilty of trying to ossify (and thus control) the gains of the Reformers.[57] Thus to speak of the word of God, is 'to speak about a being and event which are not under human control and foresight'.[58] If we speak of the Bible as the word of God, we should not thereby turn it into a 'paper Pope', an 'instrument of human power'.[59] In particular we should note and beware the transformation of the authority and freedom of the word of God into a form of theological dictatorship.[60]

To speak of the word of God is *always* to speak of an event. 'It is not to contemplate a state or a fact but to watch an event

... an act of God which rests on a free decision.'[61] This principle of Barth's theology is applicable to all three forms of the word of God, to the Word incarnate, to the Bible and to Christian preaching. Concerning the first there is no difficulty in recognizing the event character of the incarnation. More difficulty attends the second and third forms. But here Barth is equally insistent. The Bible is the word of God as it becomes concretely and miraculously the grace of God in a particular human existence. The same argument is applied to preaching. And it is precisely here that dogmatics is located; dogmatics is 'the effort and concern of the Church for the purity of its doctrine. Its problem is essentially the problem of Christian preaching.'[62] But pure doctrine is itself also, somewhat strangely, said to be an event, not a text or a series of formulae or a theological system. The Church has to work hard at dogmatics, both in order to submit its preaching to searching enquiry, and to prepare the preacher to speak the truth; but if the truth is spoken, that is a particular event, 'an action of the Holy Ghost in the Church', which can not be controlled by human beings.[63] It is important for us to note here, in parenthesis, how closely interrelated for Barth are the themes of the word of God and of the problem of divine and human power, as we shall have cause to develop them below.

Dogmatics, then, is a discipline developed in the service of the Church. Because there is inherent ambiguity in the human words of Scripture and in the human words of preaching[64] there has to be a critical and clarifying discipline midway between exegesis (*explicatio*) and practical theology (*applicatio*).[65] The remarks on ambiguity pick up a theme which, as we noted in Chapter 1, is one of the major causes of conflict in the Church. Barth plainly accepts the implication that ambiguity attends human language. He also recognizes the internal diversity of Scripture.[66] But though he plainly realizes that conflict is inevitable,[67] he rejects it as a peripheral matter in order to emphasize the clarity of the word of God in Scripture, and the unequivocal character of pure doctrine in preaching.[68] The existence of ambiguity is actually said to be virtually intolerable, because the Church has received a promise that the word of God would be identical with Christian proclamation.[69] This is what determines the task of dogmatics, which is to assist the realization of that promise by on the one hand criticizing the Church's present proclamation, and by preparing the Church for the better performance of its task of witness to the deed of God.

Dogmatics is not, however, a timelessly fixed discipline. It does not consist in the discovery and canonization of propositions which express pure doctrine without error or ambiguity. This follows necessarily from the event character of the word of God. The Church is in a state of constant expectation of the contemporary occurrence of the unambiguous word of God. Its only weapon is that of 'continually listening'.[70] 'The hearing which dogmatics must demand from the teaching Church is a fresh hearing of the promise which is the basis of the Church and its message. The Word of God became flesh.'[71]

In consequence of the above position, Barth consistently argues that the writing of church dogmatics cannot be carried out according to a prescribed method. The dogmatician is a person who has to train him- or herself in both listening to the word of God, and in full involvement in the contemporary life of the Church. 'The content of dogmatics can only be an exposition of the work and action of God as it takes place in his Word.'[72] This action takes place under no human restrictions or controls; it is theonomous, an event reflecting the divine freedom. Dogmatics is autonomous from the human point of view, when by free human decision the work of God is allowed to take place within it. Neither Bible, nor confession nor Church can occupy the place reserved for the word of God alone. And the inner obedience of the theologian to that word can never be represented in objective law. There is no established theological method by which dogmatics can be made obedient. 'It is the gift of grace and of the Holy Spirit which must come from God, so that man can take it into account only as a presupposition for which he must pray.'[73]

The position which Barth occupies on the identity of Christianity could be described without any exaggeration, in the light of the above, as the apotheosis of the inwardness tradition. He recognizes, of course, that the phenomenon of Christianity exists in its various human, external features, Scriptures, law, rites, confessional documents, and ministerial offices. But none of these are anything other than ambiguous. Christianity is only truly Christianity if it attends, and in so far as it attends, to the word of God. Moreover, and this is the decisive point, this obedient attention cannot be guaranteed by any external observance whatsoever. It can only be prayed for. It is internal obedience, the obedience of the heart. That is the human side of the phenomenon. From the standpoint of the divine gift of grace, the maintenance of the true identity of Christianity is entirely the free operation of God's Holy Spirit, subject to no human control.

At once, however, a puzzle arises. For according to my analysis of the debate about the essence of Christianity, that whole attempt arises directly out of the problem of inwardness. How, then, can Barth reject the essence of Christianity tradition as the very obverse of inwardness, an unacceptable example of objectification and of human control in theology? The answer in fact confirms the depiction of Barth which we have offered. Barth regards the essence of Christianity tradition as objectivizing because he has taken up a still more extreme version of the inwardness position. Pure doctrine as an event, according to Barth, is a divinely caused event. From the human side nothing guarantees the occurrence. One may work hard for it in wholehearted obedience, but because it is dependent upon a gift of the Spirit pure doctrine can never submit to any form of human encapsulation. Even the quest for the essence of Christianity, which was the result of a recognition of the disturbing presence of the inwardness tradition upon still more objectivizing interpretations of Christianity's persisting identity, must be, from Barth's more radical standpoint, unacceptably rigid. What, in effect, Barth has done is to take Troeltsch's later thought about the changing essence of Christianity, and further radicalize it. There is, and can be, no external expression of the invariable and persisting identity of Christianity, according to Barth; this identity consists solely and entirely in the unchangeable character of the word of God. If human words and deeds realize that identity, they do so only as the Holy Spirit himself acts in the Church, at particular times and places.

We may further confirm that this is indeed how Barth ought to be interpreted by observing precisely how he treats the history of the essence of Christianity discussion. In a typical excursus he traces back the origin of the 'thin formulae by which later neo-Protestantism thought it could grasp the so-called "essence of Christianity" to the doctrine of the fundamental articles in later

Protestant orthodoxy'.[74] The examples he gives are the orthodox Lutheran, Johann Andreas Quenstedt (1617–88) and the Genevan Calvinist, François Turrettini (1623–87). The first of these claims to have identified what he termed the *fundamentum dogmaticum*, that is, that part of theology referable to no other part, but upon which all other elements of the dogmatics depend. Quenstedt describes this as consisting in propositions existing in a sort of aseity above other dogmas, articles and formulae, and subdivided into primary and secondary fundamental articles, the first of which we must know if we are to be saved, the second which we may not safely deny.[75]

To discuss the origin and history of the fundamental articles tradition would be a labour far beyond what is required here.[76] But it should be noted that it is disputed that this derivation, commonly enough made, is in fact correct.[77] At the very least we may take it as established that the eighteenth- and nineteenth-century debate about the essence of Christianity is not exclusively to be traced to the fundamental articles tradition. To be fair to Barth he does not purport to give a complete history. His point is, rather, that what once existed in Protestantism as an attempt to identify the fundamentals finished up as a very minimizing affair indeed.

In fact the evidence for this contention is even better than he realizes. For J. A. Turrettini, the son of François, issued in his *Nubes testium* of 1719 (dedicated to Archbishop William Wake) a clarion call to the Protestant churches to unite on the basis of fundamental articles.[78] This Turrettini had been directly influenced by Locke, whose redefinition of the fundamentals of the faith provided for many the *locus classicus* of the rationalistic reductionism of the eighteenth century.[79]

But that is not to say that it is adequate to characterize the entire essence of Christianity tradition as reductionist. To go no further, it is quite certainly inadequate as a description of Schleiermacher's complex and sensitive treatment of the question. If we are to explain Barth's mistake here, apart from a perfectly understandable lack of adequate historical information, it must surely be ascribed to the perspective on the essence tradition inevitable to someone standing in his position. From the standpoint of radical inwardness it would necessarily appear to be the case that propositions about the essence of Christianity represent an objectification in external form of the identity of Christianity. To prove his point Barth would naturally refer to the fundamental articles tradition which is capable of being one of the most static, objectifying and (as Barth pertinently observes) more or less arbitrary ways of specifying Christianity.[80] He is selectively blind to the other elements which also contribute to the essence tradition.

One further matter is noteworthy in Barth's treatment of this issue. His contention is that there is a 'basis, foundation and centre' to dogmatics.[81] This centre is the *present* event of the word of God, the contemporary happening in which God is God in truth and in power. 'It is round this event that the whole doctrine of Holy Scripture circles, and with it all Church dogmatics, and, with it too, preaching and the sacrament of Church proclamation.'[82] Quite apart from the metaphysical problem of time implicit in this assertion of a single divine event,[83] there remains the obvious question why there should not be a central concept or concepts corresponding to the event. If the event is to be spoken or thought about at all, it will surely be amenable to conceptualization. If there is a particular event which is spoken of as determining the discipline of dogmatics, will not dogmatics be centred upon the appropriate conception of that event? This Barth most emphatically denies, as we shall see in the next section. Here, by way of transition, we may usefully observe his delicate treatment of Protestant orthodoxy's assertion of a conceptually precise foundation.

Barth is, in fact, ready to recognize that there must always be some elements of dogma which are more important, and some which are less.[84] Quenstedt's *fundamentum dogmaticum* might be taken to correspond to the Church's ever-necessary task of addressing itself to the present. This would amount to the Church's responsibility for confession; and confession always necessitates 'a certain selection from the wealth of biblical truth and reality'.[85] Moreover dogmatics has, to a certain extent, got to be the work (and thus reflect the confession) of an individual. What then *is* Barth's objection to Quenstedt's procedure? If this element of particularity in the Church's and the individual theologian's situation and view is inevitable, how can there not be a conceptualized expression of the most important element in a dogmatics?

Barth's answer throws us back, once again, to his fundamental position. Nothing must supervene between dogmatics and the word of God.

> Traditional notions as to what is fundamental or not, central or peripheral, more or less important, have to be suspended, so that they can become a matter for vital new decision by the Word of God itself.[86]

Distinctions and choices will be made, but may not 'anticipate the fresh discrimination which the Word of God may make at any time'. High orthodoxy's doctrine of the *fundamentum dogmaticum*, like its doctrine of holy Scripture, became, according to Barth, a prison; it was the result of an arbitrary human action, and resulted in the imposition of 'a human system of beliefs'.[87]

What is particularly striking in this objection is Barth's insertion of the word 'traditional'. The *fundamentum dogmaticum* is not, however, necessarily traditional. Barth's objection to traditionalism, or the ossifying of dogma in allegedly invariable propositional statements, certainly does not meet the case. Why should not the fundamentals be precisely those doctrines which at a given time seem to a particular theologian to reflect the significance of the event of Jesus Christ for a particular context? Why should there not be a conceptual discipline, namely dogmatic theology, which systematically organizes itself according to a particular theologian's conception of what Christianity essentially is? Barth's considered rejection of this possibility was to await the publication of volume IV of the *Church Dogmatics*, and his further elucidation of 'the centre of theology'.

III

Proposition 57, opening volume *IV* of the *Church Dogmatics* on the doctrine of reconciliation, reads as follows:

> The subject matter, origin and content of the message received and proclaimed by the Christian community is at its heart the free act of the faithfulness of God in which he takes the lost cause of man ...[88]

To speak, with Barth, of the 'centre' or 'heart' of theology and of church proclamation is manifestly to use a metaphor. What does it mean to speak of the heart of the subject matter of dogmatics? According to Barth, this centre is, in fact, not occupied but empty, 'like the opening in the centre of a wheel'.[89] To receive the true consequences of there being such a centre in theology, the theologian has first and foremost to be obedient and open to the word of God. He may not be a *systematic* theologian, because such obedience precludes a system. Openness, vigilance against premature closure, confidence in the power of the object of theology, lack of anxiety and a presupposition that the promise given to the Church will be fulfilled, these are all characteristics of a properly 'centred' theologian. 'Dogmatic method consists essentially in the expectation that there will eventually be this purification and the consequent emergence of the essence of Christianity.'[90] This is Barth's only positive use of the formula, essence of Christianity, and it is ineluctably future-oriented. We do not possess this essence; we may not guess at it, nor hypothesize about it; if we leave it genuinely open then God himself will confirm or refine what we have done. To adopt the open centre of dogmatics means, simply, that the dogmatician honours, fears and loves the work of God in his word above everything else.[91]

Barth points us, in general illustration of correct dogmatic method in operation, to the example of Calvin.[92] Specifically against the supposedly more scholarly method of fundamental articles, Barth sets Melanchthon's and Calvin's method of *Loci*, or topics 'which did not pretend ... to be rooted and held together in any higher system than that of the Word of God'.[93] Nor did Calvin follow Luther in making (at least according to some interpreters) the doctrine of justification by faith the centre of this theology.[94] What he did was to gather in a certain arrangement the topics which the faith itself seems to require, adequately interrelated inasmuch as all refer to the confession of Jesus Christ, but not systematically deduced from one basic principle.

By the time Barth came to the *Church Dogmatics* he had already argued with Harnack about the sense in which Jesus is the centre of the gospel.[95] Barth here emphatically denied that it is the so-called 'historical Jesus', as reconstructed by biblical scholars working behind the text, which is the centre of theology.[96] The biblical object is not a human creation, especially not one brought into being by the theological professoriate. But a more far-reaching discovery had been made by Barth, so he believed, in his work on Anselm. Here he acquired and articulated the grounds for his assertion of the epistemological control established by the object of faith over the knowing of faith by a believer. The theologian does not master the object of faith, but is mastered by it, and thus achieves true rationality, the *intellectus fidei*, 'a real comprehension of the ontic *ratio* of faith'.[97]

Armed with this confidence, Barth subsequently described the investigations carried out in the Anselm book as 'a vital key, if not the key, to the understanding of that whole process of thought that has impressed me more and more in my *Church Dogmatics* as the only one proper to theology'.[98] The point may be briefly characterized as follows: In Anselm's work there are three uses of the term *ratio*. One applies to human rationality, 'man's knowing *ratio*'; the second to the rationality proper to the object of faith; but a third, on which he particularly focuses and which conditions the other two, is the *ratio veritatis*, the rationality of God. There is, says Barth, an ultimate *ratio* in creation, the divine rationality, in which all created things participate. Knowledge of creation by human beings, therefore, has to be by means of the action of the Truth, that is God himself. This is what Barth terms the 'noetic *ratio*'. One cannot ascribe to human rationality apart from this *ratio* a creative or normative status. But in addition to the noetic *ratio*, there is an 'ontic *ratio*', which is the truth conferred on the object in its creation. The only question is whether that truth is recognized or not. As far as the object of faith is concerned its truth is rooted in itself, and has to be acknowledged as such, though it may not be fully displayed in any one act of recognition.

> In the *Credo* and in the Bible it is hidden and must reveal itself in order to make itself known to us. It does this, however, only if and in so far as the Truth, God Himself, does it. Thus: from time to time in the event of knowing, it happens that the noetic *ratio* of the *veritas* conforms to the ontic and to that extent is or is not *vera ratio* – or (and this is normally the case *in praxi*) is to some extent *aliquatenus*.[99]

The last word of this quotation is important. Barth is not stating that by the act of God human beings may acquire absolute confidence in the pure rationality of all claims they may make for knowledge of God. Knowledge of God is an event brought about by God; but normally speaking that knowledge only achieves the desired conformity to its object *to some extent*.[100] But to what extent? The claim which is made for the rationality of a particular event of knowing sounds very strong, if it must also be claimed that conformity between human knowing and divine truth can occur only as a result of the divine activity. But the qualification *aliquatenus* returns us to the normal human realm of ambiguity and uncertainty. It is this same mixture of confidence and humility which sounds throughout the *Church Dogmatics*.[101] For the theologian above all else must seek the conformity of his or her noetic *ratio* with the ontic *ratio* of the word of God. A dogmatics which fails to make the claim that this conformity has actually taken place condemns itself to irrelevance. But, in practice, despite the claim, the most likely outcome of any specific theology is that the *vera ratio* of God himself is only expressed to some extent. Barth believes that he is in a position to say what theological method has imposed itself upon him in accordance with his understanding of obedience to God. But such method is not a law for others. It can only be a challenge or a suggestion to which attention may well need to be paid. Dogmatic method has to remain open.[102]

It is in this sense that Barth declines to use the description 'systematics' of this theology, preferring the term 'dogmatics'. Thus although the atoning work of Christ is the centre of dogmatics, it is the *act*, not the *doctrine* of atonement which is said to be central. Moreover, this is the sense in which Barth is ready to affirm that the word of God is the being (*Sein*) of the Church, and thus the heart of church dogmatics,[103] or that all theology must be christologically determined.[104] Christology is by no means to be separated from the work of Christ, and when he speaks of the 'word' of God, Barth understands word as act.[105] For him the most comprehensive statement is that revelation is the same thing as atonement.[106] This means that everything in dogmatics has to be understood 'together with this centre and with constant reference to it';[107] but it does not mean that the atonement is the *Grundanschauung*, as Schleiermacher believed.

Thus, for Barth there is a special doctrine of God not subordinated to a doctrine of atonement; there is a doctrine of creation which is not a mere preface to atonement; and there is a doctrine of God as redeemer, which is more than a mere appendix. These doctrines are not subordinated to, but co-ordinated with, atonement by reason of their common origin in the word of God. The point at the centre at which these doctrines are said to be one is invisible.[108] Extending his metaphor of centre, Barth likens the open centre at the heart of theology to a ring, the periphery of which is the word of God; from this periphery there are a certain number of lines to be drawn, constituting the substance of dogmatics.[109] But there is no comprehensive enclosure of the whole. Dogmatics is not a systematic totality.

What is the significance of this attempt to speak of a 'centre' in theology for our enquiry into the identity of Christianity? Briefly put, the answer is that Barth has tried at once to occupy a highly conservative stance in most theological questions whilst at the same time being a most radical representative of the inwardness tradition. To emphasize inwardness is, as we have noted, generally a means of facilitating a critical distance from the tradition in all its external forms. Barth accepts this consequence, and will not allow traditional dogma to determine his theology;[110] but at the same time his dogmatics *is* highly conservative. And the root of that conservatism is unquestionably the determination that the theologian should be obedient to the word of God. It is, for Barth, a matter of who is to be master. Does the theologian follow Schleiermacher and play upon Christianity 'as a virtuoso plays upon his fiddle', with a sense of free mastery?[111] Or does he follow the more demanding path, as Barth thought it, of utter obedience and responsible servanthood. It is, in other words, ultimately a question of power, of who is thought to be in control.

IV

As we have already observed more than once, there is, for Barth, a very close connection between his doctrine of the word of God and the question of the relation of divine and human power in the Church.[112] The reason for this is the desire, manifest throughout Barth's life, to convey a doctrine of the sovereignty of God. The gospel is the power of God unto salvation (Rom. 1.16), the gospel of the resurrection of Jesus Christ, apprehended and lived in the power of the Holy Spirit.

In developing this doctrine of freedom in the Church, a Church living by the word of God, Barth specifically develops the theme of the power of the word of God, a power which enters the battleground of human history as a competing and limiting power.[113] This is a hidden power, but one ultimately guaranteed to be victorious, demonstrating in the present its freedom and superiority in maintaining itself against attack, in constantly proving its distinctiveness, in assimilating alien elements and in its adaptability to different contexts.[114] Its sphere of influence is, of course, the Church, which it brings into being and maintains. There is a twofold powerful activity of the word, in overcoming human resistance to the obedience demanded of faith, and in the reconciliation of humanity with God and with each other.[115] Barth, in a later volume of the *Church Dogmatics*, relates all this to the Holy Spirit:

> The power of this Word is the power of His Holy Spirit. As this power shines in divine power and is at work in the world, there takes place in the world and its occurrence the new and strange event of the Christian community. As Jesus Christ in the power of the Holy Spirit, or the Holy Spirit as His Spirit, creates recognition, establishes knowledge, calls to confession and therefore quickens the dead, the existence of the community begins and endures.[116]

The Holy Spirit is powerfully active in the community, but the community itself has no power over it.

But the basis of all Barth proposes to say about power in the Church lies in the Christology of the *Church Dogmatics* IV/2. Having treated in IV/1 the priestly work of the Son of God (the Lord as servant, in his humiliation and obedience), the way is open for a development of the kingly work of Christ (the servant as Lord). The theme is the exaltation of the humanity of Jesus to participation in the being and lordship of God, acting as Head, Representative and Saviour of all humanity.[117] It is in this context that the theme of power receives its most explicit and remarkable development.

Jesus receives power. The way Barth speaks of this is fundamentally as 'grace addressed to human essence in Jesus Christ'.

But it is empowering to carry out his work as Mediator and Reconciler. All the acts which are carried out to accomplish the reconciliation of God and humanity are not manifestations of naked divine power, but consist in the identity of the Son of God with the man Jesus of Nazareth. 'This means that this divine power, all power in heaven and on earth, is given to this man in His identity with the Son of God.'[118]

But the giving of power to Jesus is a giving to human essence the task of serving divine power. 'Divine authority has also the form of human authority.'[119] Human essence does not possess the power, as such. That is crucial for all that Barth has to say about power in the Church. But the human essence mediates, attests, bears and serves divine authority. Thus there is a purely human history of Jesus which is necessary if God's work is to be done. And in the doing of this work the human essence common to all is empowered and exalted, acquiring even in its weakness and meanness divine authority and power.[120]

This is the essential christological background for the following section of the *Church Dogmatics* which attempts to answer the question, What is the power of the existence of the man Jesus Christ for his disciples? Here, of course, Barth is obliged to be specific, since power in the Church is, at least on the face of it, subject to observation. What account is he to give of the empowering of the Christian? The basis of the power which flows from Jesus is the resurrection, in which we are set on a new beginning.[121] But Barth strongly presses the question what it really means to say that we are in Christ, and the answer is given in the reality of a new direction or determination of human existence. A remarkable paean of praise is sung to the power of this transformation.[122] It is no mechanical force, nor power of nature, nor one cosmic force among others; it is 'absolutely unique as the power of the resurrection of Jesus Christ'.[123] It is light, liberation, knowledge, peace and many other things, but especially life, 'an exalted human life'.[124] Not to be understood as pure inwardness, it has a necessarily external character; it is body as well as soul. It is the work of the Holy Spirit dwelling within a person and controlling 'the centre and basis of his human existence, the axiom of his freest thinking and utterance, the origin of his freest vocation and action, in short the principle of his spontaneous being'.[125]

We have given only a brief account of a long and important treatment of the theme of power. But it is apparent at once that, for all Barth's concern to give the genuine meaning of the Christology and Pneumatology he has embraced, he has a real problem in being entirely specific. The transition from Christ to the Christian is the focus of his prolonged attention and he honestly wrestles with the question. But to what effect? A theologian, says Barth, ought not to be either a sceptic or a spectator. If, however, one stares naively and a little critically at the outcome of his hypnotic prose, what emerges most concretely is Barth's sense of confidence in the ultimate significance of Christian faith. The New Testament confidently assumes the reality of the power of the Spirit at work in the Christian community and in Christians; Barth will do likewise.[126] We have already seen with what confidence Barth expects the purification of Christianity as a result of faithful and obedient work by theologians.[127] It is not for nothing that in 1966, in celebration of Barth's eightieth birthday, a collection of essays was published under the single title, *Parrhesia*, confidence. But is the confidence justified? It is more than a little disarming when Barth honestly admits that the New Testament description of the effect of conversion on the person has 'the smack of hyperbole and even illusion' about it.[128] Only if we refer these grand statements to Jesus Christ, can we allow 'the little movements of our own inner and outer life' to be spoken of as effects of divine power.[129] But we should note that it is this parallelism of language which permits the most far-reaching claims to be made of divine power, whilst very little concretely emerges concerning its human effects. Confidence may well be the result of conceiving the divine power to be great. But what is the difference between that and a less exalted theological rendering, if the effects are no different?

The problem of parallel language emerges with still greater clarity in Barth's writing about the Church. The history of Christians is a 'central history' in which God is at work in his own proper cause, ruling at the heart of world occurrence.[130] The origin of the history is Jesus, its goal is Christendom, and its centre is the Holy Spirit, the source and power of the transition from Christ to Christendom.[131]

There is both an external and an internal deployment of this power. In relation to the external power of the Church in society, Barth's most characteristic thoughts are that the power is concealed and that it is opposed to all forms of compulsion.[132] The Church is not in itself a body visibly triumphant in world history, nor may Christians in their service of witness to the power of God oppose force with force.[133] The most to which Barth will commit himself, in discussing the place of law in the Church, is that by exemplifying the law of service the Church may point to the truth of the claim that Jesus Christ exercises the power to rule in the world.[134]

For obvious reasons the discussion of the internal exercise of power occupies a greater amount of Barth's attention. As a Protestant theologian he is conscious of the extreme danger of power in the Church, which in due course he identifies as the twin perils of sacralization and secularization. By sacralization he means the Church's claim to be the earthly-historical form of Jesus Christ. This is a disastrous error.

> The community is not Christ, nor is it the Kingdom of God. It is the very last purpose of the Lordship and glory of Jesus Christ (which it has to proclaim) to exalt these little men, Christendom, above all others; to set them in the right against the world; to invest them with authority and power; to magnify them in the world.[135]

Throughout the *Church Dogmatics* a running battle is conducted with the hierarchical concept of the ministry. Barth is fascinated by the process by which the doctrine of the presence of Christ transforms itself into the doctrine of the Vicar of Christ, who exercises Christ's lordship over the Church.[136] Diametrically opposed to this, his own understanding of ministry makes permanent hierarchy impossible. The government of the Church is solely by the word of God; that is no decorative flower of speech. In a remarkable passage Barth insists that the establishment of any other form of rule is a denial of the time in which the Church lives, between the ascension and the second coming; this is the time in which the government of the Church can only be determined by the word of God in the Scriptures, the Scriptures received and interpreted by the whole Church, not by a special élite of scripture scholars.[137] Of course there are scholars and there are teachers, but the Church as a whole is both a hearing and a teaching Church. 'Theologians cannot teach except as the mouthpiece of the congregation of Jesus Christ . . . of those who, as listeners, are themselves teachers.'[138]

Barth's awareness of the danger inherent in the internal distribution of power in the Church is well developed. But it does not extend to a denial of the need for canon law in the Church. On the contrary, he gives long and sophisticated consideration to the means whereby what he terms a 'brotherly christocracy' may be maintained.[139] Specifically against Sohm and Brunner he argues the necessity of the Church's existence in a specifically constituted form, and maintains that church law must be a law of service, with its roots specifically in liturgy, reformable and exemplary.[140] Canon law is necessary in the worshipping community, but it is not in the end enforceable. What Barth has given with one hand, he takes away with the other. The community is constituted by the baptized, but the baptismal qualification is inseparable from trust and confidence in the reality of the individual's desire for baptism.[141] The power of canon law cannot be established apart from this mutual confidence; but conversely the presence of this confidence gives the law a spiritual power no worldly law can ever have.[142]

What, for Barth, is the power of the theologian? We have already seen the warning given against an intellectual élite of biblical scholars. There is another well-developed aspect of Barth's work which ascribes to prayer, especially to the worship of the community, a vital role.[143] He emphasizes that the sacraments are included in the gospel, specifically to indicate that 'pure doctrine' is not a merely intellectual matter.[144]

Nonetheless the 'pull' of Barth's theological position is emphatically in the other direction. He strongly insists that speech is the primary category in which the proclamation of the Church is to be expounded. And the role which he assigns to the intellectually demanding work of Christian dogmatics is the twofold task of correcting errors in the Church's present proclamation of the gospel, and preparing for a more faithful future proclamation. Theologians, therefore, occupy the vital centre where criteria are clarified and applied, and the groundwork for the Church's ministry is prepared.

Of course, as we have continually observed, Barth denies that human beings *possess* the power of the word. It is not handed over to them simply to wield. But 'the question of the Church's ministry is decided in dogmatics'.[145] Bad dogmatics leads to bad preaching. Is this mere *hybris*, Barth muses? Not at all, he replies, provided that we recognize good dogmatics to be a matter of the free grace of God and the work of the whole Church not of one professor.[146] However, a page later Barth is again insisting that nothing whatever in the Church's life escapes the control of dogmatics.[147] Given the fact that professors of theology organize the theological curriculum, write theological text books, train ministers and future theologians, write references and vote on appointing committees, and are much in demand in church congresses and commissions, it appears on the face of it that nothing escapes the control not merely of dogmatics, but of dogmaticians.

How is it that Barth avoids making, indeed strenuously denies, so vulgar a deduction? The answer lies in what I have already called the parallelism of his language. Discussing the relationship between the being of Jesus Christ and the being of the Christian community, Barth insists on the term 'co-ordination'.[148] It is by the power of the Holy Spirit that this co-ordination occurs, so that Jesus is at once the Head of the community and its body in time and history. The holding together of eternal reality and temporal present is not a matter of identification, intermingling or confounding, nor is it changing one into the other, but a work of co-ordination, of making them parallel, and thus of bringing them into unity.[149]

Because they are parallel, divine power and human power can be said to have no features in common. Consider the following passage:

> The Christian community ... knows that it owes its origin and continuation to a very definite power, to the constant working of which it is totally directed for its own future. The power of its human and creaturely being and action, which it also has, is not to be recognized in this basic power, *nor is any other power which it might even partially control*. It can only acknowledge, recognize and confess it as the free power of God which does in fact establish and direct it in superiority from without.[150]

Parallelism, so expressed, is extraordinarily useful to Barth. It enables him to be at once utterly matter-of-fact, down-to-earth and historical in his affirmation of the sociological necessities under which the Church lives. But at the same time he is also able to be utterly theological and transcendent in the claims made for the power of God, of the word of God, and of the Holy Spirit.

This parallelism is reflected in Barth's political activities and disposition. The political rhetoric of revolution in the first edition of his commentary on Romans does not prevent him from a routine condemnation of power politics as basically dirty.[151] Contrary to the thesis which seeks to depict Barth as a strongly committed socialist, the evidence suggests that 'he aspired to a viewpoint too Olympian for politics'.[152] The consequence is that while a whole series of problems arise on the boundaries between the human and the divine, in such areas as politics, law, and church government, the humanly necessary solutions are simply not developed. Although everything is subordinated in Barth to the service which the community must render to God and to humanity, practical solutions to the difficulties are, in fact, left to pragmatism, so alarmed is Barth by the possibility of a controlling ideology.

Whether this parallelism is a strength or weakness will be variously estimated. The danger of Barth's writing, however, is surely the illusion which he unwittingly creates that he has dealt with the actual occurrence and exercise of power in the Church. Barth is so radical a representative of the inwardness tradition that nothing external can be said unequivocally to be an actual sign of the presence of divine power. What Barth seems not to appreciate is that not even confidence escapes this general impossibility, since that too can be psychologically generated. But if joyful confidence is a sure sign of the activity of the power of God at work, then there is no reason why he should hesitate with other similarly sociologically or psychologically perceptible traits, including the development of a church hierarchy and the recognition of a large quantity of social power in the office and work of a theologian. The Christian community and Christian individuals have in fact no alternative to channelling the power of God in and through psychological or sociological mechanisms. The language of sociology and the language of theology may be separate, but the reality of divine and human power is not. It is not parallel or merely co-ordinated; it is inevitably, and dangerously, mixed. Barth's treatment of the phenomenon of Christianity is remarkable in twentieth-century theology for the place which he assigns to the power of God, and for the subtlety with which he struggles to avoid an oversimple resolution of its difficulties. But in the end he leaves us with the concealment to which his parallelism leads. We have next to take up the challenge of a more balanced and realistic interpretation of the identity of Christianity, with which his remarkable achievement leaves us.

Part Three

9

Analysis of the Essence Discussion

I have made a group of 'early moderns' the centrepiece of this investigation into the identity of Christianity, because of my conviction that their discussion of the essence of Christianity is particularly instructive for our topic. But our close study of their respective arguments for or against the essence tradition has shown, if nothing else, the considerable complexity of this particular term and the variety of the uses to which it may be put.

Has anything been learnt, however, from this historical survey? Excruciating difficulties keep theologians in business, and the more ready they are with clear analyses and simple solutions the more otiose their own profession appears. Nonetheless it will obviously not do merely to wring one's hands about the perplexities surrounding the question of Christianity's identity. We need to understand both what the discussion has been about and why it has taken the precise form we have expounded. We require, in other words, a clear analysis.

The present chapter has three sections. In the first we shall refer back to the argument of the first three chapters of the book, and enquire whether and to what extent we were justified in prefacing our study of the 'early moderns' with largely biblical treatments of the themes of conflict, inwardness and power. The second section will deal with the motivations lying behind the task of attempts to resolve the problem of Christianity's essence in the nineteenth century. Then, finally, I shall propose a highly simplified interpretation of the available alternatives.

Inevitably description, analysis and prescription are inter-related activities. This is the point where, if anywhere, a justification will emerge for the method pursued in the early chapters, the particular choice made of theologians to examine, and the type of proposals to be made in the final chapters. Analysis does not necessarily make fascinating reading, but if any new door is to be opened on this peculiarly complex episode in Christian history this is the hinge on which it will swing.

I

The first justification has to concern itself with the diversity of forms of Christianity, even from its earliest days. The first chapter of this book dealt principally with the *inherence of conflict* in the actual accomplishment of what Christianity is about in the world. The point of the argument was to demonstrate that internal conflict between Christians with differing apprehensions of the gospel is not an anomalous or unusual phenomenon. On the contrary, it is, and always has been normal. Unity, peace and love are achieved by the containment of conflict within bounds, not by its elimination.

The reality of conflict between churches and between theologians in the modern western Christian Church is so obvious that we may be in danger of overlooking it. But plainly, one of the most prominent features of the essence discussion we have surveyed is the attempt to identify the source of that elusive unity by which the Christian Church may escape its fragmentation into warring sects. Schleiermacher's identification of the essence was, he believed, of an *Anziehungsprinzip*, a principle of *cohesion*.[1] It was, moreover, of potentially ecumenical significance, since, although there were indeed essences of, respectively, Catholicism and Protestantism, he held that they were due to be transcended in time.[2]

Conflict about the essence itself is, of course, ironic. Newman believed that the pontifications of Protestant theologians involving competitive and contradictory identifications of the essence were self-destructive.[3] So, also, did Barth.[4] And both Newman and Barth believed that there was a way in which mere arbitrariness could be transcended. Alas, their 'authoritative' verdicts on the issue, though similar, are by no means identical.

It was, moreover, the conflicting attempts to define the essence which drove Troeltsch to his sophisticated treatment of the methodology of essence definition. In this endeavour, however, he gets caught (so we argued) between his desire to affirm that reliable essence definition can be done by the highly qualified Protestant historians and his growing realization that all essence definition contains, in the end, a subjective *Zukunftsglaube* or belief for the future.[5] But Troeltsch is unquestionably right in his perception of the inherence of conflict in Christianity, which at a certain stage he schematizes in the form of a restless oscillation between two poles.[6] It is this very oscillation which causes him finally to abandon Harnack's idea of the essence as a kind of continuous 'red thread' in the medley of colours constituting Christian history.

There is, in other words, no way in which one can understand either what the essence tradition tried to achieve or the problems into which it ran unless one presupposes the existence and resolution of internal conflict in Christianity as an element in its background. That essence definition is in some sense too ambitious a project is the most obvious lesson to be learnt from the history. One cannot merely shrug off the complaint about the sheer arbitrariness of the competing claims, even if one suspects that the attempts to escape from arbitrariness are merely a higher form of this same characteristic, combined with elements of sheer evasiveness. In the next chapter an attempt will be made to explore a direct answer to the fact of conflict, which accepts it as inevitable but strives to set boundaries to it. This involves the argument that the essence of Christianity tradition should issue not in a single definition which purports to decide the matter, but in the delineation of boundaries in which different and competing claims can be made. How to treat the question of rival delineations of boundaries is the obvious, but by no means insoluble, objection, which we shall also have to consider.

The second introductory chapter concerned the Judaeo-Christian tradition about the heart. It is *the tradition of inwardness*, I argued, which makes it impossible to identify Christianity merely with its external features, whether myths, teaching, rites, or social embodiment. But at the same time the mysterious and elusive quality of conversion, whereby a person is transformed at the centre of his or her intentional life, precludes any definitive solution of the inherent conflicts about external features.

Our examination of the 'early moderns' abundantly confirms the importance of the tradition of inwardness for essence definition. Here again Schleiermacher leads the way. By arguing that the distinctiveness of a given religion consists in its *Glaubensweise*, its mode of faith, and by defining faith primarily in relation to consciousness of God, he makes the coherence of a religion depend on its inward shaping or toning of the human spirit. Moreover, by defining the essence of Christianity as redemption (*Erlösung*) and by giving to this notion the specific connotation of the setting free of the imprisoned God-consciousness, he ties essence definition to inwardness primarily and subordinates all externals to that.

It is with Schleiermacher too that it becomes explicit that there is an epistemological dimension to the inwardness tradition. Inwardness, as analysed by Schleiermacher, purports to give an answer to the question, How is a Christian conscious of God? It traces that consciousness to the immediacy and unity of feeling, a state prior to that of explicit knowledge. Moreover, he argues that every member of the whole human race has immediate, albeit darkened, access to God through the feeling of absolute dependence, and it is this presupposition which enables him to offer a hermeneutics not merely of the Christian tradition, but, in principle at least, of every religious tradition.

The relation of essence definition to the Enlightenment's 'turn to the subject' is, in fact, a commonplace of commentary upon the essence tradition.[7] The point, however, which needs particular emphasis is that essence definition, precisely because it is an attempt to resolve conflict about Christianity, turns naturally and literally to the 'heart of the matter'. In this it is not dependent on post-Enlightenment philosophical styles, nor even upon pietism.

The original meaning of the Greek term '*Christianismos*' confirms this. It is first used in the letters of Ignatius of Antioch to refer, not to an institution but to the manner of living of a true disciple, Christianness, including the disciple's reception of the gospel.[8] Much the same may be said of Gregory of Nyssa's celebrated 'definition' of Christianity: '*Christianismos* is imitation (*mimesis*) of the divine nature.'[9] This is by no means a casual remark; it expresses with the necessary economy the major element in Gregory's religious philosophy of the 'image', as at once the origin and goal of humanity.

As we saw in the chapter on inwardness, Augustine, like Gregory a theologian deeply imbued with Neoplatonic thought forms, is the chief mediator of the inwardness tradition to the West. The critical potential of this tradition was noted in Abelard, and it is obviously in the name of the true, inward nature of faith that Luther progressively distances himself from some of the major institutional embodiments of late medieval Catholicism. What we are dealing with, therefore, in the post-Enlightenment custom of referring the essence of Christianity to an inward disposition of the believer is an extremely long-standing gambit employed in the context of internal self-criticism, and also of platonic or platonizing philosophical presentations of Christianity.[10] In Schleiermacher both of these contexts coincide.

But it would be a mistake to restrict the essence to either of these contexts. In Harnack, for example, we have a historian whose basic concern is for the simplicity and power of the original message. He finds both, he believes, in the radical inwardness of Jesus' own gospel and the sheer effectiveness of his exemplification of it. At once, however, Harnack encounters a serious difficulty, of which his critics, not least Loisy, made much. The propositions in which he expresses Jesus' gospel of inwardness are open to being interpreted as permanent externals. Pure inwardness permanently eludes verbal embodiment.[11] It is the implicit recognition of this which enables us to identify Barth's solution as the most radical version of the inwardness tradition. The heart of Christianity, for Barth, is literally inexpressible, since it consists not of doctrines but of the disposition of openness, of expectant obedience. No mere doctrines are ever permanent or unchangeable, nor are any forms of church government. The nearest we can get to the heart of the matter is the utterance of a name, bearing in itself a particular story.[12]

Roman Catholic writers may be expected, for obvious reasons, to be more reticent in the role they assign to inwardness. But Newman is a remarkable example of the attempt to incorporate the basic features of the inwardness tradition in his response to the problem of the development of Christian doctrine. The 'idea' of Christianity is not assimilable without remainder to one central doctrine, closely though it is allied to the incarnation. More important is the epistemological thesis for which Newman wants to argue about the way in which the 'idea' takes root in a person's mind and will, and the kinds of justification which may be offered for its so doing.[13] Thus, according to him, there is 'an inward view' of doctrines, distinct from the propositional expression of them. This 'sacred impression' is the regulating principle of a believer's mind and constitutes 'the reality and permanence of inward knowledge'. Like Barth, Newman concludes that doctrines may take different forms at different periods, though in all periods and at all times the activity of theology can only take place in obedience to divine revelation.

In short the inwardness tradition can be put to many uses, and may feature in different ways in different writers. But an understanding of the discussion of the essence of Christianity is impossible apart from the New Testament's presentation of the transformation of the believer's heart and mind as an indispensable precondition of the phenomenon of Christianness in human history.

The theme of the third chapter was *power in the Church*. Its general conclusion was that the early Christian communities were highly power-conscious bodies, setting their own existence in the context of the myth of a cosmic battle, which issues in confirmation of the sovereignty of God. It is precisely this setting which lends urgency to the unavoidable task of discrimination in the conflicting alternatives open to Christians, an urgency amply demonstrated in Paul's own use of his power as an apostle. The role of theology in elucidating what is at stake in internal conflicts, I argued, necessarily bestows upon theologians a considerable measure of power in the Church. Implicit, therefore, in a theologian's interventions in discussion or decision-making about the Church's future is some view or other about his or her own power.

As applied to our examples from Schleiermacher to Barth the matter is complicated by the changing evaluation of the basic myth of God's kingly rule. Miracles occupy a diminished place in Enlightenment and post-Enlightenment Protestant theologies, Schleiermacher's not excluded. It becomes an open question to what extent a theologian considers that his or her interventions in internal conflicts matter to the future of Christianity. Nonetheless the inherited Protestant tradition, especially in Germany, was to attach great importance to the teaching authority of the university theologian.[14] The sense of this authority lingered long after the Faculties of Theology had become so widely distanced from the churches which they were supposed to serve as to be popularly regarded as centres of heresy. To university Faculties of Theology fell, in any case, the task of training candidates for the ministry, and in so doing they laid their imprint upon the future of the Church.

Schleiermacher was quite explicitly aware of the importance of theology for ministerial training, and for that reason depicted theology as a 'positive' science. Moreover the function of the definition of Christianity's essence was internally critical, or 'polemical' as he termed it. Precisely because of its role as criterion, the correct identification of the essence of Christianity was crucial to the Church's future. When Troeltsch spoke of essence definition as a *Zukunftsglaube* he was merely encapsulating a thought of Schleiermacher's. And when Barth after Troeltsch assigned to dogmatics the task of criticism of the Church's proclamation, he, too, was carrying forward a Schleiermacherian theme.

But if correct understanding of the essence or centre is so vital to the future of Christianity, then unquestionably the person who formulates that understanding (presumably correctly) is him- or herself likewise vital. To depict the theologian as a mere instrument of the truth does not make him or her any less powerful a person, any more than Paul's tracing of his authority to Christ rather than to himself makes him any less formidable as an apostle. There is an inherent power claim relating to theology and theologians in the claim for the importance of the essence identification.

Newman, we saw, is also ready to assign to theology (that is, theology 'commensurate with revelation') the 'fundamental and regulating principle of the whole Church system', regulating even the 'regal' aspect of the Church with its inbuilt proclivity towards undue power.[15] The specific merit of this observation is that it sets up within the orbit of Christianity's aspects a counterbalance against mere centralized executive authority. Loisy's fate was to experience the force of that authority, but only after having been unsuccessful in persuading a sufficient number of his fellow-theologians of the cogency of his theological position. But the consequence of Newman's view is that the theologian, particularly the one responsible for the training of the clergy, is potentially (and in certain spectacular cases, actually) caught in an internal power struggle with the episcopate and its centralized bureaucracy.[16]

It is, however, the work of Troeltsch and Barth which most startlingly confirms the importance of the theme of power for the theological definition of Christianity's essence. For Troeltsch plainly sees that the professoriate, the mandarin tradition in Germany, is by training and inclination remote from the naive sources of religious commitment.[17] His sociological sensitivity alerts him to the problem, but his philosophical objections to the most prominent forms of religious naiveté in his own day, conservative Protestantism and Roman Catholicism, cut him off from any actual realization of his solution. He is caught in a spring-loaded trap of his own devising. For it is precisely the philosophical ban under which he places conservative theologies which turns the professor into a powerful church leader. When a theologian pronounces on the question of the right which a believer has to claim to know something religiously, that theologian is necessarily both identifying the source of religious power, and him- or herself in relation to it. Epistemology itself has inescapable power–connotations in religion.

The same thesis is, if anything, plainer in Barth than in Troeltsch, if only because Barth more strongly insists on full retention of the sovereignty theme in his doctrine of God. Consciously in reaction against the milk-and-water timidity of his liberal precursors, Barth positively revels in the contemporary freedom and power of the word of God in the Church, which he attributes to the activity of the Holy Spirit. The theologian, like the preacher, must live in full confidence that the promised presence of the Spirit will be an actual presence. Moreover, the theologian's role is the exceptionally important and demanding one of holding the Church's proclamation up to the truth of the word of God.[18] Needless to say the epistemology of theology is again determinative of the theologian's position. For it is precisely the philosophical (Barth would say christological) ban under which he places liberal theologies, which turns the professor of a truly faithful dogmatics into a powerful church leader. The fact that Barth strenuously denies that such a person 'possesses' that power is (as in the case of Paul's power) wholly irrelevant to the power which is exercised.

In Barth's case, as in Troeltsch's, there is plenty of evidence of a desire to mitigate the force of this conclusion. Barth denies that he wishes to impose his theology on anyone. He insists that it is the whole community which interprets the word of God, not a professorial élite. Above all, he constantly emphasizes the significance of the Church's worship for the realization of its ministry in the world, to the extent that the praise of God appears *before* preaching in the list of the Church's ministry of speech.[19] These mitigations are of very great importance, and constitute an explicit recognition of the danger of imbalance in the internal distribution of power implied in the epistemology. But they amply confirm the thesis of the third introductory chapter, that the question of the internal distribution of power is implicit in the Church's procedures for resolving its inherent conflicts. The significance of the nineteenth- and twentieth-century discussion of Christianity's essence is unintelligible apart from this, not infrequently concealed, element in the total picture.

II

It is, however, not enough to illustrate the fact that the themes of conflict, inwardness and power occur in the essence of Christianity discussion. If we are to understand why there was a veritable rash of efforts to define the essence in the nineteenth century in particular, then we have to consider certain specific motivations which coincide to produce this remarkable episode in the history of Christian doctrine. The question, therefore, which we now have to ask and answer is, What purpose or purposes do definers of the essence of Christianity have in mind? This is by no means a new enquiry, and a number of valuable contributions have already been made to the discussion.[20] It is already evident that the answer is not likely to be a simple one. It will not do, for example, to speak of essence definition as mere reductionism, although reduction in scale is certainly one of the operative motives. It seems rather that there are a number of coinciding intentions which combine to give the essence of

Christianity debate the appearance, at least, of inevitability in its nineteenth-century context. The motives may be grouped into three major categories, those of simplification, the creation of priorities, and solution to the problem of continuity. I shall develop each of these in turn below.

Before turning to the first of these, however, it is as well to observe that books on the essence of things became a widespread cultural phenomenon of the nineteenth century. When Harnack published his *Das Wesen des Christentums* in 1900, he did so in a climate of opinion familiar both with academic and with popular treatments of the essence of things. Today, of course, essence books have greatly diminished in popularity. A glance at *Liefbare Bücher* reveals that many of the remaining titles containing the word essence are, in fact, survivals and reprints of earlier books, including one fascinating-sounding work, *Das Wesen des Panzerkraftfahrzeuge*, volume 1 of Heigl's *Taschenbuch des Tanks*. American books show much the same trend, apart from certain newer works like *The Essence of Fly Fishing*, or *The Essence of Kung Fu*, and the mysteriously entitled *The Essence of Nothing*. One may also remark on the popularity of titles such as *Essential Business Mathematics*, *Essential Stalin*, or *Essentials of Firefighting*.

What we have here is a series of titles designed to arouse potential readers' expectations that if they read this book on this topic they will learn as much as they need to know about the subject. The degree of need is not, of course, closely defined. It is doubtful, for example, whether perusal of *The Essence of Kung Fu* would enable the reader so to practise Kung Fu as to be capable of meeting all contingencies. Definition of need is, in part, a publishing convention, and is limited by the size, format, and price of the publication. The publisher analyses the market, and in so doing estimates the potential readers' needs.

Seen in this light the word essence is not in the least technical in such titles, and can be replaced by a number of others, such as (as we have already seen) essential *x*, the essentials of *x*, or the heart, spirit, nature, basis of *x*. The list is by no means exhaustive. This is, in fact, what we find in publishers' titles. Harnack's *Das Wesen des Christentums* was replaced by the English title, *What is Christianity?* Gerhard Ebeling's work, *Das Wesen des Christlichen Glaubens*, which was, like Harnack's book, given as lectures for students of all faculties, was translated as *The Nature of Faith*, presumably in order to avoid the less fashionable connotations of the word essence in English.[21] The Roman Catholic theologian, Michael Schmaus, published a similar series of lectures *Vom Wesen des Christentums*, containing an entirely straightforward exposition of Roman Catholic teaching ('Christianity, therefore, is in actuality the Church'), but this was given the English title, *The Essence of Christianity*.[22] A similar earlier work by Karl Adam had been entitled *Das Wesen des Catholizismus*, but translated into English as *The Spirit of Catholicism*.[23]

Works of this kind, despite their lack of self-conscious reflection on the term essence, have every right to use it in their titles, and publishers have every right to replace it, if they wish, with a cognate term, because the title functions untechnically as a conventional signal to a particular audience. It implies an unspoken contract between publisher and reader that a book of general accessibility has been written. It presupposes the existence of a large general readership of persons interested enough to want to acquire an overview of the subject. It could only flourish in a context where there was a sufficient number of educated people used to engaging in study. It is, of course, the nineteenth century which sees the necessary growth of educational opportunity in the western world.

The first motive, therefore, for the production of studies of the essence, nature, or spirit of Christianity is *simplification*, or abbreviation. Given the existence of a particular subject-matter *x*, it is evident that, if that subject-matter is reasonably complex, a writer or speaker could expatiate on it at considerable length. *X* may be Cubism, Kung Fu, Firefighting or one of the world's religions. In speaking of its essence one of the motivations which may play an important role is the intention to be relatively brief.

There can also be extreme abbreviation to the point where what is said or written is capable of being committed to memory. We have already remarked on Gregory of Nyssa's utterance that 'Christianity is imitation of the divine nature'. In a sentence of that kind the word 'is' might well be reinforced, tacitly, by some such phrase or term as 'essentially' or 'in a word'. The intention is not to provide an exhaustive description of the phenomenon of Christianity, nor a logical starting-point for a series of deductions; rather, it is to provide a readily memorable indication, in the manner of a signpost, of the transcendent purpose of Christian existence. It is, in other words, a rhetorical device, whose natural milieu is the teaching situation, where the demands of effective communication play an important role in the manner in which the content is presented.

Simplification has long been a motive of Christian catechesis. Thus attempts to speak in relatively brief compass of the essence of Christianity ought to be located in the continuous history of catechesis. The declaratory creeds, it has been argued, are the by-product of the Church's developing catechetical system. In early days there was no single, or universally agreed form of words, but the different summaries of the faith are of roughly similar length. The length and complexity of these documents has a natural limit in the human memory. Some of the creeds produced in the hectic wake of the Arian controversy so plainly exceeded this requirement (one to such an extent that it was known as the *Ecthesis Macrostichos*, long-lined creed), that whatever their doctrinal merits they condemned themselves to oblivion.

To speak of these brief credal statements as the essence of Christianity, as Hooker does at the end of the sixteenth century, is perfectly intelligible. Karl Rahner in the twentieth century is well justified in including in his examples of the demand for a short presentation of the Christian faith (in effect, expansions of short formulas) the books of Harnack, Ebeling, Schmaus and Adam to which we have already referred.[24] The succession of such works includes Paul VI's 'Confession of Faith of the People of God', Cardinal Gasparri's attempt to produce a world catechism under Pius XII, Martin Luther's Short Catechism and Augustine's *Enchiridion*. Indeed, 'the history of those "short formulas" is as old as Christianity itself.'[25]

It should not be thought that the multiplicity of these attempts is in itself an argument against their credibility. The very brevity of the formulas means that different readers will have to supplement what is said out of their own resources, and these resources will vary at different times and places. Rahner argues persuasively that there cannot be one universally satisfactory short formula, and he himself provides no less than three in order to meet different needs in the western world alone. Not even the Apostles' Creed, permanently binding though it may be, adequately fulfils the contemporary need, so Rahner argues, because of its assumption of the meaningfulness of the term God.[26] But whether the outcome is permanent or impermanent, simplification or abbreviation is one motive behind the production of works on, or formulas of, the essence of Christianity.

The second motive for essence definition which is actually entailed in the first is the *creation of priorities*. A good simplifier will be someone who has thought carefully about priorities. On the other hand, not everyone who thinks carefully about priorities will necessarily be engaged in simplification. The creation of priorities ought, therefore, to be regarded as a separate motivation for essence definition. A clear example of a writer on the essence of Christianity who is plainly concerned to establish priorities, but not at all with simplification, is Schleiermacher in *The Christian Faith*. It would not be correct to see the creation of priorities as his only motivation, but it is clearly enough one of them. He needs a definition of the essence of Christianity first in order to determine out of what set of conditions Christian doctrine emerges; all Christian religious affections are determined in one way or another by redemption, therefore all Christian doctrines concern redemption, its preconditions or consequences.

This example is a relatively sophisticated one relating to Schleiermacher's acute perception of the need for the hermeneutic of the Christian tradition. But, in fact, the creation of priorities is rooted in a much more elementary state of mind, the entirely natural attempt to establish an order in the intellectual world, on the analogy, it may be, of order in the social world. The question, 'Which commandment is first of all?' (Mark 12.28) is evidently intended as a request for the creation of priorities. As commentators point out, there are a number of attempts known to rabbinic literature of summaries of the most fundamental principle or principles of the law, the point of which was to establish the commandment or commandments from which all others derive.[27] The interesting point is, however, that these attempts at creating a relatively brief (and thus memorable) central core out of the mass of particular commandments was an inductive process. All the laws were by divine revelation, and all were to be kept. No one seriously believed that all the laws amounted to deductions from general principles; no one therefore minded that various authorities found now eleven, ten, six, three, two or even one principle.[28] Thus the Matthean version of Mark's story presents Jesus' reply with the comment, 'On these two commandments *depend* all the law and the prophets' (Matt. 22.40).

Elsewhere Matthew clearly states that Jesus insisted on the keeping of the entire law. This passage is remarkable in that it explicitly relates order in the intellectual world (i.e. priorities in the commandments) in obverse relation to order in heavenly society. Thus:

> Whoever then relaxes one of the least of these commandments and teaches men so, shall be called least in the kingdom of heaven; but he who does them and teaches them shall be called great in the kingdom of heaven (Matt. 5.19).

Obedience to the least commandment entails hierarchical greatness; observance merely of the great commandments entails low status in the Kingdom. But observance of both lesser and greater commandments is perfectly consistent with the request for priorities. The fact that there are certain priorities does not entail that what is lesser is of no account, or inessential.

The creation of priorities is, therefore, like simplification as old as Christianity itself, indeed older on the evidence of Judaism. It was a device extensively employed at the Reformation. The 1530 *Confessio Augustana* spoke of the doctrine that 'we obtain the grace of God through faith in Christ without any merits' as *der furnehme Artikel des Evangeliums, praecipuus evangelii locus*, the chief article of the gospel.[29] When pressed to make concessions on one matter or another, Luther's habit was to insist on agreement on the chief matters of faith and works. Where such concord can be established then other matters can be left.[30]

It is in relation to Luther, however, that the potential complexity of the creation of priorities in the substance of Christianity becomes apparent. The *Confessio Augustana*, which is largely the work of Melanchthon, though approved by Luther, is content merely to assert the central status of the 'chief article'. Luther's theological work itself, on the other hand, both argues for, and clarifies what is entailed in, such a priority. The ramifications of the chief article when applied as a criterion or hermeneutic to other doctrines, especially those involving the human mediation of the gospel (such as Church, ministry and sacraments), are of far-reaching significance. It entails both a denial of any salvific validity to such means as have been instituted by human beings on their own authority, and the attribution of pure grace to the effectiveness of such means appointed by God. The creation of priorities, in Luther's case, operated as a critical hermeneutic of received traditions.

One of Luther's modern interpreters, Gerhard Ebeling, denies indeed that Luther intends to give preference to the doctrine of justification by faith. Rather, 'the proper function of the doctrine of justification is that of giving a true significance to all other doctrines', by making the distinction between law and gospel 'the decisive standard of theological judgement'.[31] Such a distinction, Ebeling continues, cannot be carried out once for all, but has to take place in and with actual Christian proclamation of the gospel. The word of God is a living force constantly creating true apprehension of the gospel. The creation of priorities, on this account, is the precondition of knowledge of God. Priorities and epistemology have been decisively linked.

The significance of Luther's thought for Protestantism's subsequent attempts to define the essence of Christianity lies chiefly in the epistemological realm. Despite the variety of matters to which the New Testament in various places apparently gives priority, in the light of Paul it was not at all implausible to state that if a person misunderstood the meaning of faith, nothing could be clear. Moreover the verse stating that the letter kills, but the spirit gives life (2 Cor. 3.6), whatever its original meaning, invited exegesis in terms of church traditions and Christian experience. This is precisely how Schleiermacher, following an already venerable tradition, understands that 'dogmatizing love of system' (he is referring in this place to Roman Catholic orthodoxy, though he holds the same view of Protestant rationalism) which 'plainly suppresses, as much as it can, the living knowledge of God and changes doctrine into a dead letter'.[32] It is precisely in order that theology should be living that Schleiermacher develops the view of the essence of a religion as a *Glaubensweise*, a way of believing. Then the essence of Christianity, as defined, becomes the hermeneutical criterion for the received traditions of his Church. This illustrates how in the work of a sophisticated theologian the creation of priorities leads directly to the epistemology of religious faith. We could argue the same thesis in relation to Newman, to Troeltsch and to Barth. In the cases of Harnack and Loisy, who are not primarily interested in epistemological questions, the illustration of the argument demands some little digging around in the basic premises of the positions advanced.[33]

One final example of the creation of priorities within the substance of theology is the well-known reference, in the Vatican II Document on ecumenism, to the fact that 'in Catholic teaching there exists an order or "hierarchy" of truths, since they vary in their relationship to the foundation of the Christian faith'.[34] Although the document does not proceed to state the order of priorities, nor even to define the foundation, the context makes it reasonably clear that the 'mystery of Christ', expressed in trinitarian incarnational form, is the foundation.

What is the source of this concept of a 'hierarchy of truths'? It appears that the formulator of this phrase is the distinguished French Dominican, Yves Congar, in a paper read in the presence of one Monsignor Roncalli in 1146.[35] In his *La tradition et les traditions* II, Essai théologique, published in 1963, the year of Roncalli (Pope John XXIII)'s death and the year before the promulgation of the decree, Congar wrote:

> There is need ... to restore the idea, certainly traditional, of a kind of stratification within the totality of the truths of the faith, which make up an organic and structural whole. Unfortunately, the consideration of the *quo* (that is, the authority by which teaching is given its obligatory character) has gained too much of an ascendancy over the *quod* (the content or object of this teaching).[36]

Two points need to be made, the first being that Congar is careful to affirm that the hierarchy exists within an organic and structural whole. To use his own metaphor, the fact that the trunk of the tree is of very high importance to its life does not mean that twigs and leaves are not an organic part of the whole. Secondly, the distinction between the *quo* and the *quod* is not the same as that between means of knowing and object of knowledge, since on Congar's own showing it is the *quod*, the mystery of Christ, which determines how it may be known, by the Holy Spirit.[37]

The 'hierarchy of truths' is, in short, not a way of cutting down on the quantity of 'truths' to be believed, but, as Roman Catholic commentators emphasize, of intensifying and deepening the grasp on the central matters of faith.[38] As what one might call a qualitative, rather than a quantitative, consideration, it is distinct from the enumeration of 'fundamental articles', and moves rather in the direction of theological hermeneutics. It is, thus, further confirmation of the thesis that the creation of priorities leads directly to the epistemological question raised by religious faith.

The final motive for the essence of Christianity discussion which we are to examine is the *problem of continuity* in Christian theology. On the face of it there is no biblical precedent or basis for this consideration, since continuity was hardly a problem in the first decades of the Christian movement. But the criterion of apostolicity is of remarkably early origin; 'the gospel ... which we preached' (Gal. 1.8), the 'standard of teaching to which you were committed' (Rom. 6.17), 'the sound words of our Lord Jesus Christ' (1 Tim. 6.3), 'the doctrine of Christ' (2 John 9) are all expressions implying the duty of continuous transmission of a normative truth. With the challenge of Gnosticism, and the necessity of facing practical and philosophical questions for which the written or oral tradition gave no immediate answer, continuity assumed greater importance. Origen, himself notably engaged in the problem of conflicting possibilities for developing the Christian tradition into new areas of thought and activity, produced, precisely for the sake of preserving continuity, the distinction between the few and easily assimilated truths necessary for salvation, and the speculations permitted to the spiritual élite.[39]

The problem of continuity is one element of the modern problem of development of doctrine. We are not concerned here, however, with theories to account for development, but rather with the resources of Christian theology when continuity is perceived as a problem. Continuity is no problem, so long as there can be confident affirmation of the identity of the witness of the contemporary Church with that of the apostolic Church. Plainly criticism disturbs that confidence, and of the many episodes in which critics have unfavourably contrasted the present with the past the protest of the sixteenth-century Reformers was the most serious. Rival claims were made with serious plausibility on both sides. All the reformed churches claimed continuity with the apostles, but it was Anglicanism, with its more traditionalist cast of mind, which developed with special emphasis, as we have already seen, the fundamental articles apologetic.[40] Hooker's essence of Christianity was, therefore, at once an abbreviation of the whole Christian tradition and an ostensible solution to the problem of continuity.

With the Enlightenment, however, the problem of continuity acquired two further dimensions. First, it became imperative to deal convincingly with aspects of biblical history which were repulsive or unacceptable to the enlightened mind, such as the deficient morality of the Old Testament or the miraculous in both Testaments. Secondly, it soon became necessary to provide a more differentiated account of the history of the Bible itself.[41] Both of these problems turned the Protestant appeal away from a mere reference to the biblical text, to a less formal and external criterion, such as biblical faith. Theologies, not excluding biblical theologies, were necessarily history-relative; what endures might be said to be biblical religion. The contrast between religion and theology, which we find extensively deployed in the works of Semler, enables the enlightened theologian both to pass criticism upon the highly cerebral traditional theology of the day, and yet with plausibility to claim continuity with the popular religious impulse of Christianity.[42] Pietism was the natural home for such convictions, and Schleiermacher the apotheosis of the enlightened pietist, a '*Herrnhüter* of a higher order'.[43]

It is, however, an easily made mistake to confine the essence of Christianity apologetic to post-Enlightenment Protestantism. Obviously the solution which this apologetic offered to the new problem of continuity explains to some extent the currency of the idea among Protestants of that age and outlook. But the problem of continuity was by no means restricted to Protestants. Once the solution of Bossuet to the Protestant challenge that Rome had changed the apostolic faith had yielded ground under the force of new historical studies of the early eighteenth century, Roman Catholicism itself was in need of a new theory to the problem of continuity.[44] It is no accident that in the *Brief Introduction to the Study of Theology, with reference to the scientific standpoint and the Catholic system*, published by the Tübingen theologian, Johann Sebastian Drey, in 1819, we read, 'the basis of scientific theology is a philosophical construction of the essence of Christianity'.[45] A work whose form and expression is unthinkable without the impulse provided by Schleiermacher, it offered a theory of development, in which Christianity is conceived as a systematic whole,[46] the outworking of a basic perspective or intuition (*Anschauung*) constituting its fundamental idea (*Grundidee*).[47] This fundamental idea is explored first historically, then philosophically, and finally is evaluated. There is both an inner essence of Christianity and an outer, or historical essence. The latter historical essence is made up of both the original revelation and the means of its transmission.[48] Drey then argues for a congruence between the idea of Christianity as a religious system, and the idea of the Church. The fundamental idea of the Christian Church is that it constitutes the necessary development (*Ausbildung*) of the Christian idea into an objective external phenomenon, a religious association, 'in which the basic religious intuition acquires empirical reality and objective significance'.[49] As Drey makes clear in another work of the same date, entitled *Vom Geist und Wesen des Katholizismus*, the principle of the inner spiritual development is none other than the Holy Spirit, the 'common spirit' (*Gemeingeist*, a word Schleiermacher was to use later in *The Christian Faith*).[50]

Whether or not a direct historic link can be forged between Drey and Newman, via Drey's pupil Möhler, to whom Newman refers but whom he may not have read for himself, there is an obvious connection between Drey's use of *Das Wesen des Christentums*, and Newman's idea of Christianity.[51] The connection consists not in slavish imitation; Newman's information about Möhler was too imprecise for that. It consists rather in a correspondence between the fundamental problem to which essence and idea were respectively designed to address themselves. In both cases the question is continuity in history. The great phenomena of history must, argues Drey in words which remarkably resemble those to be used subsequently by Troeltsch, be grasped as the struggle of a single principle of spirit to express itself.[52] In Newman the idea of Christianity is not so much a theory of development, as 'an hypothesis to account for a difficulty'[53] – the difficulty being, precisely, that the history of Christianity contradicts the natural assumption or presumption 'that the external continuity of name, profession, and communion, argues a real continuity of doctrine'.[54] Idea and essence belong to the same problem context, despite the fact that the Roman Catholic discussion of the source of continuity has to take account in a more structured way of interpreting the documents in which the doctrine of the Church is incorporated. It is, however, a mistake to say that the essence of Christianity is a purely Protestant problem, as though it were solved for Roman Catholics by their doctrine of the Church. The truth is rather that for both Protestants and Roman Catholics the question of the essence of Christianity involves both the doctrine of the Church and the source of its continuity in history. For neither is there any simplistic solution. For both there are inherent problems of conflict, of inwardness and of the reality of power. Both belong to a single tradition of reflection, albeit with different conventional gambits, and both tend to be guided by certain implicit models or metaphors by which the complexities of the history of the Church can be grasped. Our final task is to refer briefly to certain of these, so as to identify some hidden assumptions in the metaphorical language in which they are commonly embedded.

III

As we have seen, in and with the rise of historical consciousness the confident affirmation of the identity of the witness of the contemporary Church with that of the apostolic Church becomes problematic. Having already been a matter of acute controversy between Roman Catholics and Protestants in the preceding centuries, from the eighteenth century onwards Roman Catholic and Protestant continuity claims became internally, as well as externally, controversial. In Chapters 1 to 3 of this book I have offered to exhibit the elements which solutions to these controversies are bound to take into account; this was confirmed in the first section of this present chapter. In the immediately preceding section of this chapter, I have attempted to outline the three motives whose coincidence made essence of Christianity discussion especially popular in the nineteenth century. Here I want to offer a simplified interpretative grid with which to handle the different solutions. Basic to this grid is the distinction

between two gambits, which I shall respectively entitle the externality tradition and the inwardness tradition. By externality,
I mean the tradition which sees the identity of Christianity as
lodged in certain external features, especially in the external
dimensions we have listed;[55] by the inwardness tradition, I mean
the reiterated appeal to that inner, spiritual reality of personal
lives being transformed by God. These traditions come into play
when there is conflict about the identity of Christianity, that is,
all the time. But they are not equally balanced, because, as I
argued earlier, in a situation of conflict, words whose meaning
has been as carefully defined or delimited as possible, are our
sharpest tool for making the necessary distinctions.[56] In a situation of conflict, therefore, the externality tradition has an at
least apparent, advantage. When a conflict arises, at once re-
course is had to the already existing words in which the content
of Christian teaching has been summarized. Theologians may
also have already begun to interpret, in words, the meaning of
certain myths and rituals. They most likely have also begun to
explain with some precision, the right of certain persons to
adjudicate when dispute arises. If we add to this the fact that the
Roman world was governed, bureaucratically, by the literate,
and that part of Paul's authority derived from his native intelli-
gence, we have a picture of the extent to which the externality
tradition, armed with the power of education, starts at a considerable advantage in a situation of conflict.

Characteristically the externality tradition throws up a long
and complex history of propositions in which the Christian faith
is expressed. J. N. D. Kelly, in his comprehensive review of early
Christian creeds, has shown that there is a line of development
from the sense of the content of Christian preaching in the New
Testament period, through the catechetical tradition to the
writing in the late second century which refers to the 'rule of
faith' or 'the canon of the truth'. This 'common body of doctrine,
definite in outline and regarded by everyone as the possession of
no individual but of the Church as a whole',[57] is in Irenaeus
spoken of (in a revealing phrase) as 'the substance (*dynamis*) of
the tradition'.[58] Kelly's own (metaphorical) term for this
doctrinal content is 'the Church's central message, the kernel of
its doctrinal deposit'.[59]

The externality tradition is in its happiest days when this

common body of doctrine was both brief and readily memorable. The writing is already on the wall when Origen distinguishes in *de Principiis* between the articles of faith which are essential to salvation, and those which may legitimately be regarded as speculative. Speculation may involve error, and error will need to be guarded against. Who can say in advance what is the limit of the truth? The result is that what the leaders of the Church may decide is of the truth is not necessarily expressible with brevity. To the creeds may be added explanatory letters and documents, carefully weighed and universally agreed.

Nor is the externality tradition the exclusive preserve of the Catholic, especially the Roman Catholic tradition. As we have seen, Protestant orthodoxy likewise produced its attempted clarification of the fundamental articles, and a distinction between that which everyone must believe (in practice what more than one Protestant denomination did believe) and that which might safely be controverted.

But the externality tradition is, by itself, clearly and in principle inadequate and impossible. It leads to what has been contemptuously dismissed as *Denzinger-Theologie*; the sort of theology which looks up a topic in the collection of authoritative documents, and expounds what is taken to be their significance. It is profoundly unhistorical, it ignores the 'inside' of Christian profession, and it devalues the non-verbal dimensions of Christianity as a religion. It is always inadequate for new questions, and at the very least it requires authoritative contemporary expounders, whose reasons and arguments are bound to involve certain non-traditional features.

But if the externality tradition is in principle inadequate by itself, the more so is the inwardness tradition. This is involved in a massive, and apparently insurmountable, difficulty. The inwardness tradition is embodied in an appeal to a non-verbal reality, the inner, spiritual occurrence of lives being transformed by God. But it must do so in sentences. The lives themselves may be transformed by the indwelling power of the Holy Spirit. But there is a theology of the Holy Spirit and there are normal means of the Holy Spirit's operation, the preaching of the Church, the sacraments and ascetical discipline. When there is conflict about the work of the Holy Spirit or the content of preaching, or the efficacy of the sacraments or the appropriateness of an ascesis, then the analytic discipline of theology, and the written resources of the tradition come into their own. Denzinger is pulled off the shelf; or the Institutes; or the Thirty-Nine Articles; or the Westminster Confession; or the sermons of Wesley. The inwardness tradition may sense that no words can capture the reality of the love of God shed abroad in the heart; it may feel deeply that what decides is not, finally, doctrinal orthodoxy but holiness. But it is trapped. On the one hand, it is involved in conflict which requires a solution; on the other, it experiences an inarticulate yearning which can never achieve the clarity of definitiveness for a solution.

A third element, therefore, enters the grid, poised between the externality and the inwardness traditions, and incorporating an element of each in some kind of interplay. I shall refer to this as the dialectical tradition, because, as was argued in Chapter 2, the incorporation of inwardness as a conscious element in explanations of the phenomenon of Christianity entails the impossibility of the final resolution of conflicts. It is here that the models for continuity begin to be of some importance. The continuity of Christianity is, after all, highly complex. It is not a physical continuity, like the continuity of a mountain. If one sees Christianity as an institution, it is clear that, like many institutions, it is open to radical alterations of character – we have only to think of the history of the railway corporations. There is, moreover, the internally complex character of the relation of Christianity's dimensions; discontinuity can result not merely by change imposed from without, but by disproportion within. Accordingly if continuity is claimed for the Christian tradition, it requires metaphoral or analogical illumination. The unfamiliar must be interpreted or explained by the more familiar; the grid can be expanded with the help of a catalogue of analogies or models.

As one would expect the externality tradition, which starts, as I have argued, with a strong advantage when it comes to the resolution of conflict, threw up its own analogy for the continuity of the Christian religion. It is the analogy of the permanence and durability of a specific quantum of hard matter. Thus with some obvious biblical allusions, the substance of the tradition, the dogmas or fundamental articles can be spoken of as a store of treasure (cf. Matt. 19.21; 2 Cor. 4.7; Col. 2.3), which can be handed down from generation to generation and which remains unvaryingly the same. The continuity is physical in the most elementary sense, and the assumptions which allow the 'deposit' (*paradosis*) of the gospel to be considered as such are those of a classicist culture which sees all knowledge as a permanent and culturally invariable possession to be handed on from generation to generation.

There are two ways of conceiving this substance; one is to suppose that it is exclusively invariable, that is to say that once the propositions have been definitively established as constituting the body of the tradition, nothing may be either added or subtracted from it. The other is to suppose that they are inclusively invariable, that is to say, that once they belong to the body of the tradition they do so even though other things may be added to them. The first of these two positions is the closest to the purely physical model, and it underlies the fundamental articles tradition (which, as we have seen, Anglican apologists for the undivided Church of the first six centuries deployed to maximum effect). It is noticeable that the language of addition and subtraction is employed by those who use the analogy in this way. Because the fundamental articles are a precisely determined quantum, the attachment of an extra sentence may well constitute an addition to the quantity of material (and that, indeed, was the Anglican charge against Romanism). On the other hand, because what is added are words, not physical objects, it is always possible to argue that the extra words represent no addition, but are, rather, a mere unveiling of an idea already implicitly present in the original. By the word 'implicit', one means logically implicit, a meaning itself capable of considerable further exploration in the light of the fact that a syllogism may contain, in its major or minor premise, a statement which is true but not revealed.[60]

This discovery is, in effect, the death of the analogy. Since the propositions of the faith are not in fact a specific quantum of physical material, the notion of addition to, or subtraction from, the substance of the faith is much more complex than the analogy can allow. Substances do not have the fascinating and perplexing ambiguity of words; words, indeed, especially the verbal images with which religious language abounds, have an almost reproductive capacity to beget more words by association. Hence the externality tradition develops, in due course, an organic model (rightly so called) to help interpret the process of internal multiplication. The model, at its simplest, is that of a living plant. Again with an obvious reference to biblical passages of growth, such as the mustard seed (Mark 4.30ff), the changes which characterize the Christian Church are interpreted by a model which guarantees continuity within them. A daffodil bulb does not grow into a lily; an acorn does not produce a fir tree. The essential quality of this model is the mysterious, but determinate pattern of the principle of growth. The model is appropriate only for those thinkers who find little or no difficulty in identifying the phenomenon at its various stages of growth. It is a model, in other words, for the externality tradition. Although it allows, indeed requires, outside influences to play upon the seed and young plant, there is no possibility of radical mutation. Growth or death are the only options; preservation of type is assured, and no particular care has to be taken to identify the essential from the inessential, or to distinguish the more important from the less important. In the resultant tree, every branch, twig and leaf is an integral part of the whole (even if it is admitted that the main trunk is more important on the *hierarchia veritatum*). Hence it amounts to a modification of the analogy of treasure appropriate for the externality tradition. The modification consists in saying that the gospel is contained entire in every stage of growth from seed, young plant, to mature plant, without addition or subtraction. The only question to be decided is what does, and what does not, belong to the organism.

The second gambit, the inwardness tradition, has naturally much greater difficulty in specifying the continuity of the Christian gospel. It is for this reason that Karl Barth, the most radical representative of the inwardness tradition, uses the analogy of the opening in the centre of a wheel. True inwardness is an imageless void. It is, to use biblical terminology, the Spirit 'which blows where it wills' (John 3.8), leaving a sound but having no physical source or goal. The moment it becomes locally identifiable, a reference to one aspect or another of the externality tradition becomes inevitable, and the inwardness tradition passes over into the dialectical.

Thus the dialectical tradition has developed models with two elements in them, an external and an internal, held together in some kind of relation. I have collected hitherto three basic types, each with an obvious root in biblical language (and it may well be that there are more).

(a) Foundation – superstructure. Both the Gospels and the Epistles speak of laying foundations, in Paul's case of a permanent and invariable fundament, namely Jesus Christ himself (1 Cor. 3.11–15). In this passage, the building erected on the foundation, which has been laid by Paul, is put up by other builders who have to beware of how they build in the light of judgement to come. That it is possible to build wrongly on the foundation is the whole point of this model. There is, therefore, a useful distinction here between foundation and subsequent building, which enables a 'return to fundamentals' to involve an implicit or explicit criticism of contemporary teaching. The model does nothing, however, to aid the specification of the relationship between the foundation and the superstructure. Precisely because once again the durable element in Christian profession is spoken of as a physical entity, it falls into the problems of the first kind of externality analogy, to which it is linguistically related. But the model has this at least in its favour, that it draws attention to the *problem* of building. There is, implicit in the elucidation of Christian discipleship, a structural task, whose successful completion has to be repeatedly carried out, is not necessarily easy, and always involves danger.

(b) Spirit – body. This model has the merit of the implication of life, and thus of continuous adaptability within continuity. In the very next verse following his references to foundations and building, Paul affirms that the Corinthian church is God's temple, where the Spirit of God dwells (1 Cor. 3.16). This thought, as the letter to the Corinthians develops it, is of vital importance inasmuch as it enables Paul, in later chapters, to specify the marks of the Spirit-filled Church (chs. 12–14). Furthermore, when the temple imagery is used by the author of 1 Peter, it is developed in a theory of 'spiritual sacrifices', offered by a 'holy priesthood'. On this model the continuity of the Church lies entirely in the presence of the Holy Spirit, and the proof of the presence of the Holy Spirit lies in its demonstration of holiness and other marks of the Spirit-filled life, including its proclamation 'of the triumphs of him who has called you out of darkness into his marvellous light' (1 Pet. 2.9).

This model is of considerable significance for the subsequent history of the Church for the following reason. It made possible both of two diverging tendencies. On the one hand, to the extent that the identification of the visible Church with the Body of Christ was felt to be secure, so much the stronger was the power of that Church, inhabited as it was claimed to be by the Holy Spirit itself. Hence, on the view of the Church as an institution, the Spirit is bound to the body of the Church, as the soul of man is bound to his body. At the same time, however, in as much as the body of the Church is not a physical body, with an indisputable point of reference in physical continuity, those who assert that the Church, though claiming to be authentically the Church of Christ, is actually unfaithful to him, have a ready-made model for identifying the *true* Church, by its superior demonstration of the life-signs of the Spirit. This is, indeed, the procedure of the Donatists, of numerous reform–movements in the medieval period, and of the Reformers themselves. On this development, in as much as the Spirit of God is free, he is not bound to a particular institution.

If we consider that both of these developments are equally possible on the basis of the body–spirit model, it is clear that the weakness of the model lies in the application of the term 'body' to the Church.[61] Similarly its strength lies in the clarity with which the continuity of the faith is identified, not in any external achievements of the Church, such as a visible hierarchy, or declarations or definitions, but in the gift of God himself and the response which this gift elicits.

(c) Centre – circumference. The model of centrality is one of the most persistent and effective of the ways in which the dialectical tradition depicts that which stands for the permanent in the Christian gospel. The root of the model is less, therefore, a question of the mathematical point around which a centre is drawn, than the inner location of the heart. The inwardness tradition spoke of a change of heart; what, therefore, occurs 'there' is the 'centre'. As the place where the essential transforming work of God is carried out (cf. 2 Cor. 1.22; 4.6; Rom. 5.5), the heart is the place where Christian identity is fashioned. In this respect the model of centre and circumference is clearly exchangeable with that of spirit and body.

However, this basic model gives rise to a number of variants, which have their origin in the diversity of forms in which what lies at the centre relates to what is external. The most celebrated of these is the kernel and the husk. The implication of this model is, naturally, the disposability of the husk. A different model is suggested by Harnack, who, as we have seen, prefers to speak of the relation of bark and sap, emphasizing thereby at once the life-giving character of the sap, and the capacity of a live tree to protect itself with the successive layers of bark necessary to its survival. On this model that which does not belong to the centre is, nonetheless, essential. In both models, however, the important point is that it is that which lies at the heart of the organism which constitutes its permanence. The difference between these two is that the kernel–husk model is non-living, whereas the sap–bark model is living. The latter is, accordingly, more capable of coping with the problem of historical development, as it increasingly came to be identified in the nineteenth century.

The grid and the models are a highly simplified way of charting and illustrating the complex territory which the problem of continuity requires one to survey. The grid amounts to scarcely more than the observation that somehow the externals of Christianity need to be related to the inner reality of conversion and commitment. To point to the various metaphors scarcely achieves more than an observation of the danger of the uncritical use of language.

This chapter, however, offered to do no more than analyse the elements of the essence discussion. The substantive problems remain to be tackled in what follows.

IO

The Unity
of Christianity

Is Christianity one thing? The general terms used to designate
intellectual positions in philosophical questions, such as
idealism, realism, phenomenalism, empiricism, existentialism
and so forth, are generally recognized to be a source of danger.[1]
They are inherently imprecise, and very frequently become opprobrious slogans. Nevertheless experience shows how difficult
it is to avoid them, and the history of philosophy unquestionably
does contain instances of schools of thinkers working at problems on the basis of a set of agreed principles.

The history of religions is not, of course, the same thing as the
history of philosophy. Religions, or at least many religions, aim
to produce followers or disciples. There seems to be no reason
why such disciples should resent or mistrust the use of a generalizing term to designate the phenomenon of their common allegiance. No matter what the origin of the term Christianity, why
should the followers of Jesus Christ be ashamed to be called
Christians?

Nonetheless, after so many centuries of Christian history, with
the example of so many divisions and subdivisions of this form
of religious allegiance before us, there surely is a problem about
the oneness of Christianity. This religion has demonstrated a
remarkable capacity to splinter itself into distinguishable forms.
Smart indeed asserts that there are only 'mini-essences' of forms
of Christianity, not one single essence.[2] Quite apart from the
organized confessions, both major and minor, within the
families shades of theological opinion lend themselves to further
qualifying designations. The phenomenon of multiple qualification seems to know no limit. Thus there is within Christianity,
Anglican Christianity; not merely is there Anglican Christianity,

there is catholic Anglican Christianity; not merely catholic Anglican Christianity, but liberal catholic Anglican Christianity; nor are we in any way quibbling if we insist on identifying within liberal catholic Anglican Christianity, a form of theological opinion we can designate neo-liberal catholic Anglican Christianity.[3]

Pluralism in theology is certainly no new phenomenon in the history of Christianity, nor is it necessarily in itself proof of the fact that Christianity is not one thing. The argument of the second chapter was designed precisely to take seriously the *inherent* variety of forms of Christianity. If there is such a thing as Christian unity, it will necessarily be in the form of a containment of diversity within bounds.

We may speak of a synchronic unity of Christianity, that is, the unity of the forms of Christianity in existence at any one time; and of the diachronic unity of Christianity, that is of the historically changing forms of Christianity. But at any one time, the form which a particular expression of Christianity may take will be the outcome of an historical process of development. In the end, the most serious problems for speaking of Christianity as one thing are caused by its continuity, or lack of continuity, over time.

Thus the first task of this chapter is to specify a way of speaking of the diachronic unity of Christianity which is not open to certain obvious objections. Once we have clarified the limited use to which such an understanding of Christianity would be put, it will then be possible to enlist the idea of 'an essentially contested concept' as a means of accounting for the phenomenon of internal dispute about Christianity.

I

In the previous chapter, as part of the analysis of the essence of Christianity discussion we discovered the problem of continuity to be one of the motivations for attempting to identify Christianity's essence. We also presented a series of metaphors in which the continuity of Christianity has been rendered in the form of dialectical interplay between two elements. But it might well be argued that throughout the above analysis the *fact* of Christianity's inner unity and continuity has merely been assumed. This assumption, of course, reflects the basic confidence of all the theologians whom we studied, with the exception of Ernst Troeltsch. Is it not time that we took Troeltsch's challenge more seriously? *Is* Christianity one thing, even one highly complex thing? Does not the very use of a single term, Christianity, cast an aura of spurious unity over its irreducible diachronic, and hence synchronic, pluralism?

The first problem we must face in relation to continuity has recently been discussed largely under the general term 'cultural relativism'.[4] Unfortunately for the clarity of this discussion, critical appraisal reveals that relativism itself is not one thing. Nonetheless there is undoubtedly a problem. Christians have patently not believed an identical and unvarying set of propositions to be true in the same sense over the nearly twenty centuries of their history. The Christian writings of the past which have proved central sources of inspiration for generations of believers contain for modern readers an uneasy mixture of familiar and unfamiliar tones. The Scriptures especcially seem to lend themselves to a variety of readings, according to whether the interpreter is concerned to domesticate the thought forms so as to approximate them to present concerns and interests, or to emphasize their strangeness and unfamiliarity. Exaggeration and selective blindness are by no means unreal dangers, and theologians who study the Christian past have to submit to a severe self-discipline in identifying their own predilections and setting them on one side, so far as possible.

The qualification, 'so far as possible', is, surely, important. The effort required to undeceive oneself is, in principle, a continuous process, not an achieved state. Theologians who proclaim the relativity of all stand-points in theological matters do not escape from the relativity of their own proclamation. There can be no generally valid proof of cultural relativism nor can one ever be sure that one's reading of the evidence in detail is free of presuppositions. The important point to grasp is that there is *no* perspective on Christianity which relativizes all other perspectives. So long as it is grasped that any platform which we may construct from which to survey the material before us is constructed out of substances which themselves have been fashioned from a survey of the material, the interesting questions turn out to be not purely methodological, but substantial. If one perpetually asks what the criteria are for theological positions, one does not arrive at a bedrock method, but an infinite (and infinitely boring) methodological regression.

An illustration of this point is to hand in the case of Friedrich Schleiermacher. Originally presenting his hundred pages of prolegomena to dogmatics as 'above' dogmatics, or at least as impartial with respect to the particular content of dogmatics, he was vulnerable to those critics who pointed out that there was a dogmatic background to his supposedly neutral definition of 'Church'. Barth, as we have seen, baldly stated that despite his own intentions Schleiermacher's prolegomena were indeed dogmatics; were, unfortunately, heretical dogmatics.[5] Barth's own prolegomena, by contrast, were to be presented as part of the church dogmatics, and entailed a preliminary justification of the Trinitarian standpoint of the Reformed Church. This should by no means be regarded as a Barthian oddity. The basic tradition of Roman Catholic theology is to include the elements of ecclesiology inside the sections dealing with fundamental theology.[6] There can be no treatment of faith or revelation apart from the doctrine of the Church. The precise position to be assigned to the Church may vary from theologian to theologian.[7] But the methodology of dogmatics and the dogmatics themselves are plainly to be written with each other in view.

Similarly the question of the continuity of Christianity cannot be resolved by a purely methodological enquiry into the conditions of its sheer historicity. In order to get the argument under way we need to have material before us. There are, thus, two tasks to be undertaken. First, a viewpoint upon Christianity has to be constructed, a platform from which it may be surveyed, consciously subject to the conditions of provisionality enunciated above; and secondly, this viewpoint has exhaustively to be tested against actual Christian history, to discover whether it is of any explanatory interest or value. This specification of tasks is, in fact, the same as Schleiermacher's self-imposed prescription for determining the essence of Christianity. What he described as the 'critical method' for defining the essence of Christianity, was the twofold activity of offering an hypothesis (based on a wide-ranging comparative treatment of Christianity as a religious movement) and testing the hypothesis against Christian history. The development of this programme remains a remarkable achievement in the history of Christian thought, as fruitful outside Protestantism as within it. But what is undertaken here as a version of Schleiermacher's programme has one self-imposed limitation and a no less important variation.

The limitation is that under no circumstances can one offer an exhaustive testing of the hypothesis to be advanced. Schleiermacher's testing of his definition in *The Christian Faith* in fact hardly amounted to more than a few paragraphs on aspects of Christian history. Newman's testing of his hypothesis concerning continuity of idea was considerably more thorough, but hardly such as to inspire general confidence that he had seriously entertained the possibility of discontinuity by sheer over-accumulation. The quantity of issues to be interpreted, once the decrees and definitions of the Holy See have to be included in one's perspective, practically elude even the most devoted efforts of a single scholar. Harnack and Troeltsch, with their respective surveys, *The History of Dogma* and the *Social Teaching of the Christian Church*, similarly afford attempts at the confirmation of an hypothesis about the identity of Christianity, the second in conscious correction of the over-intellectual bias of the first. They abundantly illustrate what is involved in the serious testing of hypotheses about the unity and continuity of Christianity. In both cases the complexity and difficulty of the treatment of particular issues does nothing to encourage their successors to launch on an immediate personal quest for the confirmation of the original hypothesis.

There is a point, however, in a less ambitious project, in variation of Schleiermacher's own. Instead of striving for a definition of Christianity of enormous generality, it seems to me possible to enquire under what conditions can Christianity be grasped as one thing. A specification of these conditions would amount to an hypothesis about Christianity's identity, in principle capable of being tested by a variety of investigations. It would not be necessary or even profitable at once to launch into a massive history of Christianity from the point of view of that hypothesis. The function of the hypothesis seems to be somewhat less pretentious in character. The formation of a hypothesis about the identity of Christianity has the function of making explicit what in any case is implicit. That is to say, it brings out for inspection those assumptions which are made when a person conceives of Christianity, when there takes place an imaginative construal of the religion as a whole.[8]

It is here that it is pertinent to ask again what grounds we have for thinking of Christianity as one thing. Are we not in danger of being misled by the mere occurrence of a single term, Christianity? Ought we not to recall the fact that there are competent theologians who have come to the conclusion that it is not one thing? But it is undeniable that there is, from the standpoint of Christianity itself, a strong predisposition in favour of conceiving Christianity in terms of a continuous identity. This has, as Troeltsch correctly observed, in the first instance a social-psychological background. Religions have a centring function for the personality.[9] Mol defines this in terms of commitment and the hierarchy of values.[10] Smart interprets worship as orientation upon a single focus.[11] Disciples are, therefore, naturally predisposed to believe that that in which they invest their highest aspirations is itself a unity (of however internally complex a kind).

Moreover Christians have particular theological reasons for thinking of this unity as a unity over time. In contrast to the teaching of certain other religions, it is repeatedly said in the tradition of Christian theism that God is internally self-consistent. The undeviatingness of God, in his will, and especially his 'steadfast love', for his people is a constantly reiterated theme in the Christian understanding of God, deeply rooted in both Old and New Testaments. One scholar goes so far as to say that 'in the combination of power and steadfast love the nature of the Old Testament belief in God is summarized'.[12] Untypical though the terminology of the single New Testament passage to affirm the divine immutability may be ('Every good endowment and every perfect gift is from above, coming down from the Father of lights, with whom there is no variation or shadow due to change'; Jas. 1.17), it unquestionably reflects the sense of God's 'essential fidelity to himself and to his promises, which guarantees constancy and continuity in his action', characteristic of the Old and New Testaments.[13]

The observation of this fidelity is vital for any argument about continuity. The ultimate ground for insisting on the need for minimal continuity in the identity of Christianity lies in the integrity of its witness to the undeviatingness of God. Of course it is conceivable that, though God himself is undeviating, Christians may have varied widely in how they have understood and spoken of him. Nor is it in principle impossible that Christians have misled generations of people in speaking of the character of God in the way in which they have done, though Christians would be bound to consider it a profoundly significant objection to the truth of Christianity if this were to have been the case. The vision of God and the imitation of God lie deeply at the root of Christian spirituality. If the Christian depiction of the character of God has been for long periods of time seriously at fault, the Christian Church is in effect responsible for the systematic deformation of human lives on a scale which puts the propaganda efforts of twentieth-century dictators into the shade. The resistance, therefore, to the idea that there are no continuities in the development of the Christian tradition is rooted in the stubborn insistence that the family resemblance between Christians, their synchronic unity, lies in their conformity to the immutable, diachronic image of his Son, 'who is the likeness of God' (2 Cor. 4.4).

It is perhaps worth clarifying further the nature of the defence of the need for continuity in the Christian tradition which is being offered here. It takes the following form:

1   God himself is undeviatingly good. His will for humanity is subject to no variation; he is not arbitrary in his regard for, and treatment of different persons; his world is such that, although life itself is sometimes devastatingly uneven in human experience, the divine comparison and the divine judgement are steady and true. This kind of speech about God is recognizably anthropomorphic; but its function in Christian theology is to rule out the possibility of a contrary position, which is known best in the Greek myths and legends, in which the gods cannot be relied upon not to play cruel tricks upon mortals and where there is no guarantee of justice after death.

2   To the undeviating goodness of God the Christian gospel bears witness, in order that people may have reliable knowledge of the kind of world in which they are alive and may shape their life's course accordingly. Agnosticism on this point undermines too much to be tolerable. The character of God is the essential basis on which is framed the practical understanding of the

world, which is said to be his creation. This is especially the case for self-knowledge and knowledge of other people. In Christian faith knowledge of others, like knowledge of oneself, is of those who are fundamentally the living subjects of the love of God, of his goodness and of his judgement. We know how to behave because we know what is expected of us.

3   The Christian gospel must therefore be undeviating in the sense that it must be capable in all circumstances of creating that response to God which is the proper practical expression of knowledge of his character. From this, however, it does not follow that the identical response can only be created in all circumstances by the identical verbal utterances. This formulation of the view which has to be defended rests on the need for an *identity of response*, if the diachronic continuity of Christianity is to be defended at all.

It is plainly not possible to submit this claim to thorough examination here and now. But it should be noted that in principle the argument is falsifiable by the production of sufficient quantities of evidence from history. If, for example, it were possible to show an inner connection between the proclamation of the Christian gospel and the various forms of racial and sexual intolerance which have disfigured Christian history, then the rational defence of Christianity would become impossible. It is perhaps less implausible to claim that the falsification of the Christian claim for continuity has not yet been carried out successfully, than to purport to verify the claim in detail. The making of the claim, however, I believe to be a theological necessity.

This argument for minimal continuity is a good deal more circuitous than, for example, the criterion of apostolicity used in the early Church. It may be taken to imply no more than the fact that, for Christians at least, the term Christianity stands for the deeds of the immutable God in performing human salvation. Christianity from the Christian standpoint is the response appropriate to the undeviating goodness of God. It is this undeviatingness which furnishes the presumption in favour of the continuity of the symbols of Christianity, its doctrines, its rites, and its social embodiment. Although in order to remain the same it is certain that it must change in response to the changing context, it is equally certain that there must be a presumption in favour of the maximum amount of visible continuity.

The further pursuit of Schleiermacher's programme of seeing Christianity as one thing raises one final objection, which he did not face because it would have constituted a challenge to an assumption made both by himself and most of his contemporaries. This is the objection that those concerned with the continuity of Christianity have generally all too little interest in the question of truth. We may identify this position as the consequence of the radical concentration, characteristic of modern philosophy, upon the problems of epistemology. From this point of view to practise hermeneutics upon the Christian tradition, however subtly carried out, is an evasion of the insistent demands of the truth. Moreover, any project which attempts to uncover the nature of the identity of Christianity, before enquiring what grounds there may be for the assertion of any of its doctrines, is – so the argument goes – basically frivolous.

This position has a certain robust common sense about it. It takes the epistemological blows on the chin. The question of truth is primary, and its claims peremptory. If the truth leads one out of orthodox Christianity, whatever that may be, so be it. Characteristically the defender of this view will admit that the major problem for theology is the truth of any theistic position whatsoever; and that since Christian faith most certainly entails the defence of theism, and may or may not entail the defence of the primacy of the Bishop of Rome or the penal substitutionary theory of the atonement or of two-nature Christology, the epistemological question which has to be faced is not about the essentially Christian character of certain particular doctrines, but whether or not Christian theism is defensible. The weightier matters of theology cannot be neglected for the lesser. The basic question is whether *any* Christian position is true, not whether one brand of Christian position is more characteristically Christian than another.

Because I do not approve of, or hold this view, let me try and state at least one of its advantages and strengths. In particular, it has the considerable merit of taking the basic objections to theology with real seriousness. Christians are sometimes intellectually elusive. If you demonstrate to them the impossibility of reconciling the love of God and the doctrine of the culpability of original sin, they will try to redefine sin. If you prove that the proofs for the existence of God are no such thing, they will explain that they were not meant to be. If you show the incompatibility of belief in the humanity and divinity of Jesus at one and the same time, they will resort to talk about mystery, or paradox, or 'truths held in tension'. The history of theology is such that anyone with a reasonable knowledge of its twists and turns will have little difficulty in moving from one protective cover to another, and claiming that each position successively is Christian in some adequately convincing sense. Faced with this hydra, the controversialist must be excused for desiring to aim a blow below the point where new heads may spring up; the natural instinct is, therefore, to treat it as though it had feet, and cut off its point of contact with any kind of reality whatsoever. It is not Calvinism, or Roman Catholicism, or neo-Protestantism which is mistaken, but any form of Christian theism. If there is no God, the doctrine of election and the theology of infant baptism are alike groundless. What we need to know, then, are the grounds for believing in God, not whether propositions about God are Christian or not.

However, I reply: The concept of a *basic* objection is evocative of the model of foundation and superstructure. A basic objection is an objection to a basic belief or reality. The objection as advanced does not really circumvent the question we are considering, which is, what is properly spoken of as Christian. In appearing to tackle basic objections with seriousness, it simply makes assumptions about the nature of the position which is being attacked. It may be true that some beliefs are more central than others, that the communicability of the love of God to humanity is more important than the Immaculate Conception of the Blessed Virgin; but what tells us (or may tell us) that this is so, is no mere assumption, or hunch, but a careful enquiry into the identity of Christianity, and such an enquiry includes the discovery of what may be basic to it.

While we have not by any means disposed of the objector's position with this elementary observation, it is worth indicating what is involved in an alternative stance. There is a justification for treating with seriousness the question of the identity of

Christianity which by no means neglects the problem of the truth of Christian statement. The view I wish to defend is that the identification of what is really, genuinely, essentially, fundamentally, basically, Christian plays an indispensable (and, I think, sometimes neglected) role in discovering what to defend and how.

This position can be illustrated as follows: let us suppose that we are concerned about the problem of speaking of the power of God. The basic objection to all such talk is the non-occurrence of patent acts of divine power, even in apparently desperate situations. Where, then, *is* God's power? One possibility to which I have referred earlier, is systematically to evacuate the power claim which the Christian is supposed to defend. By overlooking the general power context of the preaching of the Kingdom of God, by dispensing with the miraculous (including the resurrection) on the basis of the allegedly essential presuppositions of historical enquiry, and by devising suitably minimizing explanations of the unmistakable signs of power–consciousness in the primitive communities, it can be made to seem as though the problem is less acute than it is. For a depotentiated Christianity neither Auschwitz, nor Hiroshima, nor Vietnam, is much of a difficulty. Nor, of course is the cross itself. Nor is Paul saying anything profound when he reports God's words to him about his thorn in the flesh, 'My grace is sufficient for you, for my power is made perfect in weakness' (2 Cor. 12.9); rather, he is conducting an exercise in self-acceptance, or making the best of a bad job. In the end of the day depotentiated Christianity is indistinguishable from Stoicism.

Against the procedures which precipitate such a devastating evacuation of the content of the Christian position one may hold the real justification for attempting to discern what is genuinely Christian. It is only when some at least preliminary sense has been generated of the permeation of the theme of the power of God in the doctrines of the resurrection and of the Holy Spirit, in the worship and sacraments of the Church, and the corporate confidence of Christian believers faced with death and its institutionalized embodiments, that the dimension of the demand for grounds for speaking of the power of God will become apparent. There is no necessity which dictates that those concerned for the identity of Christianity have no concern for its truth. It may indeed happen, just as it may happen that those who raise epistemological problems not infrequently make very short work of describing the position whose cogency they are questioning.

I conclude, therefore, with a simple summary of the position which we have reached. It is perfectly reasonable to enquire under what conditions Christianity is one thing. Such an enquiry performs a useful service in bringing into the open the natural assumptions about its diachronic and synchronic unity. The specification of these conditions would be a conscious construction or standpoint on Christian history, neither ruled out of court by historical relativism nor convicted of being a subtle deviation from the question of truth.

II

This standpoint obviously rests on the possibility of speaking of the Christian position *as a whole*. We have already seen just how important a motif this was for Schleiermacher and Newman. But if our investigation has taught us nothing else, it ought to have shown us that, even if such writers agree that one *can* take such a holist perspective and speak with Schleiermacher of the 'principle of adhesion' or with Newman of 'one comprehensive moral fact', they do not agree on what that principle, idea or fact is. The *dis*agreement is chronic and on the face of it this conclusion tells against the position for which I appear to be arguing. If there can be such a diversity of judgements about what Christianity is, does this not greatly diminish the point of striving to learn what the position is?

There appear to be only three possible responses to this situation. The first is the obvious procedure of simply affirming a single authoritative solution which admits neither of ambiguity, nor of dispute. This would constitute the externality tradition in its rawest form. There could be no place for genuine causes of uncertainty, because in that case what Christianity entailed would return to the sphere of disputed judgements. Such a view is contrary to the implications of inwardness, as we have traced them from New Testament times onwards. The assertion of a single authoritative version of Christianity is a profoundly non-historical response, a mere assertion in the face of an overwhelming quantity of contrary evidence.

The second response is simply to abandon any attempt to defend even minimal continuity in the Christian tradition. This also runs into acute difficulties. It is contrary to the well-grounded instinct for requiring the symbols of Christian faith to reflect the immutability of the God to whom they point. It leads, as I have already argued in the case of Troeltsch, to a severe internal difficulty about the role of an élite corps of intellectuals in shaping the future direction of Christianity. Its depotentiation of Christianity is profoundly contradictory to both the theology and the sociology of power in the Church, and in its embracing of uncertainty it destroys too much of the original Christian hallmark of confident participation in a victorious struggle against the powers of evil in the world.

This leaves us with a third possibility, closely corresponding to what I have called the dialectical tradition. This response proposes that the phenomenon of dispute within Christianity has certain conditions about it which make it dispute about one thing. This does not necessarily imply that all participants in the dispute share the *same* convictions in common. Rather there is agreement that the existence of dispute about any element of the Christian tradition is not in and of itself a ground for denying that there is unity in Christianity. Disputes are not necessarily contrary to the constructive intentions of the faith. Therefore we need to examine whether such an understanding of the constructive potential of controversy is a reasonable response to the phenomena of Christian history.

To provide us with a way of tackling this question I wish now to refer to an exceptionally interesting proposal made by Professor W. B. Gallie in his book, *Philosophy and the Historical Understanding*.[14] Here, in the course of an argument designed to show the necessity of knowledge of the history of philosophy for philosophy, he develops the notion of an essentially contested concept. The essentially contested concept is, typically, a term which occurs again and again in the history of the discussion of a subject and yet is the subject of a chronic series of disputes. A historical understanding of the use of these terms is a necessary prerequisite for their philosophical clarification; yet they remain rooted in history in a way which explains the persistent resurgence of disputes about them. As examples of essentially contested concepts, Gallie mentions the concepts of science, fine arts, religion, justice and democracy. About these there has always been, and there ought always to be, sharp dispute; their essential contestability proves the need for philosophy of a vitally combative kind.

Gallie's argument pursues the further delineation of the perennial character of the contests about these concepts, by describing an imaginary game in which there are no definitive rules for finally determining the winner. The example need not concern us, since it is merely a device for introducing the formal conditions which, Gallie believes, characterize the genuine disputes about essentially contested concepts. These concepts, he believes, are 'sustained by perfectly respectable arguments and evidence',[15] although they are not resolvable by argument. What distinguishes them from pointless verbal wrangles are seven conditions: (1) that the concept is appraisive in signifying or accrediting some valued achievement; (2) that the achievement is of an internally complex character; (3) that the explanation of its worth therefore includes reference to respective parts or features of the whole; (4) that the accredited achievement be capable of considerable modification in the light of changing circumstances; (5) that each party to the contest recognize that its own use of the concept is contested by others, and agree to participate both aggressively and defensively; (6) that there be an acknowledged exemplar from whom the concept is derived and whose authority is agreed; and (7) that there be a plausible case to be made for supposing that the fact of contest enables the original exemplar's achievement to be sustained and developed in optimum fashion.

Of the examples Gallie has mentioned he selects the concept of religion as an illustration, noting in particular the different emphases in the various religions arising from the fact that they assemble the elements of cult, doctrine, personal salvation, social cohesion, moral comfort and metaphysical illumination in differing ways. The concept of Christianity, he says, embodies the seven formal conditions of an essentially contested concept. Thus: (1) it is used appraisively of a spiritual achievement; (2) it relates to an achievement of an internally complex kind, capable of being rendered in various ways (as the history of doctrine amply demonstrates); (3) these different accounts of it do refer to parts or features of the whole; (4) it is, moreover, an open concept in the sense that history requires different modifications of it (Gallie uses as an illustration the attitude taken by Christianity to slavery in the ancient world, and in modern times); (5) the concept is also deployed both defensively and aggressively; (6) the source and its authority is obvious; and (7) there is an approach to the optimum realization of Christianity through the different, competing interpretations of it.

Before we pass to a discussion of Gallie's proposals, one aspect of his further consideration of the nature of the argument between rival uses of the concept is worth noting. From the first he recognizes the fact that an alternative view of the use of such concepts is that their justification amounts to unconscious rationalization or special pleading concerning opinions whose capacity to evoke intellectual tenacity is of psychological origin. This would, he admits, explain the fact that argument is not necessarily sufficient to accomplish a change of view. Why is it, one might ask (at least in Birmingham) that everyone is not equally impressed with the arguments deployed in *The Myth of God Incarnate*?[16] Is it because they are logically invalid or historically mistaken? Or is it because certain people are so deeply sunk in the psychological quagmire compounded of the primeval slime of ecclesiastical tradition that they are incapable of recognizing a rational life-line when one is thrown to them?

Gallie offers us an interesting alternative to either of these views. There is a certain logic in the conversion of an individual from one kind of view to another, a logic which we can distinguish from a purely emotional or a psychologically manipulated change. The logic is not, however, the drawing of plain conclusions from plain facts.

> It is rather, the fact that a particular achievement revives and realizes, as it were in fuller relief, some already recognized feature of an already valued style of performance, i.e. that of the original exemplar. Because of this particular performance [he] sees, or claims to see, more clearly and more fully why he has acknowledged and followed the exemplar's style of performance all along. The scales are tipped for him not, or at least not only, by some psychologically explainable kink of his temperament, nor by some observandum whose sheer occurrence all observers must acknowledge, but by his recognition of a value which, given his particular marginal appraisive situation, is conclusive for him, although it is merely impressive or surprising or worth noticing for others.[17]

This, in my opinion, represents a more subtle and differentiated conception of the role of argument in relation to dispute about the nature of Christianity, than the rather unsatisfactory notion of proof used in some recent controversies. It also sheds useful light on what may be involved in discernment, namely, the recognition of a match between what has already come to be valued in Christian discipleship and an aspect of the exemplar's achievement.

The crucial question is, however, what it is that constitutes the fact that the players are all playing in a single game, and that the participants in the dispute are contending about the same matter. This has been the central question of this chapter from the start, but do Gallie's seven conditions supply us with further illumination? Are there any points in his argument which confirm, or in any way take further, the move towards speaking of Christianity as a whole made in the first section of this chapter?

In the first place, Gallie lays considerable stress on the condition which specifies that there must be an acknowledgement by all the contestants of the authority of the original exemplar. Although the achievement of the exemplar is from the first variously describable, the contestants are held together by the conviction that the contest has a single origin in a single, albeit internally complex, performance. For Christians that performance is the life, death and resurrection of Jesus Christ. It is certainly true that that event is internally complex, composed of teaching, example, healing, suffering, dying and being raised from death. It is certainly true that that event was, from the first, described in various ways. Moreover it is true that the bodily continuity of Jesus guarantees the statement that, from the cradle to the tomb, we have to do with a single series of public events; and, further, that all those who speak of the resurrection believe that the identity of the risen Christ was continuous with his identity as Jesus of Nazareth. There is substantial ground, therefore, for Gallie's view that the contestants who disagree about what Christianity is, are, despite their differences, disagreeing about the nature of a single 'performance'. In this case the word 'performance' might be rendered as 'life story', the connected series of events telling of the impact of Jesus Christ.

But do the contestants agree on the authority of the original exemplar? To establish this it is not, of course, necessary to show that all who dispute about the concept of Christianity must agree that Jesus is authoritative for their own personal convictions. There can be, and there are, useful commentators on the idea of the Christian religion, who do not profess themselves to be Christians. All that it is necessary to show is that the performance or achievement of Jesus has an exemplary authority for the proper way of conceiving what Christianity is. Doubtless, Gallie is too cavalier in failing to refer to the wide variety of views, even among Christians, on precisely this point. Nonetheless he is correct in his assumption; indeed the contrary position is too eccentric to detain us for long. For what a contrary position would have to show is that there is no greater reason for Christians to attend to the Gospels and Epistles than to the traditions about the Buddha, or the wisdom of Confucius or the philosophy of Plato. But what, *per contra*, defines the Christian is the attention he gives to Jesus Christ; and the quality of such attention, though by no means necessarily, or even properly, exclusive attention, is precisely that which establishes that his performance or achievement has exemplary authority for him.

It is manifest, therefore, that this *formal* characteristic of one who is a contestant about the concept of Christianity contains a statement about the status of Christology for a Christian. But precisely because it is a formal characteristic, any further articulation of the *type* of Christology becomes at once part of the contest. The achievement or performance of Jesus is of an internally complex character, and there it is initially describable in diverse ways. But at the same time there is a second element in the formal characterization, which arises from attention to Jesus, namely the reference to God as the context of the event. God is the context in the sense that, from start to finish, God is spoken of as initiating, accompanying and bringing to completion Jesus' achievement. This is not merely factually the case about Jesus' own teaching; it is formally the case with respect to contest about Christianity, in as much as the quality of the attention given to Jesus is the quality of attention given to that which is transcendent. Again no particular Christology is involved in this statement. It is merely that, formally speaking, a Christian is defined as one who gives attention to Jesus whose achievement is contextualized by God.

The importance of a formal definition of what it means to be

Christian is that it permits a title of this kind to be used intelligibly by both spectators of, and participants in, the Christian religion. But a formal definition is a long way from being an adequate rendition of the substance and quality of the disciple's attention to Jesus, and if a formal definition is treated as a sufficient expression of Christian discipleship the charge of reductionism is impossible to avoid. The purpose of a formal definition is to satisfy the minimum conditions of intelligibility required for the common use of a particular set of terms, Christian, Christianity and so forth. It does not foreclose the question of the inherent contestability of the terms, because it formally indicates the area in which the contests take place. A formal definition is both banal and boring. Christianity only becomes interesting as a concept when someone has the courage to spell out in greater or lesser detail one or other of the contestable possibilities which the definition permits.

The formal definition does not in itself foreclose discussion of the normativity of one or other of the contestable possibilities for further elucidation. Thus it provides no answer to the question: What are the rules of the games? Indeed, the whole point of using Gallie's depiction of an essentially contested concept was to draw attention to the fact that contestants characteristically do not agree about the rules of the games, but that this disagreement does not prevent them from mutual participation. Consequently it is still entirely open, on the basis of a formal definition, to argue that a particular way of specifying the disciple's attention to Jesus, for example a specific Christology or family of Christologies, is normative for the games being played. The argument that will undoubtedly break out, in this case, will be both about the Christology itself, and about the rules for determining what is, or is not normative. The mistake commonly made by participants in contests such as these is that they assume that if only one agreed about the method for solving disputes, one would know which form of Christology was normative. On the contrary, I am maintaining that one only understands the nature of the disputes if one is prepared to accept the fact that they raise both substantial and methodological questions at the same time, and that consequently methodology is not a prior discipline in theology.

III

That Christianity is to be understood as an essentially contested concept is the proposal of the previous section. How this proposal enables one to make further sense of the dialectical model (as described above) for interpreting the identity of Christianity has now to be further explored. In the first place, I want to argue that the formal definition of Christianity offered in the previous section makes particularly good sense of an interesting aspect of early Christianity, namely the persistent movement towards a series of statements in which the central content of the Christian faith comes to expression.[18]

Thus if we compare the formal statement I have just made about the achievement of Jesus being contextualized by God with the articles of the *fundamentum fidei* as taught in the early Church some interesting features emerge. There are, we argued, two aspects of the formal characterization, namely the reference to Jesus, and the context provided by reference to God. Similarly there are, in the fundamental articles tradition, two prime characteristics, the so-called *gesta Christi*, a summary of the events of the life of Christ, and a series of statements contextualizing that life with reference to God. This fact explains the second-century phenomenon of two article summaries of faith speaking of God as creator, and Jesus as the Son of God. The omission of any reference to the Holy Spirit need not be understood as naive binitarianism, *en route* to a fully developed Trinitarian theology, but a more basic articulation of the ground to be occupied by any Christian whatsoever.[19]

This confirms the argument of the previous section. In such summaries we are dealing not with a condensation of the whole content of Christian believing, but with a slightly elaborated version of a formal definition of the area which believing occupies.

I would suggest that further examination reveals the nature of the position which is being summarily indicated, as follows:

(i)   The acts of Jesus are detailed because it is being said that here the power of God is at work in the creation of new life. Articulable, of course, in a variety of ways, the point at issue is the power of God to achieve something genuinely novel in the very midst of time. One destroys Christianity when one de-potentiates God or denies that in Jesus there is any such novelty. (That, incidentally, is what the incarnation debate has ultimately to attend to, not merely to the inherent and admitted problems of two-nature Christology.) The capacity of this life story to initiate novelty in the world is represented by the context in which it is set, and this contextualization consists of two features.

(ii)   It is being said that God is the Lord of creation. Here the first article of the creeds shows a remarkable consistency. To omit or to deny it would make possible Manichaeism or fatalism; in either case God would be disempowered, and the world handed over either to malign forces or to meaninglessness.

(iii)   The second aspect of the context is, as one would expect, the other horizon. If God is Lord over beginnings, he is Lord over ends. Already prefigured in Jesus' resurrection, it is said that God is Lord over death. Here the power is simply this, that human death is not the final word on his existence, since God has the power to raise him from the dead and to make him stand under judgement.

These three elements, which together narrate the life-story of Jesus in the context provided by two horizon affirmations, constitute the basic Christian delineation of the ground occupied by Christianity. They are a Christian, that is, an insider's depiction of the area of context. They are thus characteristically fuller than a merely formal definition. At the same time they permit a wide variety of arguments to be developed both about the content of Christian belief and the norms for deciding what constitutes Christian belief.

Nonetheless the position I have outlined is open to one apparently devastating objection. Why should it be thought that a delineation of the ground occupied by Christianity should not itself be open to dispute? Is not this threefold statement merely a thinly disguised way of summarizing Christianity in a certain number of propositions which are then raised to a position of bogus invulnerability by being called the delineation of the ground occupied by Christianity? Are not these propositions in fact a highly disputable, idiosyncratic version of the essence of Christianity?

The answer to this question has to return to what was said above about the formal definition of what it means to be Christian. The purpose of a formal definition, it was said, was to provide certain minimum conditions of intelligibility required for the common use of terms, like Christian, Christianity and so forth. There are good grounds for using these terms, as I have argued above. There must be boundary conditions for their use; that is, there must be conditions under which it is ridiculous to say the word Christian properly applies to such a view, attitude or action. It is not necessary to the case for the existence of boundary conditions that the boundaries should be absolutely clear and distinct.[20] One can sensibly claim that the fact that the threefold set of propositions excludes certain contrary positions does not entail prejudgement of a whole series of contested possibilities. Nor does it preclude a still sharper definition of boundaries. To use the game analogy again, it is like designating a field as the site of a game on which some of the contestants will certainly want to draw out a precise rectangular pitch, whereas others will find it more exciting to play in ditches and hedgerows. But nobody can play with impunity on the nearby motorway.

This reply, however, is still rather a long way from being adequate to an important element in the force of the objection, which derives from the propositional character of the delineation of the boundaries. After all that has been said about the tradition of referring to the heart as the experiential centre of Christian profession, it appears that with the propositional expression of the life-story of Jesus Christ set in the context, or horizon, provided by creation beliefs and eschatology we have reverted to a purely external verdict on the identity of Christianity. It will be apparent enough that such is not my intention. But how do I propose to evade the charge that, despite my intention to offer what I have called a dialectical account of the identity of Christianity in which its outward and inward aspects are in interrelation, the delineation of boundaries has been by means of a purely external story, myth and doctrine? The answer to this must again refer to a feature of Gallie's depiction of the essentially contested concept.

On Gallie's account of the distinction between a pointless verbal wrangle and a genuinely creative dispute, it was axiomatic that each party to the contest recognize that its own use of the concept is contested by others, and yet agree to participate both aggressively and defensively. But why should they agree? Why should they not assert that it is absurd to play with others who do not recognize the same rules? Who wants to play soccer against a team determined to play American football? This, of course, transposed to the Christian arguments is precisely the question raised by ecumenism. Why should there be discussion with those who believe they know the answers in advance and the proper method for reaching definitive conclusions? It is possible, of course, that one may win some kind of tactical advantage by appearing to be willing to enter into discussion. At least one avoids the impression of intransigence, and in the process one may win over converts to one's own side.

But agreement to participate in this kind of argument seems to rest on something more than merely tactical considerations. Gallie specifies again that a plausible case ought to be able to be made out for the fact that the contest has a constructive significance, in order to enable the original exemplar's achievement to be sustained and developed in optimum fashion. That is to say, it ought to be possible to see a connection between what Jesus had in mind and achieved by way of new life possibilities, and the implicit purpose of arguments about Christianity. The simplest way of indicating what such a connection might be would be to refer to the tone of a contest. Arguments can be hard, serious and purposeful, without being acrimonious in character. The tone of the controversy is indicated in such matters as fairness to one's opponent, assumption of honourable motives and self-criticism of one's own, attempt to distinguish central from peripheral matters, and choice of vocabulary or rhetorical style. In a very large number of ways a user of words can demonstrate the intention he or she may have. The tone of a controversy is a direct indication of the hearts of the controversialists. How controversialists argue has a close bearing upon what is intended in Jesus' achievement.

I should want, therefore, to defend the threefold expression of the ground occupied by Christianity in the following way: it is, necessarily a series of propositions, constituting an external expression in story, myth and doctrine. But this external expression is interrelated with the internal experience of new life inseparable from the story, myth and doctrine. One reason for the occurrence of internal conflict is the problem of the more precise delineation of boundaries. Another reason is the inherent ambiguities in the tasks which Christianity is continuously called to carry out, and the problems which it must solve. The proper conduct of all such controversies helps it in this activity. But proper conduct means conduct which is based on an inwardly appropriated sense of what has to be achieved in the world. *It is in the process of interaction between this inward element and the external forms of Christianity that the identity of Christianity consists.*

This conclusion leaves me with one further task, which is to assign to worship a particularly crucial place in the process of interaction so defined. Without the dimension of worship, what has been described above could be carried out in a well-mannered discussion group dedicated to the promulgation and performance of a certain way of viewing the world. Christians do discuss their doctrines, and they must do so in a sensitive way; but Christianity is also a community of worshippers, and this fact makes for a decisive difference.

I I

Worship, Commitment and Identity

Gallie's discussion of an essentially contested concept deployed examples not merely from religion but also from politics, aesthetics and other fields of human activity. The clarification of a concept specific to a field of study is, of course, one thing, and being a politician, an artist or a religious person is quite another. Each of these activities has a conjoined intellectual tradition of reflection, but the intellectual work is dependent on the prior existence of living examples of politicians, artists and practitioners of religion.

It ought not to be overlooked, therefore, that Christianity is a religion not a philosophical system, and that one does not participate in Christianity by discussing its methodological problems. This unremarkable statement, which was given an airing early in this book, was justified by reference to the multifaceted character of Christianity.[1] The Christian religion, we argued, following Newman and Smart, exists in a number of aspects or dimensions. The philosophical or doctrinal aspect, with its methodological interests, can only be seen in conjunction with other aspects, such as those related to rituals or social embodiment. Discussion of the identity of Christianity, which naturally raises acute problems of method because of the inherent problem of conflict, cannot be allowed an independent existence.

The argument of this book has emphasized the fact of internal conflict in Christianity. What Christianity is, according to the conclusion of the previous chapter, is essentially contested. But at the same time we have had reason to note that internal conflict cannot be regarded with equanimity. Too much is at stake for mere toleration. Because of the tasks which Christians believe themselves to have been commissioned to carry out in the world, conflict cannot be allowed to be entirely free ranging. But it is not sufficient to recognize that the Christian Church is not a society for the good-mannered discussion of the meaning of life. One is no more likely to make that kind of mistake, than one is to confuse a discussion group on philosophical aesthetics with an art school. But the more difficult problem is to state how the Church can both be what it is, the religiously appropriate context for living the Christian life, and at the same time allow the kind of discussion and dissent which we have argued is inevitable. As we have repeatedly emphasized, it is the fact of discussion and dissent which sets off the second order activity of reflection upon the concept of Christianity. Our problem now is to locate the role of discussion and dissent in the total phenomenon of Christianity.

At this point a certain recapitulation of the whole theme of the book becomes necessary if we are to avoid the impression of wheeling on the apparently new consideration of Christian worship as a *deus ex machina* to solve our difficulties. Certainly it is true that what we have been mostly concerned with is the doctrinal content of Christianity; increasingly the discussion has revolved around the highly specialized field of the method of Christian doctrine. Why? The reason for this progressive concentration on the intellectual dimension of Christianity is, as was stated right from the start, that conflict brings it quite naturally into prominence.

For it is by means of such precision as is attainable by the careful use of words that the disagreements at issue in such diverse non-verbal matters as, for example, ritual and the structure of social relations can be clarified. There is a theology of ritual, and a theology of the Church. Neither, however, constitutes a replacement for performing rituals and for living in a structured community. Despite the intellectual tradition, those who disagree about Christianity are disagreeing not about a philosophy of life, but about an embodied religious tradition. Nonetheless at the same time the inevitable arguments about the forms which the embodied religious tradition is to take can be sharpened up methodologically, and that is one of the contributions which the intellectual tradition is able to make.

Another reason for the concentration upon the doctrinal, especially the methodological issue, is the fact that the discussion of the essence of Christianity which has formed the core of the book was largely conducted within modern Protestantism. The Protestant tradition has laid particular emphasis upon the hearing of the word, and the Reformation itself has been interpreted as the triumph of auditory over optical notions of form and thought.[2] The commission to preach the gospel to every creature, and concern for the purity of the preached word has occasionally resulted in an indifference, or even contempt, towards the sacramental life. Modern Protestant theologians are often acutely aware of this danger, and seek to avoid it.

Troeltsch, for example, realized from his study of Christian social teaching that Harnack's *History of Dogma* had seriously undervalued the embodiment of the Christian tradition in cult and community, and to that extent distorted the presentation of Christianity's essence.[3] Barth, also, stated unequivocally the importance of the sacraments precisely as a counter-weight to the danger of one-sided intellectualism.[4] These statements, however, have to be set in the context of the logic of their respective positions. It is not enough to cite them, as though their mere enunciation at once redressed the balance. It was argued above that the epistemology of their respective theologies inevitably bestows huge power upon the theologian in two, not dissimilar, ways: either by shaping the form of Christianity appropriate to each new cultural environment in the light of the scholar's detailed historical knowledge and philosophical maturity (Troeltsch), or in seeking to conform the whole life of the Church in accordance with the sole, sufficient criterion of utter obedience to the word of God (Barth). The epistemological decision in each case is crucial. And it is for that reason that, increasingly, methodology has appeared to be the area where the future of the identity of Christianity is decided.

But, as we have argued in the previous two chapters, it is an illusion to think that the methodological questions raised by disagreements over the substance and content of the Christian tradition have any absolute priority. These disagreements evidently entail different ground rules and different games, to use Gallie's analogy. There has never been one, single, universally agreed methodology for solving the inherent conflicts of Christianity, and we have every reason to suppose that there never will be.

It does not betoken, therefore, a radical change of direction if we ask, finally, whether there may be a conception of the identity of Christianity which is not committed to the attempt to resolve the problem of its unity and continuity by a methodological *tour de force*; but which is, rather, respectful in a more than theoretical manner of the multifaceted character of Christianity on which we insisted from the beginning. The last word of this book is to argue, without any detraction from the importance of the doctrinal aspect of Christianity, that the phenomenon of Christian worship makes a vital difference to the conditions under which vigorous argument of a radical kind may be regarded as a constructive contribution, not a destructive irrelevance, to the performance of Christian identity in the modern world.

I

First it is necessary to indicate what is meant here by worship. Rather than offer a definition of greater or lesser precision one may point initially to occurrences of Christian worship; that is, to assemblies of Christian men and women, baptized in the name of the Trinity, gathering on certain days at a definite time for an appointed meeting, at which virtually everything is done with prayer.[5] Characteristic of such occurrences is the fact that those who have gathered have come to invoke the name of Jesus and to be enriched by his special presence. Worship, so observed, entails congregational assembly for prayer and a common intention defined by the achievement of Jesus. Three vital conditions are incorporated. In the first place, the condition for the Christian character of what is done is satisfied by the necessary reference to the achievement of Jesus, which is recalled. *Anamnesis* (remembering, recollection) in worship is of the deeds of Jesus set in the context of God. But, secondly, that *anamnesis* is prayer and praise. It is, therefore, a recollection by means of which the intentions of the recollector are inwardly challenged, reoriented and offered up. Finally, the worship is corporate; it is an arrangement so devised as to take place at a time and place known to be convenient for those who desire to assemble. This last feature of worship is so important that it deserves extended treatment.

The communal character of worship is a direct inheritance from the Jewish matrix out of which Christian worship emerged. Commonly Christian writers exaggerate the degree of radical novelty to be attached to the Christian assemblies.[6] The evidence is very scanty, but certain facts are eloquent enough in the absence of contrary indications. The Gospels all indicate that Jesus both attended and participated in synagogue worship; Acts asserts that the apostles did likewise after the ascension (Acts 1.14),[7] and that Paul's practice was to visit the synagogue in every city in which he preached. Although we do not know precisely what words or readings Christians used in their own assemblies, such indications as we have indicate continuities with synagogue practice (use of psalms, Bible readings, the Sanctus, the Decalogue and some of the Benedictions) together, doubtless, with adaptations.[8]

This is altogether as one would expect. The history of the developing self-awareness of the new Christian movement includes the discovery of a 'new covenant' (1 Cor. 12.25; Mark 14.24) with the God of Israel, implying both continuity and novelty in its traditions of worship. As in the case of aspects of its teaching we have good reason to speak of a transformation of Judaism, so in the worship of the Christian groups new themes, new associations and a new importance given to earlier practices (especially to baptism and to table fellowship) led Christians to a transformation of Jewish worship. At no stage are we able to identify any decisive act of formal separation from Judaism, not even from temple worship. But Christians found that by doing certain additional things together, especially by meeting for prayer and the breaking of bread, and under the impact of the new causes for thanksgiving which they believed themselves to possess, the older traditions of Judaism lost their appeal and relevance. The period of transition entailed sharp internal conflict, especially over the Jewish rite of circumcision. The new ways of practising baptism and table fellowship contained formidable ambiguities concerning the outside and inside of the ritual actions. But in due course the identity of Christianity was as plainly reflected in its new forms of communal worship as in its formal professions of belief. Christians had become, in the words of the writer of 1 Peter, a chosen race, a royal priesthood, a holy nation, God's own people, that you may declare the wonderful deeds of him who called you out of darkness into his marvellous light (1 Pet. 2.9).

The simultaneous transformation of communal traditions of belief and worship is important for the much discussed question, which will be canvassed in Section III below, of whether belief is normative for worship, or vice versa. There it will be argued that this way of posing the problem is highly confused; we restrict ourselves here to ruling out certain highly simplified solutions. Thus it is not the case that early Christians suspended themselves from public worship until they had sorted out their doctrinal problems, and then applied their solutions to the creation of new liturgical forms of worship. Nor, on the other hand, is the converse true, that their instinctive urge to adopt new forms of worship compelled them, in due course, to rationalize their practices in new doctrinal constructions.

But if doctrine is not a comprehensive norm or exclusive criterion for worship, neither is it irrelevant to it. Communal worship includes the use of rituals which plainly imply doctrines. Practices such as circumcision, which constitute an important part of communal identity, may imply, or at least be taken to imply, doctrines about the relation of God and humanity which are, from the new perspective, actually false. If the doctrines have been rejected for good reasons, these same reasons apply to the practices. Moreover, in the event of disagreement about rituals, it is necessary to have a verbal clarification of what is meant or intended by the practices. If the significance of the practices cannot be reduced to their verbally articulated meaning, neither, on the other hand, can they be separated from such meaning. In focusing upon worship in this last chapter, therefore, there is no implied departure from recognition of the role of doctrine. Communal worship, indeed, is a theatre in which doctrine, ethics, myth, social embodiment, ritual and inward experience are integrally related.

Hitherto I have spoken solely of the importance of communal worship. But is there not a solitary worship, secret prayer to the Father who sees in secret, in one's own room, with the door shut (Matt. 6.6)? There seems to be an unavoidable individualism in the Judaeo-Christian tradition springing directly from its emphasis upon the heart, that secret self which is known only to God and which is uniquely constitutive of a person's identity. Is it not with this unique self alone that God is ready to have dealings? Individualism, however, is a misleading designation of this selfhood. For this secret self is never wholly separated from a social context. In two ways solitary worship is set in the wider context of the community, first by reason of the fact that solitary prayer is a practice enjoined on *all* members of the community (Matt. 5.1), and secondly, in as much as the aim of solitary prayer is the bringing about of the Kingdom upon earth (Matt. 6.10). Physically solitary prayer does not psychologically isolate the individual, even as it sets him or her in a unique relation with the Father. It both implies and looks forward to a community of belief, an ethos or a tradition. In that sense the communal worship deserves to be spoken of in the first place, as the normal form of worship.

But precisely with the communality of worship, the problem of the synchronic unity of Christianity comes once more sharply into focus. The question is: In what way, if at all, does the phenomenon of communal Christian worship contribute to an identity conceived as containing an inherent series of conflicts? Are we any better served by the diversity of styles and content of communal worship than we are by the diversity of traditions of doctrine? If there are competitive and contradictory traditions in the latter, are there not at least as obviously competitive and contradictory forms of the former? Of the diversity of forms of worship there is no doubt. Because the New Testament does not provide us with an early Christian liturgy, the development of common traditions of worship has lacked the point of reference provided by the not inconsiderable knowledge we possess of the beliefs of the primitive communities. Consequently the discord between different liturgies and between different styles of their performance, both of which swiftly acquire the status of hallowed tradition, is, if anything, more extensive than discord between forms of Christian believing. On the face of it the project of finding a form of unity in Christian worship is more hopeless than that of unity in belief.

Nonetheless, the case I wish to argue is that the continuous and effective identity of Christianity is preserved in the world when the basic features of Christian worship have been recognized, and that in this context the disputes which inevitably break out about Christian doctrine and every other external dimension of Christianity, not excluding ritual itself, may themselves contribute towards an optimum realization of the achievement which Christian discipleship acknowledges.

II

We must start by attempting to understand the implications of commitment in Christianity. This is a theme upon which we have already commented on a number of occasions. It has been said, for example, on the basis of a recent sociological work, that one of the functions of sacrifice in a religion is to clarify priorities and strengthen commitments.[9] But it is not often realized with sufficient force that modern pluralistic societies present acute problems for maintaining the strength of religious commitment. Mol puts the matter thus:

> In pluralistic societies, the actual competition between a large variety of foci of identity has created dilemmas of commitment ... Lack of commitment, lack of identity, meaninglessness, anomie and alienation are all very much related symptoms of societies in which definitions of reality are no longer taken for granted because competition has relativized each and all of them.[10]

The variety of roles which are presented to an individual, irrespective of whether that person could ever come to occupy them all, constitutes a severe threat to the single-mindedness required by the performance of religious obligations. Religious observance increasingly resembles a rather inefficiently organized leisure-time activity, made available for those with a particular preference, and the practitioners of religion appear to accord it no higher priority than might be claimed by a tennis club.

One example of crisis for religious commitment in Christianity is the debate about the celibacy of the Roman Catholic clergy. Presented both to candidates for the priesthood and to the Church as a whole in terms of self-sacrifice, the person of the priest functions as a living focus for the implications of commitment to Christ. While it is recognized that it is not given to all to live in this way, the single-mindedness which the faith can evoke is publicly exemplified in the celibate priest, monk or nun.

But, of course, it is precisely celibacy which is under scrutiny at the very moment when the cohesion of Roman Catholicism is weakening.[11]

The vulnerability of Protestantism to the impact of other claims on the interest and attention of its church members is still more obvious. Lacking the sign of a celibate priesthood, the problem of how religious commitment is to be focused is reflected in a greater lack of cohesiveness. The relatively slight interest in external rituals, and the abandonment of the structure of supernatural beliefs connected with the rituals, has compounded the difficulty for Protestantism. The maintenance of inner convictions in a cultural context characterized by a plurality of beliefs and life-styles requires apparently formidable discipline. But at the same time, open theological disagreement, the fruit of the 'emancipation' of the Enlightenment, apparently corrodes the very roots of the required discipline. At once every possibility is open, and at the same time nothing seems achievable.

The religious words of both Roman Catholicism and Protestantism have evidently suffered from a progressive crisis in religious commitment. Although it is open to question whether, since the eighteenth century in western Europe at least, religious values permeated the whole of the society, it is nonetheless a new phenomenon that the traditional language of the Christian faith should have so little public currency. In these lands, and to a lesser extent in North America, the Christian Church is faced with the real possibility that it will occupy in the future the position of a minority group or groups, more or less radically at odds with the dominant ideology of the culture.

The thesis has recently been argued by Alastair MacIntyre, that the contemporary vision of the world is predominantly one which affirms, with Max Weber, an irreducible plurality of values, but at the same time strives to continue to use moral vocabulary whilst denying its objectivity.[12] For such a society the question of the ends or goals of human life are systematically unsettlable.[13] The culture as a whole comes to embody the philosophy of liberal individualism profoundly destructive of the human good. At the close of his book he envisages, with a reference to St Benedict, the necessity of 'the construction of local forms of community within which civility and the intellectual and moral life can be sustained through the new dark ages which are already upon us'.[14]

This pessimistic analysis of the moral situation is of considerable importance for Christian theology, which has for decades attempted to reconcile its traditional content with the basic premises of modernity. The pretext for these attempts has been the issue of supernaturalism, as Troeltsch and many other writers have urged. The origins and classical expression of the Christian Church lie in centuries for which, unlike our own, the supernatural world was an ever-present reality. The miraculous in Old and New Testaments was supported by tales and affirmations of the supernatural in the present. Dependence upon God was a live option, if for no other reason, because medical or political intervention was as likely to be detrimental to physical or social well-being as leaving matters to providence. But with the growth of a reasonably efficient secondary environment of public health and medical care, supported by reasonably stable centralization of political authority and community policing, such forms of dependence become less natural. The tales of the miraculous, moreover, have been replaced by tales of the uncovering of fraud, and the discovery of unsuspected mechanisms and regularities. In a world from which the supernatural has been banished as a form of causal explanation, Christianity has no grounds (other than sheer assertion) for presenting itself as the Great Exception.[15]

In the chapter devoted to the contribution of Ernst Troeltsch to the essence of Christianity debate, I expressed certain reservations about the adequacy of the historical construction which radically separates the supposedly naive supernaturalism of the pre-Enlightenment era from the assumptions of modernity. But it is impossible to deny that the modern challenges to Christianity are unprecedented and far-reaching, affecting issues of a quasi-factual kind, such as whether or not crop-disasters, famine or plague are to be attributed to 'natural causes' or to the activity of divine judgement. The arguments against over-simplifying the issue of supernaturalism are too numerous to rehearse here, though it is apparent, from Troeltsch's work itself, that there must be a metaphysical basis for *any* claim that Christianity is exceptionally interesting or valuable.

Nonetheless I am by no means disposed to minimize the

271

impact which the philosophy of liberal individualism, as MacIntyre portrays it, has had upon whole-hearted religious commitment, exemplified in the Christian tradition of sainthood. It is here, rather than in an overdrawn contrast between modern and pre-modern world views, that the major dissuasives to Christian discipleship are encountered. The assault is both overt and covert.

The *overt* opposition to religious commitment takes the form of an argument to the effect that all such standpoints entail an abdication of rationality. The case can be argued in both moderate or stronger versions. The moderate view is that, though all moral and religious over-beliefs are irrational, they are humanly unavoidable. The proper course is, therefore, to preserve the area of rationality in as uncontaminated a form as possible. The stronger version presents a somewhat paradoxical demand for a prior commitment to rationality.[16] On this account, what the modern world has taught us is that when religious claims are testable, they prove to be false; and when not testable, are indistinguishable from fancy. Once we discover that, even if only occasionally, religions have taken refuge in untruths, we are obliged to submit them in their entirety to rational investigation. Nor can this commitment to rational enquiry itself be regarded as merely one form of commitment among many, since it is the criterion for commitment. We can tell the difference between these forms of commitment, because no one (we are assured) would attempt to argue that the commitment to rationality ought itself to be subject to the criterion of, say, religious commitment.

The overt challenge to Christianity is justified at least to this extent that certain propositions, maintained as true by Roman Catholics and Protestants, have, as the result of careful investigation, been abandoned as untenable. That Christianity has lent itself to the perpetration of religious fraud, and to the suppression of critical investigations, is undeniable. The discovery that Christian institutions are capable of sponsoring either error or deceit imposes a *moral* obligation to pursue historical enquiry to whatever conclusions it may lead.[17]

But it will be noticed at once that the acknowledgement of a moral criterion as a condition of making religious affirmations is not a modern importation into the substance of Christian commitment. What is new is the development of new techniques for discriminating between truth and falsity. The knowledge that Christian commitment entails the total rejection of the 'father of lies' is wholly traditional. It is plain enough that the impact of the new techniques is very far-reaching, particularly since theological argument and construction had accustomed itself to reliance upon the unquestionable authorities of Bible and solemn traditional definition. But at the same time it is a notable feature of modern Christian theology that traditions of various kinds survive as 'authorities', that is, they continue to count as points of reference in theological argument, despite the fact that they are unprotected in principle from being challenged and criticized.[18]

The *covert* opposition to religious commitment takes the form of a social disincentive to rule out certain possible forms of experience in favour of a Christian imperative. This may take the obvious expression of sexual experimentation outside the context of Christian marriage, or the less blatant, but no less seductive, attractions of life-styles made possible by the acquisition of wealth. The consumer-oriented society assiduously promotes the view that unspecified goods are to be derived from the consumption of labour-saving devices, better homes, packaged holidays and the like. The power of their appeal lies in the elements of truth contained in the messages. But, of course, the need financially to maintain the churches enters into competition with the desired consumption which functions as an inhibition to commitment. Christians in an affluent society seem to require constant reassurance that Jesus' instruction to the rich young man to sell all that he had and give to the poor does not apply to them.

The covert opposition to religious commitment is of immense power and pervasiveness because it can coexist with limited overt religiosity. Thus, for example, the modern world has familiarized us with the phenomenon of the Christian who threatens to abandon the practice of the faith because of minor irritants, such as the loss of a favourite landmark in the religious horizon, or a change of residence, or a new minister. When overt religious profession has finally come to depend upon a matter of taste or sentiment, then indeed it has become marginal in a person's system of priorities. The word commitment can hardly be applied to it.

The importance of this discussion of commitment for our understanding of the place of worship in the maintenance of modern Christian identity lies here. A contrast must inevitably be drawn between the absolute claim of Christian discipleship and the 'dilemmas of commitment' caused by the competition between a large variety of 'foci of identity' (Mol). The activity of worship sharpens the contrast to the point of crisis. The language of the Scriptures, the confessions of faith and traditional hymns express a single-mindedness of devotion fundamentally discordant in tone with the implications and effect of both overt and covert attacks on religious commitment. The self-sacrifice of Christ proclaimed anew at each Eucharist makes an uncompromisingly absolutist demand.

For an example we may refer to Paul's appeal to the congregation in Rome to present their bodies 'as a living sacrifice, holy and acceptable to God, which is your spiritual worship' (Rom. 12.1). The contrast hardly needs to be brought out. It is significant that the passage brings together the themes of self-dedication, sacrifice and worship. It is not necessary with Käsemann to deny that any cultic sense could or should be seen in the term worship (*latreia*).[19] The fact that Paul demands the presentation of bodies suggests rather that both external and internal worship is in mind, and that external worship includes not merely ritual but also ethical behaviour. This worship he describes as 'spiritual' (*logikē*) or rational, that is, worship consistent with the ultimate truth about human beings revealed in Jesus Christ, and issuing in the disclosure of 'what is good, acceptable and perfect' (Rom. 12.2). As C. E. B. Cranfield comments, 'cultic worship ought to be the focus-point of that whole wider worship which is the continually repeated self-surrender of the Christian in obedience of life'.[20]

The recognition of the significance of cultic worship specifically in relation to the problem of commitment advances the argument to this stage. Worship, as the surrender of the whole of the self, itself contextualizes the work of the theologian. The discussion of methodological questions arising from the conflicts entailed in maintaining the identity of Christianity do not take place on a level above that of commitment. The identity of Christianity is not, therefore, reshaped by the activity of theologians acting externally to the principle source of its continuous perpetuation. Their activity, indeed, is set in context by the continuous offering of the community's worship; and as a member of the community the theologian is challenged to see what she or he does as itself an act of self-surrender.

The natural response to such an argument would undoubtedly be that it constitutes a characteristic evasion of the claims of truth. It suggests that the Christian thinker is never to allow anything to count against the intellectual content of Christian commitment. It seems that all enquiry is to be conducted within safe parameters, and that worship is invoked to neutralize the impact of sharp intellectual disagreement. At this stage three points can be made in reply; the significance of the critical function of theology is to be explored more fully in section III.

In the first place, it cannot be held to be to the disrepute of Christian theologians that they should be known as persons with convictions. The important question is whether or not those convictions inhibit theologians from giving an accurate and sympathetic account of arguments against their preferred conclusions. The rigidity of outlook which fails to understand alternative points of view, and the indecisiveness which fails to distinguish the grounds for preferring one view to another, are not the necessary concomitants of the holding of convictions leading to a definite commitment.

Secondly, it should actually be an advantage to a theologian to believe in God, in that nothing ought to stand in the way of the acknowledgement of the truth. The Judaeo-Christian spirituality, indeed, strongly encourages the utmost honesty in dealings with God, and the tradition of the negative way affords support to those who enter the experience of doubt and despair. The *sacrificium intellectus* is less a confinement of the mental horizons to those of comfortable religiosity, than an engagement of the whole self in a quest for truth.[21]

The third consideration is of a more specific kind, connected with the degree to which the Christian commitment spoken of exists in fully articulated form. In the previous chapter it was argued that the use of the word Christian had to convey certain conventional boundaries, but that the boundaries need not themselves be precisely specifiable. To be a Christian theologian means to agree to participate defensively and aggressively in the contests which necessarily occur about Christianity. It is an advantage to an intellectual quest both to know what the initial commitments are (so as to be able to recognize counter-positions, and thus the conditions and grounds on which the initial commitment would have to be abandoned), and also to have a sense of the freedom given by the initial commitment to engage in articulating its possibilities.

On all these grounds, it is not to be thought that the commitment of which I have spoken as entailed in Christian discipleship is incompatible with the exposure to rational argument required in a scholar. There are no valid objections of a general kind to the conclusion for which we argued that worship itself contextualizes the activities of theologians. The question which now has to be faced is the particular, indeed, perennial, problem of the relation between doctrine and worship within Christianity.

III

In his extensive discussion of the Latin tag, *lex orandi, lex credendi* (literally, law of praying, law of believing), Geoffrey Wainwright draws attention to the fact that the balance of the two laws enables one to construe them together as meaning the dominance of prayer over faith, or faith over prayer.[22] The history of theology abundantly illustrates the mutual influence which worship has had upon doctrine, and doctrine upon worship. But the history of theology does not solve the systematic question of their normative relations: Ought worship to provide the criterion for doctrine, or doctrine for worship?

The position for which argument is to be advanced here is based on the premise that this is a confused question, and that the problem could not possibly be solved if posed in that form. Doctrine and worship are not comparable in such a way that one might constitute the criterion for the other, or vice versa in precisely the same sense. If by 'doctrine' we mean, as we customarily do, the account given of the fundamental relations between God and humanity, then, of course, worship is a doctrinally-loaded activity. Doctrine could then appropriately be said to be a criterion for worship in that, if true worship was being offered, it would embody the truth of the doctrinally formulated relationship between God and humanity. That is to say, the truth of true worship would be articulable as doctrine.

Worship, on the other hand, could be the criterion for doctrine in a quite different way, if for example it could be shown (which is far from certain) that a particular account of the God–humanity relation was incapable of being the basis of the activity of worship.

In practice, the dispute between these supposed alternatives has resolved itself into a contrast and comparison, not between doctrine and worship, but between doctrine and liturgies. Here the situation is much plainer, since liturgical texts and doctrinal texts are comparable entities, and it can be reasonably asked whether, for example, a reference to a liturgical text constitutes an appropriate argument in doctrine, and vice versa. The dominant tradition in both Roman Catholicism and in Protestantism is to affirm the criterial status of doctrine, albeit for different reasons. In Roman Catholic thought the centralization of doctrinal and liturgical control in the Papacy facilitated the application of logical argument of a juristic kind to the public worship of the Church. The Protestant Reformation, on the other hand, overthrew the traditional liturgies precisely in the name of pure doctrine; but in doing so they provoked a response of an identical character in the Tridentine Reformation. The teaching *magisterium* of the Church and the sole sufficiency of the word of God proved to be rival authorities of a doctrinal kind in the intense disputes relating to the Eucharist, characteristic of the post-Reformation period.[23] Thus the Western experience of the relation of doctrine and liturgy is fundamentally characterized by a disequilibrium in favour of doctrinal purity, which is abundantly capable of accommodating (in the case of Roman Catholicism) an argument of some weight to be derived from established liturgical or pious usage.

The force of this tradition must be conceded. After all, liturgical texts are human compositions written by persons professing doctrinal ideas. Such texts plainly can and do imply doctrines, to which truth conditions attach. The Te Deum Laudamus, for example, implies the doctrines of Athanasian incarnationism. Other liturgical texts contain Arian doctrines, and one's preference for one text or another will depend upon one's doctrinal convictions. These convictions, moreover, will be formulated in the light of arguments, some of which may relate to matters of fact, such as whether or not it is probable that Jesus referred to himself as Son of God, and ought, or ought not, therefore, to be so addressed in a liturgy.

But what I wish to concede here must be rather more sharply outlined. It is true that Christian beliefs, including beliefs which play an important part in liturgies, are accessible to rational criticism of various kinds. All Christian belief has moral import, that is to say, it concerns the delineation of the conditions of the human good; it is, therefore, in principle exposed to moral criticism. It may also be true that all Christian belief entails historical affirmations concerning Jesus, which are in principle accessible to falsification. Moreover the range and complexity of the basic texts containing the original symbolism of the early years of Christianity are such that acute problems of internal coherence and consistency arise for rational consideration. Finally, because of the comprehensive nature of language to do with God, Christian theology is constantly exposed to critiques provided by various forms of specialism in the natural and social sciences, critiques whose range is intrinsically controversial, but nonetheless real and effective.

It is thus no part of my case that Christian doctrines should be shielded from criticism. There is a critical function to be performed by theologians. If the honouring of relics gives rise to fraud, then historical and moral criticism is right to expose it. If the liturgy of benediction is based on reasoning from faulty premises, or illicit reasoning from true premises, then again critical theology has a right to discredit it.

But none of these concessions affects the nub of the argument concerning the relation of worship and doctrine. For whereas a liturgy is (conventionally at least) a text, worship may be expressed non-verbally, in, for example, a physical movement or an offering. The relationship between doctrine and worship does not therefore need to be that of texts of competing degrees of authoritativeness; it can, rather, be genuinely complementary, as I propose now to show. The fundamental axiom of this position is the perception, by no means an innovation in the history of Christianity, that all Christian doctrinal belief is worshipping belief. Doctrine in Christianity is the expression in words of the terms of the divine-human relation; and these expressions are as a whole subject to the conviction that humanity is engaged in the worship of the Creator.

278

Barth, who, as we have seen, repeatedly insisted that the theologian be a person given to prayer, precisely on the grounds that such prayer expresses that openness to God which is the heart of all true theological method, put the matter of the communal ministry of praise thus:

> What is more worthy or urgent for any man than to praise God? But the great majority of men seem not, or not yet, to do this. The community does, not reproaching others for their failure, nor of course posturing before them, but provisionally, in their place, anticipating what in the light of the consummation will one day be the work of all creation ... All its ministries, whether of speech or action, are performed well to the extent that they all participate in the praise of God enjoined upon it. We may also add that if its praise of God as a specific act of speech is well done it is also itself quite definitely a saving, helpful, purifying and restoring action, and as such an act of witness in the world.[24]

I have depicted Barth as a theologian whose instincts are in tension with the logic of his own position, which brings about the exaltation of preacher and theologian to a dizzy eminence in the community. But his insight that true theology is necessarily connected with confidence and joy in God is more securely established, when rooted in the community's instinctive life of praise, expressed in its communal worship.

This, again, is not to deny that doctrines may be incorrectly formulated and open to the criticisms we have already described. But a doctrine which is not formulated in such a way as to be the vehicle of worship of the creature is open to the most fundamental criticism of all, that it has lost touch with its origins. The relevance of a consciously speculative essay in metaphysics to the life of prayer was noted in the case of Teilhard de Chardin's *Milieu Divin* by Donald MacKinnon, who wrote thus:

> The idiom of *Naturphilosophie*, however vulnerable to the critical philosopher, finds its home in religious exercise: metaphysical idiom is consciously bedded down again in the religious life in which it takes its origin. But if this is in one sense, for metaphysics, a loss of the kind of autonomy which men sought to gain for it when presenting it as a set of rationally defensible, unconditionally valid truths concerning the nature of what is, in another sense the insertion of

such highly self-conscious reflection concerning the universe around us into religious meditation bestows upon the latter a quality of intellectual rigour and seriousness that it very easily loses, that it indeed has lost, and is continually in threat of losing.[25]

The mutual enrichment of theology and spirituality, with the attendant danger, of course, of mutual loss, is a project of the utmost importance in contemporary Christianity.

Thus closely to associate worship and doctrine is by no means to inhibit the development of the intellectual implications of doctrine with the utmost intellectual rigour. But there can be no kind of requirement that the texts of communal worship should reflect the necessarily provisional conclusions reached in doctrinal investigations. Here the considerations recently advanced in favour of regarding the Christian story and its attendant symbols as the 'raw material' of theology are of importance.[26] Even if it be true that elements of that story can give rise to theological misunderstanding, and even if these misunderstandings can be avoided by the promulgation and reception of doctrinal decisions made by competent authorities, it still does not follow that such decisions should be incorporated in liturgical texts, much less made central to them.

Theological history, however, has a number of contrary indications. In Western Christianity the most striking examples of dogmatic insertions into liturgical practice are the Athanasian Creed and the rival eucharistic doctrines of the Reformed and Tridentine churches. The liturgical movement of the last two centuries is chiefly responsible for the recovery of a less didactic, and necessarily more ambiguous form of eucharistic liturgy. But the symbols which constitute much of the raw material of liturgies are not to be thought of as doctrinally inadequate because they are open to an indeterminate range of associations. On the contrary, the plurality of possible points of contact with the diverse life experiences of a congregation is an advantage in a liturgy, whose function is not to determine with precision what shall be thought by all, but to unlock the prison doors of conventional and mundane habits of mind. The Church's educational task is certainly aided by a liturgy, but liturgies should never be conceived of primarily as instruments of instruction.

A corollary of the same point is that theologians are always learners, and that participation in the communal worship of the Christian community is a means of their further education. To cut oneself off from such a community is to invite the danger of self-projection as guardian of the criteria of truth. Here it is perhaps relevant to add that theologians who wish to become sensitive to the sources of the identity of diverse Christian groups, are under an obligation to seek a varied experience of worship. If the separated systems of communication constituted by the different denominations are not to be endlessly self-perpetuating and self-justifying, conventional lines of theological argument will need to be challenged by unfamiliar experiences and perceptions.

A final consideration relevant to the case for the complementarity of belief and worship must be made in relation to the integrating element provided by the rituals of a common form of worship. Rituals (which here must be taken to include the recital of liturgical texts) have the function of restoring a system of meaning by constant repetition and recommittal to memory, and by the reabsorption of individuals into the common fabric.[27] They are the counterpoint to the detachment of rational thought, and are the appropriate means for the expression of profound commitment. The constant rehearsal, therefore, of what in the previous chapter I called the formal definition of Christianity (the deeds of Jesus, set in the context provided by creation beliefs and eschatology) is the natural substance of the rituals of worship. So too is the bodily enactment of the sacrificial self-dedication of Christ at his last supper with his disciples, 'on the night on which he was betrayed' – by one of them. Participation in such rituals not merely perpetuates the identity of Christianity, it serves to indicate that the theologian is genuinely qualified to engage in the conflicts which the preservation of that identity necessarily entails.

The rituals of worship have one other less frequently noted characteristic, of importance to the theme of commitment. While it is true that participation in the Christian ritual celebration of the last supper is the focal point of the worshipper's self-dedication, that act needs some protection from the insidious snares of self-importance, fanaticism and even masochism. Here it seems that the very bodiliness of rituals, and the frequency of their repetition, constitute a necessary distancing from the transcendence of that which is sought or intended. There is, even, an ironic element in physical rituals which can be employed by a discerning worshipper in the inevitable moments when convictions fail.

Thus the arrangement of human ceremonial, designed, of course, to express awe and reverence in the presence of the holy, may simultaneously evoke and not evoke the glory of God. The person of the priest may likewise be, and not be, a fitting symbol of the presidency of Christ at his table. The music of a liturgy, and not infrequently the extempore utterances of participants, constantly plunge into banality and pretentiousness, while even simultaneously expressing human longing. The irony which the cult evokes may, paradoxically, be a more liberating experience of transcendence than strivings for immediacy, spontaneity and sincerity. Indeed, it may even be the case that Christian culture requires cultic rituals precisely to save it from the fashionable mythology of authenticity.[28]

IV

We are now in a position to bring together the various strands of the argument of the two previous and the present chapters. It will be recalled that a central requirement for the preservation of the identity of Christianity was a dialectical interplay between external and internal elements. The attempt permanently to locate Christian identity in a specifiable quantum of propositions, rites or institutional embodiments was seen to be a failure in its ability either to account for the fact of conflict or to assign to conflict any positive significance. What Christianity entails was seen to be essentially contested.

But at the same time certain minimum conditions for participating in the contest needed to be fulfilled, and these (the narration of the life story of Jesus in the context provided by two horizon affirmations) were seen to correspond closely to the articles of the *fundamentum fidei* as handed down in the early Church. Now it has been argued that participation in the communal worship of the Christian community fulfils the requirement of the internal element, namely that the heart of the believer also be engaged in the maintenance of Christian identity, by means of an inwardly appropriated sense of what needs to be achieved in the world. Thus the identity of Christianity consists in the interaction between its external forms and an inward element, constantly maintained by participation in communal worship. But this attempted definition is inadequate without a closer comment upon the relationship between external forms and communal worship.

The bulk of this book has concerned, as has repeatedly been acknowledged, the doctrinal tradition. This is, of course, one external form; in Newman's reckoning, it is one of three, in Smart's one of five (the sixth being, it will be remembered, experience). The reason for thus concentrating upon doctrine has been the fact that doctrinal argument has come to assume extraordinary importance in the chronic series of internal conflicts to which Christianity has given rise. But doctrine is only one such form; if we take Smart's categories, Christianity subsists also in myths and ethical teachings, in rituals and social embodiments. It is not necessary further to consider myths and ethical teachings, both of which are closely related to doctrines as well as being, like doctrine, verbal. The ritual and social embodiment of the Church require, however, further discussion.

What, we must ask, is the relationship between the consideration we have given to worship, and the subsistence of Christianity in the external forms of rites and social embodiment? For Christianity, the major rituals are the sacraments, and the sacraments (especially those of baptism and Eucharist) are principally concerned with belonging to the worshipping community. In other words, as an external form of Christianity, ritual is, like doctrine, also related dialectically to the inwardness of worship. As with doctrine, there is a restless interplay between outside and inside giving rise to conflicts, characteristically about 'intention' on the one hand or 'ritualism' on the other. As we saw in the sections dealing with baptism and the Eucharist in Chapter 2,[29] no permanent resolution of those difficulties can be identified in the New Testament, and the history of Christianity gives rise to continuous controversy about the efficacy of rites.

The social embodiment of Christianity, its existence as a human organization, shows precisely the same characteristics. On the one hand its existence is defined precisely in relation to worship ('You are a chosen race ... that you may declare the wonderful deeds of him who called you out of darkness into his marvellous light', 1 Pet. 2.9); on the other, the regulations governing the conduct of worship give rise to conflict. The entitlement to be regarded as a genuine member of the Church is defined by the rite of baptism; the entitlement to be regarded as a leader in the Church is defined by the various rites of commissioning and ordination. But once again the externally perceptible rituals are incapable of preventing the rise of conflicts concerning the internal qualification of the baptized or ordained to be regarded as genuinely entitled to exercise power as either members or leaders. Moreover the question of the consent of the membership to be led is an unavoidable issue in assessing the authority of the leaders of the community. In Christian doctrine this gives rise to the vexed question of the 'reception' of authoritative decisions, another example in the context of the social embodiment of Christianity of the same dialectic between internal and external elements.

The question of the communal character of worship raises yet another issue of complexity and importance, namely the unity of the diverse acts of worship. Diversity of cultures, and diversity of experience within cultures, make it practically impossible and actually undesirable that the Church should use a single liturgical text. But common symbolic forms have a vital capacity to create unity, or rather to set boundaries on the range of diversity, and a Church which sets store upon harmony and reconciliation will plainly not give unrestricted licence to local idiosyncrasies. What is required for the unity of the Church is a coherent family of liturgies with a common character; and coherence requires authorization proceeding from a single competent authority. As Barth saw clearly, the conduct of communal worship requires a framework of canon law, and a legally competent authority to administer it. There can be no avoidance of the inevitable discriminations which have to be made in agreeing on what and who can and cannot be authorized.

Worship, in other words, is the source of communal organization. Needless to say, by worship one means, in this context, not merely the recitation of liturgies, but the whole life of self-offering of which liturgical participation is the focus. But the conclusion is important because it extends the dialectic of external forms and internal meaning. The attempt to define Christianity by reference to the (external) content of its doctrines required a reference to the (internal) forum of worship; but worship itself requires the reference to the (external) conditions of organizational existence and the conduct of authorized rites. But this organization and these rites necessarily refer to interior states of mind, so that tension and conflict are set up, requiring (external) doctrinal discriminations, which again require reference to inwardness characteristic of the tradition of worship. Christian identity is, therefore, not a state but a process; a process, moreover, which entails the restlessness of a dialectic, impelled by criticism.

A final word must be said about the role of the theologian, a question which at an earlier stage I identified as constituting the sub-plot of the argument of this book. If this argument has in any way carried conviction, then the project of complete doctrinal agreement, together with full agreement on the appropriate means for resolving disputes, is inherently implausible. Christianity does not possess, and cannot aspire to, that degree of settled precision. Unity has only ever meant the containment of diversity within bounds.

But what bounds? The argument of this chapter has been that internal doctrinal conflict may actually serve a constructive purpose in the Church so long as there is a tradition of communal worship, centrally authorized, in which the symbols and rituals of the Christian faith are openly spoken and performed, and the whole Christian community opened up to the interior dimension of the self-offering of Jesus. It is when this is being carried out that theologians may have the confidence to make the necessary experiments and to risk making the necessary mistakes. The potential tyranny of intellectuals, with their superior articulacy and natural concern for the epistemology of the arguments on which they are called to adjudicate, is qualified by the context in which they are now seen to be working. There is no single method, nor fundamental epistemological decision by the adoption of which the correct result for the preservation of Christian identity can be guaranteed. Theologians participate in the inevitable contests which arise about Christian identity, and they do so using a variety of methods and reaching a variety of conclusions. Some of these conclusions may be inconsistent with traditional ways of thinking, and the leadership of the Church may deem it necessary to sponsor reasoned rebuttals. But the state of internal argument is neither surprising, nor is it unhelpful to the mission of the Church, so long as those involved continue recognizably to be disputing about one and the same thing, namely Christianity, and so long as they continue to participate in that interior movement of the heart represented by the Church's public worship.

Theologians ought not to conceal from themselves, or from others, the power which they undoubtedly exercise in their interventions in the life of the Church. But neither, on the other hand, ought they to arrogate to themselves the power which belongs properly to the community as a whole, that of preserving the identity of Christianity by means of committed participation in the Church's worship in word and deed. The processes of internal argument ought never to come to predominate over the achieving of the Church's major tasks. While there can be no convenient moratorium in these disputes during which the Christian community may put its house in order, every participant in an internal conflict ought to have regard to the mobilization of resources for the infinitely greater external struggles in which it is involved. The theologians' commitment in those larger battles is determined, with that of the Christian community as a whole, by that worship which longs for the coming of God's Kingdom. The context of communal worship permits doctrinal dispute. But dispute is not an end in itself; rather it is a means of drawing all things into a unity with Christ.

Notes

INTRODUCTION

1 G. Wingren, *Theology in Conflict* (Edinburgh 1958), p. 166.

2 'The Essence of Christianity', *Religious Studies* 7 (1971), pp. 291–305; and *Christian Theology Today* (London 1971), esp. chaps. 3 ('Pluriformity and the Essence of Christianity') and 5 ('The Character of Christ').

3 'Ernst Troeltsch and Christianity's Essence', in J. P. Clayton, ed., *Ernst Troeltsch and the Future of Theology* (Cambridge 1976), pp. 139–71. Also a note on the differences between the 1903 and the 1913 versions of Troeltsch's essay on the essence of Christianity, in R. Morgan and M. Pye, ed., *Ernst Troeltsch* (London 1977), pp. 180f.

4 See E. Troeltsch, 'What does "Essence of Christianity" mean?', in Morgan and Pye, p. 130.

5 W. B. Gallie, 'The Function of Philosophical Aesthetics', in W. Elton, ed., *Aesthetics and Language* (Oxford 1954), p. 13

6 As, for example, in Paul Johnson, *A History of Christianity* (Hammondsworth 1980).

7 As, for example, in Ninian Smart, *The Phenomenon of Christianity* (London 1979).

8 See the debate initiated by W. Sanday's article, 'On Continuity of Thought and Relativity of Expression', *The Modern Churchman* (1915), pp. 125ff, and published as W. Sanday and N. P. Williams, *Form and Content in the Christian Tradition* (London 1916). A careful consideration of this discussion would have alerted later writers to the ambiguity of the distinction.

9 See A. Richardson, *History, Sacred and Profane* (London 1964), and Van A. Harvey, *The Historian and the Believer* (London 1967).

10 See Sarah Coakley, 'Theology and Cultural Relativism: What is the Problem?', *Neue Zeitschrift für systematische Theologie und Religionsphilosophie* 21 (1979), pp. 223–43.

11 See esp. Hans Mol, *Identity and the Sacred* (Oxford 1976).

12 An attempt at comprehensive treatment of the relevant factors in the development of the Christian tradition is to be found in E. Farley, *Ecclesial Reflection* (Philadelphia 1982).

Chapter 1
IDENTITY AND CONFLICT IN CHRISTIANITY

1   Wilfred Cantwell Smith, in *The Meaning and End of Religion* (New York 1962), p. 76.

2   *Christianos* is a Latinism, and if Acts 11.26 is correct in saying that the term was used first in Antioch, then it may have been designed by Roman officials to discredit Christians in the eyes of Herod Agrippa. See E. Peterson, 'Christianos', *Miscellanea Giovanni Mercati* I (Città del Vaticano 1946), pp. 355–72.

3   The major example in the twentieth century is Paul Tillich: 'historical research can neither give nor take away the foundation of the Christian faith', *Systematic Theology* II (London 1957), p. 130. On the contrary, if it were *Christian* faith it would be historically falsifiable. See John Powell Clayton, 'Is Jesus necessary for Christology?: An antinomy in Tillich's theological method', S. W. Sykes and J. P. Clayton, ed., *Christ, Faith and History* (Cambridge 1972), pp. 147–63.

4   See the account given by Nils A. Dahl, 'Paul and the Church at Corinth according to 1 Corinthians 1.10 – 4.21', in W. R. Farmer, C. F. D. Moule, and R. R. Niebuhr, ed., *Christian History and Interpretation*, Festschrift Knox (Cambridge 1967), pp. 313–35.

5   'The Church without Factions: Studies in 1 Corinthians 1 – 4', *Paul and the Salvation of Mankind* (London 1959), pp. 135–67. Munck summarizes as follows: 'In Paul's view there are three things that the Corinthians have misunderstood: (a) the Gospel, (b) the Christian leaders, and (c) their own position', p. 154.

6   See esp. ch. 3.

7   C. K. Barrett, 'Cephas and Corinth', in O. Betz, M. Hengel, P. Schmidt, ed., *Abraham unser Vater*, Festschrift Michel (Leiden 1963), pp. 1–12; and *The First Epistle to the Corinthians*, 2nd edn (London 1971), pp. 87f.

8   See Günther Bornkamm, 'The letter to the Romans as Paul's Last Will and Testament', in K. P. Donfried, ed., *The Romans Debate* (Minneapolis, Minn., 1977), pp. 17–31.

9   New Testament scholarship has had to take increasing account of the fact that the picture of Judaism given by Paul is not one which is found in Rabbinic literature; see, especially, E. P. Sanders, *Paul and Palestinian Judaism*, (London 1977), pp. 1–12. That Paul did not accurately represent the views of Jewish Christians is argued by H. Räisänen, 'Legalism and Salvation by the Law', in S. Pedersen, ed., *Die Paulinische Literatur und Theologie* (Århus 1980), pp. 63–83.

10   See the summary in J. Riches, *Jesus and the Transformation of Judaism* (London 1980), ch. 4.

11   M. Hengel, 'Zwischen Jesus und Paulus. Die "Hellenisten", die "Sieben" und Stephanus (Apg. 6. 1–15; 7.54 – 8.3)', *Zeitschrift für Theologie und Kirche* 72 (1975), pp. 151–206.

12   For what follows I am largely dependent on Riches, *Jesus*, chs. 5 and 6.

13 Riches provides in his account of these terms an introduction to the philosophical question of how a religion undergoes a transformation. Such a treatment has long been needed in New Testament study; see *Jesus*, ch. 2.

14 cf. C. K. Barrett, *The Second Epistle to the Corinthians* (London 1973), 'the existence of Christians is determined both theologically and ethically by Jesus', p. 246.

15 By Robert L. Wilken, *The Myth of Christian Beginnings* (London 1971): 'The apostolic age is a creation of the Christian imagination', p. 158.

16 Most recently by J. D. G. Dunn, *Unity and Diversity in the New Testament* (London 1977), who concludes, 'When we ask about the Christianity of the N.T. we are not asking about any one entity; rather we encounter different types of Christianity, each of which viewed the others as too extreme in one respect or another', p. 373

17 See H. Chadwick, *Early Christian Thought and the Classical Tradition* (Oxford 1966).

18 Both Tertullian and Jerome can be found to express this view, but both are far from consistent in practice; see Chadwick, *Early Christian Thought*, pp. 1–3.

19 As in the justly celebrated analysis of H. Richard Niebuhr, *Christ and Culture* (New York 1951); oddly, after making a penetrating analysis of the variety of solutions to the problem, Niebuhr does not reflect on why Christianity gives rise to this variety.

20 Friedrich Schleiermacher, *On Religion*, Speeches to its cultured Despisers (ET John Oman, New York 1958), pp. 242–5.

21 See G. W. H. Lampe, '"Grievous Wolves" (Acts 20.29)', in B. Lindars and S. S. Smalley, ed., *Christ and Spirit in the New Testament*, Festschrift Moule (Cambridge 1973), pp. 253–68.

22 cf. C. K. Barrett's comment on this passage: 'The institutional tradition begins as soon as it becomes apparent that the people of God have a life to live in the conditions of space and time, and this has already happened in the New Testament' ('Conversion and conformity: the freedom of the spirit and the institutional church', in Lindars and Smalley, *Christ and Spirit*, p. 381). For further discussion, see ch. 2, below.

23 *An Essay on the Development of Christian Doctrine* (edn of 1878; New York 1960), p. 59; the reference is Chapter 1, I, 3. Compare also the reference to the political, doctrinal and devotional aspect of Christianity, p. 308 (ch. 6, III, 23, n. 182), and to the 'doctrines, rites, and usages in which Christianity consists', p. 309 (ch. 7, 'Continuity of Principles'). The doctrine of the threefold office of Christ was formulated and popularized by Calvin (Institute II, 15; edn of 1559), and its impact on ecclesiology is everywhere visible in the documents of Vatican II (cf. esp. *Lumen Gentium*, 9–13). See also Chapter 5, note 65.

24 *The Via Media of the Anglican Church*, I (London 1877) p. xi. (See Chapter 5, note 2.)

25 N. Smart, *The Religious Experience of Mankind* (London 1971), p. 31.

26 Smart, *Religious Experience*, p. 17.

27 This is the position advanced by N. H. G. Robinson in *The Groundwork of Theological Ethics* (London 1971).

28 Smart, *Religious Experience*, p. 28.

Chapter 2
THE TRADITION OF INWARDNESS

1 'Truth in the inward parts' is the translation which Coverdale introduced in the 1539 revision of his 1535 translation of the Psalter for the Great Bible. It is directly derived from Sebastian Munster's 1534–5 Latin translation of the Hebrew Psalter, 'veritatem exigis in interioribus'; see E. Clapton, *Our Prayer Book Psalter* (London 1934), p. 119.

2 Hans Mol, *Identity and the Sacred* (Oxford 1976), ch. 15. The author lays particular emphasis on the fact that sacralization is a continuous process in which societies engage in order to limit infinite adaptation to changing conditions, cf. pp. 5ff.

3 Mol, *Identity*, p. 216.

4 Mol, *Identity*, p. 226.

5 Mol, *Identity*, p. 216.

6 'Knowing the wherewithal of the commitment of a person, a group, or a society, makes the person, the group, or the society predictable. The predictability in turn improves security and stability'; Mol, *Identity*, p. 216.

7 In what follows I am principally dependent on the following: A. R. Johnson, *The Vitality of the Individual in the Thought of Ancient Israel* (Cardiff 1964); H. W. Wolff, *Anthropology of the Old Testament* (London 1974); F. Baumgartel and J. Behm, 'Kardia' etc., in G. Kittel, ed., *Theological Dictionary of the New Testament* III (Grand Rapids, Mich., 1965), pp. 605–14; R. Bultmann, *Theology of the New Testament* I (London 1952), para. 20; R. Jewett, *Paul's Anthropological Terms* (Leiden 1971); and *'Kardia'*, art. in H. Balz and G. Schneider, ed., *Exegetisches Wörterbuch zum Neuen Testament* II (Stuttgart 1980), pp. 615–19.

8 e.g. the stories of Jacob and Esau (Gen. 27), the sons of Jacob (Gen. 34), and the men of Gibeon (Josh. 9).

9 e.g. in Ps. 15 (a psalm used, it is thought, during the celebration of the festival cult in Jerusalem), there are enquiries concerning the interior and external qualities required for dwelling 'on thy holy hill' (vv. 1–3, cf. Ps. 34.3 – 4). See H. Ringgren, *The Faith of the Psalmists* (London 1963), p. 109. H. J. Kraus has suggested, in connection with Ps. 17.3 and Ps. 139.1 and 23–4, that a whole night was spent in self-examination, *Worship in Israel* (Oxford 1966), p. 212.

10 Johnson, *Vitality*, pp. 76–7.

11 cf. the phrases 'the heart of the sea' and 'the heart of the heaven' used to illustrate impenetrable depths. Similarly the heart of a human being is

12   concealed from others and known only to God; thus, 1 Sam. 16.7 and Prov. 15.11. See Wolff, *Anthropology*, p. 43.

12   Thus Yahweh is the one who uniquely 'tries the hearts' (Ps. 7.9; Prov. 17.3; Jer. 11.20; 20.12).

13   Mere rote-worship is scandalous (Isa. 29.13).

14   cf. Ps. 51.17. Note also the demand for the removal of the 'foreskin of the heart' (Jer. 4.4; Deut. 10.16). It is particularly significant that the rituals of both sacrifice and circumcision are subject to a metaphorical extension so as to apply to 'the heart'.

15   Ezek. 11.19.

16   Thus Isa. 29 is quoted in Mark 7.6 (cf. Matt. 15.8, 9), and becomes the occasion for stressing the internal origins of religious defilement (cf. Matt. 23.27f). God is tester of the hearts according to 1 Thess. 2.4; Heb. 4.12; Rev. 2.23.

17   Jewett, *Paul's Anthropological Terms*, p. 448.

18   Thus Gal. 4.16. According to W. D. Davies, for Paul the indwelling of Christ is the New Torah written in the heart, *Paul and Rabbinic Judaism* (London 1962), p. 226. cf. the adoption of the thought of a circumcised heart (Rom. 2.29), and the necessity of an act of God (Rom. 6.17), based on faith (Rom. 10.6–13) and consisting in the Holy Spirit (Rom. 5.5).

19   2 Cor. 4.16; Rom. 7.22; and Eph. 3.16. On the inconsistency of Paul's anthropological terms see C. E. B. Cranfield, *The Epistle to the Romans* I (Edinburgh), p. 363; cf. R. Bultmann, *Theology*, pp. 220–2. Where Romans 7 refers 'the inmost self' to the mind (*nous*), Eph. 3, Pauline in thought if not in authorship, links the same phrase to the heart (*kardia*).

20   1 Pet. 3.3–4.

21   Rom. 2.29. A similar view that God is the agent in spiritual circumcision and that he internally implants a Holy Spirit is found in Jubilees 1.23f.

22   In addition to the word 'baptism', which in the New Testament refers to the external ritual of baptism in water, there is the phrase 'baptism with the Holy Spirit' (Mark 1.8 – Luke and Matthew add 'with fire', Luke 3.16 = Matt. 3.12 – Acts 1.5; 11.16), or by the Spirit (1 Cor. 12.13). There is, in other words, both a visible and an invisible baptism. Two uses analogically relate to the water-rite by means of the symbolism of death, the baptism of martyrdom (Mark 10.38 = Matt. 20.22, cf. Luke 12.50), and baptism into the death of Christ (Rom. 6.3). 1 Pet. 3.21 draws a contrast between the mere physical washing of baptism and an appeal to God 'for a clear conscience'. Commentators differ on whether water baptism creates the possibility of an appeal to God, and thus saves, or expresses the *prior* appeal of a clear conscience, and thus saves. See Bultmann, *Theology* I, p. 316, and the discussion in J. D. G. Dunn, *Baptism in the Holy Spirit* (London 1970), pp. 215–19.

23   The fact that Christians have the Spirit, or are the dwelling-place of the Spirit, is, according to Paul, the most distinctive mark of their standing before God (1 Cor. 2.12; 3.16; 6.19; 2 Cor. 1.22; 4.13; 5.5; Gal. 3.2, 5;

Rom. 5.5 and Rom. 8 *passim*); see E. P. Sanders, *Paul and Palestinian Judaism* (London 1977), pp. 447ff. Not surprisingly the Holy Spirit and baptism are brought together; 'for by' (or, 'in') 'one Spirit we were all baptized into one body' (1 Cor. 12.13). But the passage does not clarify the relation between the ritual of water-baptism (assuming that to be the reference, though this is disputed by some) and the inward reality of the indwelling of the Holy Spirit. When commentators discuss the issue they are forced to use later categories in order to determine Paul's meaning (e.g. Cranfield, *Romans* I, pp. 302–4 where the author twice denies that Paul could have held an *ex opere operato* view of baptism).

24   cf. 1 Cor. 10.1–13.

25   See Ps. 40.8; Ps. 50.14, 15 and 23; Ps. 51.17; Ps. 141.2. See R. J. Daly, *The Origins of the Christian Doctrine of Sacrifice* (London 1978), pp. 41–4.

26   Though the Rabbis do not attack the sacrificial system, it is normal teaching to deny any magical efficacy in sacrifice and to require that it be accompanied by repentance; see Sanders, *Paul*, p. 168. No real crisis seems to have been caused by the ending of temple sacrifice; so G. F. Moore, *Judaism in the first Centuries of the Christian Era* I (Cambridge, Mass., 1927), p. 114 and Sanders, *Paul*, p. 164.

27   On Mark 14.24 (= Matt. 26.28), see M. Hengel, *Atonement* (London 1981), pp. 53f. The early Church laid hold on those OT passages giving the strongest grounds for criticism of sacrifice (e.g. Hos. 6.6, quoted in Matt. 12.7, and Ps. 40.6–8, quoted in Heb. 10.5–10).

28   See the discussion and literature cited in C. K. Barrett, *1 Corinthians*, p. 235.

29   cf. J. N. D. Kelly on the symbolist and conversionist interpretations of the 'unquestioningly realist' view taken of the presence of Christ in the sacrament, *Early Christian Doctrines*, 2nd edn (London 1960), p. 440. Also J. Pelikan, *The Christian Tradition* I; The Emergence of the Catholic Tradition 100–60 (Chicago 1979), pp. 167–71.

30   *In Joan Evang.* IV, xl, 10; cited by J. Burnaby, *Amor Dei* (London 1938), p. 98.

31   *Conf.* i, 1, 1.

32   *Enarr. in Ps.* xxxvii, 4; and *in Ps.* cii, 2.

33   *De Civ. Dei* X, 5, ET *Concerning the City of God* (Pelican Books) by H. Bettenson (Harmondsworth 1972), p. 377.

34   *De Civ. Dei* X, 6 (ET p. 380).

35   *De Civ. Dei* X, 19 (ET p. 399).

36   Burnaby, *Amor Dei*, p. 124.

37   *De Civ. Dei* XXII, 10.

38   *De Civ. Dei* XIX, 23; compare *Serm.* 272.

39   On the appeal to Augustine in subsequent eucharistic controversies see J. H. Srawley, art. 'Eucharist', in J. Hastings, ed., *Encyclopaedia of Religion and Ethics* V (Edinburgh 1912), pp. 555ff.

40 *de libero arbitrio*, ii, 53, cited in Burnaby, *Amor Dei*, p. 185.

41 For what follows see E. Gilson, *The Spirit of Medieval Philosophy* (London 1950), ch. 17.

42 Peter Abelard, *Ethics*, ed. and tr. D. E. Luscombe (Oxford 1971), p. 45.

43 Gilson, *Medieval Philosophy*, p. 344.

44 Abelard, *Ethics*, pp. 79, 85, 105 and 115.

45 *Ministerial Priesthood*, Chapters (preliminary to a study of the Ordinal) on the Rationale of Ministry and the Meaning of Christian Priesthood (London 1897). Cited hereafter as *MP*.

46 'The Christian Ministry', in *Saint Paul's Epistle to the Philippians* 1st edn (London 1868). Citations here are from the twelfth edition of 1900, published after Lightfoot's death in 1889. Cited hereafter as *CM*.

47 *MP*, p. vi.

48 *MP*, p. viii.

49 *CM*, p. 234, arguing by means of the connection between John and Polycarp and Ignatius.

50 *CM*, p. xiv.

51 *CM*, p. 181. The tone is set by the very first sentence: 'The kingdom of Christ, not being a kingdom of this world, is not limited by the restrictions which fetter other societies, political or religious.'

52 *CM*, p. 181.

53 *CM*, p. 182.

54 *CM*, p. 184. Virtually the same position is expressed by R. Murray sj in *Authority in a Changing Church* (London 1968), pp. 19–20, and endorsed by N. L. A. Lash, *Voices of Authority* (London 1976), pp. 21–2.

55 *MP*, p. 39.

56 *MP*, pp. 45–6.

57 *MP*, p. 58.

58 *MP*, pp. 59–60, correcting the imprecise assumption of Charles Gore that anything said by Lightfoot not to be of the essence of the Church's life, would automatically be regarded as 'inessential'. C. Gore, *The Church and the Ministry* (London 1886), p. 355.

Chapter 3
POWER IN THE CHURCH

1 C. S. Dessain, ed., *The Letters and Diaries of John Henry Newman* XXV (London 1974), p. 418. Cited by N. L. S. Lash, *Newman on Development* (London 1975), p. 102.

2 Compare the thesis of E. Käsemann, 'The Canon of the New Testament and the Unity of the Church', *Essays on New Testament Themes* (London 1964), pp. 95–107, accepted by Dunn, *Unity and Diversity*, pp. 376–7, that to recognize the canon of the New Testament is to affirm the internal diversity of Christianity.

3   See E. D. Watt, *Authority* (London 1982), p. 7.

4   D. H. Wrong, *Power*, Its Forms, Bases and Uses (Oxford 1979), p. 2.

5   Wrong, *Power*, pp. 23f.

6   The inclusion of authority as an instance of power seems to me inevitable. To say 'a person may have authority without power' (A. Dulles, *The Survival of Dogma* [New York 1973], p. 80, cited by N. L. A. Lash, *Voices of Authority* [London 1976], pp. 16–17) seems to be a mistake based on too narrow a definition of power. See also S. Lukes, 'Power and Authority', in T. Bottomore and R. Nisbet, ed., *A History of Sociological Analysis* (London 1979), pp. 633–76.

7   It should be noted that the fact that argument is not regarded as being *formally* present in a typical authority relationship, does not mean that reasons of various kinds are never alleged by subordinates. See Watt, *Authority*, ch. 4.

8   The point is strongly made by H. V. von Campenhausen, *Ecclesiastical Authority and Spiritual Power in the Church of the First Three Centuries* (London 1969), p. 62. Cited hereafter as *EASP*.

9   Though in general E. Käsemann's stimulating picture of the opposition between Paul and Luke's view of the Church is to be criticized on the sociological grounds developed below, his support may be claimed for the view that Paul's views on the Church had to yield to 'historical necessity'; 'Paul and Early Catholicism', *New Testament Questions of Today* (London 1969), p. 247.

10 In addition to von Campenhausen's masterly review, see most recently, E. Schillebeeckx, *Ministry* (London 1981), pp. 5–37.

11 *To the Corinthians*, 40.

12 von Campenhausen argues that the concept of apostolic succession such as we find in Clement is not present in Ignatius, *EASP*, pp. 97–8.

13 *To the Trallians*, 3.

14 *To the Philadelphians*, 7.

15 *EASP*, p. 46, referring to such passages as 2 Cor. 1.24; Gal. 5.13; and 1 Cor. 7.23. Compare pp. 52 and 117 where von Campenhausen refers to 'the monstrous tension between his vocation and his natural self'.

16 *EASP*, p. 69. The reference in 1 Thess. 5.12 to those 'who are over you in the Lord' is taken to mean not office bearers but leaders for the time being.

17 *EASP*, pp. 86, 92, 95 and 129.

18 He dismisses Roman Catholic attempts to interpret the early Church in terms of an organized hierarchy; but he also rejects F. C. Baur's presentation of antagonistic organized parties. Neither ecclesiastical law nor politics is relevant to the situation. But his own presentation, in which the leaders of the early Church hold together by the unity of their witness to Christ and of their vocation is both idealized, and sociologically implausible; see *EASP*, pp. 28–9.

19 *EASP*, p. 31.

20 cf. *EASP*, p. 298.

21 This argument has been strongly developed by Bengt Holmberg in his *Paul and Power* (Lund 1978), basing his sociological categories largely on Max Weber. See also the brief summary of his challenge to a long tradition of German New Testament scholarship from Sohm to Käsemann in 'Sociological versus Theological Analysis of the Questions concerning a Pauline Church Order', S. Pedersen, ed., *Die Paulinische Literatur und Theologie* (Århus 1980), pp. 187–200.

22 *EASP*, pp. 58 and 64.

23 *EASP*, p. 1.

24 Von Campenhausen, *EASP*, p. 80, notes the introduction of 'the image of the shepherd, which Paul himself had never used in this way'.

25 *EASP*, p. 94.

26 Watt, *Authority*, p. 67.

27 On the relevance of pseudonymity see Schillebeeckx, *Ministry*, p. 12.

28 S. L. Greenslade, 'Heresy and schism in the later Roman Empire', in D. Baker, ed., *Schism, Heresy and Religious Protest* (Cambridge 1972), p. 4.

29 cf. above, p. 48.

30 E. Troeltsch, *The Social Teaching of the Christian Churches*, 2 vols. (London 1931). Cited hereafter as *STCC*.

31 ET of 3rd German edn, *History of Dogma*, 7 vols. (London 1897–9). ET of 2nd German edn, *The Mission and Expansion of Christianity in the first Three Centuries*, 2 vols. (London 1908).

32 *STCC*, pp. 986f.

33 *STCC*, p. 53.

34 *STCC*, p. 51.

35 *STCC*, p. 69.

36 *STCC*, p. 70.

37 *STCC*, p. 71.

38 The term 'Altkatholizismus' had been used by Albrecht Ritschl in his *Die Entstehung der altkatholischen Kirche* (Bonn 1850), but it appears to be Troeltsch who is responsible for the popularization of 'Frühkatholizismus'. See S. Schulz, *Die Mitte der Schrift, Der Frühkatholizismus im Neuen Testament als Herausforderung an den Protestantismus* (Stuttgart 1976); and H.-J. Schmitz, *Frühkatholizismus bei Adolf von Harnack, Rudolf Sohm und Ernst Käsemann* (Düsseldorf 1977).

39 *STCC*, p. 90.

40 *STCC*, p. 91.

41 *STCC*, p. 92. This statement closes with a reference acknowledging indebtedness to Loisy's *L'Evangile et l'Eglise*; see below, Chapter 6.

42 ET in R. Morgan and M. Pye, ed., *Ernst Troeltsch, Writings on Theology and Religion* (London 1977), pp. 182–207.

43 Ernst Troeltsch, Writings, p. 184.

44 Amongst the recent literature are the following: J. G. Gagei, Kingdom and Community: the Social World of Early Christianity (Englewood Cliffs, N.J., 1975); H. C. Kee, Christian Origins in Sociological Perspective (Philadelphia 1980); A. J. Malherbe, Social Aspects of Early Christianity (Louisiana 1977); and esp. the numerous articles and books of G. Theissen, e.g., The First Followers of Jesus (ET London 1978), and The Social Setting of Pauline Christianity (ET Philadelphia 1982).

45 The fundamental treatment is by W. Grundmann, art. 'dunamai, dunamis' etc. in G. Kittel, ed., Theological Dictionary of the New Testament II (Grand Rapids, Mich., 1964), pp. 284–317; cf. also art. 'exestin, exousia', etc., pp. 562–75. Among more recent work is C. H. Powell, The Biblical Concept of Power (London 1963); O. Betz, art. 'Might, Authority' in C. Brown, ed., New International Dictionary of New Testament Theology II (Exeter 1971) pp. 601–11; G. Friedrich, art. 'dunamis' in H. Balz and G. Schneider, ed., Exegetisches Wörterbuch zum Neuen Testament I (Stuttgart 1980), pp. 860–7, cf. also art. 'exousia', II, pp. 23–9. M. Hengel, Christus und die Macht (Stuttgart 1975) is a study principally concerned with the relationship of Christianity to political power, culminating in a discussion of Luther's 'Two Kingdoms' doctrine.

46 See N. Perrin, Jesus and the Language of the Kingdom (Philadelphia 1976), pp. 16–21.

47 Psalms of Solomon 2, 32–6, cited by Moore, Judaism I, p. 433.

48 Sanders, Paul and Palestinian Judaism, p. 236.

49 Perrin, Jesus and the Language of the Kingdom, p. 28.

50 Riches, Jesus, p. 100.

51 C. K. Barrett, The Holy Spirit and the Gospel Tradition (London 1966), ch. 5, 'Jesus as Miracle-Worker – The Words DUNAMIS and EXOUSIA', pp. 69–99.

52 Barrett, Holy Spirit, p. 78.

53 Barrett, Holy Spirit, p. 127; J. Jeremias, New Testament Theology (London 1971), p. 233; W. G. Kümmel, Theology of the New Testament (London 1974), p. 37.

54 H. Conzelmann, History of Primitive Christianity (London 1973), p. 55 and pp. 148–51.

55 Jeremias, NT Theology, pp. 238f.

56 H. K. Nielsen, 'Paulus' Verwendung des Begriffs Dunamis. Eine Replik zur Kreuzestheologie', in S. Pedersen, ed., Die Paulinische Literatur und Theologie (Århus 1980), p. 157.

57 See, for a separation of five differing motifs of conflict and victory (dynamistic, traditional apocalyptic, moral-martyrological, forensic, and dramatic-mythical), R. Leivestad, Christ the Conqueror (London 1954), esp. ch. 4.

58 E. Käsemann, who recognizes the existence and function of law, 'oriented towards the Last Day and grounded in it' in the earliest days of the

Church, believes that later church law understood order as end in itself; 'Sentences of Holy Law in the New Testament', *New Testament Questions of Today* (London 1969), p. 80. But he does not make clear how *any* law can be adequately protected from misuse. The mere statement of its eschatological function is plainly inadequate.

59 Two relatively slight exceptions are the brief treatment of power by Paul Tillich in *Love, Power and Justice* (London 1954), and an essay by Karl Rahner, 'The Theology of Power', *Theological Investigations* IV (London 1966), pp. 391–409.

60 Mol, *Identity*, p. 232.

61 Unquestionably the most important representative of this tendency is Jürgen Moltmann in three works, *The Crucified God* (London 1974), *The Church in the Power of the Spirit* (London 1977) and *The Trinity and the Kingdom of God* (London 1981). In each of these works there is an attack on what he terms 'political and clerical monotheism', based on what is presented as the trinitarian implications of the 'crucified God', cf. *The Church in the Power of the Spirit*, p. 305, *The Trinity and the Kingdom of God*, pp. 191–202. But throughout Moltmann's work the concept of power almost always connotes domination, and authority and obedience are contrasted with consensus and harmony. A more realistic appraisal of power would suggest that no church order is free of the dominating impulse, and that harmony can exist only in the presence of consent to a form of government, whatever that government is.

62 Perrin, *Jesus, and the Language of the Kingdom* (Philadelphia 1976), pp. 198f. quoting his own Presidential Address to the Society for Biblical Literature, *Journal of Religion* 93 (1974), p. 13.

Chapter 4
SCHLEIERMACHER ON THE ESSENCE OF CHRISTIANITY

1 Hans Wagenhammer, *Das Wesen des Christentums* (Mainz 1973), pp. 25f.

2 Heinrich Scholz, Vorrede to F. Schleiermacher, *Kurze Darstellung des theologischen Studiums* (Darmstadt 1969), pp. xiiff.

3 *Brief Outline on the Study of Theology* (Richmond, Virginia, 1966), p. 19. Cited hereafter as *BO*.

4 *On Religion, Speeches to its Cultured Despisers* (New York 1958), p. 50. Cited hereafter as *OR*.

5 *OR*, p. 51.

6 *OR*, p. 217. The passage reads: 'That you may not be misled by the false ideas that prevail; that you may estimate by a right standard the true content and essence (*Wesen*) of any religion; that you may have some definite and sure procedure for separating the inner (*das Innere*) from the outer (*Das Äusserliche*), the native from the borrowed and extraneous, and the sacred from the profane, forget the characteristic attributes of single religions and seek, from the centre outward, a general view of how the essence of a positive religion is to be comprehended and determined.'

7   *OR*, p. 218.

8   *OR*, p. 220.

9   See below, p. 199, and also S. W. Sykes, 'Barth on the Centre of Theology', in S. W. Sykes, ed., *Karl Barth. Studies of his Theological Method* (Oxford 1979), pp. 17–54.

10   *Reden über die Religion*, ed. G. C. B. Pünjer (Brunswick 1879), p. 256. This passage was then altered in the second edition of the speeches, and again in the third. First the term *Anschauung* was dropped, then *Universum*, until finally the determining characteristic of a religion is made to turn on the relation to the highest being expressed in it. In these alterations we have in miniature the progress of Schleiermacher's terminology.

11   *OR*, p. 11.

12   F. D. E. Schleiermacher, *Hermeneutics* (Missoula 1977), edited by Heinz Kimmerle, who also produced a useful survey of literature in his 'Afterword of 1968', pp. 229–234. See Hans-Georg Gadamer, 'The Problem of Language in Schleiermacher's Hermeneutic', in R. W. Funk, ed., *Schleiermacher as Contemporary*, Journal for Theology and Church 7 (1970), pp. 68–84.

13   The fourth of his speeches *On Religion* is on 'Association in Religion', and the whole conception of 'ethics', a discipline described in the *BO* as the 'science of the principles of history' (p. 30), is designed to interpret the forms of human social organization of which 'church' is one. The 'propositions borrowed from ethics' with which *The Christian Faith* opens amounts to an outline of the socio-psychological function of religion; *The Christian Faith* (Edinburgh 1928), pp. 5–31. Hereafter cited as *CF*.

14   *BO*, p. 24.

15   'Der Standpunkt der philosophischen Theologie in Beziehung auf das Christentum überhaupt ist nur über demselben zu nehmen', *Kurze Darstellung*, p. 14.

16   *Heidelberger Jahrbücher* (1822), p. 525; referred to by Scholz, *Kurze Darstellung*, pp. xviiif.

17   *BO*, p. 29.

18   *BO*, p. 20.

19   *BO*, p. 21.

20   *BO*, p. 23.

21   *BO*, p. 31.

22   *BO*, p. 20.

23   *BO*, p. 21.

24   *BO*, p. 24.

25   *CF*, p. 4.

26   The number three is taken from the subdivisions found in the Introduction to *The Christian Faith*, where propositions are 'borrowed' from ethics, the philosophy of religion and apologetics (pp. 5–76). In the *Brief Outline*

the position is not quite so clear. Ethics is mentioned in para. 29 (p. 27) and philosophy of religion in para. 23, while philosophical theology is taken to be a theological discipline including apologetics (paras. 32–68). The reconstruction of the divisions of the preparatory disciplines which I propose in my text is based on the second edition of *The Christian Faith*, which has most claim to be considered Schleiermacher's mature view of the matter.

27   *CF*, p. 5.

28   *BO*, p. 25, para. 23.

29   *CF*, pp. 31–52.

30   Curiously, Islam is given as the example of an 'aesthetic' religion on the grounds of the 'strongly sensuous content of its ideas', *CF*, p. 37.

31   *BO*, p. 25, para. 24.

32   *CF*, p. 4.

33   *BO*, p. 29, para. 32.

34   *CF*, p. 52.

35   *CF*, p. 47.

36   'As it were by way of experiment' is Schleiermacher's own way of speaking of what he has done, *CF*, p. 59.

37   *CF*, p. 57.

38   *CF*, p. 97.

39   *CF*. p. 97. See further, Klaus-Martin Beckmann, *Der Begriff der Häresie bei Schleiermacher* (München, 1959), esp. pp. 14–26.

40   *CF*, p. 97.

41   *BO*, p. 39, para. 67.

42   *CF*, p. 101.

43   *CF*, p. 105.

44   *CF*, p. 103.

45   *CF*, p. 102.

46   *BO*, p. 44, para. 83.

47   *BO*, p. 50, para. 103.

48   *BO*, p. 51, para. 110.

49   *BO*, p. 52, para. 113.

50   *BO*, pp. 31f, paras. 38–40.

51   *BO*, p. 31.

52   *BO*, p. 33, para. 45.

53   *BO*, p. 33, para. 46. 'Die geschichtliche Stetigkeit in der Folge des Christentums auf das Judentum und Heidentum' is misleadingly rendered by Tice, 'the historical continuity of Christianity from age to age'.

54   *BO*, p. 33, para. 47. Both of these concepts are said to be 'conceptually related to the continuity of what is essential in Christianity: canon ... insofar as this continuity finds expression in the production of ideas, and

sacrament . . . insofar as it finds expression in the ongoing tradition of the Christian community'.

55 *BO*, p. 34, para. 48.

56 *BO*, p. 34, para. 49.

57 *OR*, pp. 242f.

58 *BO*, pp. 35f, para. 54.

59 *BO*, pp. 36f, paras. 56–8.

60 *BO*, p. 37, para. 59.

61 *BO*, p. 67, para. 178.

62 *CF*, p. 88. Dogmatic Theology is the science which systematizes the doctrine prevalent in a Christian Church at a given time.

63 See Wagenhammer, *Das Wesen des Christentums*, pp. 206–25, esp. pp. 210f.

64 See E. Farley's description of this requirement for a modern theology not conforming to the traditional Roman Catholic and Protestant 'way of authority', and his consideration of the essence of Christianity gambit in Part II of his *Ecclesial Reflection* (Philadelphia 1982), chs. 8 and 9.

65 K. Rahner, *Foundations of Christian Faith* (London 1978), pp. 8ff.

66 Farley, *Ecclesial Reflections*, p. 202, makes the bold statement that this historical enquiry subtly pervades Schleiermacher's programme.

67 On the ambiguous significance of Schleiermacher's self-imposed programme as a systematician, see S. W. Sykes, 'Theological Study: The Nineteenth Century and After', in B. Hebblethwaite and S. Sutherland, ed., *The Philosophical Frontiers of Christian Theology*, Festschrift MacKinnon (Cambridge 1982), pp. 95–118.

Chapter 5
NEWMAN ON THE IDEA OF CHRISTIANITY

1 The correspondence on Newman's side has now been published in a critical edition by Louis Allen, *John Henry Newman and the Abbé Jager* (London 1975); cited hereafter as *Jager*.

2 J. H. Newman, *Lectures on the Prophetical Office of the Church viewed relatively to Romanism and Popular Protestantism* (London 1837); this was reissued with a new preface and notes in *The Via Media of the Anglican Church* I (London 1877); cited hereafter as *VM I*.

3 J. H. Newman, *An Essay on the Development of Christian Doctrine* (London 1845). The work was revised lightly in 1846; for the changes see N. Lash, *Newman on Development* (London 1975), Appendix, pp. 207–8. In 1974 Pelican books brought out an edition of the first edition, with an introduction by J. M. Cameron. Cameron has modernized the spelling and punctuation of the text, and altered the footnotes. Rather than follow this edition, I have decided to cite the original printing of the first edition in the following way: *Dev*[1], followed by chapter, section and subsection numbers, with the page number in brackets; e.g. *Dev*[1].1.3.2 (p. 66). The

introduction is cited as *Dev¹*, Int. For the citation of the third edition see footnote 6 below.

4 *Newman's University Sermons*, with introductory essays by D. M. MacKinnon and J. D. Holmes (London 1970), reprinted from the third edition of 1871. Cited as *US*.

5 *VM* I, pp. xv–xciv.

6 The third edition of *An Essay on the Development of Christian Doctrine* (London 1878) has been frequently reissued. Because it has been so thoroughly broken up by Newman into sections and subsections it can be cited without reference to any pagination, as follows: *Dev³*, 6.1.17. Where a chapter is introduced by one or more sub-sections before the first section-heading, such sub-sections are referred to as, e.g., *Dev³*, 7.0.1. The sub-sections of the Introduction are referred to as, e.g., *Dev³* Int. I have adopted this usage from Professor Lash's valuable study of the *Essay* which includes an index of references to both editions.

7 Erskine's book was entitled *Remarks on the Internal Evidence for the Truth of Revealed Religion*, and was published in 1820. Abbott's was *The Corner Stone* (London 1834).

8 Reprinted in J. H. Newman, *Essays Critical and Historical* I (London 1871), pp. 30–99, with a note, pp. 100–1, indicating that the cause of the essay was concern at the progress of liberal theology in Oxford. Cited as *ECH* I.

9 According to J. Artz, *Newman-Lexikon* (Mainz 1975), art., 'Schleier-macher', Newman had read nothing of Schleiermacher for himself. However, if, as it seems, he had read the whole of the relevant sections of *The Biblical Repository*, Nos. 18 and 19 for April and June of 1835 – the basis of his brief comment on Schleiermacher – he would not have been un-informed. Of the two articles, pp. 265–329 consisted of a long introduction to the topic, pp. 329–53 of the first and pp. 1–80 of the second article contained a translation of Schleiermacher's essay on Sabellian and Athanasian trinitarian theology, and pp. 80–116 a further comment by the translator. Nonetheless it is hardly surprising that Newman penetrated no further into Schleiermacher than was necessary to produce the following proposition as a partial summary of his thought: 'that the one object of the Christian Revelation, or Dispensation, is to stir the affections, and soothe the heart'.

10 *ECH* I, p. 41.

11 *ECH* I, p. 42.

12 *ECH* I, p. 45.

13 *ECH* I, p. 47.

14 *ECH* I, p. 48.

15 *ECH* I, p. 33.

16 *ECH* I, p. 53.

17 *ECH* I, p. 63.

18 *ECH* I, p. 51.

19 *ECH* I, p. 52.

20 *ECH* I, p. 52.

21 Bk III, i, 4. Note that what is here in view is the unity of the visible Church. Even when in III, iii, 3, Hooker goes on to define 'necessary' as 'requisite for man's salvation', the context continues to be that of the integrity of the Church of God.

22 See A. G. Dickens, *The English Reformation* (London 1964), pp. 78–9, 322–3, and 346.

23 III, i, 5; and III, iii, 3.

24 The text of Article VI of the 39 Articles omits the clause, 'although it be some time received of the faithful as godly, and profitable for an order and comeliness'.

25 *Jager*, p. 35.

26 *Jager*, p. 36.

27 *Jager*, p. 83.

28 *Jager*, pp. 83–4.

29 *Jager*, pp. 88–9. cf. VM I, p. 256.

30 *Jager*, p. 89. cf. VM I, p. 257.

31 *Jager*, p. 89. cf. VM I, p. 257.

32 See *Jager*, p. 19.

33 The letter is printed in Froude's *Remains*, and reprinted in *Jager*, Appendix III, pp. 172–83.

34 VM I, pp. 254–5.

35 US, p. 316.

36 US, p. 329. Lash is certainly correct to say that the argument about fundamentals is not overthrown by the argument of the Sermon. See Lash, *Newman on Development*, pp. 130 and 195. One way of describing what has occurred, however, is to say that the traditional theory of fundamentals and non-fundamentals has been modified by Newman in such a way that the previous category of non-fundamentals is shown to contain both matters of belief deserving, at least, of acquiescence and matters of opinion and debate. A better way of pointing out the change is to observe that Newman's epistemology has alienated him from the crude realism with which the traditional theory was often expressed.

37 On the fixed laws upon which human nature proceeds, see US, p. 328 and *Dev*[1] I. I (p. 30).

38 US, p. 319f.

39 See his criticism of Wiseman's encomium on the Roman system and its 'principle', VM I, p. 101.

40 US, p. 318.

41 US, p. 335.

42   *US*, p. 317.

43   *US*, p. 320.

44   *US*, pp. 330–2, subsequently quoted in *Dev*[1], 1.2 (pp. 55ff).

45   *US*, p. 66.

46   *US*, p. 328.

47   *US*, p. 340.

48   *US*, p. 338.

49   *US*, p. 332.

50   *US*, p. 334.

51   *Dev*[1], 1, Int. (p. 26).

52   *Dev*[1], 1, Int. (p. 3).

53   *Dev*[1], 1, Int. (p. 32).

54   *Dev*[1], 1.1. (pp. 34f).

55   *Dev*[1], 1.3.1 (pp. 63f).

56   *US*, p. 336.

57   *Dev*[1], 1.3.2. (p. 66).

58   It is certainly true that Newman strives to rebut what might be called 'reductionism' in the Protestant attempts to identify a 'leading idea', in as much as they isolate one doctrine or aspect of the whole, and thus tear apart the organic unity of the 'one idea' which creeds and doctrines are trying to express. In the light of our examination of Schleiermacher's use of the concept of 'essence of Christianity' it can be argued that the question of 'reductionism' is not necessarily entailed by the mere use of that concept.

59   *Lash*, pp. 140f.

60   *Dev*[2], 1.1.3.

61   *Dev*[2], 1.2.10, and 7.1.3.

62   *Dev*[2], 1.2.10.

63   *Dev*[2], 7.1.3.

64   Quoted by Lash, from a manuscript in the Birmingham Oratory Archives (*BOA* D.7.6), *Newman on Development*, p. 198.

65   *VM* I, p. xl. John Coulson, *Newman and the Common Tradition* (Oxford 1970), pp. 166–8, refers the threefold office of Christ to Eusebius, *Ecclesiastical History* 1.1.3: 7–20 and to the canon of the Mass of Christ for Maundy Thursday. Neither of these seems to me as obvious a source for Newman's thought as the Calvinist theology in which Newman was reared; for this tradition the idea of the threefold office was a theological commonplace. See F. F. Müller, 'Jesu Christi dreifaches Amt', art. *Realencyklopädie für protestantische Theologie und Kirche* VIII (Leipzig 1900), pp. 733–41.

66   *VM* I, p. xlvii.

67   cf. *Dev*[2], 6.3.3.21, note 182, and 7.0.1 for the same threefold division.

68 By David Newsome in *Two Classes of Men*, Platonism and English Romantic Thought (London 1974), pp. 71f.

69 For the references to the Newman literature, see Lash, *Newman on Development*, p. 48, esp. L. Bouyer, 'Newman et le Platonisme de l'âme anglaise', *Revue de Philosophie* vi (1936), pp. 285–305; and E. A. Sillem, ed., *The Philosophical Notebook of John Henry Newman* I. General Introduction to the Study of Newman's Philosophy (Louvain 1969). On Schleiermacher see R. R. Niebuhr, *Schleiermacher on Christ and Religion* (London 1965), pp. 94ff.

70 *VM* I, p. 41.

71 *ECH* I, p. 96.

72 L. Jonas and W. Dilthey, ed., *Aus Schleiermachers Leben* III (Berlin 1861), p. 436.

73 e.g. J. Coulson, *Newman and the Common Tradition*, p. 58.

74 Lash, *Newman on Development*, p. 96.

75 Cited by Lash, *Newman on Development*, p. 199, from *BOA* D.7.6, with the appropriate comment that Newman's notion of incarnation is focused on the redemptive work of Christ.

Chapter 6
HARNACK AND LOISY

1 Adolf von Harnack, *Das Wesen des Christentums* (Leipzig 1900). In 1950 a jubilee edition was brought out, edited by Rudolf Bultmann (Stuttgart 1950). The English translation, *What is Christianity?* (cited hereafter as *WC*) was the work of T. B. Saunders, *The Times* correspondent in Berlin, and friend of Baron von Hügel. Saunders subsequently wrote an account of some English reactions to Harnack, *Professor Harnack and his Oxford Critics* (London 1902), and was closely involved in von Hügel's attempt to protect Loisy by publicity in *The Times*; see L. F. Barmann, *Baron Friedrich von Hügel and the Modernist Crisis in England* (Cambridge 1972), pp. 119f. The 1902 French translation of *Das Wesen des Christentums, L'essence du Christianisme* (Paris), was the work of a young Liberal Catholic, Blanche Calmard du Genestoux; it was said to be rather mediocre, or even 'deplorable', and was newly translated in 1907; see E. Poulat, *Histoire, dogme et critique dans la crise moderniste* (Paris 1962), p. 46.

2 Adolf Harnack was forty-nine years of age in 1900, and had held chairs in Giessen and Marburg, before being called to Berlin in 1888. The massive *Lehrbuch der Dogmengeschichte* (1885–90) had made Harnack famous, and a controversy over the Apostles' Creed, in which he argued against literal acceptance, brought him notoriety. From 1890 Harnack was a member of the *Preussische Akademie der Wissenschaften*, and responsible for the founding of the *Kirchenväter-Kommission*. A measure of his prominence is given by his being commissioned to write the history of the Prussian Academy for its 200-year Jubilee (published in 1900).

Loisy was forty-three in 1900, and perhaps somewhat less well known. But he had already been dismissed in 1893 from a Chair at the Institut Catholique in Paris. Author of *Histoire du canon de l'Ancien Testament* (Paris 1890) and *Histoire du canon du Nouveau Testament* (Paris 1891), he had also published lectures on biblical subjects in 1892–3, including articles on the Chaldean myths of Creation and the Deluge, *Revue des Religions* (1892), and the controversial, 'La question biblique et l'inspiration des écritures', *Enseignement biblique* (1893).

3   Already in 1966, Roger Aubert was speaking of 'a sudden and general revival of interest' in Modernism, 'Recent Publications on the Modernist Movement', *Concilium*, vol. 7, no. 2. (Sept. 1966), p. 47, referring to the issue of A. Houtin and F. Sartiaux's damaging *Alfred Loisy, sa vie, son oeuvre*, ed. E. Poulat, (Paris 1960), to Poulat's own fine work referred to in note 1 above, and to P. Scoppola's *Crisi modernista e rinnovamento cattolico in Italia* (Bologna 1961). For further literature on Loisy, see R. de Boyer de Sainte Suzanne, *Alfred Loisy: Entre la foi et l'incroyance* (Paris 1968), J. Ratté, *Three Modernists* (London 1968), Part One; A. Vidler, *A Variety of Catholic Modernists* (Cambridge 1970), chs. 2 and 3; Barmann, *von Hügel*, chs. 4 and 5; B. Reardon, *Liberalism and Tradition, Aspects of Catholic Thought in Nineteenth Century France* (Cambridge 1975) chap. 12; T. M. Loome, *Liberal Catholicism, Reform Catholicism, Modernism* (Tübingen 1979); G. Daly, *Transcendence and Immanence, A study in Catholic Modernism and Integralism* (Oxford 1980). On Harnack, see G. Wayne Glick, *The Reality of Christianity* (New York 1967), a full length study of Harnack's thought; W. Pauck, *Harnack and Troeltsch. Two Historical Theologians* (New York 1968); C. J. Kaltenborn, *Adolf von Harnack als Lehrer Dietrich Bonhoeffers* (Berlin 1973); Karl H. Neufeld sj, *Adolf von Harnack – Theologie als Suche nach der Kirche* (Paderborn 1977), and *Adolf von Harnacks Konflikt mit der Kirche* (Innsbruck 1979).

4   A notable exception is the dozen pages of nuanced exposition in Poulat, *op. cit.*, pp. 46–58. Poulat particularly acknowledges that Harnack's work is 'aisé à lire et difficile à bien entendre, du moins pours les lecteurs français formés dans la tradition catholique (de même que la réponse de Loisy se révélera difficile pour ses lecteurs protestants les mieux intentionnés)', p. 56. Poulat is nonetheless castigated for his ignorance of the German language and for making *French* modernism the norm for modernism as such, Loome, *op. cit.*, p. 141.

5   On the ambiguity of the definition of 'modernism' see N. Lash, 'Modernism, aggiornamento and the night battle', in *Bishops and Writers*, ed. A. Hastings (Wheathampstead 1977), pp. 51–79. Loome, *op. cit.*, devotes the first part of his book to an attempt to establish new conventions in the use of the terms 'modernism', 'modernist crisis', and 'modernist movement', cf. esp. pp. 193–6. Both he and Daly, *op. cit.* pp. 4ff, are driven to the expedient of saying that modernism is a tradition of critical scholarship (going back to the seventeenth century) which challenged prevailing orthodoxies, and was largely defined by the strenuous antagonism it elicited. It is thus inescapably imprecise.

6   *Theologische Literaturzeitung* 29 (1904), p. 59.

7   A. Harnack, *Outlines of the History of Dogma*, (ET 1893, published as Beacon Paperback, Boston 1957), p. 251. Cited hereafter as *OHD*.

8   Introduction to the fifth edition of *L'Évangile et L'Église* (Paris 1929).

9   See 'Harnacks Verhältnis zu Ritschl', in Kaltenborn, *Adolf von Harnack*, pp. 13–14; and Karl H. Neufeld, *Adolf von Harnack* (Paderborn 1977), pp. 43ff.

10 So A. R. Vidler, *Twentieth Century Defenders of the Faith* (London 1965), p. 38.

11 R. Lloyd in *The Church of England*, 1900–1965 (London 1966) states flatly: 'The Modernists might be very learned, but they seemed to be talking very great nonsense. It is for these reasons that in writing or talking about Modernism today one instinctively uses the past tense', p. 262.

12 H. D. A. Major, *English Modernism. Its Origin, Methods and Aims* (Cambridge, Mass., 1927), chap. 3, pp. 18–42.

13 O.D.C.C. (2nd edn Oxford 1974), p. 620. Much the same summary occurs in A. M. Ramsey, *From Gore to Temple* (London 1960), p. 61. A recent *Concise History of the Catholic Church* (New York 1979) by T. Bokenkotter goes still further in asserting that Harnack 'presented Jesus as a kind of nineteenth-century liberal reformer preaching a nondogmatic religion based on the brotherhood of man and the fatherhood of God', p. 360. How far these works fall short of any kind of reasonable assessment of Harnack may be seen by the penitence hinted at by A. R. Vidler in 1964, in his *Twentieth-Century Defenders of the Faith*: 'It is commonly said – and I am afraid I used to say this myself – that in Harnack's view the essence of Christianity consisted in belief in the Fatherhood of God and the brotherhood of man. But no such vulgar summary can do justice to the subtlety of the book's theme', p. 14.

14 So J. Macquarrie, *Twentieth-Century Religious Thought* (London 1963), p. 182: 'His most famous book, *L'Evangile et l'Eglise*, is a shattering criticism of the view of Christianity held by Harnack'.

15 *Mémoires pour servir à l'histoire religieuse de notre temps*, i (Paris 1930), p. 210, citing an entry in his diary dated 11 July, 1892. Loisy himself continued to insist publicly on the utmost dissimilarity between his own and Harnack's programme, and there is no reason to doubt his sincerity. What one questions is his judgement.

16 It is reasonably clear that the source of this view of the controversy is Loisy himself; but in the English-speaking world, George Tyrrell's brilliant epitome of 'The Christ of Liberal Protestantism' has been too uncritically accepted; *Christianity at the Cross Roads* (London 1909), reissued (and endorsed) by Alec Vidler in 1963, esp. pp. 46–9. One notes the repeated anti-Germanisms in such rhetorical flourishes as, 'the Pearl of Great Price fell into the dustheap of Catholicism, not without the wise permission of Providence, desirous to preserve it till the day when Germany should rediscover it and separate it from its useful but deplorable accretions'. Daly, *Transcendence and Immanence*, pp. 55–68 and 146–9, agrees that

both Loisy and Tyrrell greatly exaggerated their differences from, and sought to minimize their similarities to, Liberal Protestantism.

17 In an essay on Loisy, reprinted in A. Fawkes, *Studies in Modernism* (London 1913), pp. 48–78. Cf. esp., 'Whether M. Loisy has refuted Professor Harnack is doubtful. They are workers in a common field and towards a common purpose; to many it will seem that the points on which they differ are fewer and less vital than those on which they are agreed. Incidentally, however, M. Loisy has subjected Harnack's method and its results to an acute and suggestive criticism.' On Fawkes, see Vidler, *A Variety of Catholic Modernists*, pp. 155–60, where Vidler is at pains to stress Fawkes' Harnackian sympathies.

18 Neufeld, *Adolf Harnacks Konflikt mit der Kirche*, makes the most that can be made of the undoubtedly stressful background of Harnack's work; but it is plain from the opening lecture that Harnack is ready to harness his reputation as a historian to the 'confession' he is about to give. Like Troeltsch after him, Harnack insisted that the determination of the essence is an historical task. See the prefaces to the editions of 1903 and 1925, in the 1950 edition, pp. xix and xxii.

19 *OHD*, p. 1.

20 *OHD*, p. 8.

21 A. Loisy, *Choses passées* (Paris 1913), p. 245.

22 See N. Lash, *Change in Focus* (London 1973), pp. 104–11, and B. Reardon, *Liberalism and Tradition*, pp. 263–7. Loisy, for all his enthusiasm for Newman's theory of development, denies that he *derived* his views from Newman. Reardon argues that Loisy's evolutionary view of development 'in spite of his relative depreciation of them owed far more to both Harnack and Sabatier, as well as to the critical writings of biblical scholars like H. J. Holzmann and Johannes Wiess', p. 265.

23 N. Lash, *Change in Focus*, pp. 109f rightly points to the problem of criteria for true and false development which Tyrrell had also seen in Loisy's work.

24 *OHD*, pp. 15f.

25 *OHD*, p. 15.

26 *OHD*, pp. 16f.

27 *OHD*, p. 17.

28 *WC*, p. 64.

29 *WC*, p. 67.

30 *WC*, p. 65. cf. pp. 71f.

31 *WC*, p. 72.

32 *WC*, p. 64.

33 *WC*, p. 80.

34 *WC*, pp. 81–127.

35 *WC*, pp. 127f.

36 *WC*, p. 147.

37 WC, p. 148.

38 WC, p. 187.

39 See D. Bonhoeffer, *Christology* (London 1966), esp. pp. 104–6. Bonhoeffer was a pupil of Harnack's, and manifestly revered his teacher. But there is no question of slavish discipleship in theological questions. What can be said in respect of Christology is that Bonhoeffer inherits from Harnack the project of a non-docetic interpretation of the divinity and transcendence of Christ. See also Kaltenborn, *Adolf von Harnack*, pp. 29–46 and 122–6.

40 WC, p. 303.

41 WC, p. 15; the distinction between kernel and husk is already used on p. 12.

42 WC, p. 220.

43 WC, p. 11. We should note here the reference to the entire history of Christianity, as integral to the discernment of its essence; for the same feature in Schleiermacher, see above p. 91. Farley also regards this passage as more characteristic of Harnack, *Ecclesial Reflection*, p. 204.

44 WC, p. 176. The context is the discussion of the process whereby, by the third century, Christianity had acquired an imposing cultus to rival that of paganism. This process, says Harnack, is not to be judged from a puritan standpoint. 'Every age has to conceive and assimilate religion as it alone can; it must understand religion for itself, and make it a living thing for its own purposes.' If there is a negative aspect to it from the modern standpoint, then it was by no means irreparable.

45 *The Mission and Expansion of Christianity in the First Three Centuries* (2nd edn, London 1908), i, p. 234. It is passages such as these, expressing a cliché in Protestant theology from Semler onwards, which make it wholly untenable to say with Daly that Harnack argued 'that the essence of the Gospel could be detached from all historical cultures', *op. cit.*, p. 68.

46 *The Gospel and the Church*, cited hereafter as GC, p. 19. *L'Évangile et L'Église* (Paris 1902), was translated into English by Christopher Home, and published in London in 1903. All the passages referred to in the notes have been checked against the original French.

47 GC, p. 16 (altered translation).

48 GC, p. 17 (altered translation).

49 GC, p. 18 (altered translation).

50 Cf. above, p. 114.

51 Loisy's polemical use of the phrase 'dissection sur le mort', GC, p. 19, to describe Harnack's analysis of the essence of Christianity is precisely what has imprinted itself on the minds of those who are, for whatever reason, reluctant to read what Harnack says for himself.

52 Note 6 above.

53 WC, p. 257.

54 WC, p. 210.

55 WC, p. 212.

56 Briefly in *The History of Dogma* (London 1897), i, p. 39, with reference to Rudolf Sohm's *Kirchenrecht* (Leipzig 1892). The major controversy with Sohm was to break out in 1909–10. See Neufeld, *Adolf Harnacks Konflikt mit der Kirche*, pp. 156–73. Loisy reviewed the dispute in *Revue d'histoire et de littérature religieuses* NS 1 (1910), pp. 492–5, dealing more harshly, as one would expect, with Sohm than with Harnack.

57 WC, p. 57.

58 WC, p. 63.

59 WC, p. 14.

60 WC, p. 8.

61 WC, p. 132.

62 WC, p. 152.

63 GC, p. 172.

64 GC, p. 176.

65 'We study history in order to intervene in the course of history'; *Reden und Aufsätze*, IV (Giessen 1911), cited in J. C. Livingston, *Modern Christian Thought* (New York 1971), p. 258.

66 pp. 14–15.

67 That the biblical question is central for Loisy may be seen in his gentle criticisms of Newman's biblical scholarship, and his insistence that the problem of revelation and development is acutest at the biblical level; A. Firmin (= Loisy), 'Le développement chrétien après le Cardinal Newman', in *Revue du clergé français* 17 (1898), pp. 13ff.

68 Modern commentators accept that Pius X's letter to Loisy, communicated on 12 March, 1904, demanding unqualified submission, and, in effect, denying Loisy's good faith, destroyed his remaining links with Roman Catholicism. The reason, I think, is not just psychological; the tenability of Loisy's ecclesiology *entailed* willingness to admit the possibility of historical criticism.

Chapter 7
TROELTSCH AND THE RELEVANCE OF EPISTEMOLOGY

1 The 1913 edition is now translated into English by Michael Pye, in R. Morgan and M. Pye, ed., *Ernst Troeltsch, Writings on Theology and Religion* (London 1977), pp. 124–79, together with a note by myself on the seventy alterations incorporated by Troeltsch into the later text, pp. 180–1.

2 Ernst Troeltsch, *Brief an F. von Hügel* p. 63.

3 Van A. Harvey, *The Historian and the Believer*, p. 17.

4 WC. p. 14f.

5 *The Absoluteness of Christianity and the History of Religions*, ET D. Reid (London 1972), p. 136; cited hereafter as AC.

6 What follows (to p. 171) is reprinted from S. W. Sykes, 'Troeltsch and Christianity's Essence', in J. P. Clayton, *Ernst Troeltsch and the Future of Theology* (Cambridge 1976), pp. 143–68, with certain omissions and corrections.

7 'Die christliche Weltanschauung und ihre Gegenströmungen', reprinted in the *Gesammelte Schriften II* (Tübingen 1913), pp. 227–327, cited hereafter as *GS*.

8 *GS* II, pp. 325–7. Compare also the article on 'Aufklärung', *Realencyklopädie für protestantische Theologie und Kirche* (PRE) II, pp. 225–41, published in 1897; and 'Über historische und dogmatische Methode in der Theologie', published in 1898 and reprinted in *GS* II, pp. 729–53, esp. p. 730.

9 *GS* II, pp. 239, 247, 271 and 317.

10 *GS* II, p. 238.

11 'Aufklärung', *PRE* II, p. 241.

12 *GS* II, p. 239.

13 *GS* II, p. 261.

14 *GS* II, p. 301.

15 *GS* II, p. 403, in a passage added in 1913.

16 *AC*, p. 169. Troeltsch is referring to the fourth edition of Harnack's work (Leipzig 1901), p. 41.

17 *AC*, p. 60.

18 cf. H. Gunkel, 'Die Richtungen der alttestamentlichen Forschung', *Christliche Welt* 36 (1922), p. 66, cited by W. Klatt, *Hermann Gunkel* (1969), pp. 26–7.

19 *GS* II, p. 390, The English translation of this essay (see note 1 above), will be cited hereafter as *ET*.

20 *GS* II, p. 393. *ET* p. 130.

21 *GS* II, p. 396–7. *ET* p. 133.

22 *GS* II, p. 400. *ET* p. 136.

23 In the later version of the essay Troeltsch added that both Ritschl and Harnack are likewise dominated by a similar idea of 'progressive development' (*Fortentwickelung*) based not on the idea of incarnation, as in Hegel's case, but on the biblical idea of the Kingdom of God. In view of the objection Troeltsch was going to offer in what follows, it was a curious addition.

24 *GS* II, p. 404. *ET* p. 140.

25 cf. *GS* II, pp. 403–5. *ET* pp. 140f.

26 *GS* II, p. 405. *ET* p. 140.

27 *GS* II, p. 403. *ET* p. 139.

28 *GS* II, p. 405. *ET* p. 140.

29 *GS* II, p. 405. *ET* p. 140.

30 *GS* II, p. 405. *ET* p. 141. Added in 1913.

31 *GS* II, p. 407. *ET* p. 142.
    GS II, p. 450. *ET* p. 178.
33 *GS* II, p. 407. *ET* p. 142.
34 *GS* II, p. 411. *ET* p. 145.
35 Troeltsch indicates that so thoroughly has this view been discredited by historical writing it is not even mentioned by Rickert, *GS* II, p. 704.
36 *GS* II, p. 709.
37 *GS* II, p. 709.
38 *GS* II, p. 411. *ET* p. 145. In his *Protestantism and Progress*, Troeltsch affirms that 'the religion of the modern world is essentially determined by Protestantism' (London 1912), p. 185. The astonishing chauvinism of this statement is but the further development of the claim that only neo-Protestants like himself are capable of the necessary objectivity in evaluating the phenomenon of Christianity. Cf. my further discussion of this point in Clayton, ed., *Ernst Troeltsch and the future of Theology*, pp. 151f.
39 *GS* II p. 414. *ET* p. 148.
40 *GS* II pp. 415f (my translation; cf. *ET* p. 149).
41 *GS* II p. 416. *ET* p. 149.
42 *GS* II p. 416. *ET* p. 150.
43 *GS* II p. 423. *ET* pp. 155f.
44 *GS* II pp. 420f. *ET* p. 153.
45 *GS* II p. 419 (my translation, cf. *ET* p. 154).
46 *GS* II p. 420. *ET* p. 152.
47 *GS* II p. 422 (my translation, cf. *ET* p. 154).
48 *GS* II, p. 423 (my translation, cf. *ET* p. 155).
49 See below, p. 170, for Troeltsch's subsequently expressed belief that the essence differs in different epochs of history. The relation between the two editions (1903 and 1913) has been given a new analysis by Sarah A. Coakley, *The Limits and Scope of the Christology of Ernst Troeltsch*, Unpublished PhD Thesis (Cambridge 1982), in terms of oscillation between different understandings of historical relativism. See her article, 'Theology and cultural relativism: What is the problem?', *Neue Zeitschrift für systematische Theologie und Religionsphilosophie* 21, 3 (1979), pp. 223–43.
50 *GS* II p. 424. *ET* p. 156.
51 *GS* II p. 425. *ET* p. 157.
52 ' "Mitbedingt" heisst nicht ausschliesslich bedingt, und so bleibt der Objektivität der historischen Forschung ihr Recht gewahrt' (*GS* II, p. 425). 'This conditioning is only partial and thus the claim of objectivity in historical research is maintained' (*ET* p. 157).
53 *GS* II, p. 426. *ET* p. 158.
54 *GS* II, p. 427. *ET* p. 159.

55 *GS* II, p. 427. The original phrase was simply 'conditioned by inner experience'.

56 'The history one writes depends upon one's horizon', B. Lonergan, *Method in Theology* (London 1971), p. 247.

57 *GS* II, p. 427. *ET* p. 159.

58 *GS* II, p. 435. *ET* p. 165. 'Factual and irrational' are Rickert's terms for an individual event, the proper subject of history, *GS* II pp. 690–1.

59 A. Harnack, 'Über die Sicherheit und Grenzen geschichtlicher Erkenntnis', *Reden und Aufsätze* IV, 7, cited in J. C. Livingstone, *Modern Christian Thought* (New York 1971), p. 258.

60 *GS* II, pp. 430–1. *ET* p. 162.

61 *GS* II, p. 436 (my translation, cf. *ET* p. 167).

62 *GS* II, p. 440. *ET* p. 170, a phrase significantly qualified in 1913 by the addition of the words 'more or less close'.

63 *Die christliche Welt* 17 (1903), pp. 682–3.

64 *GS* II, p. 443. *ET* p. 172.

65 *GS* II, p. 444. *ET* p. 173.

66 *GS* II, p. 445. *ET* pp. 173f.

67 We may note that the appeal is now to the *integrity* of the historian, rather than to his or her *impartiality*.

68 *GS* II, p. 446. *ET* p. 175.

69 *GS* II, p. 428. *ET* p. 160.

70 *GS* II, p. 426. *ET* p. 168.

71 *GS* II, p. 451. *ET* p. 179.

72 *GS* II, p. 731–3.

73 *AC*, p. 55.

74 cf. Troeltsch's reply in *Theologische Literaturzeitung* 20/20 (1916), p. 449, in a review of W. Günther, *Die Grundlagen der Religionsgeschichte Ernst Troeltsch* (1914), where this charge is made.

75 *Christian Thought: Its History and Application* (London 1923), pp. 54f.

76 *GS* II, p. 758.

77 In Friedrich von Hügel, 'On the specific Genius and Capacities of Christianity', *Essays and Addresses on the Philosophy of Religion* (London 1921), p. 172. Although this essay, written in 1914, is a fairly general introduction to Troeltsch's thought, it contains some penetrating and far-reaching criticisms from a liberal catholic standpoint.

78 *GS* II, pp. 673–728.

79 *Max Weber on the Methodology of the Social Sciences*, tr. and ed. E. A. Shils and H. A. Finch (New York 1948), pp. 98f.

80 *The Social Teachings of the Christian Churches*, ET O. Wyon, vol. ii (London 1931), p. 1004.

81 *GS* II, p. 449. *ET* p. 177.

82 *GS* II, p. 449. *ET* p. 178.

83 *GS* II, p. 451. *ET* pp. 178f.

84 *American Journal of Theology* XVII (1913), pp. 1–21, esp. pp. 11f and 16. The German version published in *GS* II contains certain additions.

85 *ibid.*, pp. 12f.

86 cf. above p. 160 and *GS* II, p. 423. *ET* p. 155.

87 *GS* II, p. 451. *ET* p. 179.

88 *Die Bedeutung der Geschichtlichkeit Jesu für den Glauben* (Tübingen 1911; reprinted Munich 1969). *ET* in R. Morgan and M. Pye, ed., *Ernst Troeltsch, Writings on Theology and Religion* pp. 182–207. The *ET* cited hereafter as *Signif.*

89 *Signif.*, p. 196.

90 *Signif.*, p. 195.

91 *Signif.*, p. 197.

92 *Signif.*, p. 197.

93 *Signif.*, p. 202.

94 *Signif.*, p. 202.

95 *Signif.*, p. 199. On Troeltsch as a member of an academic body, highly conscious of its role in the state, see F. K. Ringer, *The Decline of the German Mandarins, The German Academic Community, 1890–1933* (Cambridge, Mass., 1969). He believed that the task laid upon neo-Protestantism was the accomplishment of the second act of the reformation.

Chapter 8
BARTH AND THE POWER OF THE WORD

[All references to Barth's *Church Dogmatics* (Edinburgh 1936–74) will be in the form CD, followed by volume and part number in roman and arabic numerals respectively. Of CD I/1 there is an earlier translation (Thompson, 1936) and a later (Bromiley, 1975). Bromiley's is used here.]

1 cf. §⁴ in CD I/1, p. 88: 'The presupposition which makes proclamation proclamation and therewith makes the Church the Church is the Word of God.' cf. also CD I/2, pp. 743ff. For what follows see F. Schmidt, *Verkündigung und Dogmatik in der Theologie Karl Barths* (Munich 1964).

2 Also included in proclamation (*Verkündigung*) is, in addition to preaching, sacrament, CD I/1, p. 80; and indirectly prayer, worship, confession, instruction, pastoral activity and theology, though the task of theology is said not to be that of proclamation, CD I/2, p. 750. cf. also the list of twelve ministries (*Diensten*) in CD IV/3, 2, pp. 865–901. See H. Stoevesandt, 'Der ekklesiologische Horizont der Predigt', in E. Busch, J. Fangmeier and M. Geiger, ed., *Parrhesia*, Karl Barth zum achtzigsten Geburtstag (Zürich 1966), pp. 408–27.

3 As T. H. L. Parker points out, it is not merely Anglicanism which is

missing from Barth's theological perspective, but English theology as a whole, *Karl Barth* (Grand Rapids, Mich., 1970), pp. 112f.

4 'The Need of Christian Preaching', in K. Barth, *The Word of God and the Word of Man* (New York 1957), p. 101; cited hereafter as *WW*.

5 *WW*, p. 101.

6 *WW*, p. 103.

7 'Moderne Theologie und Reichgottesarbeit', *Z.Th.K.* (1909), p. 319f. Cited in E. Busch, *Karl Barth* (London 1976). The latter cited hereafter as *KB*.

8 *KB*, p. 51.

9 *KB*, p. 61.

10 'The Righteousness of God', *WW*, pp. 9–27, cf. esp. pp. 21–4.

11 *KB*, p. 91.

12 *WW*, p. 34.

13 *WW*, p. 41.

14 *WW*, p. 50.

15 In a book of sermons by himself and Thurneysen published in 1917 under the title, *Suchet Gott, so werdet ihr leben* (Seek God and you will live), Barth wrote that human need is for a God who is really God, 'not a notion, not a view, but the power of life which overcomes the powers of death', *KB*, p. 102.

16 *The Epistle to the Romans* (Oxford 1935), p. 35, cited hereafter as *ER*.

17 *ER*, p. 37. Here Barth shows the impact of the highly critical posthumous publication of Franz Overbeck (1837–1905), *Christentum und Kultur* (Basel 1919), which contained a sharp attack on Harnack. Barth reviewed this work very positively in 1920 (ET *Theology and Church* [London 1962], pp. 55–73). The correspondence between himself and Eduard Thurneysen at this time demonstrates its importance, see, *Karl Barth – Eduard Thurneysen, Briefwechsel* I (1913–21) (Zürich 1973), and II (1921–30) (Zürich 1974). Cf., for an evaluation of the complex relationship with Overbeck's criticism of Christianity, H. Schindler, *Barth und Overbeck* (Darmstadt 1974).

18 *ER*, p. 37.

19 *ER*, pp. 37f.

20 *ER*, p. 39.

21 *ER*, p. 40.

22 *ER*, p. 195.

23 *ER*, p. 9.

24 H. M. Rumscheidt, *Revelation and Theology*, An analysis of the Barth–Harnack correspondence of 1923 (Cambridge 1972), p. 32; cited hereafter as *B–H*.

25 *WW*, p. 112.

26 *WW*, p. 114.

27 *WW*, pp. 124f (altered translation).

28 *WW*, p. 131.

29 *WW*, pp. 134f.

30 T. F. Torrance, *Karl Barth*, An Introduction to his early Theology, 1910–1931 (London 1962), p. 41.

31 *KB*, p. 115.

32 *Revolutionary Theology in the Making*, Barth – Thurneysen Correspondence 1914–1925 (London 1964), p. 128.

33 *B–H*, p. 29.

34 *B–H*, p. 31.

35 *B–H*, pp. 32 and 35.

36 Rumscheidt, *B–H*, p. 134 makes the reasonable assumption that the reference is to Overbeck of whose importance to Barth Harnack was already aware. Cf. also Dietrich Braun, 'Der Ort der Theologie', in Busch, Fangmeier and Geiger, ed., *Parrhesia*, esp. pp. 37f.

37 *B–H*, p. 36.

38 *B–H*, p. 39.

39 *B–H*, p. 43.

40 *B–H*, p. 47.

41 *B–H*, pp. 52–3.

42 *Revolutionary Theology*, p. 76.

43 *CD* I/2, pp. 762f.

44 cf. esp. 'The Task of the Community' and 'the Ministry of the Community' in §72, *CD* IV/3, 2, pp. 795–901.

45 Karl Barth, 'Nachwort' in H. Bolli, ed., *Schleiermacher – Auswahl* (Munich 1968), p. 291.

46 Bolli, *Schleiermacher*, p. 297.

47 *CD*, I/1, p. 38.

48 Karl Barth, *Protestant Theology in the Nineteenth Century* (London 1972), p. 454. For what follows see S. W. Sykes, 'Barth on the Centre of Theology', in S. W. Sykes, ed., *Karl Barth, Studies of his Theological Method* (Oxford 1979), pp. 32f.

49 The implications of this suggestion have been fruitfully explored by P. Rosato, *The Spirit as Lord*, The Pneumatology of Karl Barth (Edinburgh 1981).

50 *CD*, I/2, p. 862.

51 *CD* I/2, p. 861.

52 *CD* I/2, p. 861.

53 *CD* I/2, p. 862.

54 See above, p. 104.

55 CD I/2, p. 866.
56 This comes out particularly in the especially combative *CD* I/1. On secularization and sacralization see *CD* IV/2, pp. 669ff.
57 For example, in their treatment of Scripture, *CD* I/2, pp. 514–526.
58 CD I/2, 527.
59 CD I/2, p. 525.
60 CD I/2, p. 768.
61 CD I/2, p. 527.
62 CD I/2, p. 766.
63 CD I/2, p. 768.
64 CD I/2, p. 712 and pp. 798f.
65 CD I/2, p. 772.
66 CD I/2, p. 674.
67 CD I/2, p. 712.
68 CD I/2, p. 798.
69 CD I/2, p. 799.
70 CD I/2, p. 804f. Here Barth is ready to acknowledge the probability of tension between established forms of doctrine favoured in the Church's teaching and the potentially revolutionary character of dogmatics.
71 CD I/2, p. 806.
72 CD I/2, p. 856.
73 CD I/2, p. 859.
74 CD I/2, pp. 863–6.
75 CD I/2, p. 863.
76 But cf. the most useful work of U. Valeske, *Hierarchia Veritatum* (Munich 1968), tracing the background to the reference in article 11 of the decree on ecumenism to 'the hierarchy of truths'.
77 Esp. by Wagenhammer, *Das Wesen des Christentums*: 'Talk about the essence of Christianity is not an expansion of the distinction of fundamental articles developed in scholastic theology, but a separate strand which critically accompanied the tendency to orthodoxy in Church theology, and at the same time aggravated it', p. 62. This is putting the matter too sharply. There is no doubt that the fundamental articles were spoken of as the 'essence of Christianity', for example by Richard Hooker.
78 N. Sykes, *William Wake* II (Cambridge 1957), p. 73; and M. Geiger in R. Rouse and S. C. Neill, *A History of the Ecumenical Movement 1517–1948* (London 1954), pp. 105–9.
79 J. Locke, *The Second Vindication of the Reasonableness of Christianity* etc. (*from J. Edward's reflections*). By the author of the *Reasonableness of Christianity* etc. (London 1697). Cf. E. Hirsch, *Geschichte der neuern evangelischen Theologie* II (Darmstadt 1968), p. 389.

80 This tradition also lends itself to authoritarianism. In Whitgift's reply to Cartwright (*Works*, Parker Society [London, 1852] II, p. 571) and in Archbishop Laud (*Works* II, pp. 286–7), the distinction was used to assist the argument that the Church had the right to be obeyed on the non-fundamentals; see R. H. Bainton, *Studies on Reformation* (London 1964), p. 223.

81 *CD* I/2, p. 866.

82 *CD* I/2, p. 503.

83 The pervasive importance of Barth's doctrine of time has been shown by R. H. Roberts in 'Karl Barth's Doctrine of Time: Its Nature and Implication', in Sykes, *Karl Barth*, pp. 88–146.

84 *CD* I/2, p. 864. Valeske, *Hierarchia Veritatum*, argues that the idea of a fundament has been present in one form or another in much of Catholic history.

85 *CD* I/2, p. 864.

86 *CD* I/2, p. 865.

87 *CD* I/2, p. 866.

88 *CD* IV/1, p. 3.

89 *CD* I/2, p. 867.

90 *CD* I/2, p. 867.

91 *CD* I/2, p. 867.

92 See, further, Sykes, *Karl Barth*, pp. 23–6.

93 *CD* I/2, p. 870.

94 *CD* IV/1, pp. 524f.

95 cf. Sykes, *Karl Barth*, p. 27.

96 *CD* I/2, p. 492.

97 K. Barth, *Anselm: Fides Quaerens Intellectum* (London 1960), p. 55.

98 Preface to 2nd edn (1958), *Anselm*, p. 11.

99 *Anselm*, p. 47.

100 The *aliquatenus* occurs at the end of chapter 1 of Anselm's Proslogion, in a prayer. 'I do not try, Lord, to attain your lofty heights, because my understanding is in no way equal to it. But I do desire to understand your truth a little (*aliquatenus*), that truth that my heart believes and loves.' (*ET* M. J. Charlesworth, *St. Anselm's Proslogion* (Oxford 1965), p. 115). Barth discusses this 'ultimate disquiet and ultimate peace' in *CD* I/1, pp. 230–2.

101 For example, in Barth's instructive discussion of Luther's claim that a 'true preacher' ought not to ask forgiveness of his sins, but say boldly, *haec dixit dominus*, thus saith the Lord, *CD* I/2, p. 747ff.

102 *CD* I/2, p. 859.

103 *CD* I/2, p. 869.

104 *CD* I/2, p. 123.

105 *CD* I/1, p. 144. E. Jüngel appropriately discusses the sense in which the term 'language-event' (*Fuchs*) accurately represents Barth's intention in speaking of the prophetic office of Christ, *The Doctrine of the Trinity* (Edinburgh 1976) pp. 1f.

106 *CD* I/2, p. 871.

107 *CD* I/2, p. 872.

108 *CD* I/2, p. 877.

109 *CD* I/2, p. 869.

110 'Even the trinitarian God of Nicene dogma, or the Christ of the Chalcedonian definition, if seen and proclaimed in exclusive objectivity and with no regard for this accompanying phenomenon [sc. living Christian witness], necessarily becomes an idol like all the others', *CD* IV/3, 2, p. 655.

111 *Protestant Theology*, p. 446.

112 See above, pp. 180 and 191.

113 *CD* I/2, p. 674.

114 *CD* I/2, pp. 680–3. These 'demonstrations' of the power of Christianity are remarkably similar to Newman's arguments for development, see above p. 112.

115 *CD* I/2, pp. 687–8.

116 *CD* IV/3, 2, p. 752.

117 *CD* IV/2, p. 3.

118 *CD* IV/2, pp. 96–7.

119 *CD* IV/2, p. 98.

120 *CD* IV/2, p. 99.

121 *CD* IV/2, pp. 265 and 302.

122 *CD* IV/2, pp. 304ff.

123 *CD* IV/2, p. 310.

124 *CD* IV/2, p. 316.

125 *CD* IV/3, 2, p. 538.

126 *CD* IV/1, p. 331.

127 *CD* I/2, p. 867.

128 *CD* IV/2, p. 582.

129 *CD* IV/2, pp. 583f.

130 *CD* IV/2, pp. 334f.

131 *CD* IV/2, pp. 338f.

132 *CD* I/2, p. 679, and *CD* IV/3, 2, p. 528.

133 *CD* IV/3, 2, p. 628.

134 *CD* IV/1, p. 722.

135 *CD* IV/2, p. 669.

136 *CD* I/1, p. 97.

137 *CD* I/2, pp. 693 and 714f.

138 *CD* I/2, p. 798.

139 *CD* IV/2, p. 676.

140 *CD* IV/2, p. 691–726.

141 *CD* IV/2, p. 701. Needless to say this is entirely consistent with Barth's attack on infant baptism in *CD* IV/4.

142 *CD* IV/2, p. 707.

143 *CD* IV/3, 2, pp. 865ff and 882ff.

144 *CD* I/2, p. 750.

145 *CD* I/2, p. 767.

146 *CD* I/2, p. 768.

147 *CD* I/2, p. 770.

148 *CD* IV/3, 2, p. 760.

149 *CD* IV/3, 2, p. 761.

150 *CD* IV/3, 2, p. 786 (my emphasis).

151 W. R. Ward, *Theology, Sociology and Politics*. The German Protestant Social Conscience, 1890–1933 (Berne 1976), p. 180.

152 Ward, *Theology*, p. 187.

Chapter 9
ANALYSIS OF THE ESSENCE DISCUSSION

1 cf. above p. 84.

2 cf. above p. 93.

3 cf. above p. 114.

4 cf. above p. 189.

5 cf. above p. 160.

6 cf. above p. 159.

7 See H. Hoffmann, 'Die Frage nach dem Wesen des Christentums in der Aufklärungstheologie', in *Harnack-Ehrung* (Leipzig 1921), pp. 353–65; H. Hoffmann, 'Zum Aufkommen des Begriffs "Wesen des Christentums"', *ZKG* 45 (1927), pp. 452–9; C. H. Ratschow, art. 'Wesen des Christentums' in *RGG* ³1 (Tübingen 1975), pp. 1721–9; R. Schäfer 'Welchem Sinn hat es, nach einem Wesen des Christentums zu suchen?', *ZThK* 55 (1968), pp. 329–47; and K. Rahner, art. 'The Essence of Christianity' in *Sacramentum Mundi* I (New York 1968), pp. 299–311.

8 *Letter to the Magnesians* 10. Lightfoot translates: 'It is monstrous to talk of Jesus Christ but to practice Judaism. For Christianity (*Christianismos*) did not believe in Judaism, but Judaism in Christianity.' W. Cantwell Smith insists, rightly, that for Ignatius the imitation of Christ is a central theme, but he goes too far in evacuating the term Christianity of doctrinal content, *The Meaning and End of Religion*, pp. 73 and 265–6.

9 De Profess. Christi, W. Jaeger et al., ed., *Gregorii Nysseri Opera Ascetica*

(Leiden 1952), p. 136. *ET* by V. W. Callahan, *St Gregory of Nyssa Ascetical Works*, The Fathers of the Church, vol. 58 (Washington DC 1967), p. 85. See the discussion of Wagenhammer, *Das Wesen*, pp. 86–9.

10 Wagenhammer speaks of it as 'an expression of Christian idealism', *Das Wesen*, p. 77.

11 cf. above p. 146.

12 See now especially D. Ford, *Barth and God's Story* (Frankfurt 1981).

13 cf. above p. 112.

14 See *Das Geistliche Amt in der Kirche*, Gemeinsame Römisch-Katholische/ Evangelisch – Lutherische Kommission (Paderborn 1981), p. 41, where the need for Lutherans to re-examine the problem of the teaching office and of teaching authority is openly acknowledged.

15 cf. above p. 117.

16 The Apostolic Constitution on Ecclesiastical Universities and Faculties (*Sapientia Christiana*), issued by Pope John Paul II, asserts the duty of the bishops to supervise the teaching in the Universities and Faculties of Theology, especially in the controversial areas of doctrine and ethics.

17 cf. above p. 171.

18 cf. above p. 205.

19 cf. *CD* IV/3, p. 865ff.

20 cf. note 7 above.

21 *ET* by Ronald Gregor Smith (London 1961).

22 *ET* by J. H. Smith (Dublin 1961), p. 23.

23 *ET* by J. McCann (London 1934).

24 See the bibliography to his *Sacramentum Mundi* article, vol. i, p. 311.

25 On Rahner's treatment of the short formula, see *Theological Investigations* IX (London 1972), pp. 117–27; *Theological Investigations* XI (London 1974), pp. 230–44; and, largely repeating the latter, *Foundations of Christian Faith* (London 1978), pp. 448–60. This concern is specifically rooted in the quest for simplicity. See *Theological Investigations* V (London 1966), pp. 35f. Also Valeske, *Hierarchia Veritatum*, pp. 33–43.

26 *Theological Investigations* XI, p. 231.

27 D. E. Nineham, *The Gospel according to St. Mark* (Pelican, Harmondsworth, 1963), p. 324.

28 See Moore, *Judaism* II, p. 88, and Sanders, *Paul and Palestinian Judaism*, pp. 113f.

29 *Confessio Augustana* XXVIII, 52.

30 See F. Hildebrandt, *Melanchthon – Alien or Ally?* (Cambridge 1946), pp. 83f.

31 G. Ebeling, *Luther* (London 1972), p. 113. I fail to see, however, how turning a doctrine into a criterion of all others does not involve giving it preference. Compare also the view of E. Schlink that the central article

of the *Confessio Augustana* is the christological article (III). In support
he refers to the fact that Luther's Short Catechism does not mention
justification at all; see 'Der ökumenische Charakter und Anspruch des
Augsburgischen Bekenntnisses' in H. Meyer, ed., *Die Augsburgische
Bekenntnis im ökumenischen Kontext* (Stuttgart 1980), p. 8. In view of the
fact that there are no less than three different ways in which the pre-
eminence of the doctrine about faith is affirmed in the *CA*, I believe
that the correct explanation of the evidence is the relatively unsystematic
and occasional character of Luther's writings, and of the *CA* itself. When
Luther wants a critical criterion for other doctrines, especially in
ecclesiology, he deploys justification by faith. But among the variety of
things said by Luther in various places to be the basic, foundational, chief,
head, or highest article of faith are belief in the creator, in the Trinity,
in faith and love, in Christ, in the work of Christ in redemption, or in
forgiveness of sins, or in justification, in the death and resurrection of
Christ, or in the resurrection; see U. Valeske, *Hierarchia Veritatum*,
p. 108.

32 *On Religion*, p. 110.

33 See the penetrating remarks on Loisy's epistemology by Christoph
Theobald, in 'L'entrée de l'histoire dans l'univers religieux et théologique
au moment de la "Crise Moderniste"', J. Greisch, K. Neufeld, and
C. Theobald, *La Crise Contemporaine* (Théologie Historique 24)
(Paris 1973), pp. 28–42.

34 Decree on Ecumenism, I, 11, in *The Documents of Vatican II*, ed. W. M.
Abbott (London 1967), p. 354.

35 Y. Congar, 'On the "Hierarchia Veritatum"', in D. Neiman and
M. Schatkin, ed., *The Heritage of the Early Church*, Festschrift Florovsky
(Rome 1973), pp. 409–20. And cf. also 'Articles fondamentaux', in
Catholicisme I (Paris 1948), pp. 882ff, where Congar affirms: 'Il y a une
perspective et comme un *étagement* ou une *hiérarchie* dans la révélation.'

36 Y. Congar, *Tradition and Traditions* (London 1966), pp. 518f.

37 *Tradition and Traditions*, pp. 386f.

38 Valeske, *Hierarchia Veritatum*, pp. 66f.

39 cf. the well-known distinction between the duller folk (*pigriores*), and
those who merit the higher gifts of the Spirit of word, wisdom and
knowledge, *Traité des Principes*, Sources Chrétiennes 252 (Paris 1978),
Preface 3, pp. 78ff. H. Crouzel rightly denies that this distinction meant
that Origen was content to be an ivory tower theologian, *Origène et la
'Connaissance Mystique'* (Paris 1961), p. 475.

40 cf. above p. 105, and further P. E. More, 'The Spirit of Anglicanism' in
P. E. More and F. M. Cross, ed., *Anglicanism* (London 1962), pp. xxiv–
xxix, and H. R. McAdoo, *The Spirit of Anglicanism* (London 1965), chs.
9 and 10 on the appeal to antiquity.

41 Wagenhammer, *Das Wesen*, 3. Teil III, 'Die Entdeckung der Geschichtlichkeit und die Frage nach dem Wesen des Christentums', pp. 206ff.

42 cf. esp. on Semler T. Rendtorff, *Kirche und Theologie* (Gütersloh, 1970), pp. 32–36.

43 Schleiermacher to George Reimer, 30 April 1802, in *The Life of Schleiermacher*, as unfolded in his Autobiography and Letters (London 1860), p. 283.

44 O. Chadwick, *From Bossuet to Newman* (Cambridge 1957), chap. 3.

45 J. S. Drey, *Kurze Einleitung in das Studium der Theologie* ed. F. Schupp (Darmstadt 1971), pp. 153–4.

46 Drey, *Kurze Einleitung*, § 225, p. 151.

47 Drey, *Kurze Einleitung*, § 230, p. 154.

48 Drey, *Kurze Einleitung*, §§ 231–2, pp. 155f.

49 Drey, *Kurze Einleitung*, § 268, p. 181.

50 Text in J. R. Geiselmann, *Geist des Christentums und des Katholizismus*. Ausgewählte Schriften katholischer Theologie im Zeitalter des deutschen Idealismus und der Romantik (Mainz 1940), p. 229; see Harold Wagner, *Die eine Kirche und die vielen Kirchen*, Ekklesiologie und Symbolik beim jungen Möhler (Munich 1977), pp. 115–18. Wagner shows (pp. 197ff) that this somewhat immanentist doctrine of the Holy Spirit, which was also taught by J. A. Möhler in his *Einheit der Kirche oder das Prinzip des Katholizismus* (Tübingen 1825) was glossed in a more orthodox manner in his *Athanasius der Grosse und die Kirche seiner Zeit* III (Mainz 1827), p. 291, as part of his attempt to free himself from identification with Schleiermacher.

51 Chadwick, *From Bossuet to Newman*, chap. 5.

52 Drey, *Kurze Einleitung*, § 175, p. 118.

53 Newman, *Development* I, Introduction (Doubleday Image book edn), p. 53.

54 Newman, *Development*, Introduction (p. 33).

55 See above p. 28.

56 See above p. 32.

57 Kelly, *Early Christian Creeds* (London 1972), pp. 23f.

58 Kelly, *Early Christian Creeds*, p. 76.

59 Kelly, *Early Christian Creeds*, p. 50.

60 On the seventeenth-century Spanish discussion of this problem see Chadwick, *From Bossuet to Newman*, chap. 2.

61 On the ambiguity of the biblical image of the body see A. Dulles, *Models of the Church* (Dublin 1976), pp. 50f.

Chapter 10
THE UNITY OF CHRISTIANITY

1 cf. G. Ryle, 'Taking Sides in Philosophy', in *Collected Papers* II (London 1971), pp. 153–69.

2 Smart, *The Phenomenon of Christianity*, chap. 7, 'Varieties of Christianity and its Offspring', p. 128.

3 Bp Charles Gore (1853–1932) would be regarded as a liberal Catholic Anglican, and such persons as E. G. Selwyn (1885–1959) and A. E. J. Rawlinson (1884–1960) represent the newer version of the same strand of thought. See A. M. Ramsey, *From Gore to Temple* (London 1960), chap 7.

4 See D. E. Nineham, *The Use and Abuse of the Bible* (London 1976), discussed by J. Barton, 'Reflections on Cultural Relativism', *Theology* LXXXII (March 1979), pp. 103–9, and (May 1979), pp. 191–9. cf. also S. Coakley, 'Theology and Cultural Relativism: What is the problem?', *NZSTR* 21 (1979), 3, pp. 223–43.

5 See above pp. 87 and 188.

6 See, for example, the dogmatic textbook of Adolf Tanqueray, *Synopsis Theologiae Dogmaticae* (3 vols. 1894–6) still in use in a twenty-sixth revised edition in the 1950s, where tractates III and IV of fundamental theology deal with ecclesiology.

7 Thus for Karl Rahner Christianity is an ecclesial religion, but the doctrine of the Church is explicitly stated *not* to be the central truth of Christianity. This is justified by reference to the hierarchy of truths, *Foundations of the Christian Faith*, pp. 323f.

8 cf. D. H. Kelsey, *The Uses of Scripture in Recent Theology* (London 1975) Part III. Kelsey refers to Gustav Wingren's argument that the most basic question a systematic theologian has to answer is, What is the essence of Christianity? See G. Wingren, *Theology in Conflict* (Edinburgh 1958), p. 163. Wingren makes clear that methods are part and parcel of the decision, not a neutral preparation for it, p. 80.

9 cf. above p. 171.

10 cf. above p. 37.

11 On the connection between worship and the focusing of the believer on the transcendent object of worship, see N. Smart, *The Concept of Worship* (London 1972).

12 H. Ringgren, *The Faith of the Psalmists*, p. 47, referring to Ps. 62.11, 12 and Ps. 68.

13 H. Küng in his discussion of 'die Unveränderlichkeit Gottes' in *Menschwerdung Gottes* (Freiburg 1970), p. 642. See Ps. 33; 102.26–8; Isa. 31.2; 40.8; Jer. 4.28.

14 London 1964.

15 Gallie, *Philosophy and the Historical Understanding*, p. 158.

16 *The Myth of God Incarnate* (London 1977) was edited by John Hick, Professor of Theology at Birmingham, with contributions from Dr Michael Goulder and Dr Frances Young of the same University. The present author was among a group to take part in a colloquy in Birmingham, supported by the Cadbury Trust, which discussed the implications of the original essays. The proceedings of this second round of debate were subsequently published in M. Goulder, ed., *Incarnation and Myth*, The Debate Continued (London 1979).

17 Gallie, *Philosophy and the Historical Understanding*, p. 186.

18 J. N. D. Kelly, *Early Christian Creeds*, chaps. 1–3.

19 J. N. D. Kelly shows that 'binitarian' patterns of confession in the first three centuries are not to be regarded as fragments of more fully developed Trinitarian statements, *Early Christian Creeds*, pp. 28 and 94. My proposal offers to account theologically for why this should have come about. It would be better to refer to the 'binitarian' confessions as bi-partite, since they are by no means non-Trinitarian. Compare the 'short formula' or 'brief theological creed' offered by Karl Rahner, which like-wise makes no explicit reference to the Holy Spirit, but which is implicitly Trinitarian, *Foundations of Christian Faith*, pp. 454ff.

20 cf. R. Bambrough's statement that 'an indefinite boundary is still a boundary, and a boundary that may be crossed', *Reason, Truth and God* (London 1969), p. 101.

Chapter 11
WORSHIP, COMMITMENT AND IDENTITY

1 cf. above p. 28.

2 According to T. F. Torrance, *Theological Science* (London 1969), pp. 22ff.

3 cf. above p. 152.

4 cf. above p. 205.

5 P. Brunner, *Worship in the Name of Jesus* (St Louis 1968), p. 22.

6 It is extremely instructive in this respect to compare F. Hahn's *The Worship of the Early Church* (Philadelphia 1973), which makes the most of the case for radical novelty, with C. F. D. Moule's earlier *Worship in the New Testament* (Richmond, Virginia, 1961) which strongly emphasizes the continuity with Judaism.

7 On the assumption that what is translated in the RSV as 'devoted themselves to prayer' should be taken as meaning 'the place of prayer' (*he proseuche*), or synagogue, see K. Lake and H. J. Cadbury, *The Beginnings of Christianity*, ed. F. J. Foakes Jackson and K. Lake, IV (London 1933), p. 10.

8 G. J. Cuming, 'The Divine Office, I: The First Three Centuries', in C. Jones, G. Wainwright and E. Yarnold, ed., *The Study of Liturgy* (London 1978), pp. 353–7.

9 Mol, *Identity*, p. 227.

10 Mol, *Identity*, p. 12.

11 Mol, *Identity*, p. 230.

12 Alastair MacIntyre, *After Virtue* (London 1981), p. 103.

13 MacIntyre, *After Virtue*, p. 112.

14 MacIntyre, *After Virtue*, p. 245.

15 The phrase is Henry Drummond's, in *Natural Law in the Spiritual World* (1st edn London 1883), p. 33. The book was translated into German, *Das Naturgesetz in der Geisteswelt* (Leipzig 1886), and read (and admired) by

Troeltsch. See *Vernunft und Offenbarung bei Johann Gerhard und Melanchthon: Untersuchung zur Geschichte der altprotestantischen Theologie* (Göttingen 1891), p. 2.

16 On rationality and commitment see Mol, *Identity*, p. 223–6.

17 See, esp., V. A. Harvey, *The Historian and the Believer*, and 'The Ethics of Belief Reconsidered' in *The Journal of Religion* (1979), pp. 406–20.

18 As D. H. Kelsey successfully shows in his *The Uses of Scripture in Recent Theology* (London 1975), Part II. Edward Farley's *Ecclesial Reflection* is the most thorough modern exposition of Troeltsch's basic standpoint, in support of the view that 'the house of authority' has collapsed.

19 E. Käsemann, *New Testament Questions of Today* (London 1969), pp. 191f.

20 C. E. B. Cranfield, *The Epistle to the Romans*, vol. ii (Edinburgh 1979), p. 602.

21 For two modern examples of theologians relating the phenomenon of open questioning to the basic concerns of theology, see W. Pannenberg, 'The Question of God', in *Basic Questions in Theology* II (London 1967), pp. 201–33, and B. J. F. Lonergan sj, *Method in Theology* (London 1972), pp. 101–24.

22 G. Wainwright, *Doxology* (London 1980), p. 218.

23 cf. the encyclical of Pope Pius XII, *Mediator Dei* (1947), in which the liturgy is firmly stated to be 'subject to the Church's supreme teaching authority' (*ET Christian Worship* [London n.d.], p. 26). From the Lutheran side, Peter Brunner, who is Barth's preferred authority on the theology of worship, affirms that 'the church's doctrine on worship will determine which liturgical order it employs', *Worship in the Name of Jesus*, p. 24.

24 *CD* IV/3, 2, p. 865.

25 D. M. MacKinnon, 'Teilhard's Achievement', in N. Braybrooke, ed., *Teilhard de Chardin, Pilgrim of the Future* (London 1965), p. 62.

26 See the suggestive study of D. Ritschl and H. O. Jones, *'Story' als Rohmaterial der Theologie*, Theologische Existenz heute 192 (Munich 1976).

27 Mol, *Identity*, p. 244.

28 As Lionel Trilling remarks, 'In an increasingly urban and technological society, the natural processes of human existence have acquired a moral status in the degree that they are thwarted.' Anything resembling a mechanical process, and that would include the order and repetition of a liturgy, is 'felt to be inimical to the authenticity of experience and being', *Sincerity and Authenticity* (London 1974), p. 128.

29 cf. above pp. 40ff.

Bibliography

Adam, K., *The Spirit of Catholicism*. London 1934.

Allen, L., *John Henry Newman and the Abbé Jager*. London 1975.

Aubert, R., 'Recent Publications on the Modernist Movement', *Concilium*, vol. 7, no. 2 (1966).

Bainton, R. H., *Studies on the Reformation*. London, 1964.

Bambrough, R., *Reason, Truth and God*. London 1969.

Barmann, L. F., *Baron Friedrich von Hügel and the Modernist Crisis in England*. Cambridge 1972.

Barrett, C. K., 'Cephas and Corinth', in O. Betz, M. Hengel, and P. Schmidt, ed., *Abraham unser Vater*, Festschrift Michel (Leiden 1963), pp. 1–12.

— 'Conversion and conformity: the freedom of the Spirit and the Institutional Church', in B. Lindars and S. S. Smalley, ed., *Christ and Spirit in the New Testament*, Festschrift Moule (Cambridge 1973), pp. 359–81.

— *The First Epistle to the Corinthians*, 2nd edn, London 1971.

— *The Second Epistle to the Corinthians*. London 1973.

— *The Holy Spirit and the Gospel Tradition*, London 1966.

Barth, K., *Anselm: Fides Quaerens Intellectum*, London 1960.

— *Karl Barth – Eduard Thurneysen, Briefwechsel* I (1913–21), Zürich 1973; II (1921–30), Zürich 1974.

— *Church Dogmatics*, 13 vols. Edinburgh 1936–74.

— 'Nachwort', in H. Bolli, ed., *Schleiermacher-Auswahl*, Munich 1968.

— *Protestant Theology in the Nineteenth Century*, London 1972.

— *The Epistle to the Romans*, 6th edn, Oxford 1935.

— *Theology and Church*, London 1962.

— *The Word of God and the Word of Man*, New York 1957.

Barton, J., 'Reflections on Cultural Relativism', *Theology* LXXXII (1979), pp. 103–9 and 191–9.

Beckmann, K. M., *Der Begriff der Häresie bei Schleiermacher*, Munich 1959.

Bonhoeffer, D., *Christology*, London 1966.

Bornkamm, G., 'A Letter to the Romans as Paul's Last Will and Testament', in K. P. Donfried, ed., *The Romans Debate* (Minneapolis 1977), pp. 17–31.

Bouyer, L., 'Newman et le Platonisme de l'âme Anglaise', *Revue de Philosophie* vi (1936), pp. 285–305.

Brunner, P., *Worship in the Name of Jesus*, St Louis 1968.

Bultmann, R., *Theology of the New Testament*, London 1952.

Burnaby, J., *Amor Dei*, London 1938.

Busch, E., *Karl Barth*, London 1976.

Campenhausen, H. U. von., *Ecclesiastical Authority and Spiritual Power in the Church of the First Three Centuries*, London 1969.

Cases, S. J., 'The Problem of Christianity's Essence', *American Journal of Theology* (1913), pp. 541–62.

Chadwick, H., *Early Christian Thought and the Classical Tradition*, Oxford 1966.

Chadwick, O., *From Bossuet to Newman*, Cambridge 1957.

Clapton, E., *Our Prayer Book Psalter*, London 1934.

Clayton, J. P., 'Is Jesus necessary for Christology: an Antinomy in Tillich's Theological method', in S. W. Sykes and J. P. Clayton, ed., *Christ, Faith and History*, Cambridge 1972, pp. 147–63.

Coakley, S. A., 'Theology and Cultural Relativism: What is the Problem?' *Neue Zeitschrift für Systematische Theologie und Religionsphilosophie* 21 (1979), pp. 223–43.

— *The Limits and Scope of the Christology of Ernst Troeltsch*, Unpublished PhD Thesis, Cambridge 1982.

Congar, Y., 'Articles fundamentaux', *Catholicisme* I, Paris 1948.

— 'On the "Hierarchia Veritatum'', in D. Neiman and M. Schatkin, ed., *The Heritage of the Early Church*, Festschrift Florovsky, Rome 1973, pp. 409–20.

Conzelmann, H., *History of Primitive Christianity*, London 1973.

Coulson, J., *Newman and the Common Tradition*, Oxford 1970.

Courth, F., *Das Wesen des Christentums in der liberalen Theologie: dargestellt am Werk Fr. Schleiermachers, Ferd. Chr. Baurs und A. Ritschls*, Frankfurt 1977.

Cranfield, C. E. B., *The Epistle to the Romans* I. Edinburgh 1975; II. Edinburgh 1979.

Cremer, A. H., *A Reply to Harnack on the Essence of Christianity*, New York 1903.

Cuming, G. J., 'The Divine Office, I: The First Three Centuries', in

C. Jones, G. Wainwright and E. Yarnold, ed., *The Study of Liturgy*. London 1978.

Dahl, N. A., 'Paul and the Church at Corinth according to 1 Corinthians 1.10–4.21', in W. R. Farmer, C. D. F. Moule and R. R. Niebuhr, ed., *Christian History and Interpretation*, Festschrift Knox (Cambridge 1967), pp. 313–35.

Daly, G., *Transcendence and Immanence, A Study in Catholic Modernism and Integralism*, Oxford 1980.

Daly, R. J., *The Origins of the Christian Doctrine of Sacrifice*, London 1978.

Davies, W. D., *Paul and Rabbinic Judaism*, London 1962.

Deegan, D. L., 'The Ritschlian School, The Essence of Christianity and Karl Barth', *Scottish Journal of Theology* 16 (1963), pp. 390–414.

Dessain, C. S., ed., *The Letters and Diaries of John Henry Newman*, *XXV*, London 1974.

Dickens, A. G., *The English Reformation*, London 1964.

Drey, J. S., *Kurze Einleitung in das Studium der Theologie*, Darmstadt 1971.

Drummond, H., *Natural Law in the Spiritual World*, London 1883.

Dulles, A., *Models of the Church*, Dublin 1976.
— *The Survival of Dogma*, New York 1973.

Dunn, J. D. G., *Baptism in the Holy Spirit*, London 1970.
— *Unity and Diversity in the New Testament*, London 1977.

Ebeling, G., *Luther*, London 1972.
— *The Nature of Faith*, London 1961.

Farley, E., *Ecclesial Reflection*, Philadelphia 1982.

Fawkes, A., 'Recent Theories of Development in Theology', *Edinburgh Review* 198 (1903), pp. 52–81.
— *Studies in Modernism*, London 1913.

Ford, D., *Barth and God's Story*, Frankfurt 1981.

Gadamer, H. G., 'The Problem of Language in Schleiermacher's Hermeneutic', in R. W. Funk, ed., *Schleiermacher as Contemporary* (Journal for Theology and Church 7) (New York 1970), pp. 68–84.

Gallie, W. B., *Philosophy and the Historical Understanding*, London 1964.

Geiselmann, J. R., *Geist des Christentums und des Katholizismus*, Mainz 1940.

Gemeinsame Romisch-Katholische/Evangelisch-Lutherische Kommission, *Das Geistliche Amt in der Kirche*, Paderborn 1981.

Gilson, E., *The Spirit of Medieval Philosophy*, London 1950.

Glick, G. W., *The Reality of Christianity*, New York 1967.

Gogarten, F., *Was ist Christentum?*, Göttingen 1956.

Gore, C., *The Church and the Ministry*, London 1886.

Greenslade, S. L., 'Heresy and Schism in the later Roman Empire', in D. Baker, ed., *Schism, Heresy and Religious Protest* (Cambridge 1972), pp. 1–20.

Hahn, F., *The Worship of the Early Church*, Philadelphia 1973.

Hamilton, W., *The New Essence of Christianity*, New York 1961.

Harnack, A. von, *History of Dogma*, 7 vols. London, 1879–99.

— rev. of A. Loisy, *Evangelium und Kirche*, 2nd edn, *Theologische Literaturzeitung*, 29 (1904), pp. 59–60.

— *The Mission and Expansion of Christianity in the First Three Centuries*, 2 vols. 2nd edn, London 1908.

— *Outlines of the History of Dogma*, Boston 1957.

— 'Über die Sicherheit und Grenzen geschichtlicher Erkenntnis', *Reden und Aufsätze IV*, Giessen 1911.

— *Das Wesen des Christentums*, ed. R. Bultmann. Leipzig 1900; Stuttgart 1950.

— *What is Christianity?* 3rd edn, = ET of above, London 1904.

Harvey, V. A., 'The Ethics of Belief Reconsidered', *Journal of Religion* (1979), pp. 406–20.

— *The Historian and the Believer*, London 1967.

Hengel, M., *The Atonement*, London 1981.

— 'Zwischen Jesus und Paulus. Die "Hellenisten", die "Sieben" und Stephanus (Apg. 6.1–15; 7.54–8.3)', *Zeitschrift für Theologie und Kirche* 72 (1975), pp. 151–206.

Hilderbrandt, F., *Melanchthon – Alien or Ally?* Cambridge 1946.

Hirsch, E., *Das Wesen des Christentums*, Weimar 1939.

— *Geschichte der neuern evangelischen Theologie*, 5 vols. Darmstadt 1968.

Hoffmann, H., 'Die Frage nach dem Wesen des Christentums in der Aufklärungstheologie', *Harnack-Ehrung: Beiträge zur Kirchengeschichte*, Leipzig 1921, pp. 353–65.

— 'Zum Aufkommen des Begriffs "Wesen des Christentums"', *Zeitschrift für Kirchengeschichte* 45 (1927), pp. 452–9.

Holmberg, B. 'Sociological versus Theological Analysis of the Questions concerning a Pauline Church Order', in S. Pedersen, ed., *Die Paulinische Literatur und Theologie*, Århus 1980, pp. 187–200.

— *Paul and Power*, Lund 1978.

Hooker, R., *Of the Laws of Ecclesiastical Polity*, Everyman Edition, London 1907.

Hügel, F. von, 'On the Specific Genius and Capacities of Christianity', *Essays and Addresses on the Philosophy of Religion* (London 1921), pp. 144–94.

Jeremias, J., *New Testament Theology I*, London 1971.

Jewett, R., *Paul's Anthropological Terms*, Leiden 1971.

Jonas, L., and Dilthey, W., ed., *Aus Schleiermachers Leben in Briefen*, 4 vols. Berlin 1858–63.

John Paul II, *Sapientia Christiana* (1979), *ET*, The Apostolic Constitution on Ecclesiastical Universities and Faculties. London n.d.

Johnson, A. R., *The Vitality of the Individual in the Thought of Ancient Israel*. Cardiff 1964.

Johnson, P., *A History of Christianity*, Harmondsworth 1980.

Jüngel, E., *The Doctrine of the Trinity*, Edinburgh 1976.

Kaftan, J., *Das Wesen der Christlichen Religion*, Basle 1881.

Kaltenborn, C. J., *Adolf von Harnack als Lehrer Dietrich Bonhoeffers*, Berlin 1973.

Käsemann, E., *Essays on New Testament Themes*, London 1964.

— *New Testament Questions of Today*, London 1969.

Kelly, J. N. D., *Early Christian Creeds*, London 1972.

— *Early Christian Doctrines*, 2nd edn, London 1960.

Kelsey, D. H., *The Uses of Scripture in Recent Theology*, London 1975.

Kraus, H. J., *Worship in Israel*, Oxford 1966.

Küng, H., *Menschwerdung Gottes*, Freiburg 1970.

Lacey, T. A., *Harnack and Loisy*, London 1904.

Lake, K., and Cadbury, H. J., *The Beginnings of Christianity*, vol. IV, London 1933.

Lampe, G. W. H., 'Grievous Wolves' (Acts 20.29), in B. Lindars and S. S. Smalley, ed., *Christ and Spirit in the New Testament*, Festschrift Moule (Cambridge 1973), pp. 253–65.

Lash, N. L. A., *Change in Focus*, London 1973.

— 'Modernism, Aggiornamento and the Night Battle', in A. Hastings, ed., *Bishops and Writers*. Wheathamstead 1977.

— *Newman on Development*, London 1975.

— *Voices of Authority*, London 1976.

Leivestad, R., *Christ the Conqueror*, London 1954.

Lightfoot, J. B., 'The Christian Ministry', *St. Paul's Epistle to the Philippians*. 1st edn, London 1868.

Lloyd, R., *The Church of England, 1900–1965*, London 1966.

Locke, J., *The Second Vindication of the Reasonableness of Christianity* etc. (from J. Edward's reflections), London 1697.

Loisy, A., *Choses passées*, Paris 1913.

— = Firmin, A., 'Le développement chrétien après le Cardinal Newman', *Revue du Clergé français* 17 (1898), pp. 5–20.

— *L'Évangile et L'Église*, 5th edn, Paris 1929.

— *The Gospel and the Church* (= ET of above). 2nd edn, London 1908.

— *Mémoires pour servir à l'histoire religieuse de notre temps* 1, Paris 1930.

Lonergan, B. J. F., *Method in Theology*, London 1972.

Loome, T., *Liberal Catholicism, Reform Catholicism, Modernism*. Tübingen 1979.

Lukes, S., 'Power and Authority', in T. Bottomore and R. Nisbet, ed., *A History of Sociological Analysis* (London 1979), pp. 633–76.

Major, H. D. A., *English Modernism, Its Origin, Methods and Aims*, Cambridge, Mass., 1927.

Moberly, R. C., *Ministerial Priesthood*, London 1897.

Mol, H., *Identity and the Sacred*, Oxford 1976.

Moltmann, J., *The Church in the Power of the Spirit*, London 1977.

— *The Crucified God*, London 1974.

— *The Trinity and the Kingdom of God*, London 1981.

Möhler, J. A., *Athanasius der Grosse und die Kirche seiner Zeit* III, Mainz 1827.

— *Einheit der Kirche oder das Prinzip des Katholizismus*, Tübingen 1825.

Moore, G. F., *Judaism in the first centuries of the Christian era*, 2 vols. Cambridge, Mass., 1927.

More, P. E., 'The Spirit of Anglicanism', in P. E. More and F. M. Cross, ed., *Anglicanism* (London 1962), pp. xix–xl.

Moule, C. F. D., *Worship in the New Testament*, Richmond, Virginia 1961.

Munck, J., *Paul and the Salvation of Mankind*, London 1959.

Murray, R., *Authority in a Changing Church*, London 1968.

McAdoo, H. R., *The Spirit of Anglicanism*, London 1965.

MacIntyre, A., *After Virtue*, London 1981.

MacKinnon, D. M., 'Teilhard's Achievement', in N. Braybrooke, ed., *Teilhard de Chardin, Pilgrim of the Future*, London 1965.

Macquarrie, J., *Twentieth-Century Religious Thought*, London 1963.

Neufeld, K. H., *Adolf von Harnacks Konflikt mit der Kirche*, Innsbruck 1979.

— *Adolf von Harnack – Theologie als Suche nach der Kirche*, Paderborn 1977.

Newman, J. H., *An Essay on the Development of Christian Doctrine*, London 1845; 3rd edn, London 1878; reprinted New York 1960).

— *Essays Critical and Historical I*, London 1871.

— *Lectures on the Prophetical Office of the Church viewed relatively to Romanism and Popular Protestantism* (= *The Via Media* (London 1877), London 1837.

— *Newman's University Sermons*, ed. D. M. MacKinnon and J. D. Holmes, London 1970.

— *The Via Media of the Anglican Church I*, London 1877.

Newsome, D., *Two Classes of Men*, London 1974.

Niebuhr, H. R., *Christ and Culture*, New York 1951.

Niebuhr, R. R., *Schleiermacher on Christ and Religion*, London 1965.

Nielsen, S. K., 'Paulus' Verwendung des Begriffs *Dunamis*. Eine Replik zur Kreuzestheologie', in S. Pedersen, ed., *Die Paulinische Literatur und Theologie* (Århus 1980), pp. 137–58.

Nineham, D. E., *The Use and Abuse of the Bible*, London 1976.

Pannenberg, W., *Basic Questions in Theology, II*, London 1967.

Parker, T. H. L., *Karl Barth*, Grand Rapids, Mich., 1970.

Pauck, W., *Harnack and Troeltsch. Two Historical Theologians*, New York 1968.

Pelikan, J., *The Christian Tradition I: The Emergence of the Catholic Tradition, 100–600*, Chicago 1971.

Perrin, N., *Jesus and the Language of the Kingdom*, Philadelphia 1976.

Peterson, E., 'Christianos', *Miscellaneous Giovanni Mercati, I* (1946), pp. 355–72.

Pfleiderer, O., 'Das Wesen des Christentums', *Zeitschrift für wissenschaftliche Theologie* 36 (1893), pp. 1–41.

Pius XII, *Mediator Dei*, ET *Christian Worship*, London n.d.

Poulat, E., *Histoire, dogme et critique dans la crise moderniste*, Paris 1962.

Rahner, K., 'The Essence of Christianity', *Sacramentum Mundi I* (New York 1968), pp. 299–311.

— *Foundations of Christian Faith*, London 1978.

— 'The Need for a "Short Formula" of Christian Faith', *Theological Investigations IX* (London 1972), pp. 117–27.

— 'The Theology of Power', *Theological Investigations* IV (London 1966), pp. 391–409.

Räisänen, H., 'Legalism and Salvation by the Law', in S. Pedersen, ed., *Die Paulinische Literatur und Theologie* (Århus 1980), pp. 63–83.

Ramsey, A. M., *From Gore to Temple*, London 1960.

Ratschow, C. H., 'Wesen des Christentums', *Die Religion in Geschichte und Gegenwart*. 3rd edn I (Tübingen 1975), pp. 1721–9.

Reardon, B., *Liberalism and Tradition, Aspects of Catholic Thought in Nineteenth Century France*, Cambridge 1975.

Rendtorff, T., *Kirche und Theologie*, Gütersloh 1970.

Richardson, A., *History, Sacred and Profane*, London 1964.

Riches, J., *Jesus and the Transformation of Judaism*, London 1980.

Ringer, F. K., *The Decline of the German Mandarins, The German Academic Community 1890–1933*, Cambridge, Mass., 1969.

Ringgren, H., *The Faith of the Psalmists*, London 1963.

Ritschl, D. and Jones, H. O., *'Story', als Rohmaterial der Theologie*, Theologische Existenz heute, 192, Munich 1976.

Roberts, R. H., 'Karl Barth's Doctrine of Time: Its Nature and Implication', in S. W. Sykes, ed., *Karl Barth, Studies of his Theological Method* (Oxford 1979), pp. 88–146.

Robinson, N. H. G., *The Groundwork of Theological Ethics*, London, 1971.

Rolffs, E., *Harnacks Wesen des Christentums und die religiösen Strömungen der Gegenwart*, Leipzig 1902.

Rosato, P., *The Spirit as Lord, The Pneumatology of Karl Barth*, Edinburgh 1981.

Rumscheidt, H. M., *Revelation and Theology, an analysis of the Barth-Harnack Correspondence of 1923*, Cambridge 1972.

Sanday, W., *An Examination of Harnack's What is Christianity*, London 1901.

— and Williams, N. P., *Form and Content in the Christian Tradition*, London 1916.

Sanders, E. P., *Paul and Palestinian Judaism*, London 1977.

Saunders, T. B., *Professor Harnack and his Oxford Critics*, London 1902.

Schäfer, R., 'Welchem Sinn hat es, nach einem Wesen des Christentums zu suchen?', *Zeitschrift für Theologie und Kirche* 55 (1968), pp. 329–47.

— *Wesen des Christentums, Historisches Wörterbuch der Philosophie I*, ed. J. Ritter (1971), pp. 1008–16.

Schillebeeckx, E., *Ministry*, London 1981.

Schindler, H., *Barth und Overbeck*, Darmstadt 1974.

Schleiermacher, F. D. E., *The Christian Faith*, Edinburgh 1928.

— *Hermeneutik*, ed. H. Kimmerle, Heidelberg 1968.

— *Hermeneutics: The Handwritten Manuscripts*, = ET of above, Missoula, Montana 1977.

— *Kurze Darstellung des theologischen Studiums*, with Foreword by H. Scholz, Darmstadt 1969.

— *Brief Outline on the Study of Theology*, = ET of above, Richmond, Virginia 1966.

— *Reden über die Religion*, ed. G. C. B. Pünjer, Brunswick 1879.

— *On Religion, Speeches to Its Cultured Despisers*, = ET of above, New York 1958.

— *The Life of Schleiermacher, as unfolded in his Autobiography and Letters*, London 1860.

Schmaus, M., *The Essence of Christianity*, Dublin 1961.

Schmidt, F., *Verkündigung und Dogmatik in der Theologie Karl Barths*, Munich 1964.

Schmitz, H. J., *Frühkatholizismus bei Adolf von Harnack, Rudolf Sohm und Ernst Käsemann*, Düsseldorf 1977.

Schulz, S., *Die Mitte der Schrift, Der Frühkatholizismus im Neuen Testament als Herausforderung an den Protestantismus*, Stuttgart 1976.

Seeberg, R., *The Fundamental Truths of the Christian Religion*, London 1908.

Sillem, E. A., *The Philosophical Notebook of John Henry Newman, I: General Introduction to the Study of Newman's Philosophy*, Louvain 1969.

Smart, N., *The Religious Experience of Mankind*, London 1971.

— *The Phenomenon of Christianity*, London 1979.

— *The Concept of Worship*, London 1972.

Smith, W. C., *The Meaning and End of Religion*, New York 1962.

Söhngen, G., 'Vom Wesen des Christentums', *Die Einheit in der Theologie*, Munich 1952.

Srawley, J. H., 'Eucharist', in J. Hastings, ed., *Encyclopaedia of Religion and Ethics* V (Edinburgh 1912), pp. 555–6.

Stoevesandt, H., 'Der ekklesiologische Horizont der Predigt', in E.

Busch, J. Fangmeier and M. Geiger, ed., *Parrhesia, Karl Barth zum achtzigsten Geburtstag*, Zürich 1966.

Sykes, S. W., 'Theological Study: The Nineteenth Century and After', in B. Hebblethwaite and S. Sutherland, ed., *The Philosophical Frontiers of Christian Theology*, Festschrift MacKinnon, Cambridge 1982.

— 'Barth on the Centre of Theology', in S. W. Sykes, ed., *Karl Barth. Studies of his Theological Method* (Oxford 1979), pp. 17–54.

— 'Note', in R. Morgan and M. Pye, ed., *Ernst Troeltsch* (London 1977), pp. 180–1.

— 'Ernst Troeltsch and Christianity's Essence', in J. P. Clayton, ed., *Ernst Troeltsch and the Future of Theology*, Cambridge 1976.

— *Christian Theology Today* London 1971.

— 'The Essence of Christianity', *Religious Studies* 7 (1971), pp. 291–305.

Theobald, C., 'L'entrée de l'histoire dans l'univers religieux et théologique au moment de la "Crise Modernist"', in J. Greisch, K. Neufeld and C. Theobald, ed., *La Crise Contemporaine*, Théologie Historique 24 (Paris 1973), pp. 5–85.

Tillich, P., *Love, Power and Justice*, London 1954.

— *Systematic Theology* II, London 1957.

Titius, A., 'Der Kampf um Harnack's Wesen des Christentums', *Theologischer Jahresbericht* 21 (Berlin 1902), pp. 991–1004; 22 (Berlin 1903), pp. 1124–32; 23 (Berlin 1904), pp. 834–9.

Troeltsch, E., *The Absoluteness of Christianity and the History of Religions*, London 1972.

— 'Aufklärung', *Realencyklopädie für protestantische Theologie und Kirche* II (1897), pp. 225–41.

— *Briefe an F. von Hügel, 1901–1923*, ed. K. E. Apfelbacker and P. Neuner, Paderborn 1974.

— 'Die christliche Weltanschauung und ihr Gegenströmungen', *Gesammelte Schriften*, vol. II (Tübingen 1913), pp. 227–327.

— 'The dogmatics of the Religionsgeschichtliche Schule', *The American Journal of Theology* 17 (1913), pp. 1–21.

— Review of W. Günther, 'Die Grundlagen der Religionsgeschichte Ernst Troeltsch (1914)', *Theologischer Literaturzeitung* 20/20 (1916), p. 449.

— 'The Significance of the Historical Existence of Jesus for Faith', in R. Morgan and M. Pye, ed., *Ernst Troeltsch, Writings on*

Theology and Religion (London 1977), pp. 182–207.
— *Protestantism and Progress*, London 1912.
— *The Social Teaching of the Christian Churches*, 2 vols. London 1931.
— 'Über historische und dogmatische Methode in der Theologie', *Gesammelte Schriften* II (Tübingen 1913), pp. 729–53.
— *Vernunft und Offenbarung bei Johann Gerhard und Melanchthon: Untersuchung zur Geschichte der altprotestantischen Theologie*, Göttingen 1891.
— 'What does "Essence of Christianity" Mean?', in R. Morgan and M. Pye, ed., *Ernst Troeltsch, Writings on Theology and Religion* (London 1977) pp. 124–79.

Torrance, T. F., *Karl Barth, An Introduction to his early Theology, 1910–1931*, London 1962.
— *Theological Science*, London 1969.

Trilling, L., *Sincerity and Authenticity*, London 1974.

Tyrrell, G., *Christianity at the Cross Roads*, London 1909.

Ullmann, K., *Über den unterscheidenden Charakter oder das Wesen des Christentums*, Hamburg 1845.

Valeske, U., *Hierarchia Veritatum*, Munich, 1968.

Vidler, A., *A Variety of Catholic Modernists*, Cambridge 1970.
— *Twentieth Century Defenders of the Faith*, London 1965.

Wainwright, G., *Doxology*, London 1980.

Wagenhammer, H., *Das Wesen des Christentums*, Mainz 1974.

Wagner, H., *Die eine Kirche und die vielen Kirchen, Ekklesiologie und Symbolik beim jungen Möhler*, Munich 1977.

Ward, W. R., *Theology, Sociology and Politics. The German Protestant Social Conscience, 1890–1933*, Berne 1976.

Watt, E. D., *Authority*, London 1982.

Weber, M., *Max Weber on the Methodology of the Social Sciences*, ed. E. A. Shils and H. A. Finch, New York 1948.

Wilken, R. L., *The Myth of Christian Beginnings*, London 1971.

Wingren, G., *Theology in Conflict*, Edinburgh 1958.

Wobbermin, G., 'Loisy contra Harnack', *Zeitschrift für Theologie und Kirche* 15 (1905), pp. 76–102.

Wolff, H. W., *Anthropology of the Old Testament*, London 1974.

Wrong, D. H., *Power, Its Forms, Bases and Uses*, Oxford 1979.

Index

NOTE: Entries under K. Barth, A. von Harnack, J. H. Newman, F. D. E. Schleiermacher and E. Troeltsch include details of their works mentioned in the book, as well as a thematic breakdown of the contents of the relevant chapter.

Abbott, Jacob 104–5
Abelard, Peter 45, 214–15
Adam, K. 222
    The Spirit of Christianity
        (1934) 221
Alexander the Great 18
Anglican Church:
    its 'threefold ministry' 48
    in relation to Newman 103ff, 120
Anselm of Canterbury 198
Apollos 14, 55
apostleship: Paul's a credential 54ff
    preserves identity of the
        Church 60
Arian controversy 125–6, 222, 277
Aristotle: *Metaphysics* 22
Athanasius of Alexandria 125–6,
    277
Augustine of Hippo 24, 42–5,
    214–15
    City of God 43
    Enchiridion 222

baptism
    water-baptism 40–2, 46, 62
    words of 108
bark-sap metaphor (Harnack)
    see models and images of spiritual
        life

Barrett, C.K. 14, 67ff, 70
Barth, Karl 5, 81–2, 85, 101, 131,
    149–50, 173, 174–208, 211–38
    passim, 242–3, 264, 274, 284
    Fides Quaerens Intellectum
        (1931) 177
    The Epistle to the Romans (various
        editions) 174–208 *passim*
    Church Dogmatics (1936–74)
        177, 187, 197, 204 and 174–208
        passim
    I/2 189
    IV/1 177, 196–200, 201
    IV/2 201
    IV/3 201
    'Moderne Theologie und Reich-
        gottesarbeit' (essay, 1909) 178
    Lectures:
    'The Righteousness of God' and
        'The New World within the
        Bible' (1916) 179
    'Biblical Questions, Insights and
        Vistas' (1920) 184
    'The Need and Promise of
        Christian Teaching' (1922) 182
    Barth and the power of the
        Word 174–208
    primacy of preaching (*Predigt*)
        174
    freedom and power 175, 205ff

Barth and the power – *cont.*
the epistemological dilemma 175
'pure doctrine' 177
preacher's role 178–9
power of God as *krisis* 180
radical discontinuity 181
significance of the historical
quest 184
epistemology 185
differences with Harnack 185–7
with Schleiermacher 186–8
faith 185ff
dogmatics 188–96
inwardness 193
'centre of theology' 196–200
the theme of power 200–8
Christology of *Church Dogmatics*
IV/2 201
Jesus and power 201ff
internal and external power of the
Church 204
the power of the theologian 205ff
parallelism 206–8
Barth, Peter 179
Baur, F.C. 14, 154
Benedict of Nursia 270
Bengel, J.A. 181
Bible: versions of
Coverdale, Luther, Septuagint,
Vulgate, NEB 36
internal diversity 60
Bonhoeffer, D. 135
Bossuet, J.B. 228
Brunner, Emil 187, 205
Die Mystik und das Wort
(1924) 187
Burnaby, J. 44
Butler, Joseph 105

canon, biblical, canon criticism 94
Calvin, Jean 187, 190, 197
Institutes of the Christian Religion
(1536) 233

Campenhausen, Hans von,
*Ecclesiastical Authority and
Spiritual Power* 57–8
'centre of theology' (Barth) 176ff,
196–200
charisma, theology of, not
normative 58
Christ
see Jesus Christ
Christ, Pneuma– 62–3
Christian Platonism 119
Christianity:
a religion, not a philosophical
system 28, 239, 262
its ethical teaching 35, 40–5
its unitary nature 114ff, 239–61
unity in worship 268–86 *passim*
correlation of external to internal
experience 37 and *passim*
its Jewish matrix 12
normative 94
rites and usages 29ff, 35, 40–5,
118, 270, 281–2
early controversy 11–26
definition of 11–12 and *passim*
inner cohesion 27, 84, 212, 240ff
authority and personalization 33,
59, 73
its internal dimension 35–50
awareness of its own
power 65–73
its social embodiment 283–4
Church:
Lightfoot's 'ideal Church' 48–50
a worshipping body 7–8, 85–90ff,
261
an offered sacrifice 43, 274
authority 95, 106
power 51–77, 216–29
ambiguity in decision-making 35
office under Christ 117
political influence 75
pluralism 11–34
abuses 45

Church – *cont.*
'preaching Christ' an essence-
definition 29
clarifier of biblical teaching 46
leadership after Paul 56ff
see also Christianity
Church of England
see Anglican Church
Church, Pauline, issues in:
Corinth 13–14, 16, 20–1, 24, 25,
53–7ff, 68
Galatia 15, 16, 53
Jerusalem 15, 17
Rome 16, 17
Thessalonica 25
Ephesus 24, 26, 59
Letter to the Hebrews 25
Clement of Alexandria 22
Clement of Rome: *1 Clement* 56–9
Coleridge, S.T. 119
commitment, religious 6, 37–40, 74,
269–76
worship commitment and identity
262–86
educators distanced from
commitment 218
see also Barth; Troeltsch
Confessio Augustana (1530) 224
conflict:
a characteristic of Christianity 6,
51–3ff, 73, 212–13
its locus 262–86
in early Christianity 11–26
inescapable in biblical scholarship
23
how conducted 125–7
conduct as a component of
definition 260
Congar, Yves, *La Tradition et les
Traditions II* (1946) 226
consecration 35–50 *passim*
context, area of, for Christianity
258ff
controversy *see* conflict

Conzelmann, H. 70
covenant 40–1, 50
new covenant 266
Coverdale, Miles 36
Cranfield, C.E.B. 274
Cranmer, Thomas 106
creeds:
Apostles' 107, 222–3
Athanasian 115
Nicene 107
criticism: canon 94
higher 22–3, 94
New Testament 12
cultural relativism 75, 241
culture, Christian response to 22, 75

Dead Sea Scrolls 67
'Denzinger-theologie' 232–3
dialectical tradition 233–8 *passim*,
251, 257, 282
dimension analysis of religion
(Smart) 28ff
discipleship 25–6, 27
produces internal controversy 29
diversity in Christianity 4
'contained diversity' amounts to
unity 11, 52
doctrinal tradition, perspective on
identity of Christianity 26–34
and *passim*
doctrine and worship 276–82
documents of the New Testament
12
differing interpretations of 45ff
dogmatics 242ff and *passim*
Drey, Johann 228–9
Brief Introduction (1819) 228
Vom Geist und Wesen … (1819)
229
Duchesne, Louis 127

Ebeling, Gerhard, *Das Wesen des
Christlichen Glaubens* 220,
222, 225

education 74–5
Encyclical *Apostolicae Curae* (Leo XIII, 1896) 47
Enlightenment (*Aufklärung*) 23, 150, 214, 228ff
episcopate, rise of 63–5
epistemology *passim*
see also knowledge; Barth; Harnack; Loisy; Newman; Schleiermacher; Troeltsch
Erskine, Thomas 104–5, 113
essence of Christianity *passim*
not solely a Protestant concern 122
the discussion analysed 211–38, 250–61
essence-books 4, 220–1
essence-definition:
misconceptions 2–3
the task defined 4, 21, 219–29
'essentially contested concept' (Gallie) 251ff, 262, 282
ethics, gospel 61–5
ethics of Christianity 30–1, 35, 40–5, 61–5 and *passim*
Eucharist 29, 32, 41–2, 46, 62
see also ritual
Evangelical authority 58
Evangelicalism 119
exegesis 144
experience, nature of 32–3
experience, religious 33ff:
historical conditioning 33
externals 37, 52
Lightfoot-Moberly debate 47–50
externality tradition 230–8 *passim*, 250ff
see also inwardness tradition

faith, mystical 62
Fawkes, Alfred 130
Feuerbach, L.A. 81
Forty-two Articles (1553) 107

Foster, George Burnham 1
Freud, S. 100
Froude, J. 108
'fundamentals' 102–22, 257

Gallie, W.B. 3, 251–6, 259–60, 262
Philosophy and the Historical Understanding (1964) 251
Gasparri, Cardinal 222
Gentiles 16–17
Gnosticism 14, 60, 140, 227
God: undeceivable 38–9
unity of 56
his kingship and power 66ff
his consistency an argument for continuity 244–7
true theology has joy and confidence in him 279
Goethe, J. W. von 151
gospel 15ff and *passim*:
many versions in early Christianity 18–19
inherent ambiguity as taught by Paul 34
Gospels, synoptic, kingdom symbolism 67ff
Greenslade, S.L. 60
Gregory of Nyssa 214, 221

Hall, Joseph 105
Harnack, A. von 1, 5, 61, 81–2, 100, 123–47, 152–4, 163, 176–7, 182, 184–7, 197, 211–38 *passim*, 243, 264
as discussed by Troeltsch 61, 123, 148–50, 152–4, 163
History of Dogma (1886–9) 61, 128, 130, 133, 137, 152, 264
The Mission and Expansion of Christianity ... (1908) 61, 137
Das Wesen des Christentums (1900) 123–47 *passim*, 152ff
What is Christianity? (1904) 5, 123

Harnack, A. von – *cont.*
'15 Questions to the Despisers of
Theology' 184
Harnack–Loisy controversy
123–47, 184:
documentation and disregard of
the controversy 124–5
caution against the received view
127ff
Harnack not reductionist 129
the purpose of *Das Wesen des
Christentums* 131
Christ the centre of faith 131
Loisy's task 131ff
shares Harnack's desire to restate
the faith 132
the identity of Christianity
133–40
Harnack's Christology 133ff
Loisy's rebuttal 138–40
basic similarities between them
140
their discussion of power 140–2
of the kingdom 141–2
critic's evaluations 142–7
Harnack's faulty exegesis 143–4
Loisy and scholarship 144–5
historical scholarship and
Christian identity 146–7
Hartmann, Eduard von 163–5
Harvey, V.A. 149
heart, the 35–50 *passim*
source of human defilement 44
Hegel 81, 90, 151ff, 165
Hellenism 18
Hengel, Martin 18
Henry VIII 106
heresies: historical 92
Arianism 222, 277
modern 75
hermeneutics 13, 76 and *passim*
Herrmann, Wilhelm 186
Hick, John (ed.), *The Myth of God
Incarnate* (1977) 252

'hierarchies of truth' (Vatican II)
226–7
hierarchy in the Church 56, 95
Higher Criticism 94
Holy Spirit 15, 57
Hooker, Richard 106–7, 222, 228
Hügel, F. von 148, 167
Hypocrisy 38

idealism, German 153
identity 3, 262–86
see also essence
Ignatius of Antioch 214
incarnation 115ff
Independent Churches 106
infallability 117
institutionalization 33
intentions 38, 42–5 *passim*, 51, 62
clamor cordis 44
interiority *see* inwardness
inwardness tradition 35–50, 99,
230–8 *passim*, 213–16
Irenaeus 106, 107

Jager, Jean-Nicholas 102–3
Jeremias, J. 70
Jerusalem, Church of 15, 17
Jesus Christ:
his person and work 18, 65ff
parabolic teaching 32
three-fold office 27, 117
not the 'founder' of Christianity
20, 62
an example and model 20–1
incarnation a 'performance-origin'
for Christianity (Gallie) 254ff
the exalted risen Christ 62–5
redemption solely through him, as
essence-definition 92
images of relationship with
believer 20
unity in Christ (Paul) 41
and *passim*
Jewel, John 105

Jewish Christians   16
Jewish matrix of Christianity   12
John XXIII, Pope   226
Judaism: interpretation of   17
  external pressures   18
  transformation of, by Christianity
  19
  its counter-attack   24
Judaizers   14, 16
  see also legalism
Justin Martyr   22

Kant, Immanuel   99, 145, 151
Käsemann, E.   274
Kelly, J.N.D.   231
kernel-husk metaphor (Harnack)
  see models and images of spiritual
  life
Kingdom of God   19, 50, 62, 65ff,
  134, 141-2, 286 and *passim*
  power–implications   65-77
knowledge: and faith   120-1
  as indwelling of Jesus   112
  grounds of religious knowledge in
  the Church   7
krisis (Barth)   180
Kümmel, W.G.   70

Lacey, T.A., *Harnack and Loisy*
  (1904)   143
language: adequacy of 36-7
  of revelation, Newman's view of
  107, 111, 120
  religious language,
  Schleiermacher's theory   85
kingdom language   67
  mythical language of cosmic
  struggle   73ff
Lash N.L.A.   114, 121
Laud, William   105
'leading idea' of Christianity
  101-21 *passim*
legalism   41
Leo XIII, Pope   47

Lessing   82
libertines   16
Liefbare Bücher   220
Lightfoot, J.B.:
  St Paul's Epistle to the Philippians
  (1868)   47-50
Lightfoot, R.H.   61
literary criticism, analogy with   30
Locke, John   107, 194
Loisy, A.   81-2, 122, 123-47, 184,
  211-38 *passim*
  L'Evangile et l'Eglise (1929)   123,
  131-2, 140
  see also Harnack–Loisy
  controversy
Lonergan, B.J.F.   161
longing, lover's   43
  amor cordis   44
  see also intentions
Luther, Martin   29, 36, 99, 185-7,
  190, 197, 214-15, 224-5
  'Short Catechism'   222

Maccabees   66
MacIntyre, Alastair, *After Virtue*
  (1981)   270-2
MacKinnon, Donald   279-80
Marx, Marxism   100
Mary, Virgin   109
Melanchthon   106, 197, 224
  Confessio Augustana (1563)   224
methodological aspect of Christianity
  26-34 *passim*
  not a prior discipline to theology
  256
Moberly, R.C.:
  Ministerial Priesthood (1897)
  47-50
models and images of spiritual life
  135-7, 234-8
'modernist crisis, the'   125
Möhler, J.A.   229
Mol, H.   244, 269, 274
moral critique of Christianity   272ff

morality *see* ethics
Moses, Mosaic law 15
Munck, Johannes 14
mystery: divine 109
  of the locus of the 'hearts desire'
    39
  of the Eucharist 44
  of the exalted and risen Lord 62
myth of Christian beginnings 21, 66

nature: human, its laws 110
  of the sacred 6
New English Bible 36
New Testament:
  documents 12, 45ff, 56
  exegesis (Johannine Comma) 144
  unity 21
  teaching on power 53, 65–77
    passim
Newman, J.H. 3, 5, 26–7, 28, 81, 99,
    101–22, 124, 127, 132, 139, 144,
    146, 148, 176–7, 189–90, 211–38
    passim, 243, 250, 262, 283
  Tract 76, *Tracts for the Times*
    (1835) and appendix (1836)
    104, 113
  *Lectures on the Prophetical Office
    of the Church* (1837) 103,
    108–9, 116
  retitled as *Via Media* (1877) 103,
    116
  'The theory of Developments in
    Religious Doctrine' (sermon,
    1843) 109, 110–12
  *An Essay on the Development of
    Christian Doctrine* (1845) 103,
    112–13
  marginalia 121
  1878 revision 103, 112–13, 114ff
Newman on the idea of Christianity
    102–22
  no systematician 99, 101, 102–22
    passim

comparison with Schleiermacher
    118–22
controversy with Jager 102–3,
    105–8
  with Erskine and Abbot 104–5,
    113
criticizes Schleiermacher on the
    Trinity 104
rejects 'leading idea' of
    Anglicanism 103, 104, 113
dissatisfied with 'fundamental
    articles' 103, 106–7
defends their scriptural basis 107
view of religious language 108,
    111, 120
seven 'detached & incomplete
    truths' 104
the Trinity 104, 105ff
episcopal and prophetic traditions
    108ff
'system' now a criterion, Catholic
    theology a 'balanced system'
    110
unitary concepts of Christianity
    110ff
inward view of doctrine 112
history a guide to defining
    Christianity 112ff
nine principles derived from
    doctrine of incarnation 115,
    118
order and disorder in Christianity,
    theology a regulating principle
    117, 121
evangelical grasp of indwelling of
    Christ 120

obedience 25, 39, 54ff
  Mary's 109
  the theologian's duty 77, 203
Origen 22, 227
  De Principiis 232
Otto, Rudolf, Schleiermacher's editor
    187

Oxford History of the Church, on
    Harnack 128

Parrhesia (1966), essays in celebration
    of Barth 203
participation, theology of 41-2
Paul the apostle 13-26 and *passim*:
    teaching on the heart 39
    a Jew and not a Jew 17
    farewell at Miletus 24, 26, 59
    ambiguities in teaching 34
    conflicts in the Church 13-21,
        53-61
    dialect between weakness and
        power 71ff
Paul VI, Pope, 'Confession of Faith of
    the People of God' (1968) 222
Perrin, Norman, *Jesus and the
    Language of the Kingdom* 76
Peter the apostle 14-16:
    proposed as true foundation of
        the Church 14, 70
Petrine Confession (Matthew 16.16)
    106
Pius XII, Pope 222
Plato 99
    Schleiermacher's translation 118
Platonism 159
    Christian Platonism 118-19
pluralism of the Church 11-34,
    240ff
Pneuma-Christ 62-3
power: defined 54
    of God 249-50
    a mark of the Christian 72
    cosmic 71-2
    ecclesiastical 4, 51-77, 88, 118,
        216-19
    sociology of 61ff
    New Testament teaching 65-73
    see also Barth; Harnack; Loisy;
        Newman; Schleiermacher;
        Troeltsch
preaching, Barth's concept of 174

Presbyterian Churches 106
priorities as definition-task 223-7
Protestantism, attitude to ritual and
    liturgy 29
Psalms discussed in the text:
    Ps.22 72; Ps.51 36ff
    Ps.69 72; Ps.73 43
    Ps.110 72; Ps.114 72;
    Ps.136 66
Psalms of Solomon 66
Psalter, Anglican liturgical 36
psychology, human, open before
    God 40
purity, personal 27, 36, 62-3
Pusey, E.B. 119

Quenstedt, Johann 194-6
Qumran 18, 19
    see also Dead Sea Scrolls

Rabbinic teaching on God's kingship
    66-7
Rahner, Karl 81, 100, 222-3
rationalism 119
Ratschow, Carl Heinz, article in *Die
    Religion in Geschichte und
    Gegenwart* (1957) 1
reductionism, Protestant 113
Reitzenstein, R. 14
religion *see* Christianity
*Religion in Geschichte und
    Gegenwart, Die*, Ratschow's
    article (1957) 1
renewal, spiritual 36
resurrection 20, 68, 71
revelation, as 'facts' 105
    language of 107
    its unitary nature 110
Rickert, Heinrich 155-6
Ritschl, Albert 81, 127-8, 152, 172
ritual 29ff, 35, 40-5, 118, 270, 281-2
Roman Catholic Church 16-17:
    doctrines 110
Rome, Church of (Pauline) 16, 17

Roncalli, Mgr (later Pope John
  XXIII) 226
Russell, Bertrand 167

sacerdotalism, Lightfoot's criticism
  50
sacralization 37, 190, 204
sacraments 62, 95
sacred, nature of the 6
sacrifice 37–8
  rituals superseded by Christ's
    death 41
  partnership in 42
Sadduceeism 18, 19
Schelling 90, 151
schism *see* controversy
Schlegel, F. 119–20
Schleiermacher, F.D.E. 2, 5, 23–4,
  81–102, 104, 118–22, 124, 144,
  146, 153–4, 157, 172, 176, 187–9,
  194, 199–200, 211–38 *passim*,
  242–3, 247, 250
  *Brief Outline on the Study of
    Theology* (1969) 82–101
    passim
  its origin in lectures on
    '*Enzyklopädie*' (1804–5,
    1810–11) 82
  The Christian Faith (1928) 83,
    85, 87, 91–2, 96–8, 187, 214, 243
  Hermeneutics (1968) 85
  *On Religion, speeches to its
    cultured despisers* (1879) 23–4,
    83, 84, 85, 187
  translation of Plato 118
Schleiermacher on the essence of
  Christianity 81–101
  a pioneer of the concept *Wesen des
    Christentums* 82
  his historical significance 98–101
  essence–definition 83, 88, 91–101
    passim, 242
  complaint against empiricism and
    the externalist tradition 89, 93

Glaubensweise 83, 84, 86, 89,
  121, 214, 225
  redemption solely by Jesus Christ,
    an essence–definition 92, 98
  validation 95, 99
  historical evidence 92, 97, 99
  'original form' of Christianity 83,
    94–5
  its present diversity 91–2
  'diseased deviations' 96, 121
  its polemical character 23–6
  no 'pure' Christianity attainable
    98
  the Church 85
  its unity 95
  Glaubensgemeinschaft 86, 89,
    100
  relationship of believing to other
    human activities 85–6, 89
  relationship of theology to pastoral
    concerns 87
  education of Church leaders 87–8
  ecclesiastical power–structures
    88
  S.'s Protestant convictions 91, 93
  Protestantism and Catholicism
    93ff
  methodological contribution to
    theology 99
  an 'unrepentant systematician'
    101
Schmaus, Michael, *Vom Wesen des
  Christentums* 221–2
secularization 174–208 *passim*
Semler 82, 98–9, 120, 144, 228
Septuagint 36
Sermon on the Mount 24
Seventy-two, the mission of the
  69–70
simplification in definition 221ff
Smart, Ninian 28–34 *passim*, 40–5,
  239, 244, 262, 283
  dimensions and aspects of religion
    28–34 *passim*, 283

Smart, Ninian – *cont.*
  on ritual and ethics 40–5
sociology of religion 13
  of theological disagreement 52
  of power 61ff
Sohm, Rudolf 140–1, 205
Steinbart 82
Stillingfleet, Edward 105
supernaturalism 150–1, 271–2
systematic theology
  see theology, systematic
systematization 101 and *passim*

Taylor, A.J.P. 167
Teilhard de Chardin, P., *Le Milieu
  Divin* 279
Tertullian 106–7
theologian's role 6–8, 76–7, 203,
  275–6, 285–6
Theologischer Jahresbericht (1901–6)
  148
theology:
  a tool for discrimination 37
  commensurate with revelation
    (Newman) 117
  related to joy in God 279
theology, systematic 12–13
Thirty-Nine Articles 233
Tillich, Paul 81
Torrance, T.F. 183–4
Tracts for the Times (1835) 104
Trinity, doctrine of 63
Troeltsch, Ernst 2–3, 5, 53, 61–5,
  81–2, 101, 123–4, 142–3, 147,
  148–73, 175–6, 184, 211–38
  passim, 193, 241, 243–4, 251,
  264, 271
  'Die Christliche
    Weltanschauung ...' (essay,
    1894) 150
  'What does "Essence of
    Christianity" mean?' (essay,
    1903) 148ff
  Barth's copy 176

Absoluteness of Christianity (1902)
  152
'Modern Philosophy of History'
  (essay, 1904) 156, 168
'The Significance of the Historical
  Existence of Jesus for Faith'
  (essay, 1911) 171, 184
'The Dogmatics of the
  "Religionsgeschichtliche
  Schule"' (essay, 1913) 168, 170
*The Social Teaching of the
  Christian Churches* (1931)
  169–70
Troeltsch and the problem of
  epistemology 148–73
  in relation to Loisy 148
  the importance of epistemology
    149–50
  'pre-Harnack' attitude 150–2
  writings on Harnack 152–68
    passim
  endorses the historical view of
    Christianity 153–4
  the various versions of 'What does
    "Essence..." mean?' 154ff
  develops circumspection 155
  claims impartiality 155–6
  two trends in Christianity 158
  explicates what was previously
    implicit in the 'essence' debate
    162
  discusses von Hartmann 163–5
  the contribution of Max Weber
    168–70
  the power inherent in Christianity
    171–3
truth: a harmonious whole 110
  a primary issue 247–8, 275
Turretini, François 194
Tyrrell, George 128, 142

unity: of Christianity 239–61
  of the Church 95
  a 'contained diversity' 11

values 38, 155
Vatican II 226
Vulgate 36

Wagenhammer, H. 82
Wainwright, Geoffrey 276
Wake, William 194
Weber, Max 58, 61, 150, 168–70,
    271
  'Objektivät' essay 168
Wernle, Paul 1
Wesley, John 233
Westminster Confession 233
White, Blanco 114
will, the 45, 62

Wingren, Gustav 1
Word of God, in Barth 174–208
Word, that which is articulable
    28–9
worship 261
  defined 265
  worship commitment and identity
    262–86
  worship and the heart 39, 43
  corporate worship 265ff
  private worship 267–8
  related to doctrine 276–82

Zelotism 18–19